VACATION & SECOND HOMES

Design 4061, page 137

465 DESIGNS FOR RECREATION

Retirement and Leisure Living
Under 500 square feet to over 5,000 square feet

HOME PLANNERS, LLC
Wholly owned by Hanley-Wood, Inc.

Published by Home Planners, LLC
Wholly owned by Hanley-Wood, Inc.

Editorial and Corporate Offices:
3275 West Ina Road, Suite 110
Tucson, Arizona 85741

Distribution Center:
29333 Lorie Lane
Wixom, Michigan 48393

Rickard D. Bailey/CEO and Publisher
Stephen Williams/Director of Sales & Marketing
Cindy Coatsworth Lewis/Director of Publications
Jan Prideaux/Senior Editor
Paulette Mulvin/Project Editor
Sara Lisa Rappaport/Manufacturing Coordinator
Paul Fitzgerald/Senior Graphic Designer
Joan Simmons/Production Artist
Matthew S. Kauffman/Project Artist
Victoria M. Frank/Publications Coordinator

Photo Credits

Front Cover: Andrew D. Lautman

Back Cover: Oscar Thompson Photography

First Printing: June 1999

10 9 8 7 6 5 4 3 2 1

Printed in the United States of America

Library of Congress Catalog Card Number: 99-94047

ISBN: 1-881955-57-5

On the front cover: What could be more appealing—a cozy cabin by a crystal clear lake.
Our Design 4061 is rustic in appearance, but so easy to spend time in. For more information and to see floor plans, turn to page 137.

On the back cover: A finer seaside home would be hard to find. This home, Design 6620,
combines casual lifestyles with the amenities of luxury living. For more information and
to see floor plans, turn to page 395.

TABLE OF CONTENTS

One-Story Traditionals 4

Two-Story Traditionals 53

Farmhouse Favorites 93

Capes, Cottages and Cabins 135

Shingle-Sided Styles 187

Multi-Level and Hillside Vacation Homes 223

A-Frame and Chalet Adaptations...................................243

Contemporary Choices 275

Sunsational Second Homes 305

Seaside Vacation Homes 363

Outdoor Projects 401

How to order blueprints for the plans in this book 432

Additional plan books 446

DESIGN 8265

Square Footage: 1,404

With the right style and just the right size, this vacation cottage will be a dream to wile away leisure time. A covered porch in the front opens to the open living and dining areas on the inside. The great room is warmed by a fireplace and shares space with the dining area and open island kitchen. A screened porch, just beyond the kitchen, makes a great spot for outdoor dining, free of pesky insects. Two bedrooms lie to the rear of the plan—a master suite with walk-in closet and private bath and a family bedroom with walk-in closet and private bath. A second-floor loft can serve as an additional bedroom or as a den or media room. The covered carport is accessed from the rear.

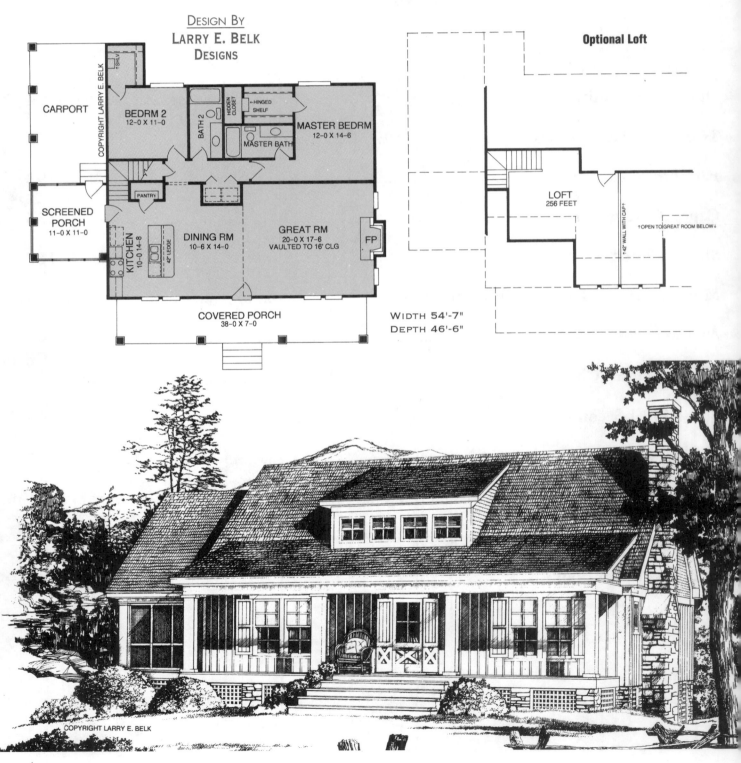

DESIGN BY
LARRY E. BELK
DESIGNS

CARPORT

BEDRM 2
12-0 X 11-0

MASTER BEDRM
12-0 X 14-6

HIDDEN CLOSET
←HINGED SHELF

BATH 2

MASTER BATH

PANTRY

SCREENED PORCH
11-0 X 11-0

KITCHEN
10-0 X 14-8

42" LEDGE

DINING RM
10-6 X 14-0

GREAT RM
20-0 X 17-6
VAULTED TO 16' CLG

FP

COVERED PORCH
38-0 X 7-0

WIDTH 54'-7"
DEPTH 46'-6"

Optional Loft

LOFT
256 FEET

↑OPEN TO GREAT ROOM BELOW↑

42" WALL WITH CAP†

COPYRIGHT LARRY E. BELK

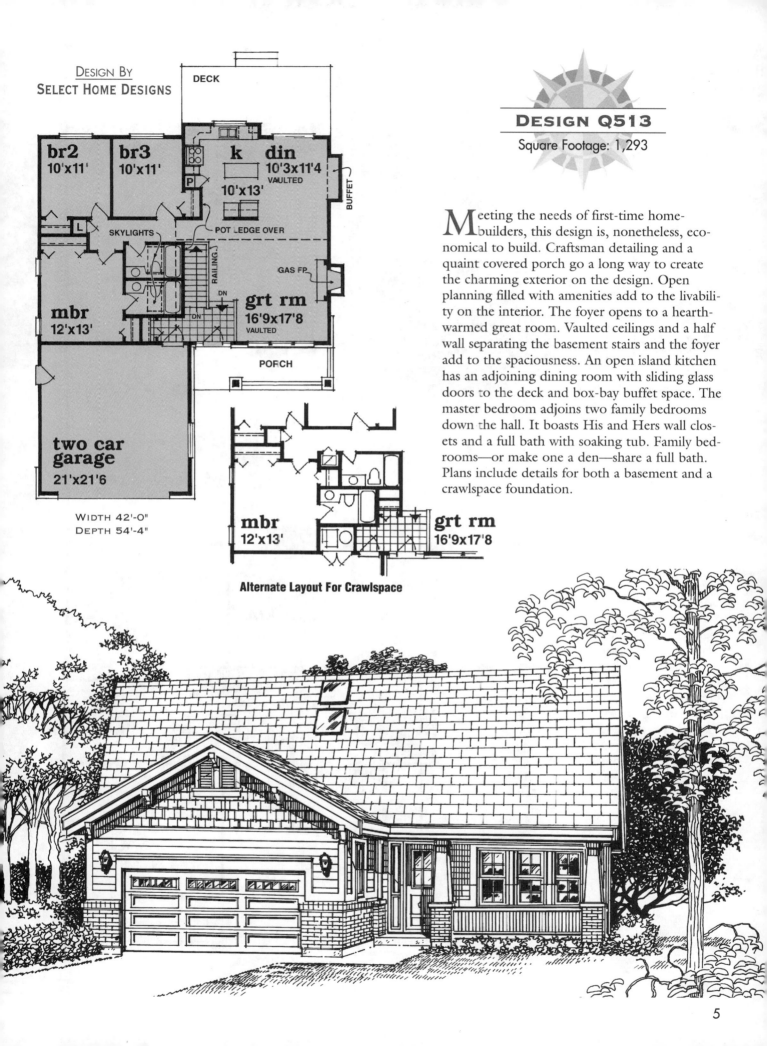

DECK

br2
10'x11'

br3
10'x11'

k
10'x13'

din
10'3x11'4
VAULTED

BUFFET

P

SKYLIGHTS

POT LEDGE OVER

RAILING

GAS FP.

mbr
12'x13'

DN

DN

grt rm
16'9x17'8
VAULTED

PORCH

two car
garage
21'x21'6

WIDTH 42'-0"
DEPTH 54'-4"

mbr
12'x13'

grt rm
16'9x17'8

Alternate Layout For Crawlspace

DESIGN Q513
Square Footage: 1,293

Meeting the needs of first-time home-builders, this design is, nonetheless, economical to build. Craftsman detailing and a quaint covered porch go a long way to create the charming exterior on the design. Open planning filled with amenities add to the livability on the interior. The foyer opens to a hearth-warmed great room. Vaulted ceilings and a half wall separating the basement stairs and the foyer add to the spaciousness. An open island kitchen has an adjoining dining room with sliding glass doors to the deck and box-bay buffet space. The master bedroom adjoins two family bedrooms down the hall. It boasts His and Hers wall closets and a full bath with soaking tub. Family bedrooms—or make one a den—share a full bath. Plans include details for both a basement and a crawlspace foundation.

DESIGN 9431

Square Footage: 1,316

DESIGN BY
ALAN MASCORD
DESIGN ASSOCIATES, INC.

An exceptional use of cedar shingles, horizontal cedar siding and brick highlights the exterior of this one-story home. The floor plan has many amenities found normally on much larger homes. Note, for example, the vaulted great room with a fireplace and the plant shelf above the entry. The master bedroom is also vaulted. The covered patio off the formal dining room lends itself to great outdoor living even in inclement weather. Opening off the entry with a pair of French doors is a den which could be used as a third bedroom.

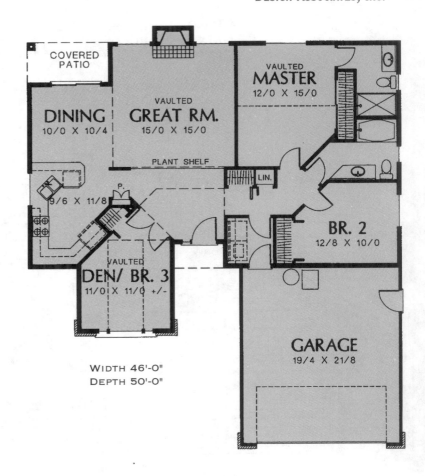

COVERED PATIO

VAULTED MASTER
12/0 X 15/0

DINING
10/0 X 10/4

VAULTED GREAT RM.
15/0 X 15/0

PLANT SHELF

LIN.

9/6 X 11/8

P.

BR. 2
12/8 X 10/0

VAULTED DEN/ BR. 3
11/0 X 11/0 +/-

GARAGE
19/4 X 21/8

WIDTH 46'-0"
DEPTH 50'-0"

This home, as shown in the photograph, may differ from the actual blueprints.
For more detailed information, please check the floor plans carefully.

Photo by Andrew D. Lautman

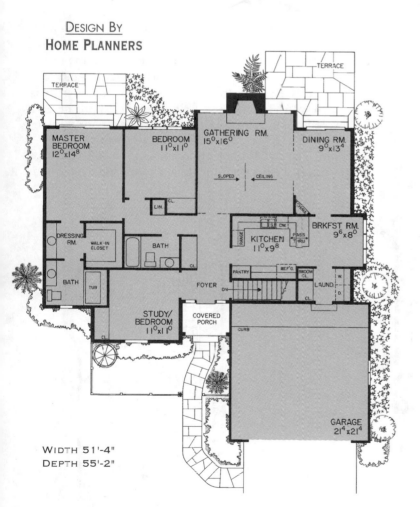

WIDTH 51'-4"
DEPTH 55'-2"

DESIGN 2878
Square Footage: 1,530

L D

This charming one-story traditional design offers plenty of livability in a compact size. Thoughtful zoning puts all sleeping areas to one side of the house apart from household activity in the living and service areas. The home includes a spacious gathering room with a sloped ceiling, in addition to a formal dining room and a separate breakfast room. There's also a handy pass-through between the breakfast room and the large, efficient kitchen. The laundry is strategically located adjacent to the garage and the breakfast/kitchen areas for handy access. A master bedroom enjoys a private bath and a walk-in closet. A third bedroom can double as a sizable study just off the foyer.

QUOTE ONE®
Cost to build? See page 434
to order complete cost estimate
to build this house in your area!

7

DESIGN Q470
Square Footage: 1,392

Traditional corner columns add prestige to this three-bedroom ranch. The vaulted living room features a gas fireplace and a built-in media center. An open kitchen with work island adjoins the dining room, which contains a large bay window and double French doors leading to the rear deck. An abundance of natural light from the skylights in the main hallways adds dramatic effects. The master suite is appointed with His and Hers wall closets and a private bath. Family bedrooms share a full hall bath. The laundry room has space for a full-sized washer and dryer with cabinets overhead. The crawlspace option allows for a convenient homework-space between the dining room and living room.

DECK

br2
10'x12'

br3
10'x12'

k
10'x12'

din
10'x12'

WORK ISLAND

R

BR

F

L

SKYLIGHT

DN

mbr
12'4x14'3

W D

SKYLIGHT

GAS F.P.

MEDIA CENTER

VAULTED
liv
13'x17'2

two car garage
21'8x21'6

DESIGN BY
SELECT HOME DESIGNS

WIDTH 44'-0"
DEPTH 52'-6"

DECK

din
9'8x15'6

HOMEWORK SPACE

H

F

GAS F.P.

VAULTED
liv
13'x17'2

Layout For Alternate Crawlspace Foundation

DESIGN BY
SELECT HOME DESIGNS

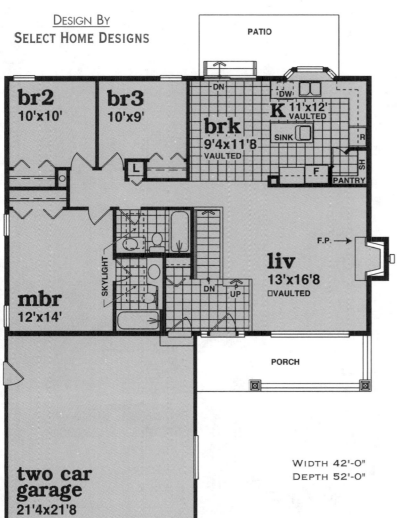

PATIO

br2
10'x10'

br3
10'x9'

DN

DW

brk
9'4x11'8
VAULTED

K 11'x12'
VAULTED

SINK

R

L

F

PANTRY

SH

mbr
12'x14'

SKYLIGHT

DN

UP

F.P. →

liv
13'x16'8
□VAULTED

two car
garage
21'4x21'8

PORCH

WIDTH 42'-0"
DEPTH 52'-0"

DESIGN Q505

Square Footage: 1,260

This economical-to-build bungalow works well as a small family home or a retirement cottage. It is available with a basement foundation but could easily be converted to a slab or crawlspace foundation. The covered porch leads to a vaulted living room with fireplace. Behind this living space is the U-shaped kitchen with walk-in pantry and island with utility sink. An attached breakfast nook has sliding glass doors to a rear patio. There are three bedrooms, each with roomy wall closet. The master bedroom has a private full bath, while the family bedrooms share a main bath. Both baths have bright skylights. A two-car garage sits to the front of the plan to protect the bedrooms from street noise.

DESIGN Q366

Square Footage: 1,538

This compact three-bedroom offers a wealth of amenities—and you can make one of the bedrooms into a den or home office, if you choose! A skylit foyer spills into a vaulted living room with a bay-window seat and corner fireplace. The dining room is open to the living room and connects directly to the kitchen where there is another bay-window seat. An angled snack bar separates the kitchen from the family room; double doors open onto the patio at the back of the house. The master bedroom offers still another bay window with window seat and has a walk-in closet and private bath. The family bedrooms—one with walk-in closet—share a full bath. Note the laundry room space in the service entrance to the two-car garage. Plans include details for both a basement and a crawlspace foundation.

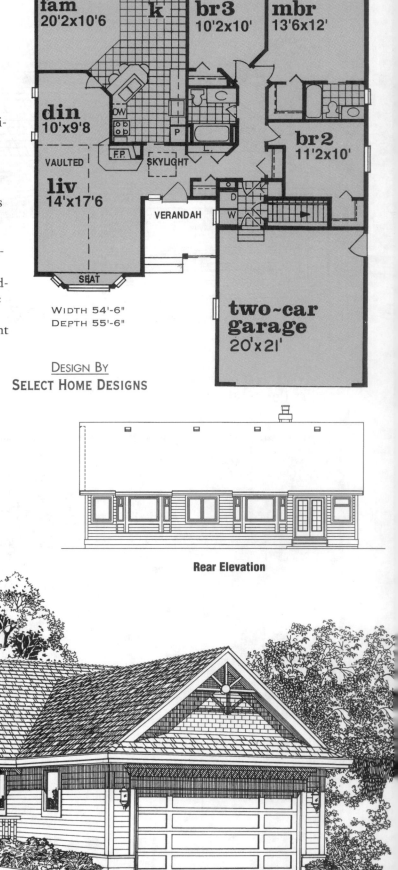

WIDTH 54'-6"
DEPTH 55'-6"

DESIGN BY
SELECT HOME DESIGNS

Rear Elevation

B. NATHAN

© 1998 Donald A. Gardner Architects, Inc.

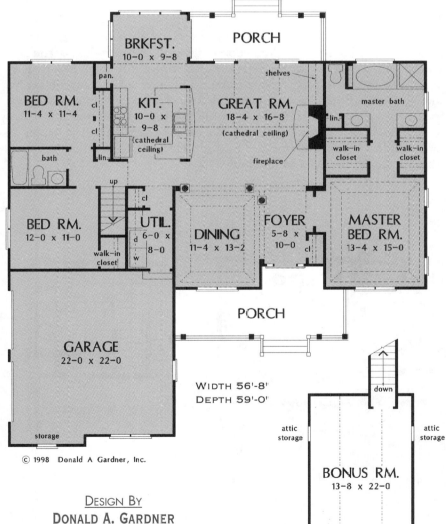

BRKFST.
10-0 x 9-8

PORCH

pan.

BED RM.
11-4 x 11-4

cl

cl

KIT.
10-0 x
9-8

(cathedral
ceiling)

lin.

shelves

GREAT RM.
18-4 x 16-8

(cathedral ceiling)

fireplace

master bath

lin.

walk-in
closet

walk-in
closet

bath

BED RM.
12-0 x 11-0

up

walk-in
closet

UTIL.
6-0 x
8-0

cl

d

w

DINING
11-4 x 13-2

FOYER
5-8 x
10-0

cl

MASTER
BED RM.
13-4 x 15-0

PORCH

GARAGE
22-0 x 22-0

WIDTH 56'-8"
DEPTH 59'-0"

storage

© 1998 Donald A Gardner, Inc.

down

attic
storage

attic
storage

BONUS RM.
13-8 x 22-0

DESIGN BY
DONALD A. GARDNER
ARCHITECTS, INC.

DESIGN 7682

Square Footage: 1,762
Bonus Room: 316 square feet

Craftsman details add architectural interest to the exterior of this charming home. Inside, it is graced by volume ceilings, decorative columns, clerestory windows and handy built-ins. The foyer introduces a formal dining room with a tray ceiling and the roomy great room with cathedral ceiling and fireplace. The kitchen and sunny breakfast nook are nearby; the kitchen boasts an island workcenter. The master suite is on the right and has a tray ceiling, double walk-in closets and private bath with dual sinks, whirlpool tub and separate shower. Family bedrooms are on the left, tucked behind the two-car garage. They share a full bath. Bonus space over the garage can be developed later for an additional bedroom or home office.

11

DESIGN Q500

Square Footage: 1,253

DESIGN BY
SELECT HOME DESIGNS

Horizontal siding and quaint window boxes lend a country appeal to the exterior of this design. If you choose this cute one-story home, you'll have the option of a powder room or a main-floor laundry room layout. The central foyer leads to a roomy living room with masonry fireplace and box-bay window. The nearby country kitchen has a long, L-shaped counter and a bay-window dining area. A rear door leads to the patio (basement stairs are directly opposite this door). Three bedrooms angle off the central hall. The master has a large window overlooking the rear yard and His and Hers wall closets. Family bedrooms face to the front of the house.

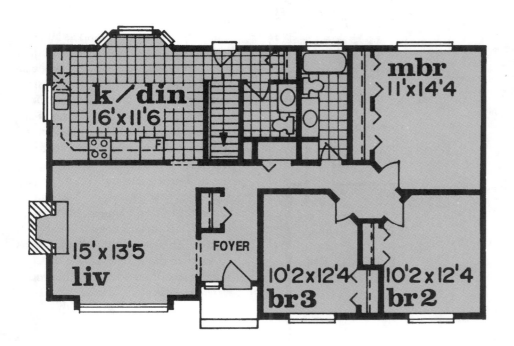

k/din
16'x11'6

mbr
11'x14'4

15'x13'5
liv

FOYER

10'2x12'4
br3

10'2x12'4
br2

Optional Laundry

D W

WIDTH 46'-0"
DEPTH 29'-6"

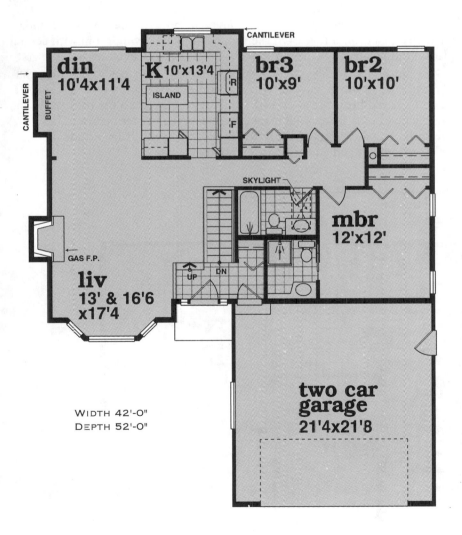

din
10'4x11'4

K 10'x13'4
ISLAND

br3
10'x9'

br2
10'x10'

CANTILEVER

CANTILEVER

BUFFET

R

F

SKYLIGHT

mbr
12'x12'

GAS F.P.

liv
13' & 16'6
x17'4

UP   DN

two car garage
21'4x21'8

WIDTH 42'-0"
DEPTH 52'-0"

DESIGN Q504

Square Footage: 1,253

DESIGN BY
SELECT HOME DESIGNS

A multi-paned bay window, nestled in a gabled roof, adds charm to this bungalow and gives it a touch of elegance. The covered front entry shares a foyer with access from the two-car garage. A coat closet here is handy. The stairway to the basement is also found here. A large living/dining area is to the left. The living room has a fire-place and bay window; the dining room has a buffet alcove. The kitchen is con-veniently located to serve the dining room and enjoys a view over the sink to the rear yard. A master bedroom and two family bedrooms are on the right side of the plan. The master has a pri-vate bath, while the family bedrooms share a full bath with skylight. A two-car garage sits to the front of the plan to help shield the bedrooms from street noise.

DESIGN Q445

Square Footage: 1,360

DESIGN BY
SELECT HOME DESIGNS

Smaller in size, but big on livability, this one-story home has amenities and options usually found only in larger homes. Begin with the covered veranda and its entry to a central foyer. On the right is a vaulted living room with central fireplace. On the left is a bedroom—or make it a den. A hall closet holds coats and other outdoor gear. The country kitchen lives up to its name. It features an open-railed stair to the basement, an L-shaped work counter, a breakfast snack island and a bayed breakfast nook with double-door access to the back yard. The two family bedrooms share a full main bath, while the master bedroom has a private bath. A two-car garage sits to the side of the plan. Plans include details for both a basement and a crawlspace foundation.

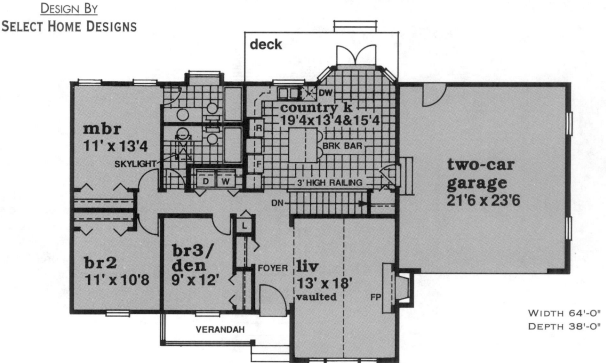

deck

country k
19'4x13'4&15'4

mbr
11' x 13'4

SKYLIGHT

BRK BAR

DW

R

F

D W

3' HIGH RAILING

two-car
garage
21'6 x 23'6

DN

br2
11' x 10'8

br3/
den
9' x 12'

L

FOYER

liv
13' x 18'
vaulted

FP

VERANDAH

WIDTH 64'-0"
DEPTH 38'-0"

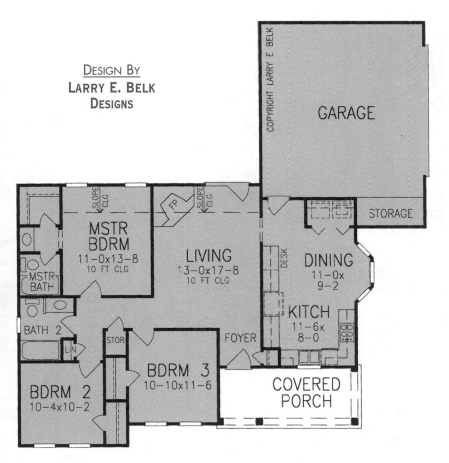

MSTR BDRM
11-0x13-8
10 FT CLG

LIVING
13-0x17-8
10 FT CLG

GARAGE

STORAGE

DINING
11-0x
9-2

KITCH
11-6x
8-0

MSTR BATH

BATH 2

LIN

STOR

FOYER

BDRM 3
10-10x11-6

BDRM 2
10-4x10-2

COVERED PORCH

WIDTH 51'-10"
DEPTH 53'-6"

DESIGN 8246
Square Footage: 1,170

This charming country home gives a nod to the past but speaks to the future as well, with an interior design for family living. A sloped ceiling lends a sense of spaciousness to the living room, which also features a corner hearth and a door to the outside. The U-shaped kitchen serves a convenient dining area, well lit by a bay window. A hall bath serves two family bedrooms, while a generous master suite has a private bath with a compartmented vanity and a walk-in closet. The two-car garage provides additional storage space and a service entrance that leads to the kitchen. Please specify crawlspace or slab foundation when ordering.

DESIGN Q512

Square Footage: 1,319

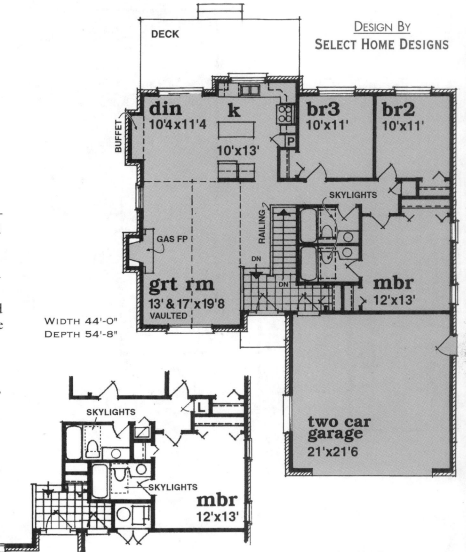

DESIGN BY
SELECT HOME DESIGNS

DECK

din
10'4x11'4

k

br3
10'x11'

br2
10'x11'

BUFFET

10'x13'

P

SKYLIGHTS

GAS FP

RAILING

DN

DN

DN

grt rm
13' & 17'x19'8
VAULTED

mbr
12'x13'

WIDTH 44'-0"
DEPTH 54'-8"

two car
garage
21'x21'6

SKYLIGHTS

L

SKYLIGHTS

mbr
12'x13'

Alternate layout for crawlspace

Charming and economical to build, this brick ranch design is ideal for first-time homeowners or retirement couples. A tiled foyer leads past the open-rail staircase to the basement into a vaulted great room. Here a gas fireplace warms the living and entertaining area. The dining room has buffet space and sliding glass doors to the rear deck. An L-shaped island kitchen is nearby and overlooks the rear deck. Three bedrooms include two family bedrooms sharing a full bath with soaking tub. The master suite has two wall closets and a private bath. If needed, the basement could be developed later into living or sleeping space. A two-car garage sits in front of the bedrooms to shelter them from street noise. Plans include details for both a basement and a crawlspace foundation.

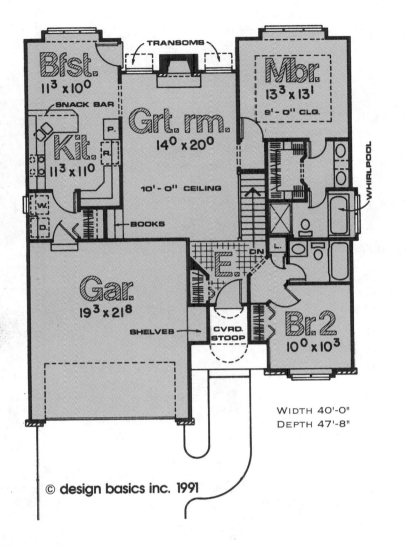

At only 1,205 square feet in size, this home feels considerably larger. The angled entry of this design features two plant shelves and a roomy closet. Straight ahead, the vaulted great room provides a window-flanked fireplace, a built-in bookcase and easy access to the kitchen and dinette. This area offers a snack bar, a wrapping counter and a pantry. The secondary bedroom extends privacy for guests or it could easily serve as a den. The master bedroom is highlighted by a box ceiling and a bath with a whirlpool and dual sinks. The two-car garage accesses the main house via a laundry area and holds storage shelves.

DESIGN BY
DESIGN BASICS, INC.

WIDTH 40'-0"
DEPTH 47'-8"

© design basics inc. 1991

G. MacDonald

DESIGN 9200

Square Footage: 1,604

Thoughtful arrangement makes this uncomplicated three-bedroom plan comfortable. The living and working areas are grouped together for convenience—a great room with cathedral ceiling, dining room with wet bar pass-through and kitchen with breakfast room. The sleeping area features a spacious master suite with a skylight and whirlpool in the bath, and a walk-in closet. Two smaller bedrooms accommodate guests graciously. A convenient service entrance leads from the garage, through the laundry room and into the kitchen. An alternate elevation is available at no extra cost.

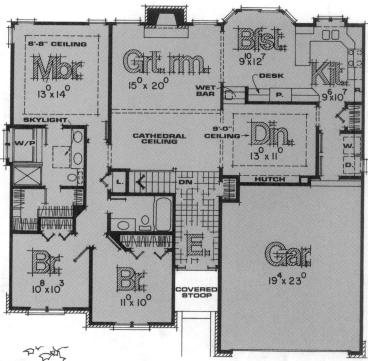

8'-8" CEILING

Mbr
13⁰ x 14⁰

SKYLIGHT

W/P

Br
10⁸ x 10³

Br
11⁰ x 10⁰

Grt. rm.
15⁰ x 20⁰

CATHEDRAL CEILING

DN

COVERED STOOP

WET BAR

Bfst
9¹⁰ x 12⁷

DESK

P.

9'-0" CEILING

Dn
13⁰ x 11⁰

HUTCH

Kit
9⁶ x 10⁷

W.
D.

Gar
19⁴ x 23⁰

WIDTH 48'-8"
DEPTH 48'-0"

DESIGN BY
DESIGN BASICS, INC.

QUOTE ONE®

Cost to build? See page 434 to order complete cost estimate to build this house in your area!

Alternate Exterior

S. MacDonald

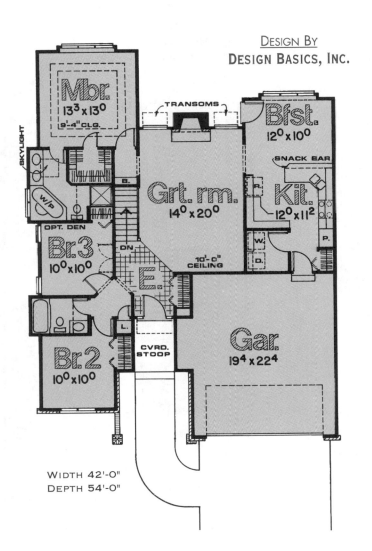

Mbr.
13³ x 13⁰
9'-4" CLG.

TRANSOMS

Bfst.
12⁰ x 10⁰

SKYLIGHT

SNACK BAR

Grt. rm.
14⁰ x 20⁰

Kit.
12⁰ x 11²

OPT. DEN

10'-0"
CEILING

Br. 3
10⁰ x 10⁰

DN

Br. 2
10⁰ x 10⁰

CVRD.
STOOP

Gar.
19⁴ x 22⁴

WIDTH 42'-0"
DEPTH 54'-0"

DESIGN 9256
Square Footage: 1,347

Though it may appear oversized, this plan is really quite compact and economical. From the ten-foot ceiling in the entry to the spacious great room with fireplace, it has on open feeling. A snack bar and pantry in the kitchen complement the work area. Bright windows light up the entire breakfast area. To the left side of the plan are three bedrooms, two of which share a full bath. The master suite has a boxed window, built-in bookcase and tiered ceiling. The skylit dressing area features a double vanity and there's a whirlpool in the bath. The double garage features storage space and accesses the main house via an entry near the laundry area.

This home, as shown in the photograph, may differ from the actual blueprints. For more detailed information, please check the floor plans carefully.

Photo by Andrew D. Lautman

DESIGN 2947

Square Footage: 1,830

LD

DESIGN BY
HOME PLANNERS

Quote One®

Cost to build? See page 434 to order complete cost estimate to build this house in your area!

This charming one-story traditional home greets visitors with a covered porch. A galley-style kitchen shares a snack bar with the spacious gathering room where a fireplace is the focal point. An ample master suite includes a luxury bath with a whirlpool tub and a separate dressing room. Two additional bedrooms, one that could double as a study, are located at the front of the home.

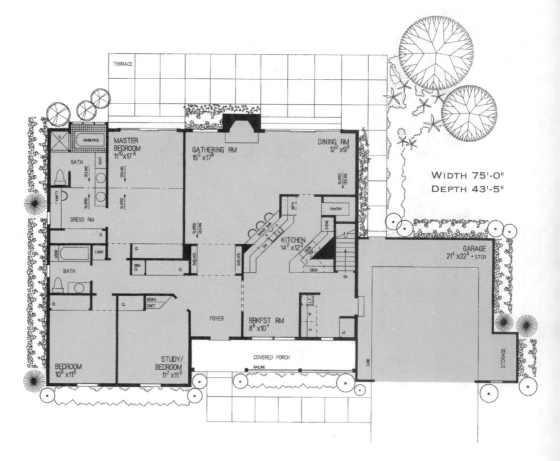

WIDTH 75'-0"
DEPTH 43'-5"

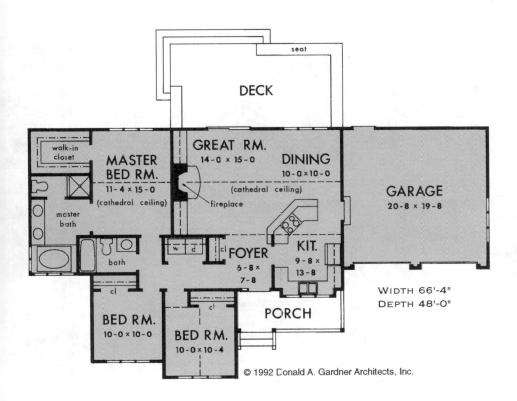

seat

DECK

GREAT RM.
14-0 x 15-0

DINING
10-0 x 10-0

(cathedral ceiling)

fireplace

walk-in closet

MASTER BED RM.
11-4 x 15-0
(cathedral ceiling)

master bath

bath

GARAGE
20-8 x 19-8

w d cl

FOYER
6-8 x 7-8

KIT.
9-8 x 13-8

cl

cl

BED RM.
10-0 x 10-0

BED RM.
10-0 x 10-4

cl

PORCH

WIDTH 66'-4"
DEPTH 48'-0"

© 1992 Donald A. Gardner Architects, Inc.

DESIGN 9664
Square Footage: 1,287

DESIGN BY
DONALD A. GARDNER ARCHITECTS, INC.

This economical plan offers an impressive visual statement with its comfortable and well-appointed appearance. The entrance foyer leads to all areas of the home. The great room, dining area and kitchen are all open to one another, allowing visual interaction. The great room and dining area both have a cathedral ceiling. The fireplace is flanked by bookshelves and cabinets. The master suite has a cathedral ceiling, walk-in closet and master bath with double-bowl vanity, whirlpool tub and shower. Please specify basement or crawlspace foundation when ordering.

QUOTE ONE®
Cost to build? See page 434 to order complete cost estimate to build this house in your area!

© 1992 Donald A. Gardner Architects, Inc.

B. NATHAN

DESIGN 9679

Square Footage: 1,512

DESIGN BY
DONALD A. GARDNER
ARCHITECTS, INC.

A multi-pane bay window, dormers, a cupola, a covered porch and a variety of building materials all combine to dress up this intriguing country cottage. The generous entry foyer leads to a formal dining room and an impressive great room with a cathedral ceiling and a fireplace. The kitchen includes a breakfast area with a bay window overlooking the deck. The great room and master bedroom also access the deck. An amenity-filled master suite is highlighted by a master bath that includes a double-bowl vanity, a shower and a garden tub. Two additional bedrooms are located at the front of the house for privacy and share a full bath.

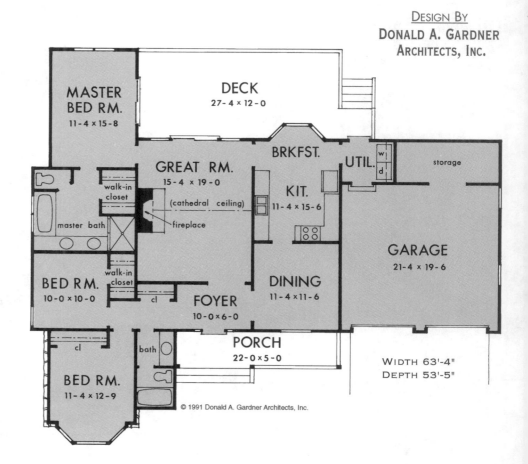

MASTER BED RM.
11-4 x 15-8

DECK
27-4 x 12-0

GREAT RM.
15-4 x 19-0

(cathedral ceiling)

fireplace

walk-in closet

master bath

BRKFST.

KIT.
11-4 x 15-6

UTIL.

w d

storage

GARAGE
21-4 x 19-6

BED RM.
10-0 x 10-0

walk-in closet

cl

FOYER
10-0 x 6-0

DINING
11-4 x 11-6

cl

bath

BED RM.
11-4 x 12-9

PORCH
22-0 x 5-0

WIDTH 63'-4"
DEPTH 53'-5"

DESIGN BY
DONALD A. GARDNER
ARCHITECTS, INC.

DESIGN 9726
Square Footage: 1,498

spa

DECK

MASTER
BED RM.
13-4 x 13-8

master
bath

skylights

walk-in
closet

storage

w
d

fireplace

BRKFST.
11-4 x 7-4

BED RM.
11-4 x 11-4

GREAT RM.
15-4 x 16-10
(cathedral ceiling)

KITCHEN
11-4 x 10-0

GARAGE
20-0 x 19-8

cl

bath

cl

FOYER
8-2 x 6-6

cl

DINING RM.
11-4 x 11-4

BED RM./
STUDY
11-4 x 10-4

PORCH

WIDTH 59'-8"
DEPTH 50'-8"

This charming country home utilizes multi-pane windows, columns, dormers and a covered porch to offer a welcoming front exterior. Inside, the great room with a dramatic cathedral ceiling commands attention; the kitchen and breakfast room are just beyond a set of columns. The tiered-ceiling dining room presents a delightfully formal atmosphere for dinner parties or family gatherings. A tray ceiling in the master bedroom contributes to its pleasant atmosphere, as do the large walk-in closet and the gracious master bath with a garden tub and a separate shower. The secondary bedrooms are located at the opposite end of the house for privacy. Please specify basement or crawlspace foundation when ordering.

DESIGN Q440

Square Footage: 1,092

DESIGN BY
SELECT HOME DESIGNS

Compact, yet efficient, this one-story home opens with a quaint covered porch to a convenient floor plan. The great room has a vaulted ceiling and warming hearth for cozy winter blazes. The step-saving galley kitchen is pure country with space for a family-sized dining area and sliding glass doors to the rear deck. The master bedroom has an angled entry and windows overlooking the rear yard. It shares a full bath that has a split entry with two family bedrooms (note the art niche at the entry to Bedroom 2). If you choose the crawlspace option, you'll gain space for a washer and dryer and a spot for a built-in media center. The two-car garage is reached through a side door in the kitchen. Plans include details for both a basement and a crawlspace foundation.

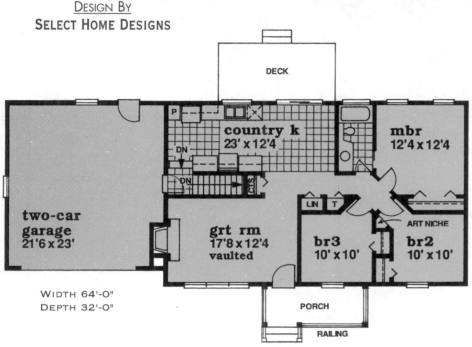

WIDTH 64'-0"
DEPTH 32'-0"

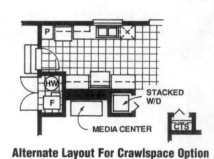

Alternate Layout For Crawlspace Option

24

Porch gables and fishscale siding bring back classic memories of yester-year in this cozy one-story. The covered entry is vaulted and protects an entry to a vaulted living room with box-bay window and fireplace. The kitchen and dining area are to the front and feature an open-railed stair to the basement and a U-shaped work area with pantry. The laundry area is nearby. It contains access to the two-car garage with workshop. Bedrooms line the rear of the plan. The master bedroom has a wall closet, a bayed window seat and private bath with box window. Two family bedrooms—one with walk-in closet—share access to a skylit main bath. Extra storage is available in a linen closet and coat closet in the center hall. Plans include details for both a basement and a crawlspace foundation.

DESIGN Q442
Square Footage: 1,282

DESIGN BY
SELECT HOME DESIGNS

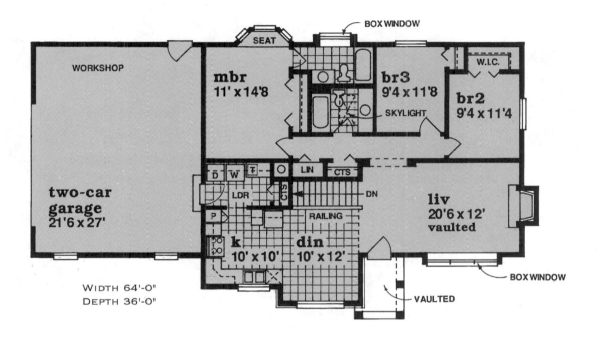

BOX WINDOW

SEAT

WORKSHOP

mbr
11' x 14'8

br3
9'4 x 11'8

W.I.C.

br2
9'4 x 11'4

SKYLIGHT

D W T LIN CTS

two-car garage
21'6 x 27'

LDR CTS DN

P RAILING

liv
20'6 x 12'
vaulted

k
10' x 10'

din
10' x 12'

VAULTED

BOX WINDOW

WIDTH 64'-0"
DEPTH 36'-0"

DESIGN 8229

Square Footage: 1,955

DESIGN BY
**LARRY E. BELK
DESIGNS**

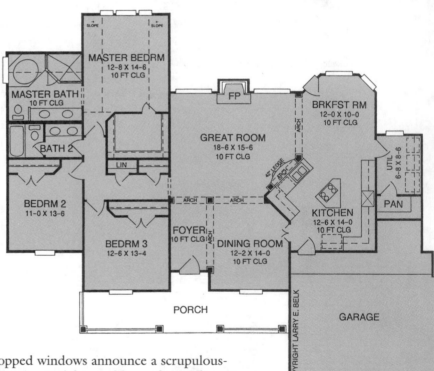

WIDTH 65'-0"
DEPTH 58'-8"

A finely detailed covered porch and arch-topped windows announce a scrupulously designed interior, replete with amenities. A grand foyer with ten-foot ceiling and columned archways set the pace for the entire floor plan. Clustered sleeping quarters to the left feature a luxurious master suite with a sloped ceiling, corner whirlpool bath and walk-in closet, and two family bedrooms which share a bath. Picture windows flanking a centered fireplace lend plenty of natural light to the great room, which is open through grand, columned archways to the formal dining area and the bay-windowed breakfast room. The kitchen, conveniently positioned between the dining and breakfast rooms, shares an informal eating counter with the great room. A utility room and walk-in pantry are tucked neatly to the side of the plan. Please specify crawlspace or slab foundation when ordering.

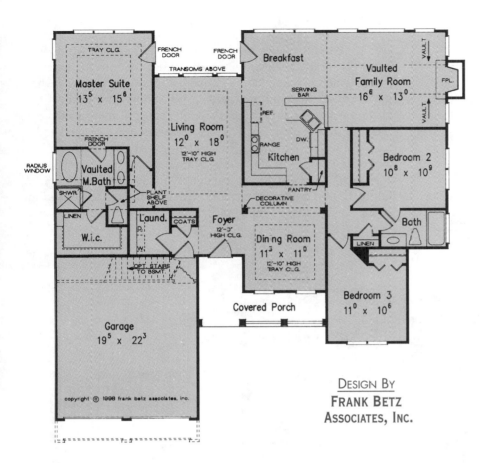

TRAY CLG.

Master Suite
13⁵ x 15⁶

FRENCH DOOR FRENCH DOOR

TRANSOMS ABOVE

Breakfast

Vaulted Family Room
16⁶ x 13⁰

VAULT

FPL

SERVING BAR

RADIUS WINDOW

FRENCH DOOR

Vaulted M.Bath

SHWR.

Living Room
12⁰ x 18⁰
12'-10" HIGH TRAY CLG.

REF.

RANGE

DW.

Kitchen

VAULT

LINEN

PLANT SHELF ABOVE

Bedroom 2
10⁸ x 10⁹

W.i.c.

Laund.

COATS

Foyer
12'-3" HIGH CLG.

PANTRY

DECORATIVE COLUMN

Bath

LINEN

OPT. STAIRS TO BSMT.

Dining Room
11³ x 11⁰
12'-10" HIGH TRAY CLG.

Garage
19⁵ x 22³

copyright © 1998 frank betz associates, inc.

Covered Porch

Bedroom 3
11⁰ x 10⁶

WIDTH 58'-10"
DEPTH 53'-6"

DESIGN BY
FRANK BETZ
ASSOCIATES, INC.

DESIGN P445

Square Footage: 1,808

All the bases are covered in this classic one-story design, from formal living to casual lifestyles. The covered porch opens to a central foyer with dining room on the right and living room straight back. Both rooms have tray ceilings. The family room is to the rear, beyond the gourmet kitchen and breakfast nook. It is warmed by a fireplace and heightened by a vaulted ceiling. Two family bedrooms are at this end of the plan. They share a full bath. The master suite is resplendent with a tray ceiling and private bath with walk-in closet. It is separated from the family bedrooms for convenience. Note the two-car garage and laundry area beyond the service entrance.

DESIGN Q441

Square Footage: 1,261

DESIGN BY
SELECT HOME DESIGNS

This compact, country home is perfect as a starter design or for empty-nesters. Detailing on the outside includes a covered porch, shuttered windows, and a Palladian-style window in the great room. The front entry opens directly into the great room, which is vaulted and features a three-sided fireplace which it shares with the country kitchen. A deck just beyond the kitchen will serve as an outdoor dining spot, accessed easily through sliding glass doors. The kitchen itself is L-shaped and has a handy work island. A nearby laundry area holds the stairway to the basement and access to the two-car garage with storage space. Three bedrooms include two family bedrooms and a full bath, plus a master bedroom with private bath. Plans include details for both a basement and a crawlspace foundation.

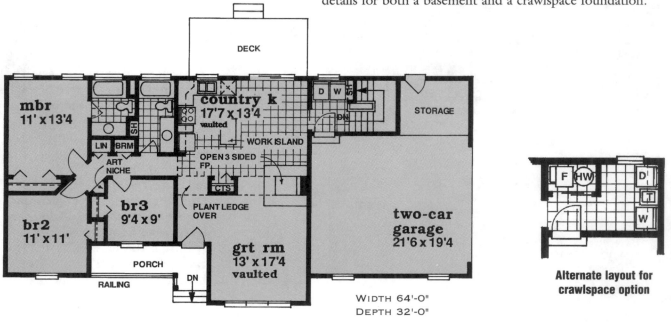

DECK

mbr
11' x 13'4

country k
17'7 x 13'4
vaulted

D W SH

STORAGE

LIN BRM

ART
NICHE

WORK ISLAND

OPEN 3 SIDED
FP

CTS

br3
9'4 x 9'

PLANT LEDGE
OVER

two-car
garage
21'6 x 19'4

br2
11' x 11'

grt rm
13' x 17'4
vaulted

PORCH

RAILING

DN

WIDTH 64'-0"
DEPTH 32'-0"

F HW D

T

W

Alternate layout for crawlspace option

28

Fine detailing and multiple roof lines give this home plenty of curb appeal. A large living room with a ten-foot ceiling and a fireplace is the focal point for this lovely small home. The dining room, with an attractive bay window, and a sunny breakfast room provide complementary eating areas. The master bedroom features a large walk-in closet, a bath with His and Hers vanities and a combination whirlpool tub and shower. Bedrooms 2 and 3 and Bath 2 complete this very livable plan. Please specify crawlspace or slab foundation when ordering.

DESIGN 8170
Square Footage: 1,402

DESIGN BY
LARRY E. BELK
DESIGNS

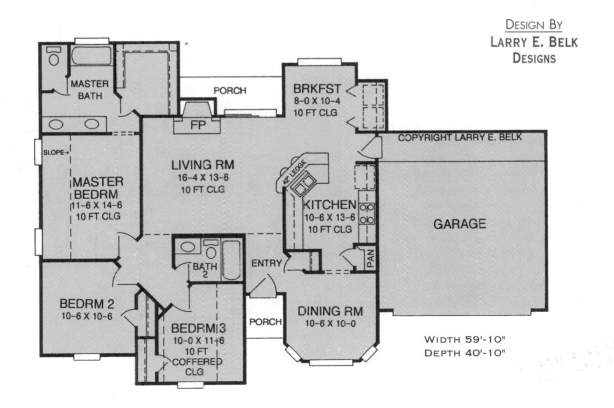

29

DESIGN T137

Square Footage: 1,770

DESIGN BY
DESIGN TRADITIONS

Wood frame, weatherboard siding and stacked stone give this home its country cottage appeal. The concept is reinforced by the double elliptical arched front porch, the Colonial balustrade and the roof-vent dormer. Inside, the foyer leads to the great room and the dining room. The well-planned kitchen easily serves the breakfast room. A rear deck makes outdoor living extra-enjoyable. Three bedrooms include a master suite with a tray ceiling and a luxurious bath. The two secondary bedrooms share a compartmented bath. This home is designed with a basement foundation.

WIDTH 48'-0"
DEPTH 47'-5"

BRKFST
8-0 X 11-6
10 FT CLG

PORCH

FP

LIVING RM
16-0 X 13-8
10 FT CLG

MASTER
BATH

W.I.C.

SLOPE

MASTER
BEDRM
11-4 X 14-6
10 FT CLG

BATH
2

BEDRM 2
12-0 X 13-0

BEDRM 3
11-0 X 13-6
10 FT
COFFERED CLG

ENTRY

PORCH

42" LEDGE

KITCHEN
10-6 X 14-0

PAN

DINING RM
10-6 X 12-0

COPYRIGHT LARRY E. BELK

GARAGE

WIDTH 59'-10"
DEPTH 44'-4"

DESIGN 8181
Square Footage: 1,500

DESIGN BY
LARRY E. BELK
DESIGNS

This bestselling traditional home is compact in size but packed with all of the amenities you'd expect in a larger home. The foyer opens to a formal dining room with a classic bay window. The adjacent kitchen opens to a breakfast nook and shares an angled eating bar with the living room, which offers a cozy fireplace flanked by picture windows. The master suite features His and Hers vanities, a whirlpool tub/shower combination and a walk-in closet. Ten-foot ceilings in the major living areas as well as in two of the bedrooms contribute an aura of spaciousness to this plan. Please specify crawlspace or slab foundation when ordering.

31

DESIGN 7695

Square Footage: 1,966
Bonus Room: 355 square feet

A striking mixture of exterior materials creates visual excitement on this cleverly designed one-story. The interior is no less thoughtful. High ceilings, built-in cabinetry and interior columns give the home a custom feel. The great room, with fireplace, resides to the rear of the plan and is the center of livability. It connects directly to the island kitchen and bayed breakfast nook. A formal dining area is at the front of the plan and is defined by columns. A master suite with all the required amenities is near a family bedroom—or make it a study. A second family bedroom is behind the two-car garage and has the use of a full bath. Extra storage space in the garage makes it exceptionally handy.

DESIGN BY
DONALD A. GARDNER
ARCHITECTS, INC.

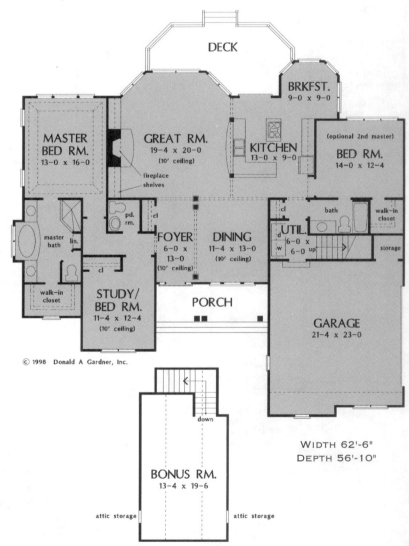

DECK

BRKFST.
9-0 x 9-0

MASTER
BED RM.
13-0 x 16-0

GREAT RM.
19-4 x 20-0
(10' ceiling)

fireplace
shelves

KITCHEN
13-0 x 9-0

(optional 2nd master)
BED RM.
14-0 x 12-4

master
bath

lin.

pd.
rm.

cl

FOYER
6-0 x
13-0
(10' ceiling)

DINING
11-4 x 13-0
(10' ceiling)

cl

bath

walk-in
closet

UTIL.
6-0 x
6-0

up

storage

walk-in
closet

cl

STUDY/
BED RM.
11-4 x 12-4
(10' ceiling)

PORCH

GARAGE
21-4 x 23-0

down

WIDTH 62'-6"
DEPTH 56'-10"

BONUS RM.
13-4 x 19-6

attic storage   attic storage

© 1998 Donald A. Gardner, Inc.

This design combines a stucco exterior with cedar shakes, a stone foundation and arched woodwork for a coveted look. Exceptional rear views are possible due to three porches in the back of the plan: at the great room, the master bedroom and one family bedroom. Thoughtful details include an island kitchen, a fireplace flanked by built-ins in the great room, outstanding baths to complement each bedroom and a bayed dining area. The utility room has access to the two-car garage where extra storage will be appreciated. Note the walk-in closets in both the master suite and the family bedroom on the right. Bonus space over the garage can become an additional bedroom in the future if you choose.

DESIGN 7699
Square Footage: 1,792
Bonus Room: 338 square feet

DESIGN BY
DONALD A. GARDNER
ARCHITECTS, INC.

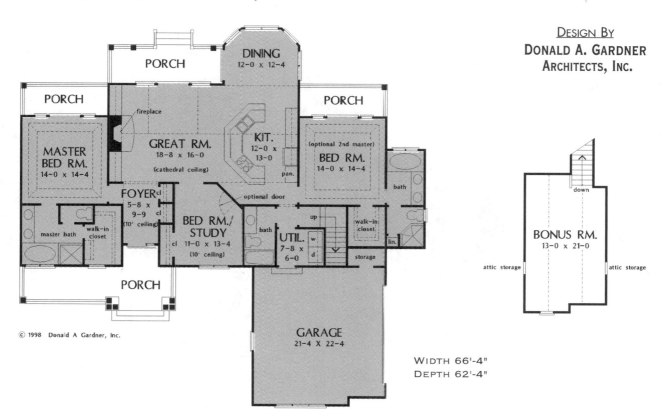

33

DESIGN 9202

Square Footage: 1,808

Discriminating buyers will love the refined yet inviting look of this three-bedroom ranch plan. A tiled entry with ten-foot ceilings leads into the spacious great room with large bay window. An open-hearth fireplace warms both the great room and kitchen. The sleeping area features a large master suite with a dramatic arched window and a bath with whirlpool tub, His and Hers vanities and a walk-in closet. Don't miss the storage space in the oversized garage.

DESIGN BY
DESIGN BASICS, INC.

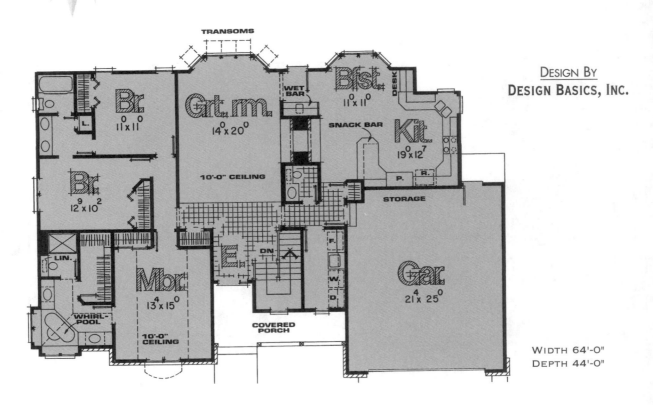

WIDTH 64'-0"
DEPTH 44'-0"

attic storage

down

BONUS RM.
railing 18-2 x 14-6

attic storage

sto.

GARAGE
22-5 x 24-0

up

seat

spa

DECK

skylights

SUN RM.
13-4 x 9-8

fireplace

GREAT RM.
19-2 x 17-6

(cathedral ceiling)

UTIL.
9-4 x
5-4

d w

pd. rm.

skylight

bath

cl

lin.

BED RM.
11-4 x 14-0

master bath

walk-in closet

cl

FOYER
6-10 x
6-10

DINING
12-0 x 12-0

KITCHEN
13-4 x 11-0

cl

BED RM.
12-8 x 11-0

cl

MASTER BED RM.
13-4 x 16-6

PORCH

BREAKFAST
13-4 x 10-8

WIDTH 67'-5"
DEPTH 75'-2"

Design 7689

Square Footage: 2,166
Bonus Room: 358 square feet

A hip roof with multiple gables and dormers, columns, keystone arches and a rich brick exterior give this traditional design distinction, while the contemporary, open floor plan creates a comfortable family home. Beautiful columns define entry to the dining room where a tray ceiling adds refinement. In the great room beyond, the cathedral ceiling adds volume, the fireplace brings warmth and French doors open to both the sun room and rear deck. With access to the skylit sun room, the master suite offers homeowners a luxurious, private retreat. Meanwhile, additional bedrooms and a full bath serve family needs. A bonus room over the garage is the perfect spot for a home office or guest suite.

Design By
Donald A. Gardner
Architects, Inc.

Design 8064

Square Footage: 1,742

Design By

Larry E. Belk
Designs

This traditional design warmly welcomes both family and visitors with a delightful bay window, a Palladian window and shutters. The entry introduces a beautiful interior plan, starting with the formal dining room and the central great room with fireplace, and views and access to outdoor spaces. Ten-foot ceilings in the major living areas give the home an open, spacious feel. The kitchen features an angled eating bar, a pantry and lots of cabinet and counter space. Comfort and style abound in the distinctive master suite, offering a high ceiling, corner whirlpool tub, knee-space vanity and compartmented toilet. An ample walk-in closet with a window for natural light completes this owner's retreat. Bedrooms 2 and 3 are nearby and share a hall bath, and Bedroom 3 offers a raised ceiling. Please specify slab or crawlspace foundation when ordering.

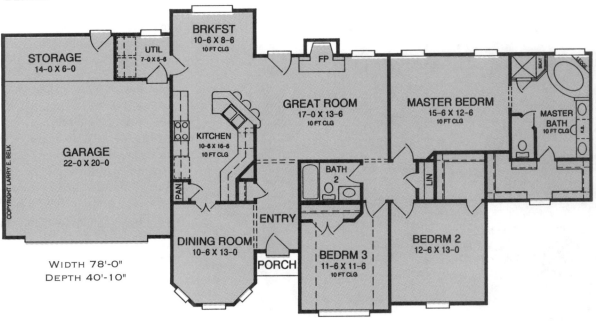

WIDTH 78'-0"
DEPTH 40'-10"

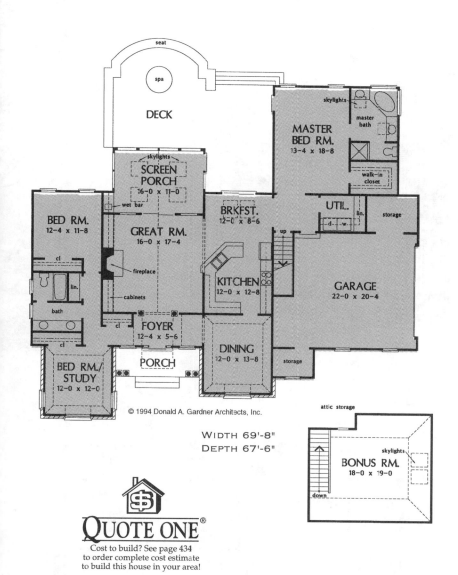

DECK

seat

spa

SCREEN PORCH
16-0 x 11-0

skylights

wet bar

BED RM.
12-4 x 11-8

cl

GREAT RM.
16-0 x 17-4

fireplace

cabinets

bath

lin.

cl

cl

FOYER
12-4 x 5-6

BED RM./STUDY
12-0 x 12-0

PORCH

BRKFST.
12-0 x 8-6

KITCHEN
12-0 x 12-8

DINING
12-0 x 13-8

up

MASTER BED RM.
13-4 x 18-8

skylights

master bath

walk-in closet

UTIL.

d. w.

lin.

storage

GARAGE
22-0 x 20-4

storage

© 1994 Donald A. Gardner Architects, Inc.

WIDTH 69'-8"
DEPTH 67'-6"

attic storage

BONUS RM.
18-0 x 19-0

skylights

down

DESIGN 9734

Square Footage: 1,977
Bonus Room: 430 square feet

DESIGN BY
DONALD A. GARDNER
ARCHITECTS, INC.

A two-story foyer with a Palladian window above sets the tone for this sunlit home. Columns mark the passage from the foyer to the great room, where a centered fireplace and built-in cabinets are found. A screened porch with four skylights above and a wet bar provides a pleasant place to start the day or wind down after work. The kitchen is flanked by the formal dining room and the breakfast room with sliding glass doors to the large, rear deck. Hidden quietly in the rear, the master suite includes a bath with dual vanities and skylights. Two family bedrooms (one an optional study) share a bath with twin sinks. Please specify basement or crawlspace foundation when ordering.

QUOTE ONE®

Cost to build? See page 434
to order complete cost estimate
to build this house in your area!

© 1994 Donald A. Gardner Architects, Inc.

B. NATHAN

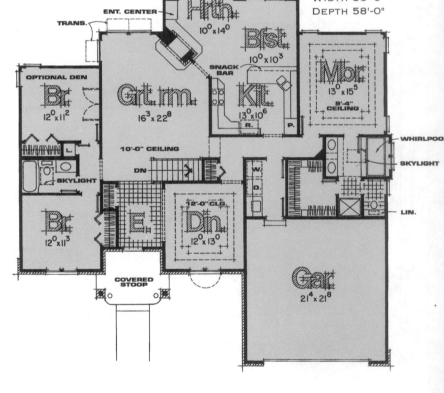

WIDTH 56'-0"
DEPTH 58'-0"

ENT. CENTER
TRANS.

Hrth
10⁰ x 14⁰

Bfst
10⁰ x 10³

SNACK BAR

Mbr
13⁰ x 15⁵

9'-4" CEILING

OPTIONAL DEN

Br
12⁰ x 11²

Gt. rm.
16³ x 22⁸

Kit
13⁰ x 10⁶

R.

P.

WHIRLPOOL

SKYLIGHT

10'-0" CEILING

DN

SKYLIGHT

W. D.

LIN.

Br
12⁰ x 11³

E

Dn
12⁰ x 13⁰

12'-0" CLG.

Gar
21⁴ x 21⁸

COVERED STOOP

DESIGN 9204

Square Footage: 1,911

DESIGN BY
DESIGN BASICS, INC.

This sophisticated ranch design shows off its facade with fanlights and elegant arches. Grace pervades the interior, starting with the formal dining room with twelve-foot coffered ceiling and an arched window. An extensive great room shares a through-fireplace with a cozy, bayed hearth room. The well-planned kitchen features a spacious work area and a snack bar pass-through to the breakfast area. Peace and quiet prevail in a secluded master suite, which offers a coffered ceiling, corner windows, whirlpool bath and skylight. On the opposite side of the plan, two family bedrooms, or one and a den, share a hall bath with skylight. An alternate elevation is available at no extra cost.

QUOTE ONE®

Cost to build? See page 434
to order complete cost estimate
to build this house in your area!

Alternate Exterior

Practical, yet equipped with a variety of popular amenities, this pleasant traditional home is an excellent choice for empty-nesters or small families. The front living room can become a third bedroom if you choose. The great room with dramatic fireplace serves as the main living area. A luxurious master suite features a ten-foot tray ceiling and a large bath with whirlpool, skylight, plant ledge and twin vanities. The kitchen with breakfast room serves both the dining and great rooms. A tandem drive-through garage holds space for a third car or extra storage. Please specify basement or slab foundation when ordering.

DESIGN 9201

Square Footage: 1,996

DESIGN BY
DESIGN BASICS, INC.

QUOTE ONE®

Cost to build? See page 434
to order complete cost estimate
to build this house in your area!

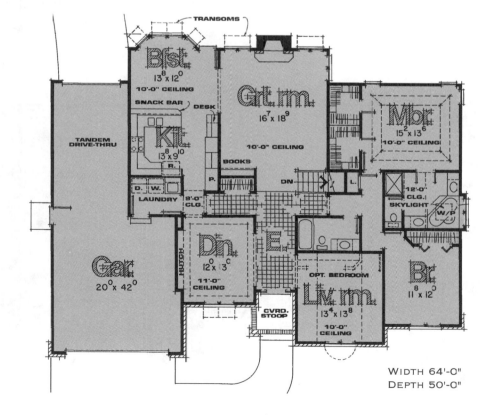

TRANSOMS

Bfst.
13⁸ x 12⁰

10'-0" CEILING

SNACK BAR

DESK

Grt. rm.
16⁷ x 18⁹

10'-0" CEILING

BOOKS

Mbr.
15² x 13⁶

10'-0" CEILING

Kit.
13⁸ x 9¹⁰

R.

D. W.

LAUNDRY

9'-0" CLG.

P.

DN.

L.

12'-0"
CLG.
SKYLIGHT

W/P

TANDEM
DRIVE-THRU

Gar.
20⁰ x 42⁰

HUTCH

Dn.
12⁰ x 13⁰

11'-0"
CEILING

CVRD.
STOOP

OPT. BEDROOM

Liv. rm.
13⁴ x 13⁸

10'-0"
CEILING

Br.
11⁸ x 12⁰

WIDTH 64'-0"
DEPTH 50'-0"

39

DESIGN 8180

Square Footage: 1,862

DESIGN BY
LARRY E. BELK
DESIGNS

The charming traditional has all the amenities of a larger plan in a compact layout. Ten-foot ceilings give this home an expansive feel. An angled eating bar separates the kitchen and great room while leaving these areas open to one another for family gatherings and entertaining. The master bedroom includes a huge walk-in closet and a superior master bath with a whirlpool tub and separate shower. A large utility room and an oversized storage area are located near the secondary entrance to the home. Two additional bedrooms and a bath finish the plan. Please specify crawlspace or slab foundation when ordering.

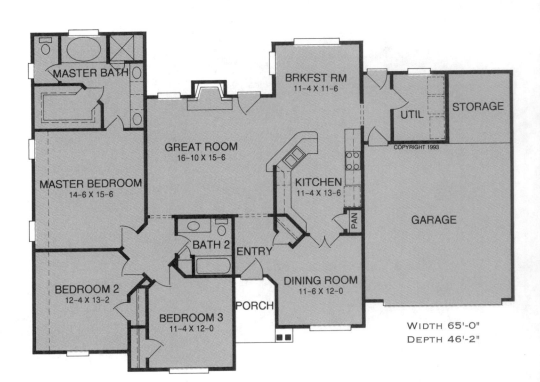

MASTER BATH

BRKFST RM
11-4 X 11-6

UTIL   STORAGE

GREAT ROOM
16-10 X 15-6

COPYRIGHT 1993

KITCHEN
11-4 X 13-6

MASTER BEDROOM
14-6 X 15-6

PAN

GARAGE

BATH 2   ENTRY

BEDROOM 2
12-4 X 13-2

DINING ROOM
11-6 X 12-0

BEDROOM 3
11-4 X 12-0

PORCH

WIDTH 65'-0"
DEPTH 46'-2"

Design 8178

Square Footage: 1,282

Design By
Larry E. Belk
Designs

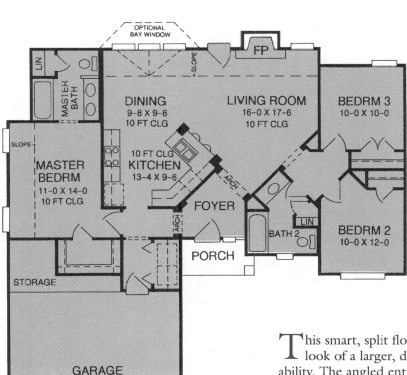

Width 48'-10"
Depth 52'-6"

This smart, split floor plan uses angles and arches to create the look of a larger, deluxe home while maintaining easy, family livability. The angled entry foyer opens through arches either to the hall leading to the master suite or to the living room. The angular living room has a fireplace, back patio door and snack bar joining the oversized kitchen. The dining room is open to both the kitchen and living room and can be enhanced with an optional bay window. The master bedroom is situated separately from the two family bedrooms for privacy and features a dual-vanity bath and walk-in closet. Please specify crawlspace or slab foundation when ordering.

DESIGN 9375

Square Footage: 2,456

DESIGN BY
DESIGN BASICS, INC.

Tapered columns at the entry help to create a majestic front elevation. Inside, an open great room features a wet bar, a fireplace, tall windows and access to a covered porch with skylights. A wide kitchen features an ideally placed island, two pantries and easy laundry access. Double doors open to the master suite where attention is drawn to French doors leading to the master bath and the covered porch. The master bath provides beauty and convenience with a whirlpool, dual lavatories, plant shelves and a large walk-in closet. Two secondary bedrooms share a compartmented bath.

Cost to build? See page 434
to order complete cost estimate
to build this house in your area!

WHIRLPOOL   LIN.   COVERED PORCH
SKYLIGHTS
TRANSOMS

Gath. rm.
17⁴ x 15⁷
10'-0" CLG.

10'-0" CLG.

Mbr.
15¹ x 17³
10'-0" CEILING

Grt. rm.
20⁰ x 16⁰
10'-0" CEILING

ENT. CENTER
SNACK BAR   DESK

WET
BAR

Kit.
13⁰ x 16⁴

Br. 3
14¹ x 11⁰
OPTIONAL DEN

DISPLAY

DN   Din.
12⁴ x 15⁴
10'-0" CEILING

P.   P.

Br. 2
12⁸ x 11⁸
10'-0" CEILING

Gar.
21⁴ x 35⁰

TRANSOMS
COVERED PORCH

WIDTH 66'-0"
DEPTH 68'-0"

© design basics inc. 1992

42

T his one-story with grand rooflines holds a most convenient floor plan. The great room with fireplace to the rear complements a front-facing living room. The formal dining room with tray ceiling sits just across the hall from the living room and is also easily accessible to the kitchen. An island, pantry, breakfast room and patio are highlights in the kitchen. A bedroom at this end of the house works fine as an office or guest bedroom since a full bath is close by. Two additional bedrooms are to the right of the plan: a master suite with grand bath and one additional secondary bedroom. A three-car garage provides extra storage space.

DESIGN 9362

Square Footage: 2,172

DESIGN BY
DESIGN BASICS, INC.

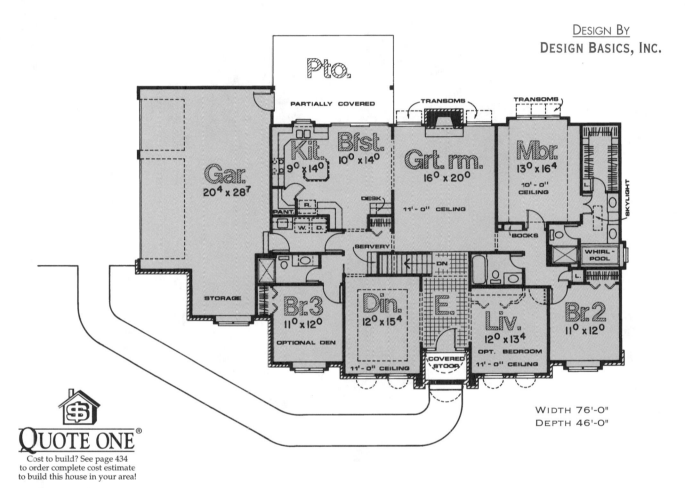

WIDTH 76'-0"
DEPTH 46'-0"

Quote One®

Cost to build? See page 434
to order complete cost estimate
to build this house in your area!

COPYRIGHT 1993 LARRY E. BELK

DESIGN 8013

Square Footage: 2,409
Bonus Space: 490 square feet

The stately elegance of this lovely home is evident from first glance. The front door, flanked by four Ionic columns, welcomes all into the foyer. Upon entering the great room through two square columns, the focus is on a large masonry fireplace. Moving from the great room, Bedrooms 2 and 3 are located off the hallway. The master suite is located at the rear of the house with a luxury master bath that includes large, walk-in His and Hers closets. The kitchen, equipped with an eating bar, a walk-in pantry and a desk, is well designed for the busy cook. The breakfast area offers a full view of the back yard with access to a spacious covered porch perfect for screening. A staircase from the kitchen area rises to an expandable second floor. With a future bedroom, game room and bath upstairs, this home will fit the needs of a growing family. This plan is available with either a crawlspace or slab foundation. Please specify when ordering.

WIDTH 85'-8"
DEPTH 68'-4"

STORAGE

DOUBLE GARAGE

BRICK STEPS

COVERED PORCH

MASTER BATH

MASTER BEDROOM
18-0 X 13-6
9 FT CEILING

BREAKFAST
10-0 X 11-6
9 FT CEILING

PWDR

UTIL

BEDROOM 2
12-4 X 12-0
9 FT CEILING

GREAT ROOM
21-4 X 17-0
9 FT CEILING

PAN

KITCHEN
14-6 X 16-0
9 FT CEILING

BATH 2

BEDROOM 3
13-0 X 11-6
9 FT CEILING

FOYER
9 FT CEILING

DINING ROOM
13-4 X 14-0
9 FT CEILING

PORCH

DESIGN BY
LARRY E. BELK
DESIGNS

FUTURE GAME RM
16-2 X 15-0

FUTURE BEDRM
11-6 X 13-0

QUOTE ONE®

Cost to build? See page 434
to order complete cost estimate
to build this house in your area!

Rear

44

This classic home exudes elegance and style and offers sophisticated ameni-ties in a compact size. Ten-foot ceilings throughout the plan lend an aura of spacious hospitality. A generous living room with a sloped ceiling, built-in bookcases and a centerpiece fireplace, offers views as well as access to the rear yard. The nearby breakfast room shares an informal eating counter with the ample kitchen, which serves the coffered-ceiling dining room through French doors. Three bedrooms include a sumptuous master suite with windowed whirlpool tub and walk-in closet, and two family bedrooms which share a full bath. Please specify slab or crawlspace foundation when ordering.

DESIGN 8183

Square Footage: 1,890

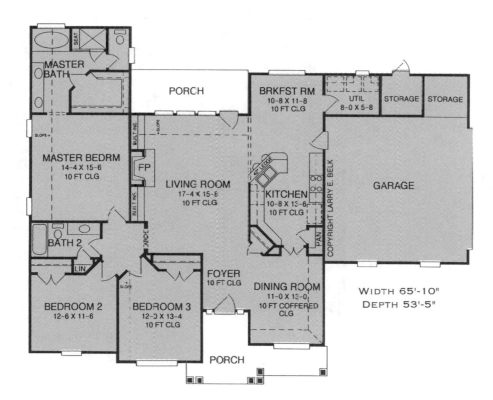

DESIGN BY
LARRY E. BELK
DESIGNS

WIDTH 65'-10"
DEPTH 53'-5"

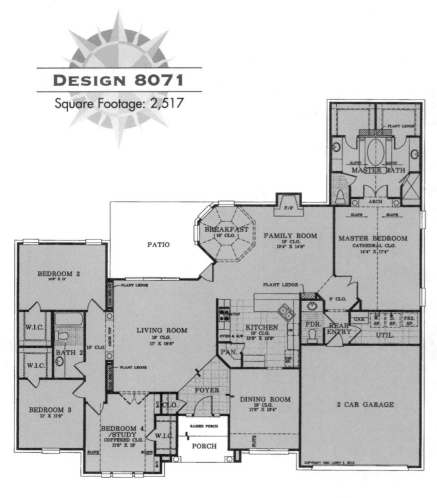

DESIGN 8071

Square Footage: 2,517

WIDTH 69'-0"
DEPTH 63'-6"

A graceful stucco arch supported by columns gives this home instant curb appeal. Stucco quoins are used to further accent its traditional brick finish. Inside, the angled foyer steps down into the living room and draws the eye to a duplicate of the exterior arch with columns. Built-in display shelves on either side provide plenty of room for books or treasures. Step down again to enter the formal dining room. The kitchen features a coffered ceiling and is conveniently grouped with a sunny bayed breakfast room and the family room, the perfect place for informal gatherings. Upon entering the master suite, the master bath becomes the focal point. Columns flank the entry to this luxurious bath with a whirlpool tub as its centerpiece, His and Hers walk-in closets, a separate shower and double-bowl vanities. This plan is available with either a crawlspace or slab foundation. Please specify when ordering.

DESIGN BY
LARRY E. BELK
DESIGNS

Elegant and classically styled, this home has great curb appeal. Inside, ten-foot ceilings give the home a spacious feel. The roomy living room features a centerpiece fireplace flanked by built-in bookcases. An angled bar opens the nearby kitchen and breakfast room to the living room. Three bedrooms, including a master suite with huge walk-in closet are on the left side of the plan. The master bath has a whirlpool spa, separate shower, compartmented toilet and double sinks. The family bedrooms share a full bath. Note the utility room connecting the two-car garage and the main house. The garage features a large storage area. Please specify slab or crawl-space foundation when ordering.

DESIGN 8257
Square Footage: 1,932

DESIGN BY
LARRY E. BELK
DESIGNS

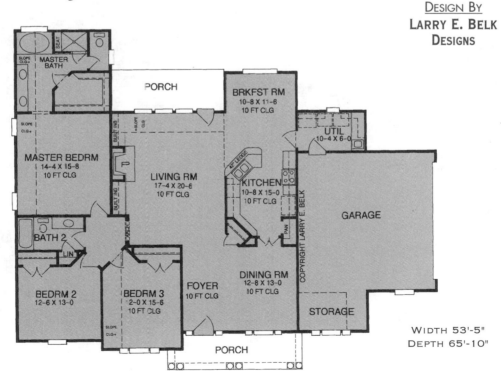

MASTER BATH

PORCH

BRKFST RM
10-8 X 11-6
10 FT CLG

UTIL
10-4 X 6-0

MASTER BEDRM
14-4 X 15-8
10 FT CLG

LIVING RM
17-4 X 20-6
10 FT CLG

KITCHEN
10-8 X 15-0
10 FT CLG

GARAGE

BATH 2

BEDRM 2
12-6 X 13-0

BEDRM 3
2-0 X 15-6
10 FT CLG

FOYER
10 FT CLG

DINING RM
12-8 X 13-0
10 FT CLG

STORAGE

PORCH

COPYRIGHT LARRY E. BELK

WIDTH 53'-5"
DEPTH 65'-10"

DESIGN P446

Square Footage: 2,007

DESIGN BY
FRANK BETZ
ASSOCIATES, INC.

WIDTH 58'-0"
DEPTH 64'-0"

Nothing can dress up a facade as well as a mixture of materials. In this case, stonework and horizontal wood siding work in tandem for a beautiful exterior. On the inside, the floor plan complements the beauty of the facade and features enough extras to make it special. The vaulted living room and formal dining room are defined and separated by columns and complement a casual great room with fireplace. A serving bar between the kitchen and the breakfast room adds possibilities to casual dining. Note the walk-in pantry in the kitchen. Both the breakfast room and master suite share a covered porch in the rear right corner. Two family bedrooms sit at the opposite end of the plan and share a full bath. Please specify basement or crawlspace foundation when ordering.

Featuring a stunning exterior of stucco, stone and cedar shakes, this home both blends with and takes advantage of the beauty of its natural surroundings. Designed for optimum openness, the common areas are defined by interior columns and ceiling heights. Windows extend dramatically across the back of the home for exceptional backyard views. The master suite features a tray ceiling, sitting alcove and private bath with dual walk-in closets, garden tub and separate shower. A bedroom/study, located adjacent to the master suite has access to a hall bath, and a third bedroom on the opposite side of the home boasts its own private bath. The plan includes a crawlspace foundation.

DESIGN 7678

Square Footage: 2,201

DESIGN BY

DONALD A. GARDNER
ARCHITECTS, INC.

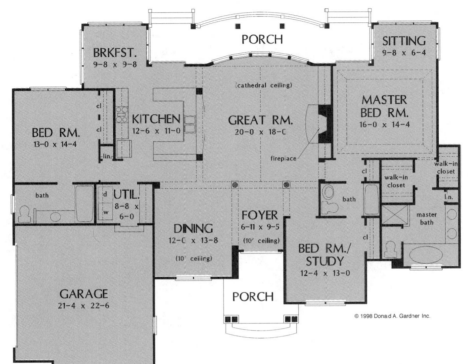

WIDTH 69'-6"
DEPTH 55'-10"

DESIGN 8253

Square Footage: 2,910

DESIGN BY
LARRY E. BELK
DESIGNS

Multiple rooflines, shutters, a bayed tower and a covered porch combine to create a fine facade for this three-bedroom home. Inside, the foyer opens onto the formal dining room to the right, with the formal living room and its fireplace directly ahead. The island kitchen easily serves the sunny breakfast room and the spacious family room, while also offering a large pantry and plenty of counter and cabinet space. Located in the left wing for privacy, the master bedroom suite features His and Hers walk-in closets and a lavish bath with a separate tub and shower. Two family bedrooms share a full bath. Please specify basement, crawlspace or slab foundation when ordering.

FAMILY ROOM
15'-0"x20'-0"
10 FT CLG

BEDROOM 2
13'-8"x13'-0"
10 FT CLG

BREAKFAST
10'-8"x12'-4"
10 FT CLG

42" LEDGE

BATH
2

MASTER BEDROOM
18'-4"x16'-0"
10 FT CLG

LIVING ROOM
17'-0"x21'-0"
12 FT CLG

KITCHEN
14'-6"x14'-0"
10 FT CLG

PDR.

BEDROOM 3
15'-4"x11'-4"
10 FT CLG

SEAT

KS

MSTR. BATH
10 FT CLG

HIS

CHEST

FOYER
12 FT CLG

DINING
14'-6"x16'-8"
12 FT CLG

UTIL.
10 FT CLG

PORCH

HERS

PORCH

COPYRIGHT LARRY E BELK

GARAGE
21'-8"x25'-6"

WIDTH 79'-8"
DEPTH 69'-6"

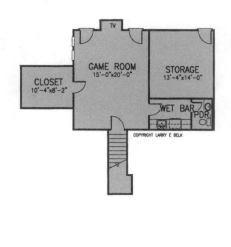

TV

GAME ROOM
15'-0"x20'-0"

STORAGE
13'-4"x14'-0"

CLOSET
10'-4"x8'-2"

WET BAR
PDR.

COPYRIGHT LARRY E BELK

50

The angles in this home create unlimited views and spaces that appear larger. Majestic columns of brick add warmth to a striking elevation. Inside, the foyer commands special perspective on living areas including the living room, dining room and the den. The island kitchen serves the breakfast nook and the family room. A large pantry provides ample space for food storage. In the master bedroom suite, mitered glass and a private bath set the tone for simple luxury. Two secondary bedrooms share privacy and quiet at the front of the house. The den may also convert to a fourth bedroom, if desired.

DESIGN 8663

Square Footage: 2,597

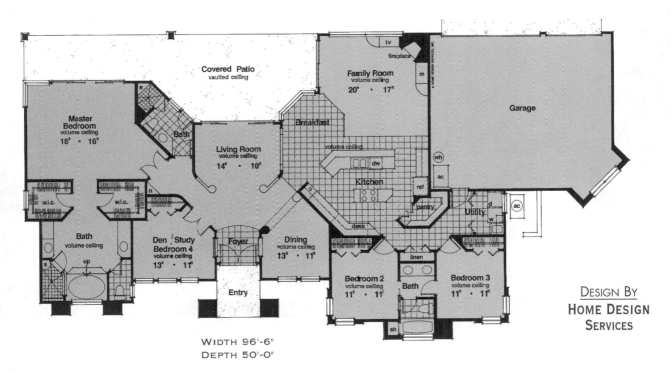

WIDTH 96'-6"
DEPTH 50'-0"

DESIGN BY
HOME DESIGN
SERVICES

DESIGN 8792

Square Footage: 3,064
Bonus Room: 366 square feet

From a more graceful era, this story-and-a-half home evokes a sense of quiet refinement. Exquisite exterior detailing makes it special. Inside are distinctive treatments that make the floor plan unique and functional. The central foyer is enhanced with columns that define the dining room and formal living room. A beamed ceiling complements the den. An indulgent master suite includes a private garden with fountain, pool access, a large walk-in closet and a fireplace through to the outdoor spa. Family bedrooms share an unusual compartmented bath. The kitchen and family room are completed by a breakfast nook. Pool access and a lanai with a summer kitchen make this area a natural for casual lifestyles. A bonus area over the garage can become a home office or game room.

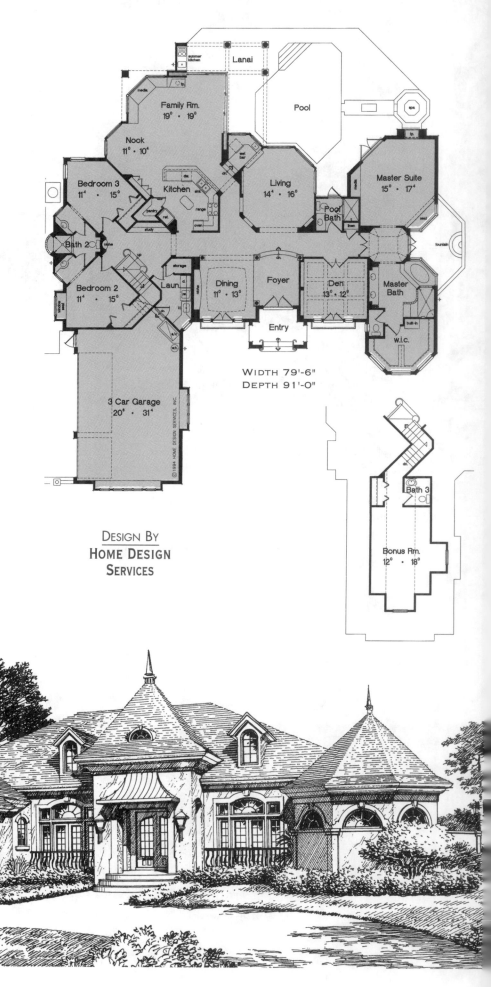

WIDTH 79'-6"
DEPTH 91'-0"

DESIGN BY
HOME DESIGN
SERVICES

DESIGN 8252

First Floor: 2,687 square feet
Second Floor: 1,630 square feet
Total: 4,317 square feet
Bonus Room: 216 square feet

DESIGN BY
LARRY E. BELK
DESIGNS

Dormer windows complement classic, square columns on this country estate home, gently flavored with a Southern-style facade. A two-story foyer opens to traditional rooms. Two columns announce the living room, which has a warming hearth. The formal dining room opens to the back covered porch, decked out with decorative columns. The first-floor master suite has His and Hers walk-in closets, an oversized shower, a whirlpool tub and a windowed water closet, plus its own door to the covered porch. A well-appointed kitchen features a corner walk-in pantry and opens to a double-bay family room and breakfast area. Upstairs, each of two family bedrooms has a private vanity. A gallery hall leads past a study/computer room—with two window seats—to a sizable recreation area that offers a tower-room bay.

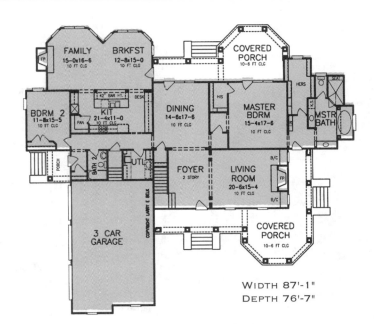

WIDTH 87'-1"
DEPTH 76'-7"

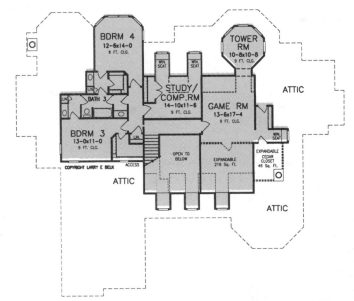

Rear

This home, as shown in the photograph, may differ from the actual blueprints. For more detailed information, please check the floor plans carefully.

Photo by Jon Riley

DESIGN 9661

First Floor: 1,416 square feet
Second Floor: 445 square feet
Total: 1,861 square feet
Bonus Room: 284 square feet

An arched entrance and windows provide a touch of class to the exterior of this plan. The dining room displays round columns at the entrance while the great room boasts a cathedral ceiling, fireplace and an arched window over exterior doors to the deck. The large kitchen is open to the breakfast nook and sliding glass doors present a second access to the deck. In the master suite is a walk-in closet and lavish bath. On the second level are two bedrooms and a full bath. Please specify basement or crawlspace foundation when ordering.

DESIGN BY
DONALD A. GARDNER
ARCHITECTS, INC.

© 1991 Donald A. Gardner Architects, Inc.

WIDTH 58'-3"
DEPTH 68'-9"

QUOTE ONE®
Cost to build? See page 434
to order complete cost estimate
to build this house in your area!

DECK

BREAKFAST
10'-4" X 10'-4"

MASTER SITTING
10'-4" x 6'-0"

MASTER BEDROOM
15'-4" X 13'-0"

GREAT ROOM
17'-0" X 17'-0"

KITCHEN
13'-4" X 17'-9"

MASTER BATH
12'-2" X 12'-8"

DINING ROOM
12'-10" X 10'-6"

FOYER
5'-6" x 13'-6"

POWDER

LAUNDRY
6'-0" X 6'-10"

W.I.C.

LIVING ROOM
11'-4" X 10'-8"

STOOP

TWO CAR GARAGE
21'-4" X 21'-4"

WIDTH 47'-10"
DEPTH 63'-10"

ATTIC STORAGE

CLOSET

BEDROOM NO. 2
11'-1" X 13'-2"

OPEN TO BELOW

LOFT
8'-4" X 9'-2"

BATH

BEDROOM NO. 3
10'-8" X 14'-0"

CLOSET

Quote One®

Cost to build? See page 434
to order complete cost estimate
to build this house in your area!

DESIGN BY
DESIGN TRADITIONS

DESIGN T014

First Floor: 1,724 square feet
Second Floor: 700 square feet
Total: 2,424 square feet

This cozy English cottage might be found hidden away in a European garden. All the charm of gables, stonework and multi-level rooflines combine to create this home. To the left of the foyer you will see the sunlit dining room, highlighted by a dramatic tray ceiling and expansive windows with transoms. This room and the living room flow together to form one large entertainment area. In the gourmet kitchen is a work island, oversized pantry and an adjoining octagonal breakfast room with a gazebo ceiling. The great room features a pass-through wet bar, a fireplace and bookcases or an entertainment center. The master suite enjoys privacy at the rear of the home. An open-rail loft above the foyer leads to additional bedrooms with walk-in closets, private vanities and a shared bath. This home is designed with a basement foundation.

© American Home Gallery, Ltd.

DESIGN 7688

First Floor: 1,904 square feet
Second Floor: 645 square feet
Total: 2,549 square feet
Bonus Room: 434 square feet

This stucco home contrasts gently curved arches with gables, and uses large multi-pane windows to flood the interior with natural light. Square pillars form an impressive entry, leading to a two-story foyer. The living room is set apart from the informal areas of the house, and could serve as a cozy study instead. The U-shaped kitchen is centrally located between the dining room and a sunny breakfast nook. Nearby, a utility room leads to back stairs and a two-car garage. The back patio can be reached from both the breakfast nook and the family room, which features a cathedral ceiling and a fireplace. The master suite is on the first floor and offers two walk-in closets and a bath with twin vanities, a garden tub and a separate shower. In addition to a bath and two family bedrooms, the second floor contains a loft and a bonus room.

DESIGN BY
DONALD A. GARDNER
ARCHITECTS, INC.

WIDTH 71'-2"
DEPTH 45'-8"

Double columns and an arch-top clerestory create an inviting entry to this fresh interpretation of traditional style. The two-story foyer features a decorative ledge perfect for displaying a tapestry. Decorative columns and arches open to the formal dining room and to the octagonal great room which has a ten-foot tray ceiling. The U-shaped kitchen looks over an angled counter to a sweet breakfast bay that brings in the outdoors and shares a through-fireplace with the great room. A sitting area and a lavish bath set off the secluded master suite. A nearby secondary bedroom with its own bath could be used as a guest suite, while, upstairs, two family bedrooms share a full bath and a hall that leads to an expandable area. Please specify crawlspace basement or slab foundation when ordering.

DESIGN 8161

First Floor: 2,028 square feet
Second Floor: 558 square feet
Total: 2,586 square feet
Bonus Room: 272 square feet

DESIGN BY
LARRY E. BELK
DESIGNS

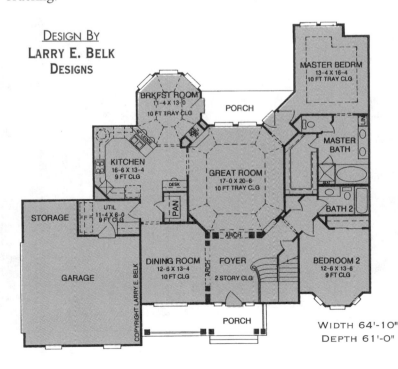

WIDTH 64'-10"
DEPTH 61'-0"

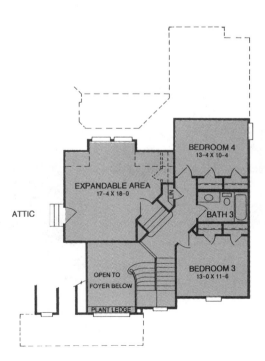

DESIGN A242

First Floor: 792 square feet
Second Floor: 768 square feet
Total: 1,560 square feet

Three solid pillars support the shed-like roof of this attractive bungalow. Inside, formal and informal gatherings will easily be accommodated. For casual get-togethers, the spacious gathering room with its fireplace and rear yard access is complemented by the nearby availability of the galley kitchen. Formal dinner parties will be a breeze in the dining room at the front of the house—or make it a formal living room if you have the need. Upstairs, two bedrooms share a full hall bath, while the master suite features a walk-in closet and a bath of its own. Look for a spa-style tub and dual vanities in the master bath.

DESIGN BY
LIVING CONCEPTS
HOME PLANNING

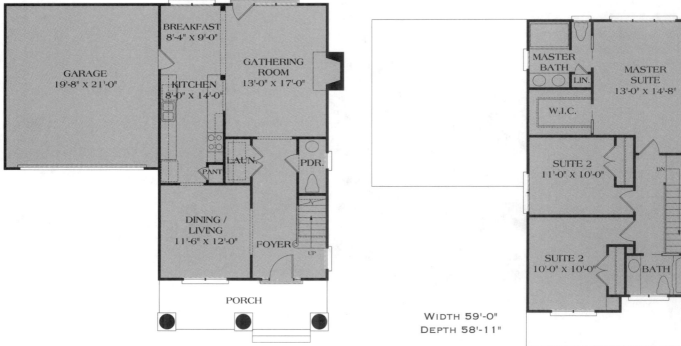

GARAGE
19'-8" x 21'-0"

BREAKFAST
8'-4" x 9'-0"

KITCHEN
8'-0" x 14'-0"

GATHERING
ROOM
13'-0" x 17'-0"

PANT.

LAUN.

PDR.

DINING /
LIVING
11'-6" x 12'-0"

FOYER

UP

PORCH

MASTER
BATH

LIN.

MASTER
SUITE
13'-0" x 14'-8"

W.I.C.

SUITE 2
11'-0" x 10'-0"

DN

SUITE 2
10'-0" x 10'-0"

BATH

WIDTH 59'-0"
DEPTH 58'-11"

Fine for a narrow lot, and fitting in perfectly with the beauty of nature, this two-story home is accented with cedar shakes and brick-based columns. The interior plan is classic by design, featuring a central hall with staircase on the right and formal dining room on the left. The gathering room is to the rear and has a fireplace and deck/patio access. An open kitchen with U-shaped work area is close by. Three bedrooms on the second floor include a master suite with walk-in closet and private bath, and two family bedrooms sharing a full bath. A two-car garage nicely rounds out the plan.

DESIGN A240

First Floor: 774 square feet
Second Floor: 724 square feet
Total: 1,498 square feet

DESIGN BY
LIVING CONCEPTS
HOME PLANNING

DECK / PATIO

LAUN.

GARAGE
19'-8" x 21'-0"

KITCHEN
7'-6" x 14'-0"

GATHERING ROOM
14'-0" x 21'-0"

PANT.

PDR.

DINING ROOM
8'-8" x 12'-0"

FOYER

UP

FRONT PORCH

MASTER SUITE
15'-0" x 12'-0"

MASTER BATH

SUITE 2
11'-0" x 9'-6"

W.I.C.

BATH

LIN.

DN

SUITE 3
10'-0" x 10'-6"

OPEN TO BELOW

PLANT LEDGE

WIDTH 43'-4"
DEPTH 42'-10"

DESIGN A241

First Floor: 792 square feet
Second Floor: 743 square feet
Total: 1,535 square feet

Bright with country details and sporting a covered porch supported by sturdy columns, this home is the essence of charm. The floor plan, though simple, is very livable and boasts sufficient space for any occasion. The entry opens to a central foyer with a dining room (or living room) on the left and gathering room at the rear. The gathering room is warmed by a hearth and opens to the rear yard. The galley-style kitchen serves a casual breakfast room with large windows for a view. The second floor holds three bedrooms, including a master suite with walk-in closet and private bath. Family bedrooms share the use of a full hall bath.

GARAGE
19'-8" X 21'-0"

BREAKFAST
8'-4" X 9'-0"

KITCHEN
8'-0" X 14'-0"

GATHERING
ROOM
13'-0" X 17'-0"

LAUN.

PANT

PDR.

DINING /
LIVING
11'-6" X 12'-0"

FOYER

UP

PORCH

DESIGN BY
LIVING CONCEPTS
HOME PLANNING

MASTER
BATH

LIN.

W.I.C.

MASTER
SUITE
13'-0" X 14'-8"

SUITE 2
11'-0" X 10'-0"

DN

SUITE 3
10'-0" X 10'-0"

BATH

WIDTH 43'-4"
DEPTH 42'-6"

Perfect for a narrow lot, this shingle-and-siding home is sure to please. With Craftsman-style influence, this bungalow has plenty to offer. The foyer opens directly into the gathering room, where a fireplace waits to add warmth and cheer to every occasion. The formal dining room is defined by graceful pillars and has a pass-through to the kitchen. U-shaped, the kitchen offers the pleasure of no cross-room traffic, as well as a window over the sink. Upstairs, two family bedrooms—or make one a study—share a full bath. The master bedroom suite offers a walk-in closet and a private bath with a dual-bowl vanity.

DESIGN A244

First Floor: 817 square feet
Second Floor: 759 square feet
Total: 1,576 square feet

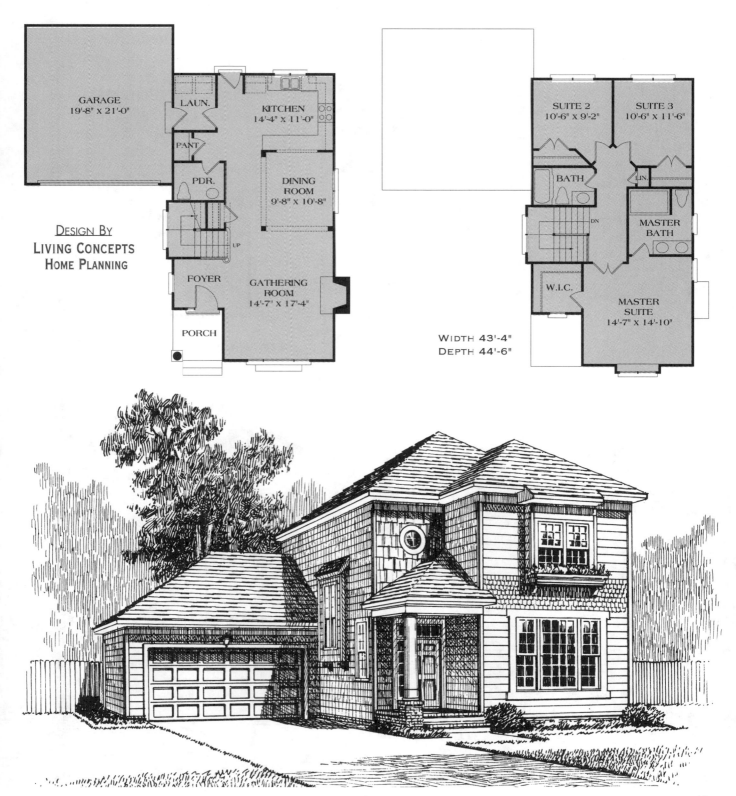

GARAGE
19'-8" x 21'-0"

LAUN.

KITCHEN
14'-4" x 11'-0"

PANT.

PDR.

DINING
ROOM
9'-8" x 10'-8"

DESIGN BY
LIVING CONCEPTS
HOME PLANNING

UP

FOYER

GATHERING
ROOM
14'-7' x 17'-4"

PORCH

SUITE 2
10'-6" x 9'-2"

SUITE 3
10'-6" x 11'-6"

BATH

LIN.

DN

MASTER
BATH

W.I.C.

MASTER
SUITE
14'-7" x 14'-10"

WIDTH 43'-4"
DEPTH 44'-6"

DESIGN 9238

First Floor: 1,421 square feet
Second Floor: 448 square feet
Total: 1,869 square feet

DESIGN BY
DESIGN BASICS, INC.

Always a welcome site, the covered front porch of this home invites entry to its delightful floor plan. Living areas to the back of the house include the great room with a stylish see-through fireplace to the hearth kitchen with bayed dinette, planning desk and large corner walk-in pantry. The formal dining room is traditionally placed at the front of the plan and is updated with a built-in hutch. A split-bedroom sleeping plan puts the master suite with whirlpool tub, walk-in closet and double vanity on the first floor away from two second-floor bedrooms and shared full bath.

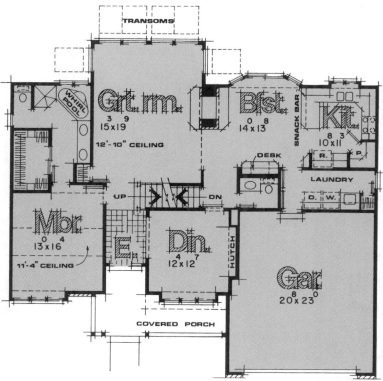

WIDTH 52'-0"
DEPTH 47'-4"

Quote One
Cost to build? See page 434
to order complete cost estimate
to build this house in your area!

62

This traditional home bespeaks comfort with a two-story great room that features a fireplace and backyard access, plus a roomy kitchen that directly serves the bayed dining area. A laundry room and a powder room complete the first floor. Upstairs, three bedrooms include a master bedroom with a walk-in closet and a bath with dual lavatories and a soaking tub. The secondary bedrooms each enjoy ample closet space and share a full bath. With a two-car garage—note the extra space for storage shelves—and a wrapping front porch, this design is sure to be a treasured family home.

DESIGN 9532

First Floor: 663 square feet
Second Floor: 740 square feet
Total: 1,403 square feet

DESIGN BY
**ALAN MASCORD
DESIGN ASSOCIATES, INC.**

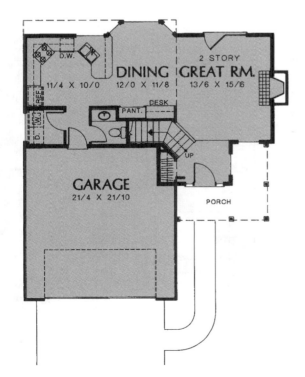

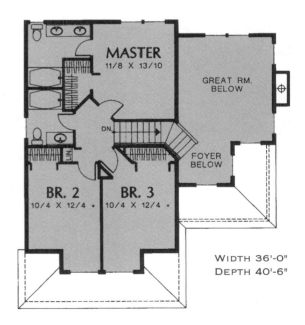

WIDTH 36'-0"
DEPTH 40'-6"

Design A243

First Floor: 817 square feet
Second Floor: 759 square feet
Total: 1,576 square feet

Lovely cedar-shake and wood siding details on the outside lend curb appeal to this smaller design. An open layout gives this design maximum livability. The spacious gathering room, just past the entry foyer, is given interest by a fireplace and flows into the dining area separated from the living area by decorative columns. The nearby U-shaped kitchen features a walk-in pantry for convenience. A powder room and laundry complete the main level. Sleeping quarters on the upper level include two family bedrooms and a master suite. The private master bath has an oversized tub and dual sinks.

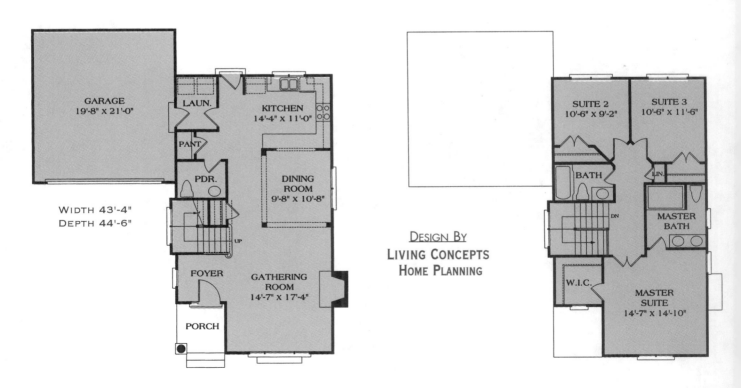

DESIGN BY
LIVING CONCEPTS
HOME PLANNING

GARAGE
19'-8" x 21'-0"

LAUN.

KITCHEN
14'-4" x 11'-0"

PANT

PDR.

DINING ROOM
9'-8" x 10'-8"

WIDTH 43'-4"
DEPTH 44'-6"

UP

FOYER

GATHERING ROOM
14'-7" x 17'-4"

PORCH

SUITE 2
10'-6" x 9'-2"

SUITE 3
10'-6" x 11'-6"

BATH

LIN.

MASTER BATH

DN

W.I.C.

MASTER SUITE
14'-7" x 14'-10"

A n innovative layout gives this plan maximum livability. The first floor is devoted to thoughtfully arranged living areas, the focal point being a generous gathering room with a fireplace. The L-shaped kitchen includes plenty of work space and offers convenient access to both the dining room and gathering room. The U-shaped staircase is open to the two-story foyer, which is accented by a plant shelf and tall arched window. Ascending to the second floor, you will find two secondary suites with ample closets and the master suite featuring triple windows that overlook the rear property.

DESIGN A239

First Floor: 774 square feet
Second Floor: 723 square feet
Total: 1,497 square feet

<u>DESIGN BY</u>
**LIVING CONCEPTS
HOME PLANNING**

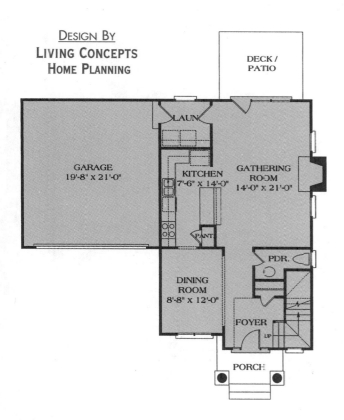

DECK / PATIO

LAUN.

GARAGE
19'-8" x 21'-0"

KITCHEN
7'-6" x 14'-0"

GATHERING ROOM
14'-0" x 21'-0"

PANT.

PDR.

DINING ROOM
8'-8" x 12'-0"

FOYER

UP

PORCH

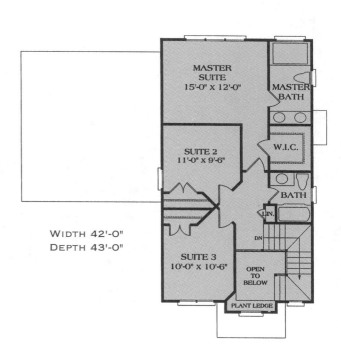

WIDTH 42'-0"
DEPTH 43'-0"

MASTER SUITE
15'-0" x 12'-0"

MASTER BATH

SUITE 2
11'-0" x 9'-6"

W.I.C.

BATH

LIN.

DN

SUITE 3
10'-0" x 10'-6"

OPEN TO BELOW

PLANT LEDGE

DESIGN A185

First Floor: 2,106 square feet
Second Floor: 984 square feet
Total: 3,090 square feet

Designed as a link-side retreat, this two-story home is elegant without being ostentatious. It begins with a facade of mixed materials—stone and siding—and features solid columns at the entry. The interior is casual in nature, with a large gathering room graced by a fireplace and rear deck, and a formal dining room defined by columns. The island kitchen connects to a golfside dining area and has a great walk-in pantry. A covered veranda can be reached from the casual dining space or from the den/guest suite. The master suite is at the opposite side of the plan. His and Hers walk-in closets lead the way to a master bath fit for a king.

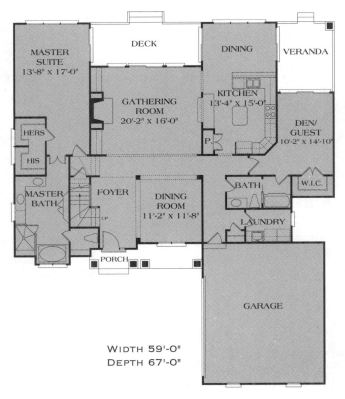

WIDTH 59'-0"
DEPTH 67'-0"

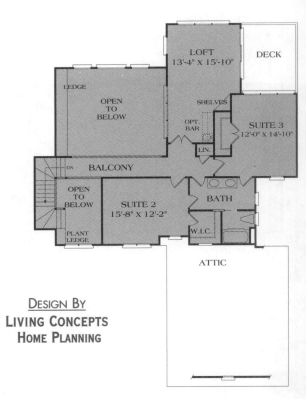

DESIGN BY
LIVING CONCEPTS
HOME PLANNING

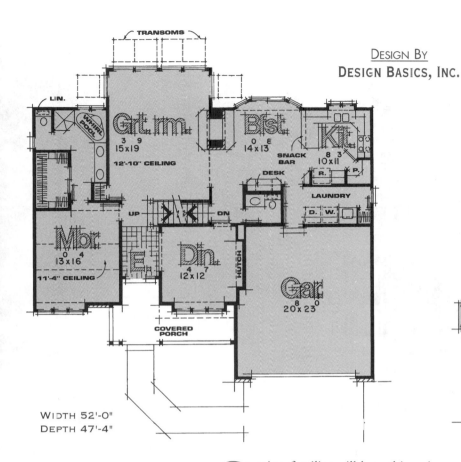

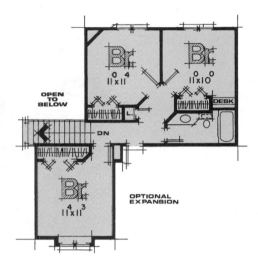

DESIGN 9206

First Floor: 1,421 square feet
Second Floor: 578 square feet
Total: 1,999 square feet

WIDTH 52'-0"
DEPTH 47'-4"

QUOTE ONE®

Cost to build? See page 434
to order complete cost estimate
to build this house in your area!

Growing families will love this unique plan which combines all the essentials with an abundance of stylish touches. Start with the living area—a spacious great room with high ceilings, windows overlooking the backyard, a through-fireplace to the kitchen and access to the rear yard. A dining room with hutch space accommodates formal occasions. The hearth kitchen features a well-planned work area and a bay-windowed breakfast area. The master suite with whirlpool tub and a walk-in closet is found downstairs while three family bedrooms are upstairs. Please specify basement or slab foundation when ordering.

This home, as shown in the photograph, may differ from the actual blueprints. For more detailed information, please check the floor plans carefully.

Photo by Design Basics, Inc.

DESIGN Q489

Entry Level: 194 square feet
Main Level: 1,178 square feet
Total: 1,372 square feet

M ain living areas are on the upper level of this two-story home. Reach this level via a 194-square-foot entry foyer with stair to the open living and dining rooms. A U-shaped kitchen separates the formal dining room and the breakfast room. Special amenities include a fireplace in the living room, a window seat in the dining room and a door in the breakfast room that leads to the rear deck. Three bedrooms—or two and a family room—are on the right side of the plan. The master suite has a private full bath. The ground floor can remain unfinished until you are ready for additional space. It includes a future bedroom and bath, a den with window seat and a large area that could become a games room or activities room.

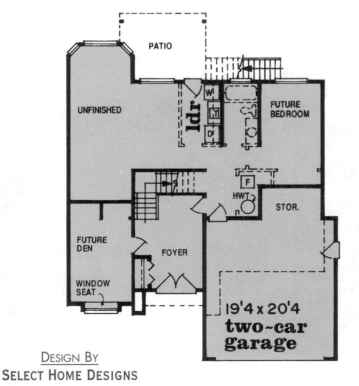

PATIO

UNFINISHED

ldr

w
D

FUTURE BEDROOM

F

HWT

STOR.

FUTURE DEN

FOYER

WINDOW SEAT

19'4 x 20'4
two-car garage

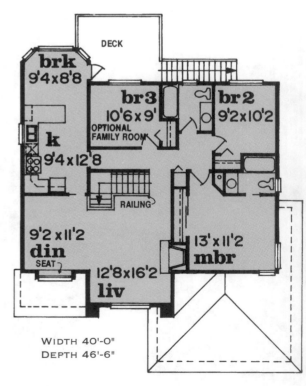

DECK

brk
9'4x8'8

br3
10'6 x 9'

OPTIONAL FAMILY ROOM

br2
9'2x10'2

k
9'4x12'8

RAILING

9'2 x 11'2
din
SEAT

12'8x16'2
liv

13'x11'2
mbr

WIDTH 40'-0"
DEPTH 46'-6"

DESIGN BY
SELECT HOME DESIGNS

Attention to detail is the key to the appeal of this unusual design. The entry opens to future space which can be developed into a recreation room and two bedrooms. The main level holds the bulk of the livability and is contained on the second floor. Both living and dining rooms benefit from the warmth of a fireplace; the living room also sports a window seat looking out to the front through a Palladian window. The family room is reached through an arched opening and has a gas fireplace and access to a rear deck. The nearby island kitchen serves a bayed breakfast nook. Bedrooms are to the right of the plan and include two family bedrooms sharing a full bath and a master suite with private bath. The master suite also has a window seat.

DESIGN Q358

Entry Level: 210 square feet
Main Level: 1,414 square feet
Total: 1,624 square feet
Bonus Space: 974 square feet

DESIGN BY
SELECT HOME DESIGNS

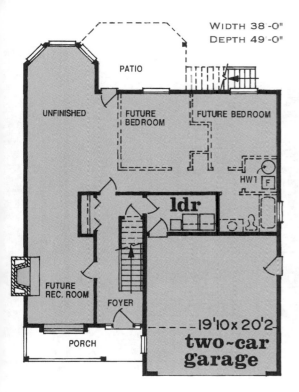

WIDTH 38'-0"
DEPTH 49'-0"

PATIO

UNFINISHED FUTURE BEDROOM FUTURE BEDROOM

HWT F

ldr

FUTURE REC. ROOM FOYER

PORCH

19'10 x 20'2
two-car garage

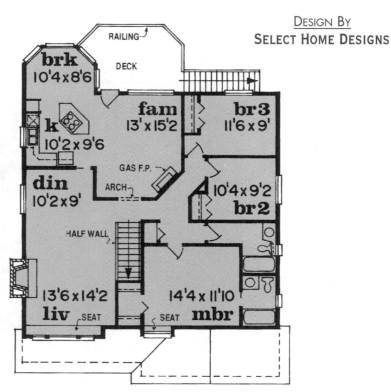

RAILING

DECK

brk
10'4 x 8'6

k
10'2 x 9'6

fam
13' x 15'2

br3
11'6 x 9'

GAS F.P.

din
10'2 x 9'

ARCH

10'4 x 9'2
br2

HALF WALL

13'6 x 14'2
liv SEAT

SEAT 14'4 x 11'10
mbr

DESIGN Q350

Entry Level: 278 square feet
Main Level: 1,286 square feet
Total: 1,564 square feet
Bonus Space: 704 square feet

Country charm prevails with a covered front porch and double chimneys in this design. The floor plan is unusual in that main living areas are on the second floor. The entry leads up a staircase which opens into the living/dining room combination. A vaulted window with seat and a fireplace adorn this area. The U-shaped kitchen, the family room and bayed breakfast nook sit to the rear and enjoy access to a deck. A master suite is also to the rear and has a walk-in closet and private bath. Two family bedrooms share a bath. Lower-level space can be developed later into a recreation room, a den and an additional bedroom with bath.

DESIGN BY
SELECT HOME DESIGNS

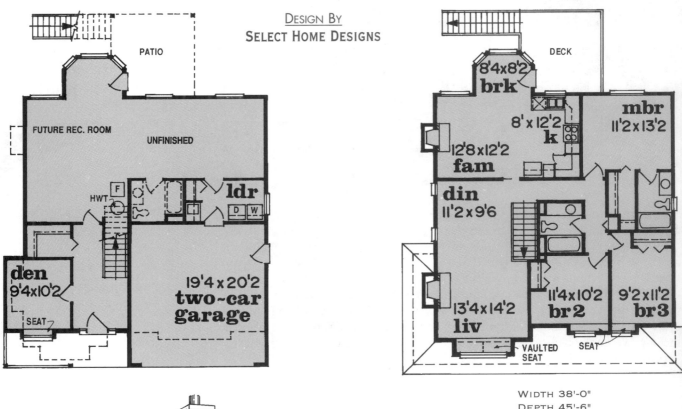

PATIO

FUTURE REC. ROOM   UNFINISHED

HWT   F   ldr   D W

den
9'4 x 10'2

SEAT

19'4 x 20'2
two-car garage

DECK

8'4 x 8'2
brk

8' x 12'2
k

12'8 x 12'2
fam

din
11'2 x 9'6

mbr
11'2 x 13'2

13'4 x 14'2
liv

VAULTED SEAT

11'4 x 10'2
br 2

SEAT

9'2 x 11'2
br 3

WIDTH 38'-0"
DEPTH 45'-6"

Build this interesting design where second-floor living space can take advantage of a great view. The lower level can remain unfinished until needed. The foyer contains 128 square feet of finished space and leads up to the living areas and bedrooms on the second floor. Living areas here are comprised of a living room/dining room combination with wide windows overlooking the front, plus a cozy fireplace. A smaller family room is to the rear with sliding glass doors to a deck. The breakfast room also has sliding glass doors, which open to the front deck. The kitchen nestles in between the formal and informal living areas. Three bedrooms sit quietly to the rear of the plan. The master suite features a walk-in closet and a private bath. A box-bay window lights the master bedroom. Two family bedrooms share a full bath.

DESIGN Q357

Entry Level: 128 square feet
Main Level: 1,391 square feet
Total: 1,519 square feet

DESIGN BY
SELECT HOME DESIGNS

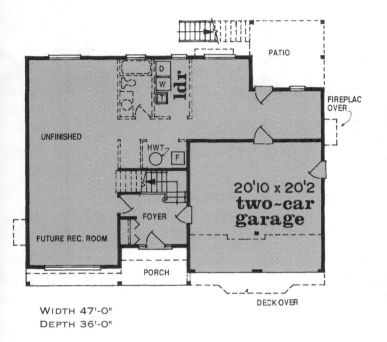

WIDTH 47'-0"
DEPTH 36'-0"

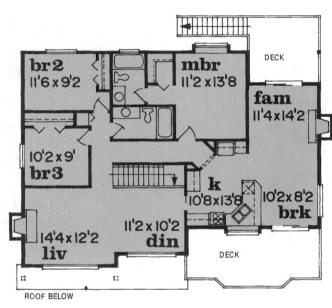

DESIGN 9525

First Floor: 1,396 square feet
Second Floor: 523 square feet
Total: 1,919 square feet

Double pillars herald the entry to this charming design. They are offset from the front door and introduce a porch that leads to the den (or make it a fourth bedroom). Living areas center on the casual life and include a great room, with a fireplace, that opens directly to the dining room. The kitchen is L-shaped for convenience and features an island cooktop. The master suite is on the first floor and sports a vaulted ceiling and bath with spa tub and separate shower. The upper floor holds two secondary bedrooms and a full bath. The open staircase is decorated with a plant shelf that receives light from double windows over the foyer.

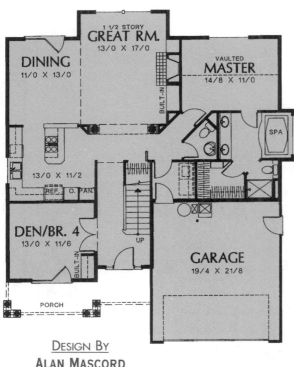

DESIGN BY
ALAN MASCORD
DESIGN ASSOCIATES, INC.

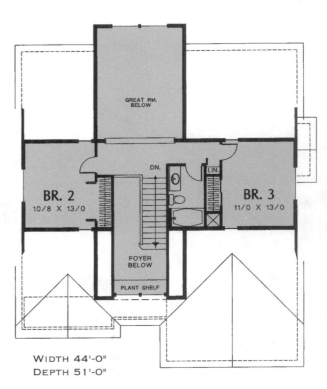

WIDTH 44'-0"
DEPTH 51'-0"

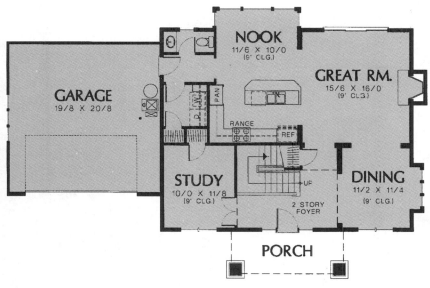

DESIGN 7471

First Floor: 1,102 square feet
Second Floor: 888 square feet
Total: 1,990 square feet

DESIGN BY
**ALAN MASCORD
DESIGN ASSOCIATES, INC.**

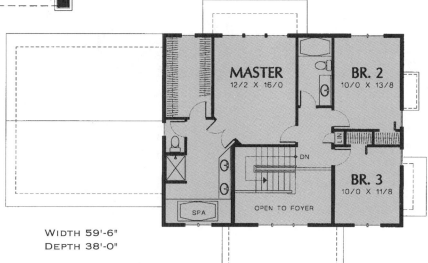

WIDTH 59'-6"
DEPTH 38'-0"

Simple design and symmetrical Crafts-man details come together to create a fine exterior for this home. The interior offers grand open spaces and cozy nooks, centered around a gourmet kitchen. Flanking the foyer are a quiet study and the formal dining room with box-bay window. The great room is to the rear and has a fireplace and access to the rear yard. The light-filled nook is nearby. A powder room and laundry area are found in a service hall to the two-car garage. Two family bed-rooms sharing a full bath and a master suite with private bath are upstairs. The master has a walk-in closet and spa-style tub.

DESIGN Q246

Entry Level: 95 square feet
Main Level: 1,107 square feet
Total: 1,202 square feet
Bonus Space: 819 square feet

This unusually designed home is planned with the bulk of the living space on the second floor. For areas with spectacular views, this is a real bonus. The entry foyer, occupying 95 square feet of finished floor space, leads up to a living and dining room with a fireplace and sliding glass door access to a beautiful sun deck. The nearby kitchen is U-shaped for convenience and has a box window over the sink. The adjoining breakfast area is perfect for casual meals. Three bedrooms line the rear of the plan. The master bedroom has a private half-bath and dual wall closets. Family bedrooms share a full bath with soaking tub. Space on the lower level will add two bedrooms, a full bath and a family room—819 square feet—when completed.

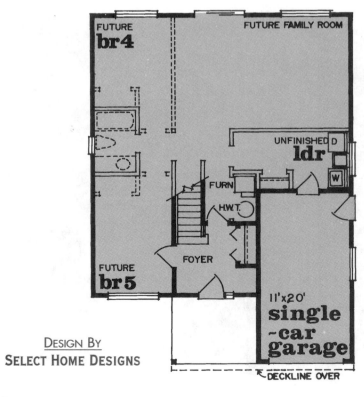

DESIGN BY
SELECT HOME DESIGNS

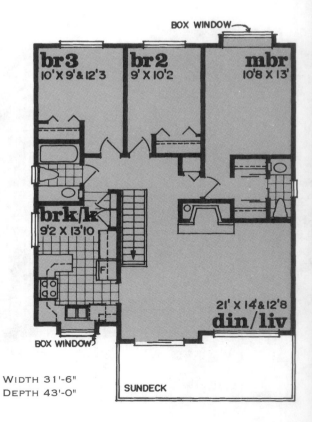

WIDTH 31'-6"
DEPTH 43'-0"

74

GARAGE

COPYRIGHT 1993 LARRY E. BELK

STORAGE   PORCH

PATIO

BRKFST
10-0 X 7-6

BEDRM 2
11-4 X 13-6

KITCHEN
12-6 X 11-6

BATH 2

↓SHOWER↓

WET BAR

DINING ROOM
11-6 X 12-0

ARCH

ARCH

ENTRY

PORCH

GREAT ROOM
15-0 X 16-0

FP

BEDRM 3
11-0 X 13-6
8 FT CEILING

BALCONY

UTL

BUILT IN

BATH
3

LIN

MASTER
BATH

LEDGE

MASTER BEDROOM
15-0 X 13-6
VAULTED CEILING

PATIO

WIDTH 24'-11"
DEPTH 73'-10"

DESIGN BY
LARRY E. BELK
DESIGNS

DESIGN 8051

First Floor: 1,078 square feet
Second Floor: 921 square feet
Total: 1,999 square feet

This charming clapboard home is loaded with character and perfect for a narrow lot. High ceilings throughout give the home an open, spacious feeling. The great room and the dining room are separated by columns with connecting arches. The efficient, U-shaped kitchen features a corner sink with a window view and a bayed breakfast area with access to the rear porch. A bedroom and a bath (with a shower tucked under the stair) are conveniently located for guests on the first floor. Upstairs, the master bedroom features a vaulted ceiling and a luxurious master bath with dual vanities, a whirlpool tub and a separate shower. Access to a covered patio from the master bedroom provides a relaxing outdoor retreat. A secondary bedroom and full bath are also located on the second floor with a large rear balcony completing this compact plan. This plan is available with either a crawlspace or slab foundation. Please specify when ordering.

DESIGN 7737

First Floor: 1,269 square feet
Second Floor: 880 square feet
Total: 2,149 square feet

DESIGN BY
DONALD A. GARDNER
ARCHITECTS, INC.

Reminiscent of the historic homes of Charleston, South Carolina, this design was created not just with narrow lots in mind, but with style and function as well. The dramatic two-story great room opens to a roomy kitchen with angled countertop and breakfast bay. The formal dining room gains distinction from its interior columns and the versatile first-floor bedroom/study has a walk-in closet. Upstairs is a master suite with tray ceiling, lavish bath and ample closet space. Across the hall is another bedroom with its own private bath and linen closet. A two-car garage is detached from the main house.

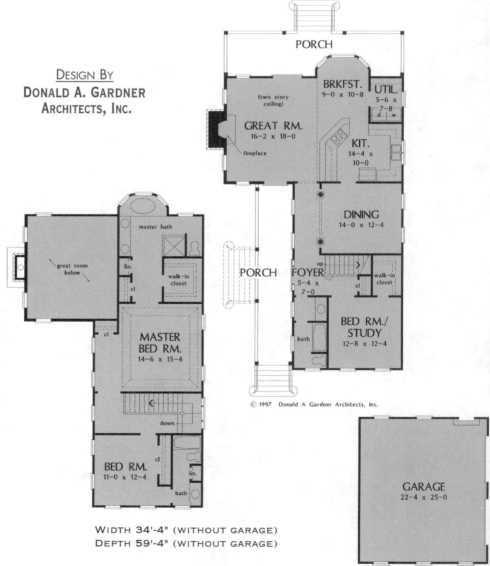

WIDTH 34'-4" (WITHOUT GARAGE)
DEPTH 59'-4" (WITHOUT GARAGE)

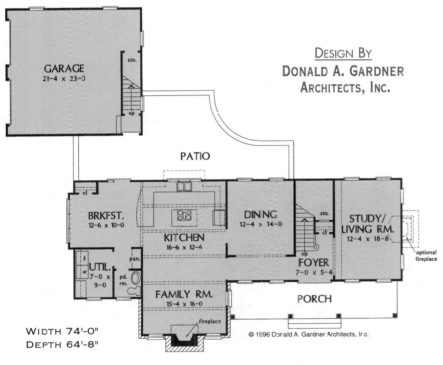

GARAGE
21-4 x 23-0

sto.

up

Design By
Donald A. Gardner
Architects, Inc.

PATIO

BRKFST.
12-6 x 10-0

cl

KITCHEN
16-6 x 12-4

DINING
12-4 x 14-0

STUDY/
LIVING RM.
12-4 x 18-8

optional fireplace

UTIL.
7-0 x 9-0

pan.

pd. rm.

FOYER
7-0 x 5-4

up

sto.

FAMILY RM.
15-4 x 16-0

PORCH

fireplace

Width 74'-0"
Depth 64'-8"

DESIGN 7621

First Floor: 1,428 square feet
Second Floor: 1,067 square feet
Total: 2,495 square feet
Bonus Room: 342 square feet

Balanced, graceful and full of life's simple pleasures, this home welcomes all to a warm inviting retreat. The family room, with fireplace, is open to the kitchen for easy, casual entertaining. The master suite is for the luxury-minded with its cathedral ceiling, dual walk-in closets and spacious bath. Numerous windows throughout the first and second floors add sun and warmth, while stone and stucco accents bring a rustic flair. Heavy timbers and brackets accent the entrance, while metal roofing and simple gable structure complete the unique, relaxed exterior. Note the bonus room over the garage which can become a home office or game room at some future time.

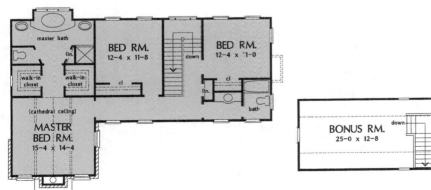

master bath

BED RM.
12-4 x 11-8

BED RM.
12-4 x 11-0

down

walk-in closet

lin.

walk-in closet

cl

cl

lin.

bath

(cathedral ceiling)

MASTER
BED RM.
15-4 x 14-4

BONUS RM.
25-0 x 12-8

down

DESIGN Q620

First Floor: 995 square feet
Second Floor: 484 square feet
Total: 1,479 square feet

What an appealing plan! Its rustic character is defined by cedar lattice, covered columned porches, exposed rafters and multi-paned double hung windows. The great room/dining room combination is reached through double doors off the veranda and features a fireplace towering two stories to the lofty ceiling. A U-shaped kitchen has an angled snack counter that serves this area and loads of space for a breakfast table—or use the handy side porch for alfresco dining. To the rear is the master bedroom with full bath and double doors to the veranda. An additional half-bath sits just beyond the laundry room. Upstairs there are two family bedrooms and a full bath. Plans include details for both a basement and a crawlspace foundation.

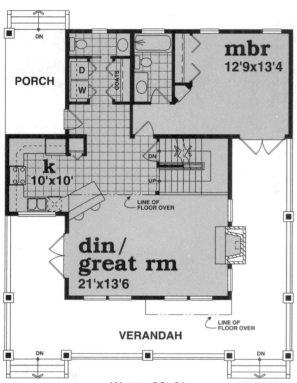

WIDTH 38'-0"
DEPTH 44'-0"

DESIGN BY
SELECT HOME DESIGNS

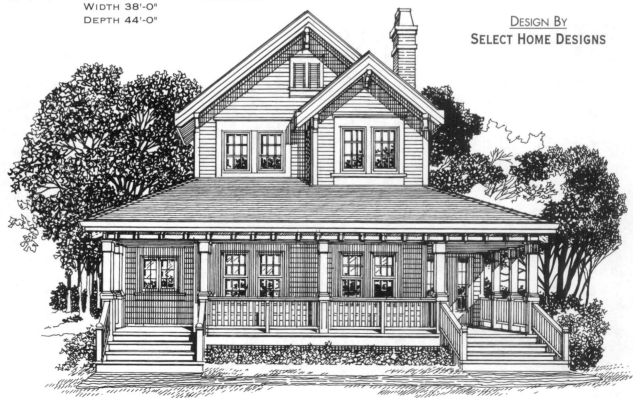

A full-length front porch, made for rocking chairs and flower baskets, adorns this modest farmhouse, which boasts an open interior designed for convenience and luxury. The central great room has a sensational cathedral ceiling and is open to a roomy kitchen that echoes the octagonal shape of the sunny breakfast bay. The master suite maintains privacy on the first floor and features a box-bay window, walk-in closet and indulgent bath. Both second-floor bedrooms have walk-in closets and dormer alcoves. The bonus room, over the garage, allows room for expansion to a home office or guest suite.

DESIGN 7727

First Floor: 1,467 square feet
Second Floor: 661 square feet
Total: 2,128 square feet
Bonus Room: 341 square feet

DESIGN BY
DONALD A. GARDNER
ARCHITECTS, INC.

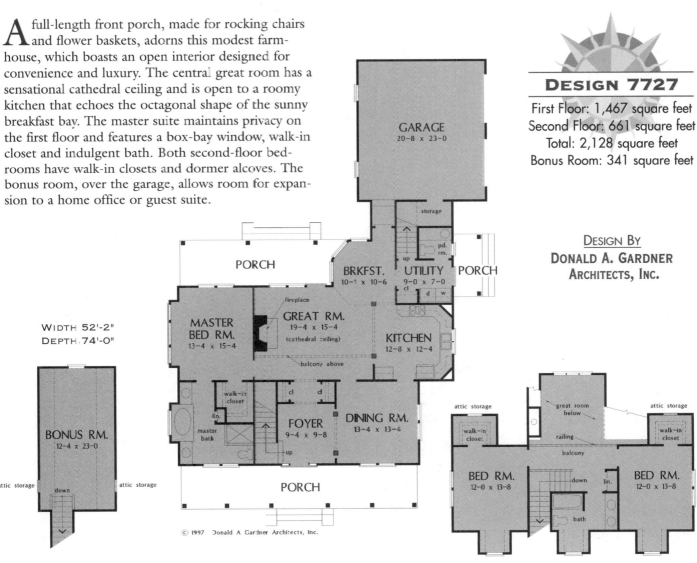

WIDTH 52'-2"
DEPTH 74'-0"

DESIGN A186

First Floor: 2,107 square feet
Second Floor: 989 square feet
Total: 3,096 square feet

Don't miss the luxury points to be found in this golfcouse plan: a rear covered deck accessed from the master bedroom, the gathering room and the casual dining area; a covered veranda accessed from the casual dining area and the den/guest suite; a columned formal dining area, a sumptuous master bath; and an island kitchen. Bedrooms are separated for privacy; each has direct access to bath. Note the two-car garage with bumped out window. It is reached through a service entrance that contains a laundry room and coat closet. A warming hearth surrounded by built-ins adorns the gathering room.

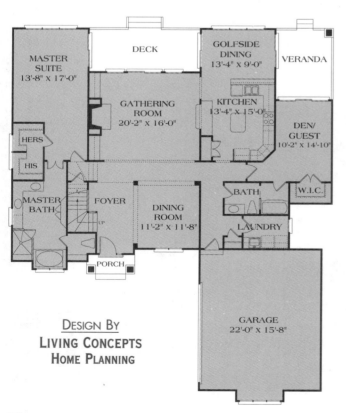

DECK

GOLFSIDE
DINING
13'-4" x 9'-0"

VERANDA

MASTER
SUITE
13'-8" x 17'-0"

GATHERING
ROOM
20'-2" x 16'-0"

KITCHEN
13'-4" x 15'-0"

HERS

HIS

DEN/
GUEST
10'-2" x 14'-10"

MASTER
BATH

FOYER

DINING
ROOM
11'-2" x 11'-8"

UP

BATH

W.I.C.

LAUNDRY

PORCH

DESIGN BY
LIVING CONCEPTS
HOME PLANNING

GARAGE
22'-0" x 15'-8"

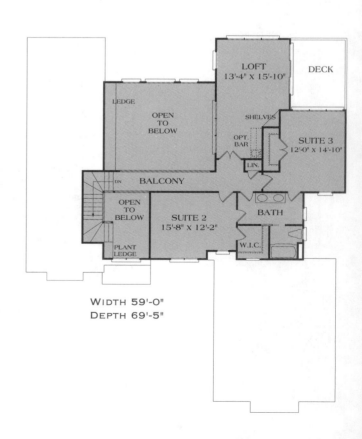

LOFT
13'-4" x 15'-10"

DECK

LEDGE

OPEN
TO
BELOW

SHELVES

OPT.
BAR

SUITE 3
12'-0" x 14'-10"

LIN.

DN

BALCONY

OPEN
TO
BELOW

SUITE 2
15'-8" x 12'-2"

BATH

PLANT
LEDGE

W.I.C.

WIDTH 59'-0"
DEPTH 69'-5"

Horizontal siding, double-hung windows and European gables lend a special charm to this contemporary home. The formal dining room opens from the foyer and offers a servery and a box-bay window. The great room features a fireplace and opens to a golf porch as well as a charming side porch. A well-lit kitchen has a cooktop island counter and two pantries. The first-floor master suite has a tray ceiling, a box-bay window and a deluxe bath with garden tub and an angled shower. A convenient powder room maintains privacy for the master suite. Two family bedrooms, each with private bath, share the second floor with a loft area that overlooks the great room. If you choose, you may build the plan with bonus space on the second floor, without the cathedral ceiling in the gathering room.

DESIGN A262

First Floor: 1,824 square feet
Second Floor: 842 square feet
Total: 2,666 square feet

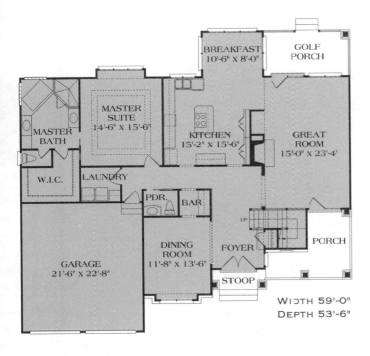

DESIGN BY
**LIVING CONCEPTS
HOME PLANNING**

WIDTH 59'-0"
DEPTH 53'-6"

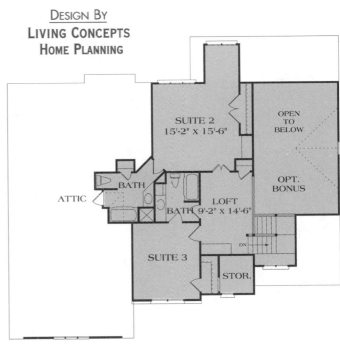

This home, as shown in the photograph, may differ from the actual blueprints. For more detailed information, please check the floor plans carefully.

Photo by Living Concepts Home Planning

DESIGN 9366

First Floor: 2,603 square feet
Second Floor: 1,020 square feet
Total: 3,623 square feet

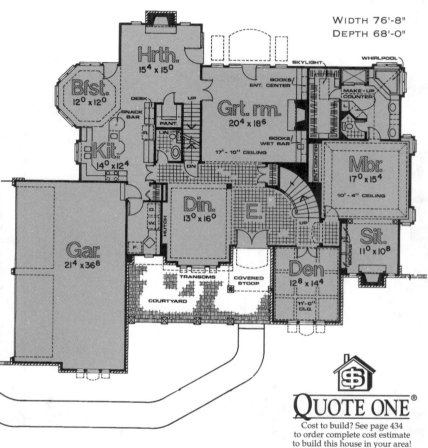

WIDTH 76'-8"
DEPTH 68'-0"

This exceptional European-style facade conceals a spectacular floor plan designed for comfort with a masterful use of space. The glorious great room, open dining room and private den—with a spider-beam ceiling—make up the heart of the home. A cozy hearth room with a fireplace rounds out the kitchen and breakfast areas. The master bedroom opens to a private sitting room with its own fireplace. Three family bedrooms occupy the second floor, each with a private bath. The four-car garage allows ample space for all the family vehicles and even a few big-boy toys. Don't miss the lovely walled courtyard in the front of the plan.

DESIGN BY
DESIGN BASICS, INC.

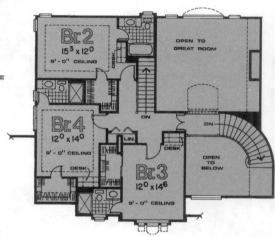

QUOTE ONE®
Cost to build? See page 434
to order complete cost estimate
to build this house in your area!

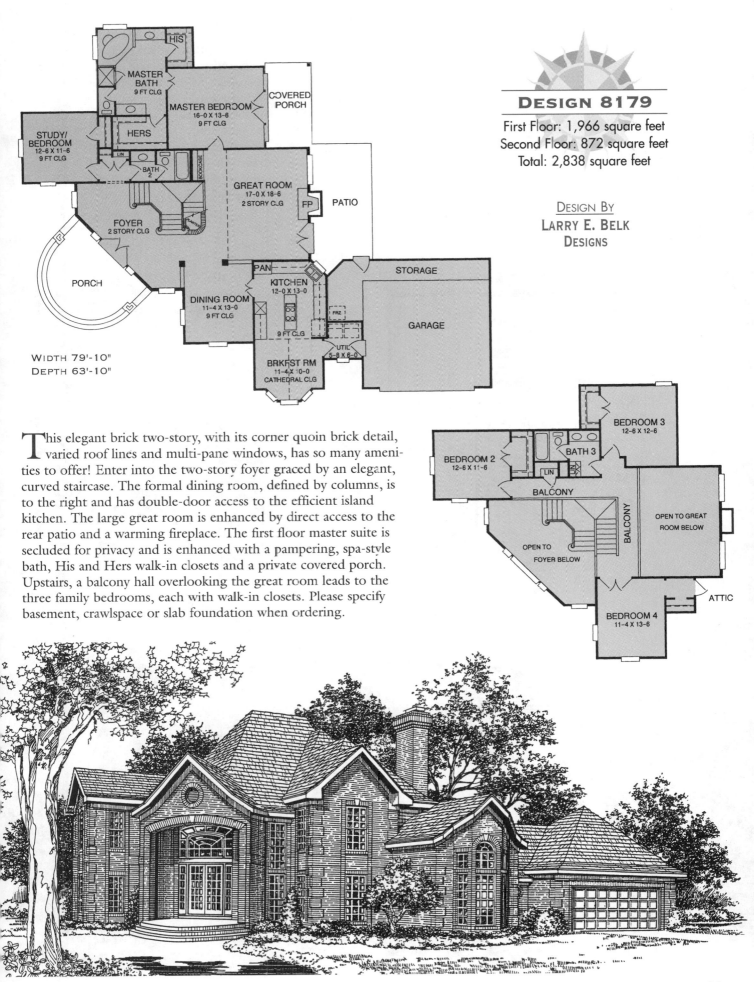

MASTER BATH 9 FT CLG

HIS

MASTER BEDROOM 16-0 X 13-6 9 FT CLG

COVERED PORCH

HERS

STUDY/ BEDROOM 12-6 X 11-6 9 FT CLG

LIN

BATH 2

BOOKCASE

GREAT ROOM 17-0 X 18-6 2 STORY CLG

FP

PATIO

FOYER 2 STORY CLG

PORCH

PAN

STORAGE

KITCHEN 12-0 X 13-0

FRZ

GARAGE

DINING ROOM 11-4 X 13-0 9 FT CLG

9 FT CLG

UTIL 5-8 X 6-0

WIDTH 79'-10"
DEPTH 63'-10"

BRKFST RM 11-4 X 10-0 CATHEDRAL CLG

DESIGN 8179

First Floor: 1,966 square feet
Second Floor: 872 square feet
Total: 2,838 square feet

DESIGN BY
LARRY E. BELK
DESIGNS

BEDROOM 2 12-6 X 11-6

BATH 3

BEDROOM 3 12-6 X 12-6

LIN

BALCONY

OPEN TO GREAT ROOM BELOW

BALCONY

OPEN TO FOYER BELOW

ATTIC

BEDROOM 4 11-4 X 13-6

This elegant brick two-story, with its corner quoin brick detail, varied roof lines and multi-pane windows, has so many amenities to offer! Enter into the two-story foyer graced by an elegant, curved staircase. The formal dining room, defined by columns, is to the right and has double-door access to the efficient island kitchen. The large great room is enhanced by direct access to the rear patio and a warming fireplace. The first floor master suite is secluded for privacy and is enhanced with a pampering, spa-style bath, His and Hers walk-in closets and a private covered porch. Upstairs, a balcony hall overlooking the great room leads to the three family bedrooms, each with walk-in closets. Please specify basement, crawlspace or slab foundation when ordering.

DESIGN Q248

Entry Level: 147 square feet
Main Level: 1,249 square feet
Total: 1,396 square feet

With the main living area on the second floor and expandable space at the entry level, this home provides plenty of space to grow. Double coat closets flank the entry, which then leads to an open staircase to the second floor. The center hall is skylit and opens to the living room with fireplace and dining room on the right. To the rear is a U-shaped kitchen and bayed breakfast room with door to the sun deck beyond. Bedrooms are on the left: a master suite with walk-in closet and two family bedrooms. The master has a private bath, while family bedrooms share a full bath. Space on the lower level could become a family room with an additional fireplace in the future.

DESIGN BY
SELECT HOME DESIGNS

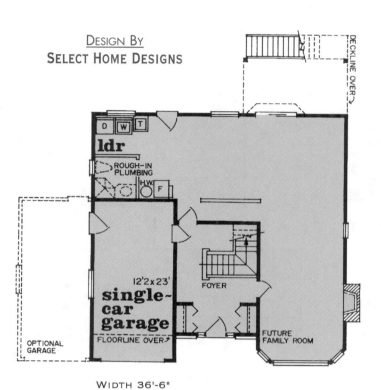

WIDTH 36'-6"
DEPTH 36'-0"

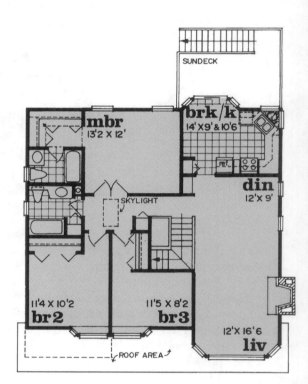

COPYRIGHT LARRY E. BELK

Designed for utmost livability, this English mini-estate is full of charm. A turret entrance leads to the vaulted foyer and the great room beyond. An adjacent kitchen features a 42-inch breakfast bar, a walk-in pantry and a planning desk. The spacious, multi-windowed breakfast room allows access to the octagonal porch, perfect for outdoor dining. Located on the first floor, the master suite includes a relaxing master bath and an enormous walk-in closet. The second floor holds an additional bedroom and full bath. A large expandable area is available off the balcony and can be used for storage or finished for additional living space. Please specify crawlspace or slab foundation when ordering.

DESIGN 8164

First Floor: 1,276 square feet
Second Floor: 378 square feet
Total: 1,654 square feet

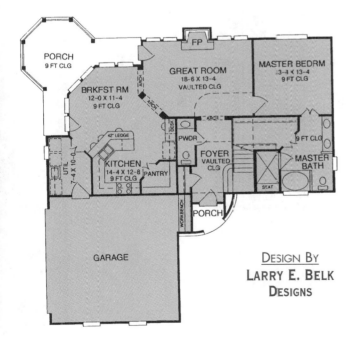

PORCH
9 FT CLG

BRKFST RM
12-0 X 11-4
9 FT CLG

GREAT ROOM
18-6 X 13-4
VAULTED CLG

MASTER BEDRM
13-4 X 13-4
9 FT CLG

FP

42" LEDGE

KITCHEN
14-4 X 12-8
9 FT CLG

PANTRY

PWDR

FOYER
VAULTED CLG

MASTER
BATH

9 FT CLG

UTIL
7-4 X 10-0

WORKBENCH

PORCH

SEAT

GARAGE

DESIGN BY
LARRY E. BELK
DESIGNS

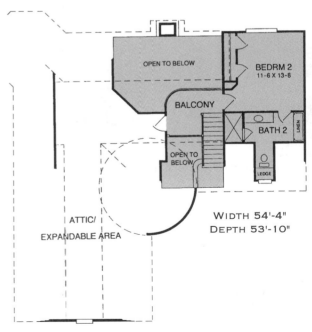

OPEN TO BELOW

BEDRM 2
11-6 X 13-8

BALCONY

BATH 2

LINEN

OPEN TO
BELOW

LEDGE

ATTIC/
EXPANDABLE AREA

WIDTH 54'-4"
DEPTH 53'-10"

DESIGN A298

First Floor: 1,882 square feet
Second Floor: 1,269 square feet
Total: 3,151 square feet
Bonus Room: 284 square feet

Offering a myriad of possibilities, this home can define your lifestyle and shape it in exciting ways. The first floor holds both formal and informal spaces for every occasion. The gathering room is the main living area, but it is complemented by a formal dining room and a casual breakfast room. The kitchen sits between the two dining options and can easily serve both. The master suite is on the first floor for convenience. A tray ceiling, bumped-out window and bath with walk-in closet, whirlpool tub, separate shower and double sinks add to its appeal. The second floor holds three family bedrooms, a recreation room and bonus space. Suites 2 and 3 share a full bath, while Suites 4 has a private bath and walk-in closet. Don't miss the huge unfinished storage area over the garage.

DECK

BREAKFAST
9'-10" x 13'-4"

GATHERING
ROOM
15'-6" x 21'-4"

MASTER
SUITE
16'-2" x 14'-0"

KITCHEN
12'-0" x 15'-6"

LIN.

W.I.C.

P.

UP

W.I.C.

MASTER
BATH

BDR.

DINING
ROOM
12'-0" x 16'-0"

FOYER

LAUNDRY

PORCH

GARAGE
20'-0" x 23'-0"

DESIGN BY
LIVING CONCEPTS
HOME PLANNING

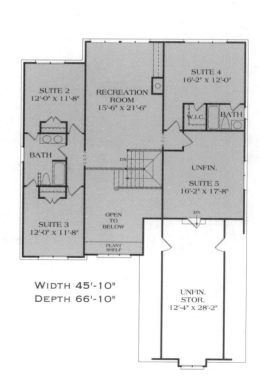

SUITE 2
12'-0" x 11'-8"

RECREATION
ROOM
15'-6" x 21'-6"

SUITE 4
16'-2" x 12'-0"

BATH

W.I.C.

BATH

DN

UNFIN.

SUITE 5
16'-2" x 17'-8"

SUITE 3
12'-0" x 11'-8"

OPEN
TO
BELOW

DN

PLANT
SHELF

WIDTH 45'-10"
DEPTH 66'-10"

UNFIN.
STOR.
12'-4" x 28'-2"

A towering entry is set off by twin gabled rooflines and a long clerestory window that lights up the foyer in this two-story home. The foyer leads to a deceptively simple floor plan that owes a great view in the back to large windows in the great room and the dining room. The great room is further enhanced by a fireplace and sits near the island kitchen for convenience. Three bedrooms on the second floor include a master suite with walk-in closet and full, private bath. The family bedrooms share a full compartmented hall bath. Note that the laundry room and large linen closet reside on the second floor near the bedrooms.

DESIGN 7512

First Floor: 655 square feet
Second Floor: 809 square feet
Total: 1,464 square feet

DESIGN BY
ALAN MASCORD
DESIGN ASSOCIATES, INC.

WIDTH 30'-0"
DEPTH 42'-0"

DESIGN 8088

First Floor: 1,904 square feet
Second Floor: 792 square feet
Total: 2,696 square feet

This charming cottage has all the accoutrements of an English manor. Inside, the angled foyer directs the eye to the arched entrances of the formal dining room and the great room with its fireplace and patio access. The master bedroom and a guest bedroom (or possible study) are located at the opposite end of the house for privacy. Two additional bedrooms, a full bath, a game room and an upper deck are located on the second floor. Please specify basement, crawlspace or slab foundation when ordering.

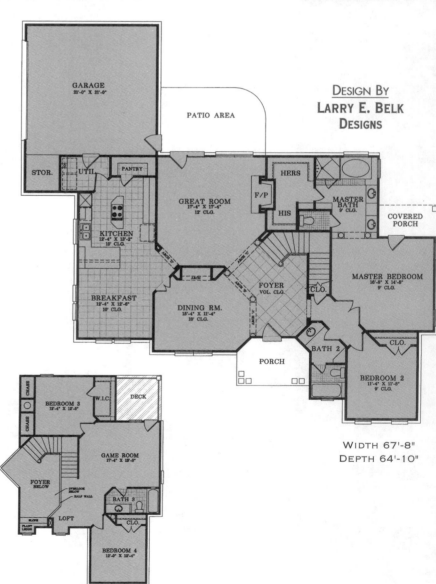

DESIGN BY
LARRY E. BELK
DESIGNS

GARAGE
21'-0" X 21'-0"

PATIO AREA

STOR.   UTIL.   PANTRY

GREAT ROOM
17'-4" X 17'-4"
12' CLG.

F/P

HERS

HIS

MASTER
BATH
9' CLG.

COVERED
PORCH

KITCHEN
12'-4" X 12'-3"
10' CLG.

BREAKFAST
12'-4" X 12'-5"
10' CLG.

DINING RM.
13'-4" X 11'-4"
10' CLG.

FOYER
VOL. CLG.

CLO.

MASTER BEDROOM
16'-8" X 14'-8"
9' CLG.

CLO.

BATH 2

PORCH

BEDROOM 2
11'-4" X 11'-8"
9' CLG.

WIDTH 67'-8"
DEPTH 64'-10"

BEDROOM 3
15'-4" X 12'-8"

W.I.C.

DECK

CHASE

CHASE

GAME ROOM
17'-4" X 15'-8"

FOYER
BELOW

OVERLOOK
BELOW

HALF WALL

BATH 3

SLOPE

PLANT
LEDGE

LOFT

CLO.

BEDROOM 4
13'-0" X 12'-4"

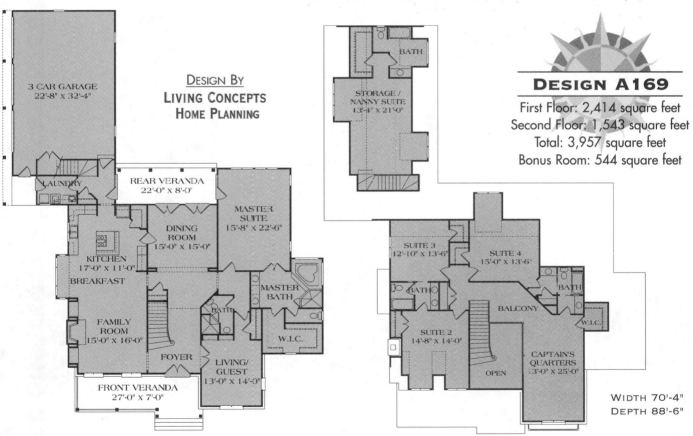

3 CAR GARAGE
22'-8" x 32'-4"

DESIGN BY
LIVING CONCEPTS
HOME PLANNING

BATH

STORAGE /
NANNY SUITE
13'-4" x 21'-0"

DESIGN A169
First Floor: 2,414 square feet
Second Floor: 1,543 square feet
Total: 3,957 square feet
Bonus Room: 544 square feet

LAUNDRY

REAR VERANDA
22'-0" x 8'-0"

DINING
ROOM
15'-0" x 15'-0"

MASTER
SUITE
15'-8" x 22'-6"

KITCHEN
17'-0" x 11'-0"

BREAKFAST

MASTER
BATH

BATH

FAMILY
ROOM
15'-0" x 16'-0"

FOYER

LIVING/
GUEST
13'-0" x 14'-0"

W.I.C.

FRONT VERANDA
27'-0" x 7'-0"

SUITE 3
12'-10" x 13'-6"

SUITE 4
15'-0" x 13'-6"

BATH

BATH

BALCONY

W.I.C.

SUITE 2
14'-8" x 14'-0"

OPEN

CAPTAIN'S
QUARTERS
13'-0" x 25'-0"

WIDTH 70'-4"
DEPTH 88'-6"

What could be finer than a country estate rendered in stone and stucco? This one adds wooden porch details and two dormer windows, then adds a great, livable floor plan. You have options in the floor plan: choose a living room for the area to the right of the foyer. Or make it a guest room with nearby full bath. The master suite is not far behind and holds a walk-in closet and bath with corner whirlpool, separate shower and double sinks. The master bedroom shares a rear veranda with the formal dining room. The kitchen and family room are linked together by a breakfast room with box-bay window. Behind all this is a three-car garage joined to the main house by the laundry room/service entrance. Three additional suites and the grand Captain's Quarters are found on the second floor. Space over the garage could become a nanny's suite or just used for storage.

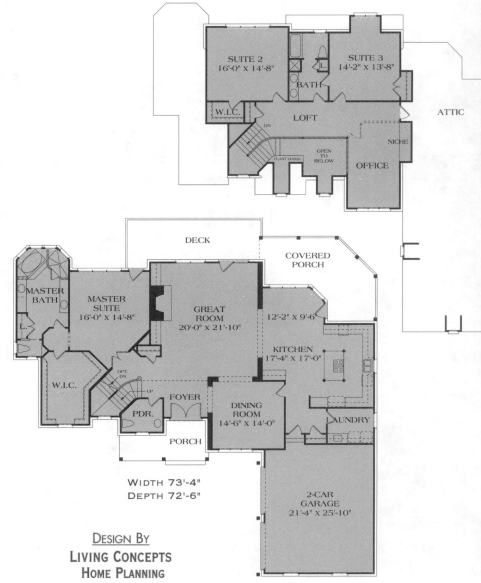

DESIGN A266

First Floor: 2,307 square feet
Second Floor: 1,009 square feet
Total: 3,316 square feet

If you're looking for superb exterior spaces, look no further than this plan. Special interior rooms? It's got those, too. Begin with a covered porch on the front, then proceed through a double door to the open foyer and huge great room. The formal dining room sits on the right and connects to the island kitchen and breakfast bay. A covered porch is just beyond, as well as a handy deck accessed by both the great room and the master bedroom. For luxury, look to the master bath, with spa tub, separate shower, twin sinks, compartmented toilet and walk-in closet. Family bedrooms are upstairs and share a full bath. A home office contains niche space and may be closed off more fully or left open to the loft area.

SUITE 2
16'-0" X 14'-8"

SUITE 3
14'-2" X 13'-8"

BATH

W.I.C.

LOFT

ATTIC

DN

PLANT LEDGE

OPEN TO BELOW

NICHE

OFFICE

DECK

COVERED PORCH

MASTER BATH

MASTER SUITE
16'-0" X 14'-8"

GREAT ROOM
20'-0" X 21'-10"

12'-2" X 9'-6"

KITCHEN
17'-4" X 17'-0"

W.I.C.

OPT. DN

UP

FOYER

PDR.

DINING ROOM
14'-6" X 14'-0"

LAUNDRY

PORCH

2-CAR GARAGE
21'-4" X 25'-10"

WIDTH 73'-4"
DEPTH 72'-6"

DESIGN BY
LIVING CONCEPTS
HOME PLANNING

This home, as shown in the photograph, may differ from the actual blueprints. For more detailed information, please check the floor plans carefully.

Photo by Design Basics, Inc.

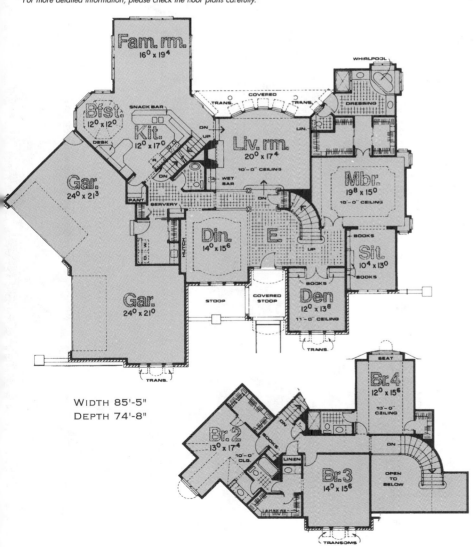

WIDTH 85'-5"
DEPTH 74'-8"

DESIGN 7246

First Floor: 2,813 square feet
Second Floor: 1,091 square feet
Total: 3,904 square feet

The stone facade of this elegant traditional evokes images of a quieter life, a life of harmony and comfortable luxury. An elegant floor plan allows you to carry that feeling inside. The tiled foyer offers entry to any room you choose, whether it be the secluded den with its built-in bookshelves, the formal dining room, the formal living room with its fireplace, wet bar and wall of windows, or the spacious rear family and kitchen area with its sunny breakfast nook. The master bedroom offers privacy on the first floor and features a sitting room with bookshelves, two walk-in closets and a master bath with a corner whirlpool tub. Three family bedrooms, each with a walk-in closet, and two baths make up the second floor.

DESIGN BY
DESIGN BASICS, INC.

91

This home, as shown in the photograph, may differ from the actual blueprints.
For more detailed information, please check the floor plans carefully.

Photo by Andrew D. Lautman

DESIGN BY
HOME PLANNERS

DESIGN 2826

First Floor: 1,112 square feet
Second Floor: 881 square feet
Total: 1,993 square feet

D

QUOTE ONE®

Cost to build? See page 434
to order complete cost estimate
to build this house in your area!

The classic American homestead is all dressed up with contemporary character and country spirit. Well-defined rooms, flowing spaces and the latest amenities blend the best of traditional and modern elements. The spacious gathering room offers terrace access and shares a through-fireplace with a secluded study. The second-floor master suite shares a balcony hallway, which overlooks the gathering room, with two family bedrooms. Dual vanities, built-in cabinets and shelves, and triple-window views highlight the master bedroom. In an alternate plan, the formal dining room and the breakfast room are switched, placing the dining room to the front of the plan.

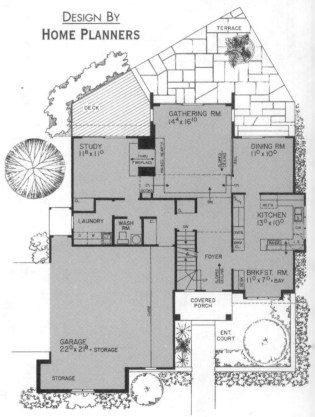

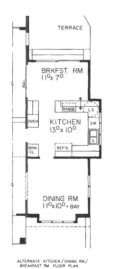

ALTERNATE KITCHEN / DINING RM./
BREAKFAST RM FLOOR PLAN

WIDTH 49'-0"
DEPTH 54'-4"

Rear

DESIGN 9622

Square Footage: 1,842

DESIGN BY
DONALD A. GARDNER
ARCHITECTS, INC.

Rear

WIDTH 92'-4"
DEPTH 61'-8"

© 1987 Donald A. Gardner Architects, Inc.

What visual excitement is created in this country ranch with the use of a combination of exterior building materials and shapes! The angular nature of the plan allows for flexibility in design—lengthen the great room or family room, or both, to suit individual space needs. Cathedral ceilings grace both rooms and a fireplace embellishes the great room with warmth. An amenity-filled master bedroom features a cathedral ceiling, a private deck and a master bath with whirlpool tub. Two family bedrooms share a full bath. An expansive deck area with hot tub wraps around interior family gathering areas for enhanced outdoor living. Please specify basement or crawlspace foundation when ordering.

© 1987 Donald A. Gardner Architects, Inc.

Design Q443

Square Footage: 1,298

Design By
SELECT HOME DESIGNS

A front veranda, cedar lattice and solid stone chimney enhance the appeal of this one-story country-style home. The open plan begins with the great room which has a fireplace and a plant ledge over the wall separating the living space from the country kitchen. The kitchen is U-shaped and has an island work counter and sliding glass doors to the rear deck and a screened porch. Vaulted ceilings in both the kitchen and great room add spaciousness. Look for three bedrooms, clustered together at the left of the plan. Family bedrooms feature wall closets and share the use of a skylit main bath. The master suite also has a wall closet and a private bath with window seat. The two-car garage is reached via the service entrance where there is a convenient laundry with utility closets. Plans for both a basement and a crawlspace foundation are included.

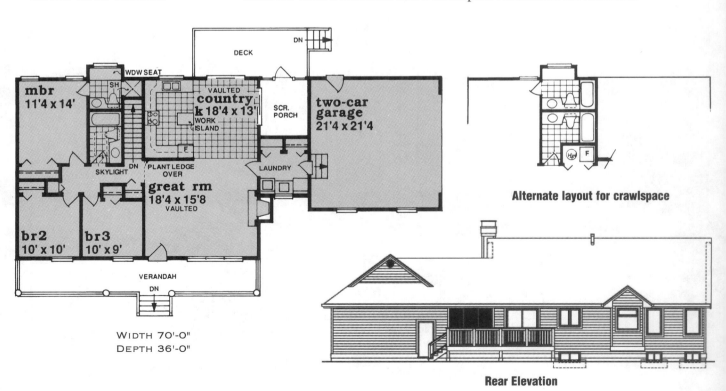

WIDTH 70'-0"
DEPTH 36'-0"

Alternate layout for crawlspace

Rear Elevation

With a graceful pediment above and a sturdy, columned veranda below, this quaint home was made for country living. The veranda wraps slightly around on two sides of the facade and permits access to a central foyer with a den (or third bedroom) on the right and the country kitchen on the left. Look for an island work space in the kitchen and a plant ledge over the entry between the great room and the kitchen. A fireplace warms the great room and is flanked by windows overlooking the rear deck. A casually defined dining space has double-door access to this same deck. Bedrooms are clustered on the right side of the plan. The master suite offers an art niche at its entry and a bath with separate tub and shower. Family bedrooms share a skylit bath. Choose either a basement or crawlspace foundation for this design—both are included in the plans.

DESIGN Q449

Square Footage: 1,578

DESIGN BY
SELECT HOME DESIGNS

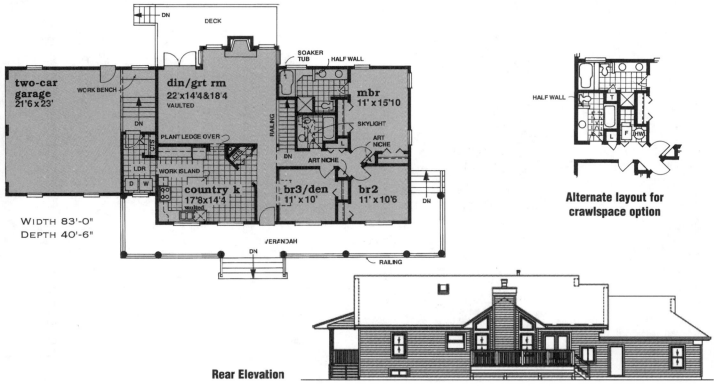

WIDTH 83'-0"
DEPTH 40'-6"

Alternate layout for crawlspace option

Rear Elevation

DESIGN Q252

Square Footage: 1,475

A railed veranda, turned posts, and filigree in the corner and at the gable points complement a lovely Palladian window on the exterior of this home. The interior opens with a skylit foyer and living and dining rooms to the right. The living room is vaulted and features a fireplace and built-in bookshelves. The dining room overlooks a covered veranda accessed through a door in the breakfast room (note the bayed eating area). The kitchen takes advantage of this veranda access, as well. It is further enhanced by an L-shaped work area and butcher-block island. The bedrooms are clustered to the left of the plan. They include a master suite with full bath and two family bedrooms sharing a full bath with double vanity. Plans include details for both a basement and a crawlspace foundation.

DESIGN BY
SELECT HOME DESIGNS

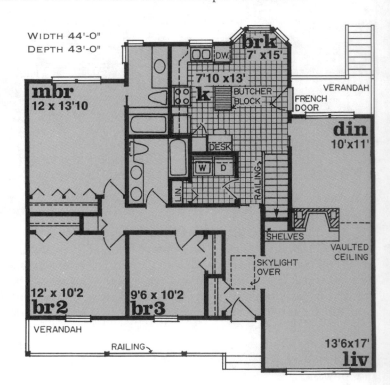

WIDTH 44'-0"
DEPTH 43'-0"

mbr
12 x 13'10

brk
7' x15'

7'10 x13'

k

BUTCHER BLOCK

DW.

VERANDAH

FRENCH DOOR

din
10'x11'

DESK

RAILING

W D

LIN

SHELVES

VAULTED CEILING

12' x 10'2
br2

9'6 x 10'2
br3

SKYLIGHT OVER

VERANDAH

RAILING

13'6x17'
liv

Rear Elevation

A covered railed veranda, shuttered windows, siding and wood detailing and a Palladian window all lend their charm to this one-story ranch. The living room shares a through-fireplace with the dining area and also has a box-bay window at the front. A U-shaped kitchen is efficient and pleasant with a window to the backyard over the sink. Garage access is through the laundry room, where you will also find stairs to the basement. The three bedrooms are on the right side of the plan. The master has two wall closets and a private bath. Family bedrooms share a full hall bath. A single-car garage sits to the side for convenience. If you choose, the basement can be developed later for additional space.

DESIGN Q346

Square Footage: 1,233

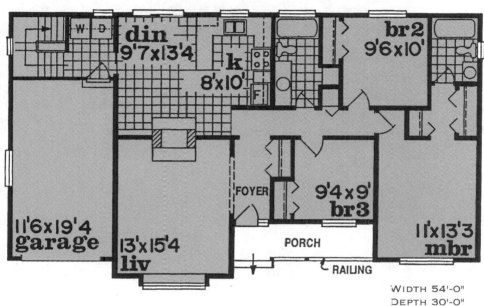

DESIGN BY

SELECT HOME DESIGNS

WIDTH 54'-0"
DEPTH 30'-0"

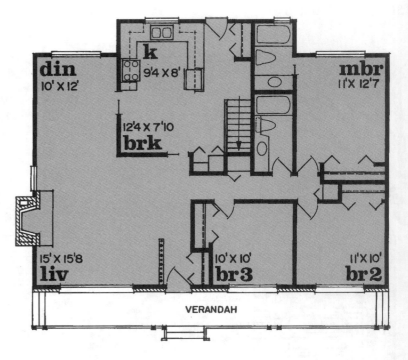

DESIGN Q222
Square Footage: 1,356

DESIGN BY
SELECT HOME DESIGNS

Charmingly compact, this easy-to-build design is ideal for first-time homeowners. The exterior is appealing with a brick facade, horizontal wood siding on the sides, a large brick chimney and a full-width covered veranda. The living room/dining room combination is warmed by a masonry fireplace and includes an optional spindle screen wall at the entry. A country kitchen has ample counter space, a U-shaped work area and dining space. Outdoor access can also be found here. Three bedrooms include a master suite with private bath and two family bedrooms sharing a full hall bath. Each bedroom has a roomy wall closet. Stairs to the basement are located in the kitchen area. Plans include details for both a basement and a crawlspace foundation.

din
10' X 12'

k
9'4 X 8'

mbr
11'X 12'7

brk
12'4 X 7'10

liv
15' X 15'8

br3
10' X 10'

br2
11'X 10'

VERANDAH

WIDTH 44'-0"
DEPTH 37'-8"

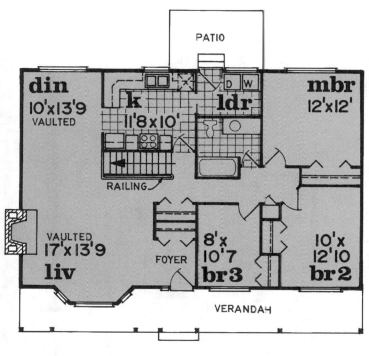

WIDTH 44'-0"
DEPTH 34'-0"

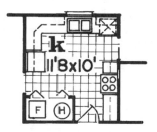

Alternate layout for crawlspace

DESIGN Q313

Square Footage: 1,254

Simple details make this starter home quite appealing. A posted front porch, with corner detail, a bay window and shuttered windows all lend a traditional flavor. The central foyer has a coat closet and opens on the left to a vaulted living room with fireplace. The dining room is also vaulted, but overlooks the backyard. An L-shaped kitchen and attached laundry share access to the back patio through a door between them. An additional hall closet sits at the beginning of its stretch to three bedrooms. Each of the bedrooms has a wall closet; two family bedrooms overlook the veranda. All three share the use of a full hall bath. Choose either a basement or crawlspace foundation—plans include details for both.

DESIGN BY
SELECT HOME DESIGNS

DESIGN Q275

Square Footage: 1,525

DESIGN BY
SELECT HOME DESIGNS

This charming country home is sized right for economy, but leaves out nothing in the way of livability. A bay window, front and rear verandas and a sweeping roof all enrich its heritage design. The front veranda opens to the center hall which leads to the large living and dining areas. A corner fireplace in the living room warms the space in cold winter months. The kitchen and bayed breakfast nook sit to the rear and open to another veranda through double doors. Two family bedrooms are at the back of the plan and share a full hall bath. The master bedroom has a bay window, walk-in closet and private bath. Plans include a single-car option, so you can add on if you choose.

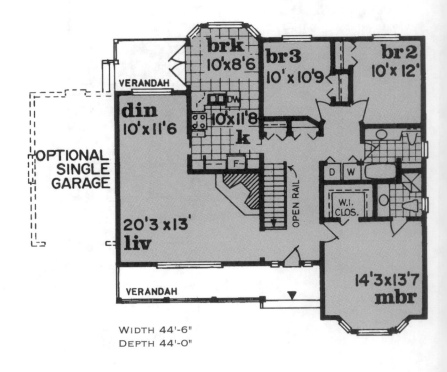

WIDTH 44'-6"
DEPTH 44'-0"

Enhanced by farmhouse details—turned spindles on a covered porch and gable trim—this compact is as pleasing as it is affordable. The entry opens to a center hall with a living room on one side and dining room on the other. The living room features a box-bay window and warming fireplace. The dining room attaches to the U-shaped kitchen. A handy laundry area with access to the two-car garage (optional) is nearby. The three bedrooms stretch out along the rear width of the home. The master suite has a private bath and wall closet. Two family bedrooms also have wall closets and share the use of a full bath. The basement may be finished later for additional living or sleeping space.

DESIGN Q273

Square Footage: 1,383

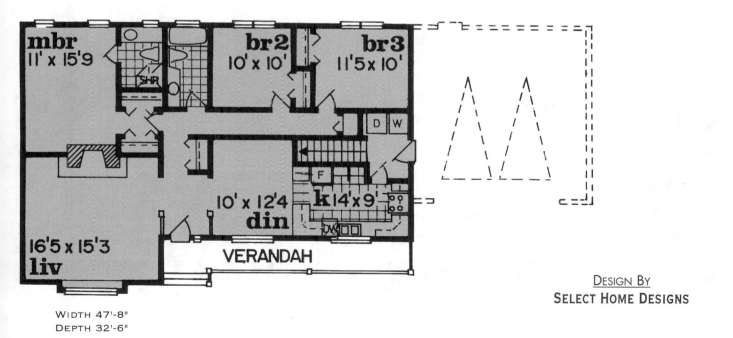

mbr 11' x 15'9"

br2 10' x 10'

br3 11'5 x 10'

SHR

D W

liv 16'5 x 15'3

10' x 12'4 **din**

k 14' x 9'

F

DW

VERANDAH

WIDTH 47'-8"
DEPTH 32'-6"

DESIGN BY
SELECT HOME DESIGNS

DESIGN Q361

Square Footage: 1,456

A covered veranda, spanning the width of this three-bedroom home, is a graceful and charming exterior detail. It leads to an entry foyer and the large living and dining space beyond. Here a warming fireplace will act as a focal point. The dining room has a small covered porch beyond sliding glass doors. The U-shaped kitchen has a breakfast bar and serves the dining room and sunny breakfast bay easily. The master bedroom is one of three at the right of the plan and features a wall closet and full bath with shower. Two family bedrooms share use of a full hall bath. A full basement, with open-rail staircase, allows for future expansion. The single-car garage has rear-yard access.

DESIGN BY
SELECT HOME DESIGNS

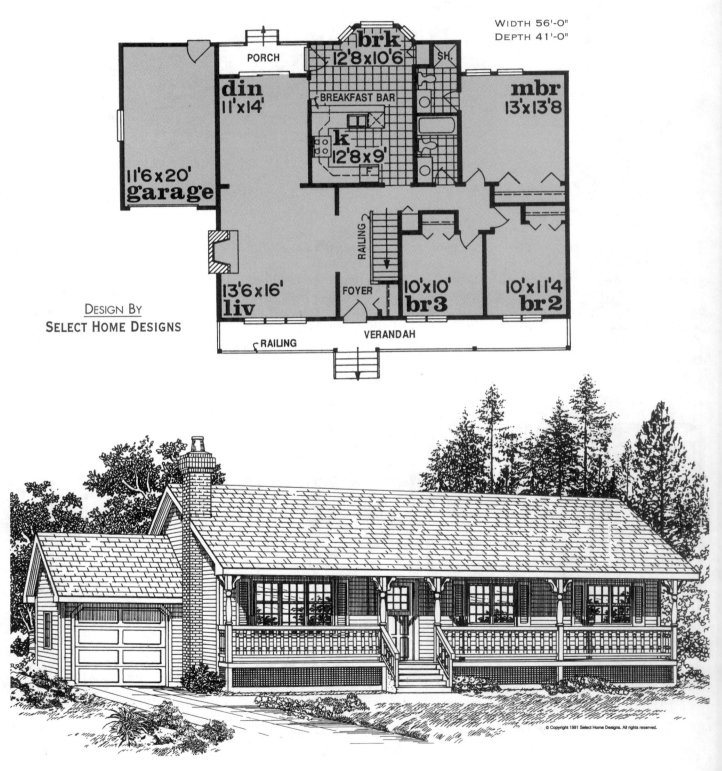

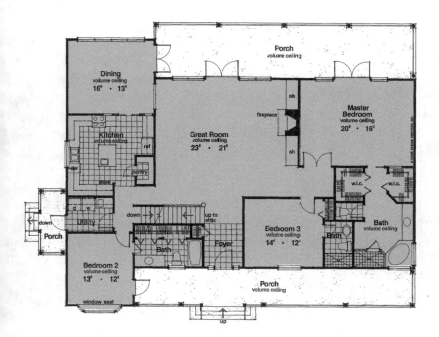

Floor plan labels:

Dining
volume ceiling
16⁰ · 13⁴

Porch
volume ceiling

Kitchen
volume ceiling

ref

desk

pantry

Great Room
volume ceiling
23⁸ · 21⁰

sh

fireplace

sh

Master Bedroom
volume ceiling
20⁸ · 16⁰

w.i.c.   w.i.c.

d   w

Utility

down

Porch

down   up to attic

Bath

Foyer

Bedroom 3
volume ceiling
14⁴ · 12²

Bath

Bath
volume ceiling

Bedroom 2
volume ceiling
13⁰ · 12⁸

window seat

Porch
volume ceiling

up

WIDTH 64'-0"
DEPTH 52'-0"

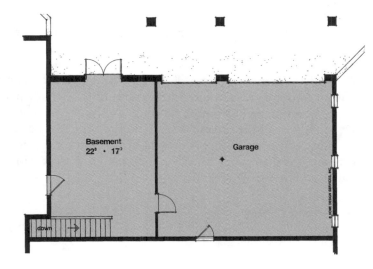

Basement
22⁸ · 17⁰

Garage

down

DESIGN 8648

Square Footage: 2,500
Bonus Space: 492 square feet

This Florida "Cracker"-style home is warm and inviting. Unpretentious space is the hallmark of the Florida Cracker. This design shows the style at its best. The huge great room, which sports a volume ceiling, opens to the expansive rear porch for extended entertaining. While traditional Cracker homes had sparse master suites, this one features a lavish bedchamber and luxurious bath with His and Hers closets and a corner soaking tub. Each of the secondary bedrooms has a private bath as well. The kitchen and dining areas also have volume ceilings; the kitchen is further graced by an island. Perfect for a sloping lot, this home can be expanded with a lower garage and bonus space in the basement.

DESIGN BY
**HOME DESIGN
SERVICES**

© 1991 Donald A. Gardner Architects, Inc.

DESIGN 9620

Square Footage: 1,310

Amulti-paned bay window, dormers, a cupola, a covered porch and a variety of building materials dress up this one-story cottage. The entrance foyer leads to an impressive great room with cathedral ceiling and fireplace. The U-shaped kitchen, adjacent to the dining room, provides an ideal layout for food preparation. An expansive deck offers shelter while admitting cheery sunlight through skylights. A luxurious master bedroom located to the rear of the house takes advantage of the deck area and is assured privacy from two other bedrooms at the front of the house. These family bedrooms share a full bath. Note the two-car garage with access to the main house and to the rear deck.

DESIGN BY
**DONALD A. GARDNER
ARCHITECTS, INC.**

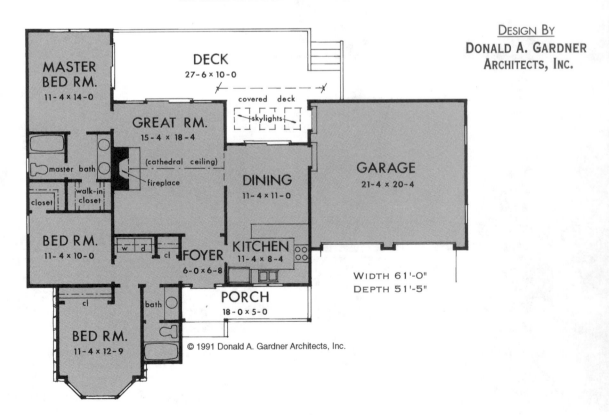

MASTER BED RM.
11-4 x 14-0

DECK
27-6 x 10-0

GREAT RM.
15-4 x 18-4

covered deck
skylights

GARAGE
21-4 x 20-4

master bath

(cathedral ceiling)

fireplace

closet

walk-in closet

DINING
11-4 x 11-0

BED RM.
11-4 x 10-0

w d

cl

FOYER
6-0 x 6-8

KITCHEN
11-4 x 8-4

cl

bath

PORCH
18-0 x 5-0

WIDTH 61'-0"
DEPTH 51'-5"

BED RM.
11-4 x 12-9

© 1991 Donald A. Gardner Architects, Inc.

104

DESIGN BY
DONALD A. GARDNER
ARCHITECTS, INC.

DESIGN 9713
Square Footage: 1,590

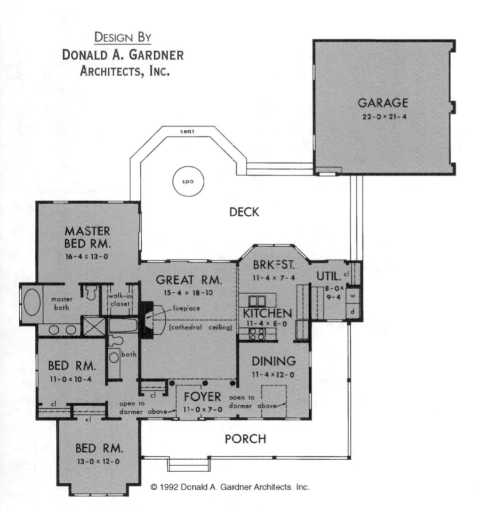

GARAGE
22-0 × 21-4

seat

spa

DECK

MASTER
BED RM.
16-4 × 13-0

GREAT RM.
15-4 × 18-10

BRK=ST.
11-4 × 7-4

UTIL. cl
8-0 ×
9-4

master
bath

walk-in
closet

fireplace

(cathedral ceiling)

KITCHEN
11-4 × 8-0

w
d

bath

BED RM.
11-0 × 10-4

DINING
11-4 × 12-0

cl

cl

open to
dormer above

FOYER
11-0 × 7-0

open to
dormer above

BED RM.
13-0 × 12-0

PORCH

WIDTH 70'-4"
DEPTH 74'-0"

The open floor plan of this country farmhouse packs in all of today's amenities in only 1,590 square feet. Columns separate the foyer from the great room with its cathedral ceiling and fireplace. Serving meals has never been easier—the kitchen makes use of direct access to the dining room as well as a breakfast nook overlooking the deck and spa. A handy utility room even has room for a counter and cabinets. Three bedrooms make this an especially desirable design. The master bedroom, off of the great room, provides private access to the deck. This design is flexible enough to be accommodated by a narrow lot if the garage is relocated.

© 1993 Donald A. Gardner Architects, Inc.

DESIGN 9702

First Floor: 1,618 square feet
Second Floor: 570 square feet
Total: 2,188 square feet
Bonus Room: 495 square feet

DESIGN BY
DONALD A. GARDNER
ARCHITECTS, INC.

A wraparound covered porch, an open deck with a spa and seating, arched windows and dormers enhance the already impressive character of this three-bedroom farmhouse. The entrance foyer and great room with sloped ceilings have Palladian window clerestories to allow natural light to enter. All other first-floor spaces have nine-foot ceilings. The spacious great room boasts a fireplace, cabinets and bookshelves. The kitchen, with a cooking island, is conveniently located between a dining room and a breakfast room with an open view of the great room. A generous master bedroom has plenty of closet space as well as an expansive master bath. Bonus room over the garage allows for room to grow.

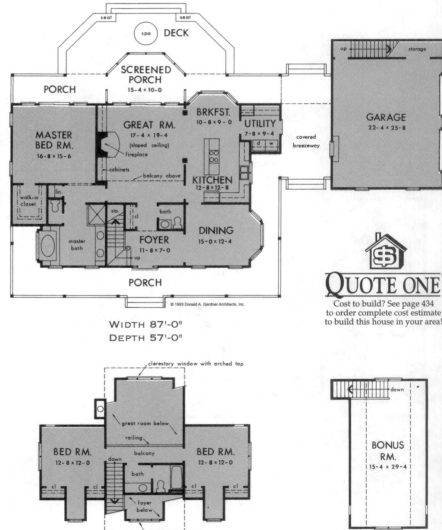

© 1993 Donald A. Gardner Architects, Inc.

WIDTH 87'-0"
DEPTH 57'-0"

Quote One®
Cost to build? See page 434
to order complete cost estimate
to build this house in your area!

106

© 1993 Donald A. Gardner Architects, Inc.

B. NATHAN

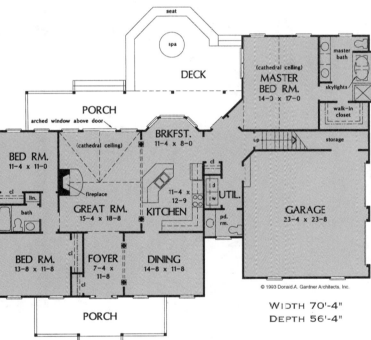

seat

spa

DECK

PORCH

arched window above door

MASTER BED RM.
14-0 x 17-0
(cathedral ceiling)

master bath

skylights

walk-in closet

BRKFST.
11-4 x 8-0

storage

BED RM.
11-4 x 11-0

(cathedral ceiling)

fireplace

cl   lin.

bath

GREAT RM.
15-4 x 18-8

KITCHEN

11-4 x 12-9

UTIL.

pd. rm.

GARAGE
23-4 x 23-8

up

BED RM.
13-8 x 11-8

cl

FOYER
7-4 x 11-8

cl

DINING
14-8 x 11-8

PORCH

© 1993 Donald A. Gardner Architects, Inc.

WIDTH 70'-4"
DEPTH 56'-4"

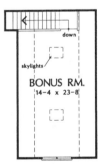

down

skylights

BONUS RM.
14-4 x 23-8

DESIGN 9749

Square Footage: 1,864
Bonus Room: 420 square feet

DESIGN BY
DONALD A. GARDNER
ARCHITECTS, INC.

Quote One®

Cost to build? See page 434
to order complete cost estimate
to build this house in your area!

Quaint and cozy on the outside with porches front and back, this three-bedroom country home surprises with an open floor plan featuring a large great room with a cathedral ceiling. Nine-foot ceilings add volume throughout the home. A central kitchen with an angled counter opens to the breakfast and great rooms for easy entertaining. The privately located master bedroom has a cathedral ceiling and access to the deck. Operable skylights over the tub accent the luxurious master bath. Two secondary bedrooms share a full hall bath. A bonus room makes expanding easy. Please specify basement or crawlspace foundation when ordering.

Rear

DESIGN 9310

First Floor: 1,505 square feet
Second Floor: 610 square feet
Total: 2,115 square feet

Many windows, lap siding and a covered porch give this elevation a welcoming country flair. The formal dining room with hutch space is conveniently located near the island kitchen. A main floor laundry room with a sink is discreetly located next to the bright breakfast area with desk and pantry. Highlighting the spacious great room are a raised-hearth fireplace, a cathedral ceiling and trapezoid windows. Special features in the master suite include a large dressing area with a double vanity, a skylight, a step-up corner whirlpool tub and a generous walk-in closet. Upstairs, the three secondary bedrooms are well separated from the master bedroom and share a hall bath.

DESIGN BY
DESIGN BASICS, INC.

© design basics inc. 1991

WIDTH 64'-0"
DEPTH 52'-0"

QUOTE ONE®
Cost to build? See page 434
to order complete cost estimate
to build this house in your area!

Stone and siding lend a rustic nature to this traditional home. A covered stoop is enhanced by a graceful arch and a glass-paneled entry. A formal dining room is served by a gourmet kitchen through a butler's pantry with a wet bar. A sunny breakfast room sits just beyond the kitchen. The great room provides a fireplace and a French door to a golf porch at the rear and covered porch at the front. An angled tub and an oversized shower highlight the master bath, while a box-bay window and a tray ceiling enhance the homeowner's bedroom. Two suites on the second floor serve the family. Each has a private bath. The loft area is perfect as a study space.

DESIGN A253

First Floor: 1,825 square feet
Second Floor: 842 square feet
Total: 2,667 square feet

DESIGN BY
**LIVING CONCEPTS
HOME PLANNING**

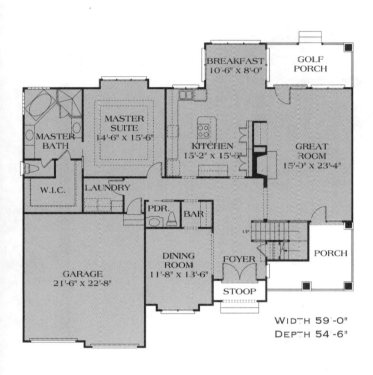

BREAKFAST 10'-6" X 8'-0"
GOLF PORCH
MASTER SUITE 14'-6" X 15'-6"
MASTER BATH
KITCHEN 15'-2" X 15'-6"
GREAT ROOM 15'-0" X 23'-4"
W.I.C.
LAUNDRY
PDR.
BAR
UP
GARAGE 21'-6" X 22'-8"
DINING ROOM 11'-8" X 13'-6"
FOYER
PORCH
STOOP

WIDTH 59'-0"
DEPTH 54'-6"

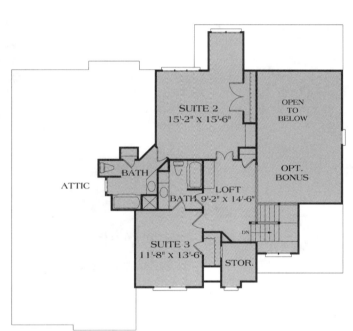

SUITE 2 15'-2" X 15'-6"
OPEN TO BELOW
ATTIC
BATH
LOFT 9'-2" X 14'-6"
BATH
OPT. BONUS
SUITE 3 11'-8" X 13'-6"
STOR.
DN

DESIGN 9251

First Floor: 1,653 square feet
Second Floor: 700 square feet
Total: 2,353 square feet

Beautiful arches and elaborate detail give the elevation of this four-bedroom, one-story home an unmistakable elegance. Inside, the floor plan is equally appealing. Note the formal dining room with bay window, visible from the entrance hall. The large great room has a fireplace and a wall of windows out the back. A hearth room, with bookcase, adjoins the kitchen area with a walk-in pantry. The private, first-floor master suite features a pampering bath that contains a large whirlpool tub and double lavatories. Upstairs quarters share a full bath with compartmented sinks.

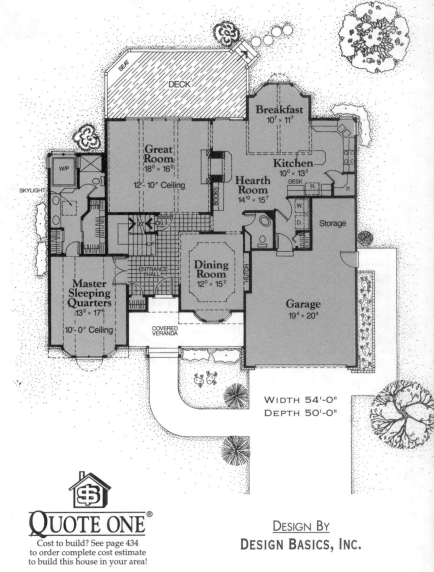

WIDTH 54'-0"
DEPTH 50'-0"

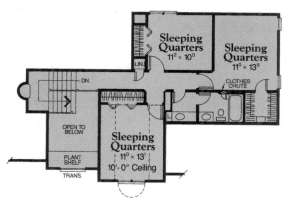

QUOTE ONE®

Cost to build? See page 434
to order complete cost estimate
to build this house in your area!

DESIGN BY
DESIGN BASICS, INC.

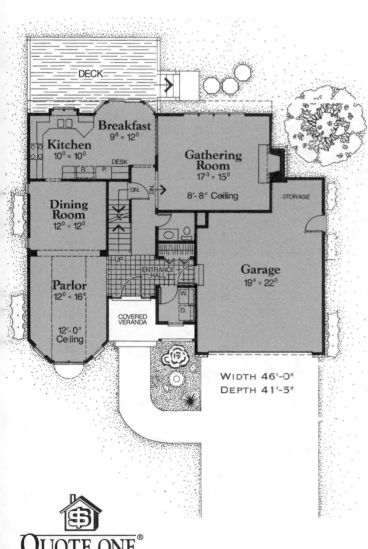

DECK

Breakfast
9⁸ × 12⁰

Kitchen
10⁰ × 10⁰

R.   P.   DESK

DN.   DN.

Dining
Room
12⁰ × 12⁰

UP

Parlor
12⁰ × 16⁴

12'-0"
Ceiling

COVERED
VERANDA

Gathering
Room
17³ × 15⁰

8'-8" Ceiling

STORAGE

ENTRANCE
HALL

W.

D.

Garage
19⁴ × 22⁰

WIDTH 46'-0"
DEPTH 41'-5"

DESIGN 9252

First Floor: 1,113 square feet
Second Floor: 965 square feet
Total: 2,078 square feet

SKYLIGHT   SKYLIGHT

W/P

9'-0" Ceiling

Master
Sleeping
Quarters
12⁰ × 17⁰

DN.

Sleeping
Quarters
11⁰ × 10⁰

Sleeping
Quarters
10⁰ × 11⁰

Sleeping
Quarters
11⁰ × 12⁸

11'-6"
Ceiling

DESIGN BY
DESIGN BASICS, INC.

Elegant detail, a charming veranda and a tall brick chimney make a pleasing facade on this four-bedroom, two-story Victorian home. Yesterday's simpler lifestyle is reflected throughout this plan. From the large bayed parlor with sloped ceiling to the sunken gathering room with fireplace, there's plenty to appreciate about the floor plan. The formal dining room opens to the parlor for convenient entertaining. An L-shaped kitchen with attached breakfast room is nearby. Upstairs quarters include a master suite with private dressing area and whirlpool tub, and three family bedrooms.

DESIGN 9588

First Floor: 1,032 square feet
Second Floor: 870 square feet
Total: 1,902 square feet
Bonus Room: 306 square feet

DESIGN BY
**ALAN MASCORD
DESIGN ASSOCIATES, INC.**

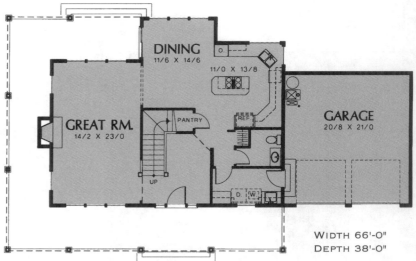

WIDTH 66'-0"
DEPTH 38'-0"

A wraparound covered porch and symmetrical dormers produce an inviting appearance to this farmhouse. Inside, the two-story foyer leads directly to the large great room graced by a fireplace and an abundance of windows. The U-shaped island kitchen is convenient to the sunny dining room and has a powder room nearby. The utility room offers access to the two-car garage. Upstairs, two family bedrooms share a full hall bath and have convenient access to a large bonus room. The master suite is full of amenities including a walk-in closet and a pampering bath.

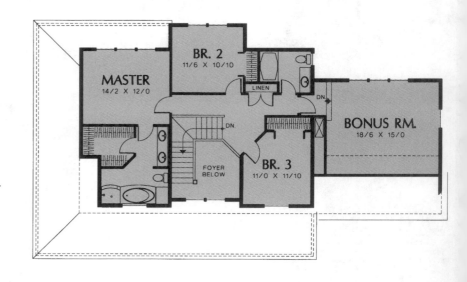

A wonderful design begins with the wraparound porch of this plan. Explore further and find a two-story entry with a coat closet and plant shelf above and a strategically placed staircase alongside. The island kitchen with a boxed window over the sink is adjacent to a large bay-windowed dinette. The great room includes many windows and a fireplace. A powder bath and laundry room are both conveniently placed on the first floor. Upstairs, the large master suite contains His and Hers walk-in closets, corner windows and a bath area featuring a double vanity and whirlpool tub. Two pleasant secondary bedrooms have interesting angles and a third bedroom in the front features a volume ceiling and arched window.

DESIGN 9235

First Floor: 919 square feet
Second Floor: 927 square feet
Total: 1,846 square feet

DESIGN BY
DESIGN BASICS, INC.

Kit.
9⁰x11⁶

Bfst.
10⁷x16⁰

Grt. rm.
18⁰x14⁰

Dn.
10⁰x13¹

Gar.
20⁰x19⁸

DN

UP

WRAPAROUND
PORCH

Mbr.
12⁰x16⁰
9'-4" CEILING

Br.
10⁰x11⁶

Br.
10⁰x11⁶

WHIRLPOOL

LIN.

Br.
10⁰x11⁸
10'-0" CEILING

DN

OPEN
TO
BELOW

PLANT
SHELF

WIDTH 44'-0"
DEPTH 40'-0"

QUOTE ONE®
Cost to build? See page 434
to order complete cost estimate
to build this house in your area!

113

DESIGN 7671

First Floor: 1,943 square feet
Second Floor: 1,000 square feet
Total: 2,943 square feet
Bonus Room: 403 square feet

DESIGN BY
DONALD A. GARDNER
ARCHITECTS, INC.

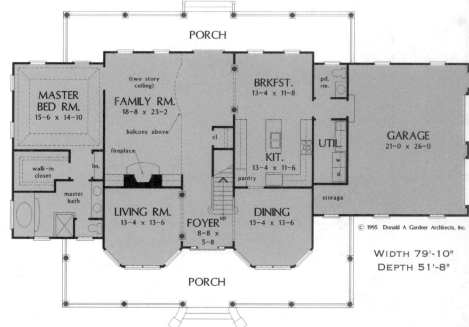

PORCH

MASTER BED RM.
15-6 x 14-10

FAMILY RM.
18-8 x 23-2
(two story ceiling)
balcony above

BRKFST.
13-4 x 11-8

pd. rm.

GARAGE
21-0 x 26-0

walk-in closet

fireplace

lin.

cl

KIT.
13-4 x 11-6

UTIL.

master bath

LIVING RM.
13-4 x 13-6

pantry

w. d.

storage

FOYER
8-8 x 5-8

DINING
13-4 x 13-6

PORCH

WIDTH 79'-10"
DEPTH 51'-8"

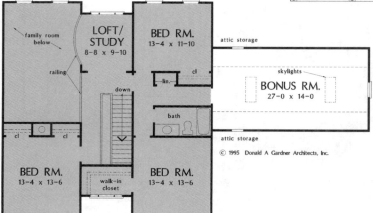

LOFT/ STUDY
8-8 x 9-10

BED RM.
13-4 x 11-10

family room below

railing

attic storage

cl

lin.

skylights

BONUS RM.
27-0 x 14-0

down

bath

attic storage

BED RM.
13-4 x 13-6

cl   cl

BED RM.
13-4 x 13-6

walk-in closet

Two symmetrical bay windows accent the formal living room and dining room of this design. The foyer leads straight back to the family room and rear porch. A fireplace, built-ins and an overhead balcony grace the family room. Between the dining room and kitchen, there's a handy pantry area. The utility room and a powder room are to the right of the breakfast room. The master suite is off the family room and includes a walk-in closet and a bath with a double-bowl vanity. Upstairs, three bedrooms share a hall bath and a loft/study that overlooks the family room.

O val windows and an appealing covered porch lend character to this 1½-story home. Inside, a volume entry views the formal living and dining rooms. Three large windows and a raised-hearth fireplace flanked by bookcases highlight a volume great room. An island kitchen with a huge pantry and two Lazy Susans serves a captivating gazebo dinette. In the master suite, a cathedral ceiling, corner whirlpool and roomy dressing area deserve careful study. A gallery wall for displaying family mementos and prized heirlooms graces the upstairs corridor. Each secondary bedroom has convenient access to the bathrooms. This home's charm and blend of popular amenities will fit your lifestyle!

DESIGN 9298

First Floor: 1,881 square feet
Second Floor: 814 square feet
Total: 2,695 square feet

DESIGN BY
DESIGN BASICS, INC.

Cost to build? See page 434
to order complete cost estimate
to build this house in your area!

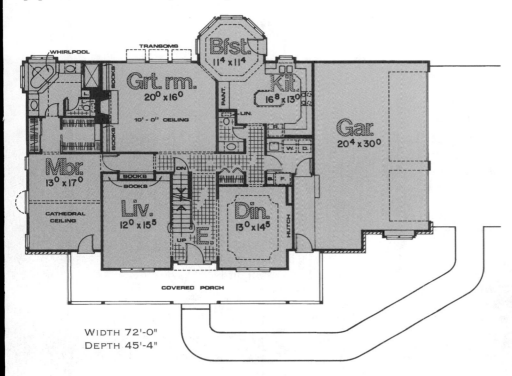

WIDTH 72'-0"
DEPTH 45'-4"

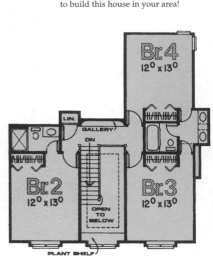

Design A301

First Floor: 1,670 square feet
Second Floor: 763 square feet
Total: 2,433 square feet

Wrought in wood siding with shingle accents, this farmhouse plan is pure country. But its floor plan is anything but rustic. The foyer offers access to the second floor at a U-shaped staircase and also provides a handy powder room for guests. The formal dining room sits on the left and connects to the gourmet kitchen through a pocket door. For more casual dining, choose the sunny breakfast room or eat at the counter which defines kitchen space from gathering room space. The master suite is on the first floor—split from family bedrooms. Its tray ceiling, walk-in closet and well-appointed bath make it very special. Two family bedrooms are on the second floor and share a full bath. A loft on the second floor overlooks the foyer and the gathering room below.

DESIGN BY
LIVING CONCEPTS
HOME PLANNING

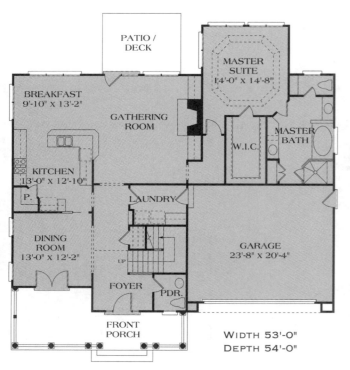

PATIO / DECK

MASTER SUITE
14'-0" x 14'-8"

BREAKFAST
9'-10" x 13'-2"

GATHERING ROOM

MASTER BATH

W.I.C.

KITCHEN
13'-0" x 12'-10"

P.

LAUNDRY

DINING ROOM
13'-0" x 12'-2"

UP

GARAGE
23'-8" x 20'-4"

FOYER

PDR.

FRONT PORCH

WIDTH 53'-0"
DEPTH 54'-0"

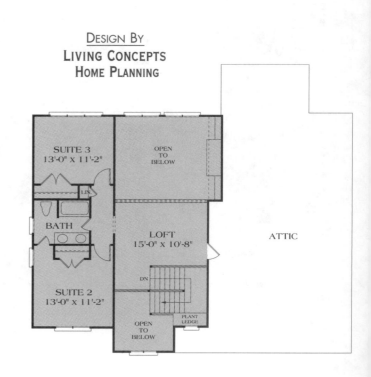

SUITE 3
13'-0" x 11'-2"

OPEN TO BELOW

LIN.

BATH

LOFT
15'-0" x 10'-8"

ATTIC

SUITE 2
13'-0" x 11'-2"

DN

PLANT LEDGE

OPEN TO BELOW

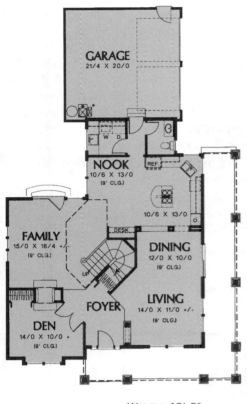

GARAGE
21/4 X 20/0

W   D

NOOK
10/6 X 13/0
(9' CLG.)

REF.

10/6 X 13/0

FAMILY
15/0 X 16/4 +
(9' CLG.)

DESK

DINING
12/0 X 10/0
(9' CLG.)

UP

FOYER

LIVING
14/0 X 11/0 +/-
(9' CLG.)

DEN
14/0 X 10/0 +
(9' CLG.)

WIDTH 43'-0"
DEPTH 69'-0"

Quote One®
Cost to build? See page 434
to order complete cost estimate
to build this house in your area!

DESIGN BY
ALAN MASCORD
DESIGN ASSOCIATES, INC.

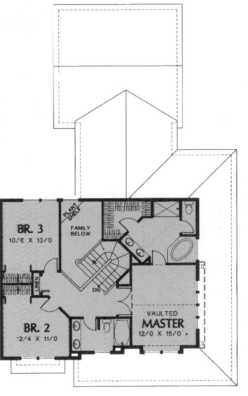

PLANT SHELF

BR. 3
10/6 X 13/0

FAMILY BELOW

DN

LINEN

BR. 2
12/4 X 11/0

VAULTED
MASTER
12/0 X 15/0 +

DESIGN 9557

First Floor: 1,371 square feet
Second Floor: 916 square feet
Total: 2,287 square feet

The decorative pillars and the wraparound porch are just the beginning of this comfortable home. Inside, an angled, U-shaped stairway leads to the second-floor sleeping zone. On the first floor, French doors lead to a bay-windowed den that shares a see-through fireplace with the two-story family room. The large island kitchen includes a writing desk, a corner sink, a breakfast nook and access to the laundry room, the powder room and the two-car garage. The master suite provides ultimate relaxation with its French-door access, vaulted ceiling and luxurious bath. Two other bedrooms and a full bath complete the second floor.

DESIGN Q501

First Floor: 1,620 square feet
Second Floor: 642 square feet
Total: 2,262 square feet

DESIGN BY
SELECT HOME DESIGNS

A wraparound veranda and extensive screened porch bring outdoor enjoyment to the owners of this fine design. A vaulted foyer introduces the interior and leads across a gallery to a vaulted living room. Special details here include a fireplace, double doors to the porch and an overlook from the upstairs gallery. A country kitchen with skylit dining area has abundant counter space and is warmed in cold months by a cozy hearth. The master bedroom resides on the first floor for privacy. It holds a skylight, access to a private deck, access to the covered porch, a walk-in closet and its own bath. Two second-floor bedrooms share a full bath and are adorned with dormer windows. Plans include details for both a basement and a crawlspace foundation.

WIDTH 60'-0"
DEPTH 54'-0"

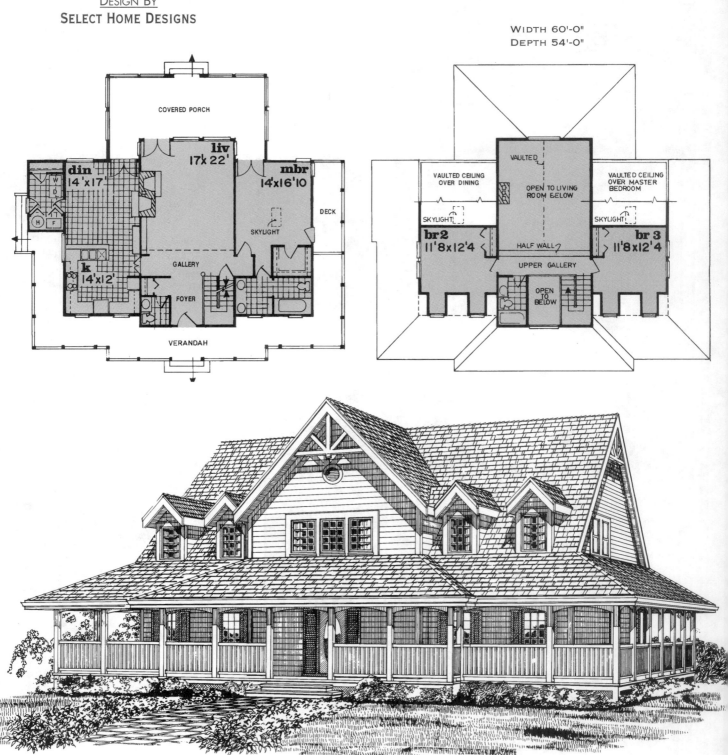

Country comes home to this plan with details such as a metal roof, horizontal siding, multi-paned double hung windows and front and rear porches. The recessed front entry leads to a two-story great room, flanked by a breakfast bar and formal dining room with access to both the front and rear porch. The great room is warmed by a fireplace and features a two-story ceiling. The master bedroom is on the first level and has a private bath and walk-in closet. A half-bath is in the laundry room. The second floor has two additional bedrooms, one with walk-in closet. If you choose, Bedroom 3 could be loft space. A full bath serves both bedrooms. Plans include both a basement and a crawlspace foundation.

DESIGN Q621

First Floor: 1,012 square feet
Second Floor: 556 square feet
Total: 1,568 square feet

DESIGN BY
SELECT HOME DESIGNS

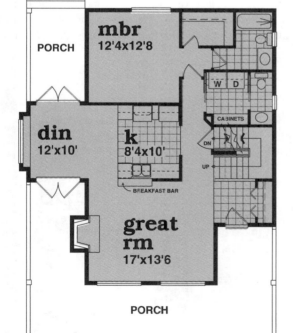

PORCH

mbr
12'4x12'8

W D

CABINETS

din
12'10'

k
8'4x10'

DN

UP

BREAKFAST BAR

great rm
17'x13'6

PORCH

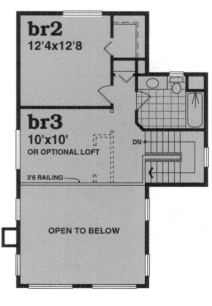

br2
12'4x12'8

br3
10'x10'
OR OPTIONAL LOFT

DN

3'6 RAILING

OPEN TO BELOW

WIDTH 34'-0"
DEPTH 48'-0"

Design Q353

Entry Level: 142 square feet
Main Level: 1,324 square feet
Total: 1,466 square feet
Bonus Space: 999 square feet

Design By
SELECT HOME DESIGNS

Rear Elevation

Using the second floor as the main living level allows for a deck in the back and future space for development into a recreation room and bedroom—or an entire in-law suite. A classic floor plan reigns on the second level with a living/dining room combination warmed by a fireplace. The open gathering space in the rear is comprised of a kitchen, breakfast bay and family room with corner fireplace. Bedrooms are on the right. They include a master suite with private bath and walk-in closet. Family bedrooms share a full bath.

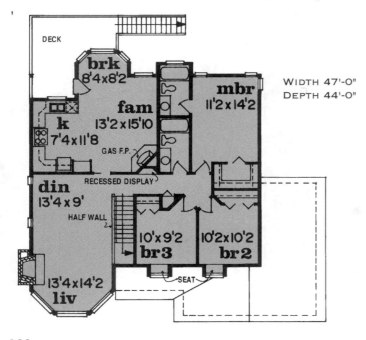

WIDTH 47'-0"
DEPTH 44'-0"

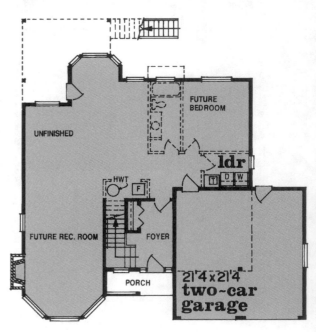

A covered veranda protects the entry of this charming home, and then wraps around to the left side where the spacious living room and dining room are found. The dining room features French-door access to the veranda; the living room is warmed by a fireplace. The open kitchen offers casual comfort for family gatherings, from the breakfast bay to the family-room area warmed by another fireplace. A covered deck sits beyond the family room. The master bedroom is on the second floor and has an intimate window seat, walk-in closet and private bath. Bedroom 3 also has a window seat. A hall bath with soaking tub serves the two family bedrooms. Plans include details for both basement and crawlspace foundations.

DESIGN Q374

First Floor: 1,092 square feet
Second Floor: 757 square feet
Total: 1,849 square feet

DESIGN BY
SELECT HOME DESIGNS

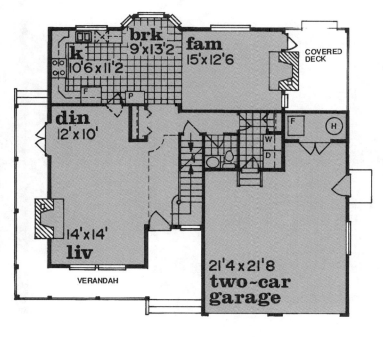

brk 9'x13'2
k 10'6 x 11'2
fam 15'x12'6
COVERED DECK
din 12'x10'
F
W
D
H
liv 14'x14'
VERANDAH
two-car garage 21'4 x 21'8

WIDTH 50'-0"
DEPTH 46'-0"

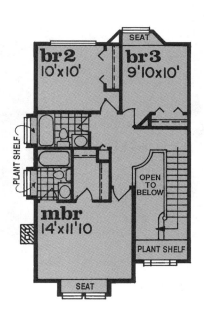

SEAT
br2 10'x10'
br3 9'10x10'
PLANT SHELF
OPEN TO BELOW
mbr 14'x11'10
PLANT SHELF
SEAT

121

DESIGN 8143

Square Footage: 2,648
Bonus Room: 266 square feet

DESIGN BY
LARRY E. BELK
DESIGNS

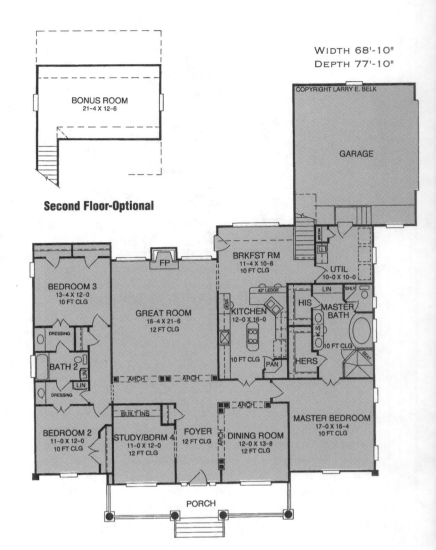

WIDTH 68'-10"
DEPTH 77'-10"

COPYRIGHT LARRY E. BELK

Second Floor-Optional

BONUS ROOM
21-4 X 12-6

GARAGE

BRKFST RM
11-4 X 10-6
10 FT CLG

UTIL
10-0 X 10-0

BEDROOM 3
13-4 X 12-0
10 FT CLG

GREAT ROOM
18-4 X 21-6
12 FT CLG

FP

KITCHEN
12-0 X 16-0

HIS

MASTER BATH

DRESSING

BATH 2

HERS

10 FT CLG

PAN

ARCH

ARCH

10 FT CLG

DRESSING

BUILT INS

BEDROOM 2
11-0 X 12-0
10 FT CLG

STUDY/BDRM 4
11-0 X 12-0
12 FT CLG

FOYER
12 FT CLG

DINING ROOM
12-0 X 13-8
12 FT CLG

ARCH

MASTER BEDROOM
17-0 X 16-4
10 FT CLG

PORCH

This Southern-raised elevation looks cozy but lives large, with an interior layout and amenities preferred by today's homeowners. Inside, twelve-foot ceilings and graceful columns and arches lend an aura of hospitality throughout the formal rooms and the family's living space, the great room. Double doors open to the gourmet kitchen, which offers a built-in desk, a snack counter for easy meals and a breakfast room with a picture window. The secluded master suite features His and Hers walk-in closets, a whirlpool tub and a knee-space vanity. Each of two family bedrooms enjoys separate access to a shared bath and a private vanity. Please specify basement, crawlspace or slab foundation when ordering.

COPYRIGHT LARRY E. BELK

A large covered front porch welcomes visitors to this home. The entrance hall opens to a formal dining room with hutch space and a living room with built-in curio cabinets. The volume great room features a handsome fireplace flanked by windows. A large kitchen provides an island counter, pantry, dual Lazy Susans and a desk. A private hall with a built-in bookcase leads to the first-floor master suite. The extravagant master bath features two walk-in closets, His and Hers vanities and a whirlpool tub. Upstairs, two of the three bedrooms feature decorator window seats. The two-car garage connects to the main house via a service entrance at the laundry room.

DESIGN 9274

First Floor: 1,780 square feet
Second Floor: 815 square feet
Total: 2,595 square feet

DESIGN BY
DESIGN BASICS, INC.

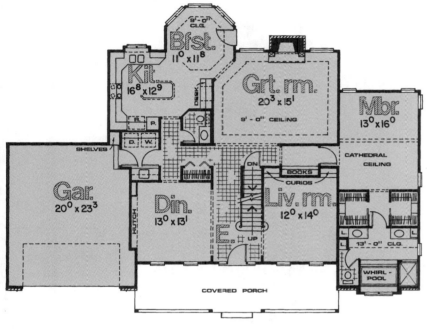

WIDTH 68'-0"
DEPTH 46'-8"

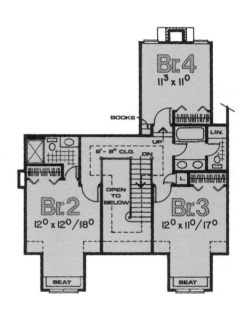

123

DESIGN A154

First Floor: 1,669 square feet
Second Floor: 706 square feet
Total: 2,375 square feet
Bonus Room: 342 square feet

DESIGN BY
LIVING CONCEPTS
HOME PLANNING

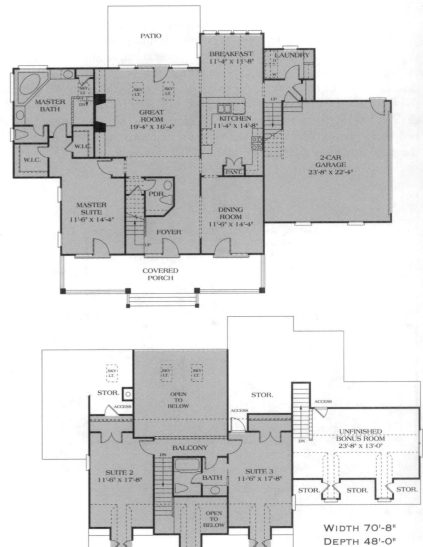

Skylights, an abundance of windows and five gable-roofed dormers flood this three-bedroom traditional country design with natural light. A balcony connects two bedrooms and a bath on the second floor and overlooks the skylit great room below with fireplace and built-in bookshelves. The nearby kitchen shares a snack-bar counter with the light-filled breakfast room. Formal dining takes place in a room just to the right of the foyer. It has access to the front covered porch, as does the master suite. Located on the first floor for convenience, the master suite features a bath with corner tub and His and Hers walk-in closets. Look for additional space to develop later in a bonus room over the two-car garage.

WIDTH 70'-8"
DEPTH 48'-0"

Looking to the past for style, the character of this winning plan is vintage Americana. A huge great room opens through classic arches to the island kitchen and the breakfast room. A corner sink in the kitchen gives the cook a view to the outside and brings in sunlight. Nearby, a small side porch provides a charming entry. The master suite is found on the first floor for privacy and features a luxury bath with separate vanities, His and Hers walk-in closets and a corner tub. The three bedrooms upstairs feature dormer windows and share a full bath. An additional 280-square-foot area is available above the garage. Please specify crawlspace or slab foundation when ordering.

DESIGN 8114

First Floor: 1,785 square feet
Second Floor: 830 square feet
Total: 2,615 square feet
Bonus Room: 280 square feet

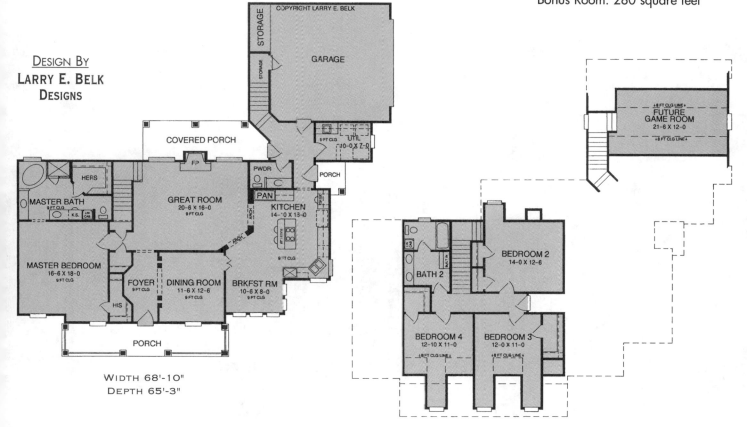

DESIGN BY
LARRY E. BELK
DESIGNS

WIDTH 68'-10"
DEPTH 65'-3"

DESIGN A141

First Floor: 2,131 square feet
Second Floor: 1,030 square feet
Total: 3,161 square feet

Double columns support the covered porch of this large four-bedroom design. A study or optional bedroom with bath is to the left of the foyer; the formal dining room is to the right. The gathering room with fireplace is at the heart of the home and features a fireplace and access to a covered wrapping porch at the rear. The kitchen and breakfast nook are nearby. Also on the first floor, the master suite is a study in luxury with a tray ceiling, walk-in closet and exquisite bath. Two family suites are on the second floor. They share a full bath and each has a walk-in closet. A loft reached by a stairway from the large, open gathering room provides an added activity center or convenient home office.

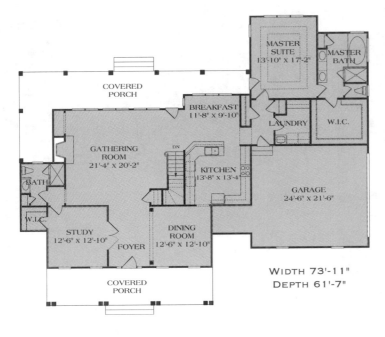

WIDTH 73'-11"
DEPTH 61'-7"

DESIGN BY
LIVING CONCEPTS
HOME PLANNING

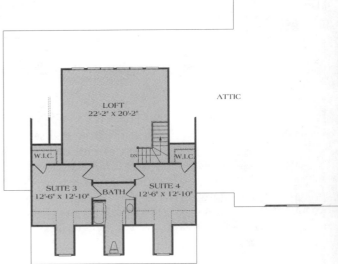

© 1991 Donald A. Gardner Architects, Inc.

A wraparound covered porch at the front and sides of this house and an open deck at the back provide plenty of outside living area. The spacious great room features a fireplace, cathedral ceiling and clerestory with an arched window. The island kitchen has an attached, skylit breakfast room complete with a bay window. The first-floor master bedroom contains a generous closet and a master bath with garden tub, double-bowl vanity and shower. The second floor sports two bedrooms and a full bath with double-bowl vanity. An elegant balcony overlooks the great room. Please specify basement or crawlspace foundation when ordering.

DESIGN 9632

First Floor: 1,756 square feet
Second Floor: 565 square feet
Total: 2,321 square feet

DESIGN BY
DONALD A. GARDNER
ARCHITECTS, INC.

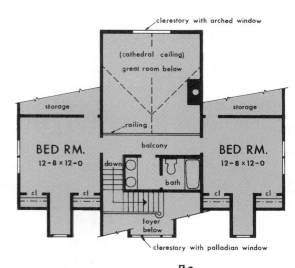

clerestory with arched window

(cathedral ceiling)
great room below

storage

storage

railing

BED RM.
12-8 × 12-0

balcony

BED RM.
12-8 × 12-0

cl

cl

down

bath

cl

cl

foyer
below

clerestory with palladian window

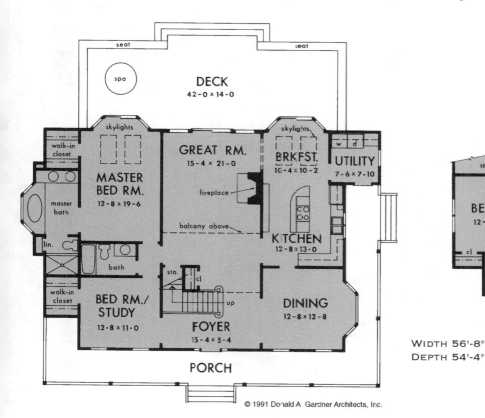

seat

seat

spa

DECK
42-0 × 14-0

walk-in
closet

skylights

GREAT RM.
15-4 × 21-0

skylights

BRKFST.
10-4 × 10-2

w d

UTILITY
7-6 × 7-10

MASTER
BED RM.
12-8 × 19-6

fireplace

master
bath

balcony above

KITCHEN
12-8 × 13-0

lin.

bath

sto.

cl

WIDTH 56'-8"
DEPTH 54'-4"

walk-in
closet

BED RM./
STUDY
12-8 × 11-0

up

FOYER
15-4 × 5-4

DINING
12-8 × 12-8

PORCH

© 1991 Donald A. Gardner Architects, Inc.

QUOTE ONE®

Cost to build? See page 434
to order complete cost estimate
to build this house in your area!

DESIGN 9621

First Floor: 1,325 square feet
Second Floor: 453 square feet
Total: 1,778 square feet

QUOTE ONE®

Cost to build? See page 434
to order complete cost estimate
to build this house in your area!

This compact design has all the amenities available in larger plans with little wasted space. In addition, a wraparound covered porch, a front Palladian window, dormers and rear arched windows provide exciting visual elements to the exterior. The spacious great room has a fireplace, a cathedral ceiling and clerestory windows. A second-level balcony overlooks this gathering area. The kitchen is centrally located for maximum flexibility in layout and features a pass-through to the great room. Besides the generous master suite with a full bath, there are two family bedrooms located on the second level sharing a full bath with a double vanity. Please specify basement or crawlspace foundation when ordering.

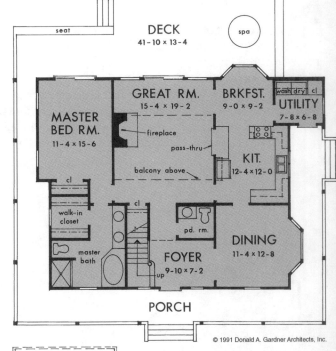

© 1991 Donald A. Gardner Architects, Inc.

WIDTH 48'-4"
DEPTH 51'-10"

Rear

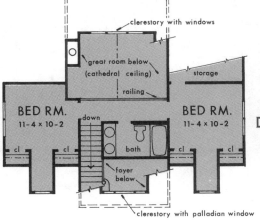

DESIGN BY
DONALD A. GARDNER
ARCHITECTS, INC.

128

© 1992 Donald A. Gardner Architects, Inc.

B. NATHAN

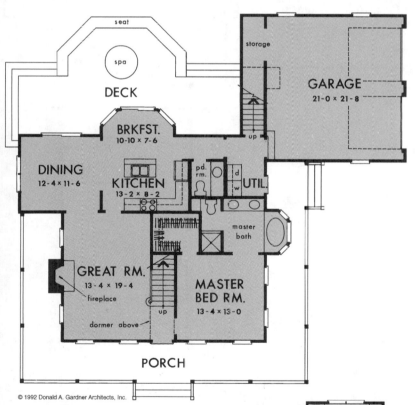

seat
spa
DECK

BRKFST.
10-10 × 7-6

DINING
12-4 × 11-6

KITCHEN
13-2 × 8-2

pd. rm.

UTIL.

d
w

storage

GARAGE
21-0 × 21-8

up

master bath

GREAT RM.
13-4 × 19-4

fireplace

dormer above

up

MASTER BED RM.
13-4 × 13-0

PORCH

© 1992 Donald A. Gardner Architects, Inc.

DESIGN 9690

First Floor: 1,145 square feet
Second Floor: 518 square feet
Total: 1,663 square feet
Bonus Room: 354 square feet

Look this plan over and you'll be amazed at how much livability can be found in less than 2,000 square feet. A wraparound porch welcomes visitors to the home. Inside lies an enormous great room with a fireplace. To the rear of the home, the breakfast and dining rooms have sliding glass doors to a large deck with room for a spa. The master bedroom contains a walk-in closet and an airy bath with a whirlpool tub. Two bedrooms are found on the second floor, as well as a bonus room over the garage.

DESIGN BY
DONALD A. GARDNER
ARCHITECTS, INC.

Cost to build? See page 434 to order complete cost estimate to build this house in your area!

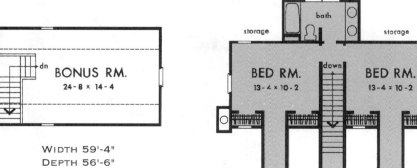

dn

BONUS RM.
24-8 × 14-4

WIDTH 59'-4"
DEPTH 56'-6"

bath

storage

storage

BED RM.
13-4 × 10-2

down

BED RM.
13-4 × 10-2

129

DESIGN 7734

First Floor: 1,778 square feet
Second Floor: 592 square feet
Total: 2,370 square feet
Bonus Room: 404 square feet

Country charm and modern convenience combine in this lovely home. The great room features a cathedral ceiling and cozy fireplace with built-ins. The centrally located kitchen, with its nearby pantry, serves the breakfast room and dining room easily. Guests will appreciate the powder room near the foyer. The master bedroom is on the first floor for privacy and is elegantly appointed with a walk-in closet and bath with whirlpool tub, shower and double vanity. A sitting room off the master suite is a special attraction. Two family bedrooms are on the second floor and share a full bath. Skylit bonus space over the garage could be developed into a home office or a game room.

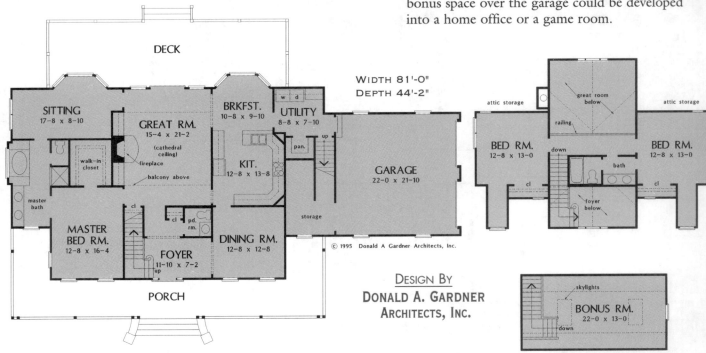

WIDTH 81'-0"
DEPTH 44'-2"

DECK

SITTING
17-8 x 8-10

GREAT RM.
15-4 x 21-2
(cathedral ceiling)
fireplace
balcony above

BRKFST.
10-8 x 9-10

UTILITY
8-8 x 7-10

w d

pan.

KIT.
12-8 x 13-8

up

GARAGE
22-0 x 21-10

walk-in closet

master bath

MASTER BED RM.
12-8 x 16-4

cl

cl pd. rm.

storage

FOYER
11-10 x 7-2
up

DINING RM.
12-8 x 12-8

PORCH

© 1995 Donald A Gardner Architects, Inc.

attic storage

great room below

railing

BED RM.
12-8 x 13-0

down

bath

BED RM.
12-8 x 13-0

cl

cl

foyer below

DESIGN BY
DONALD A. GARDNER
ARCHITECTS, INC.

skylights

BONUS RM.
22-0 x 13-0

down

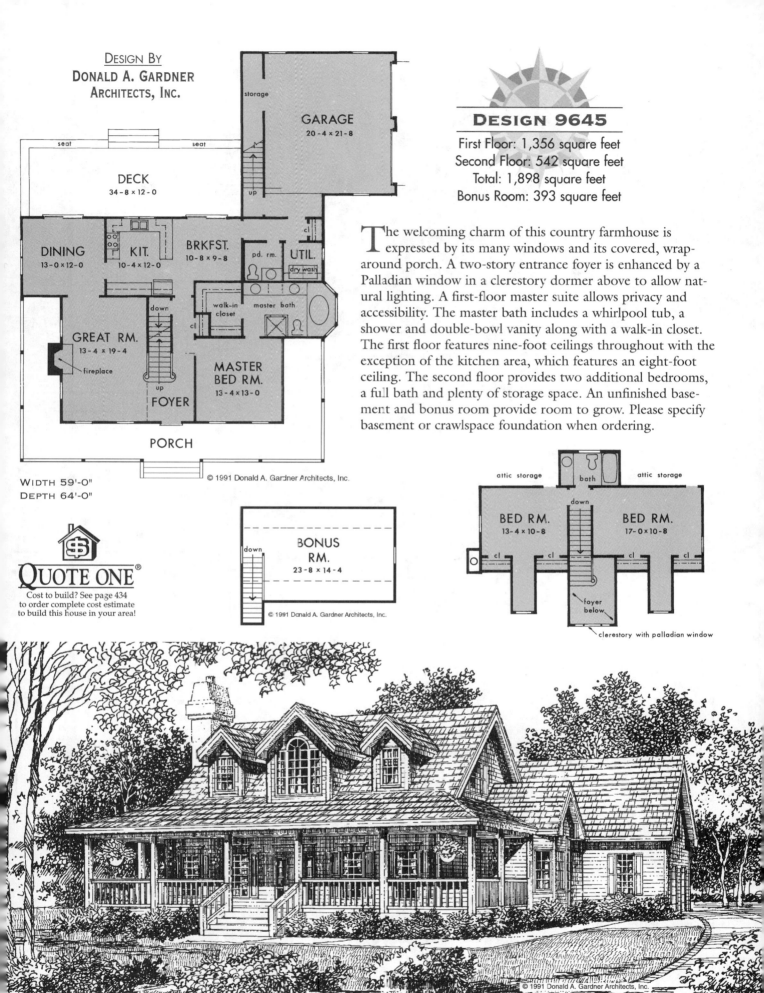

DESIGN BY
DONALD A. GARDNER
ARCHITECTS, INC.

storage

GARAGE
20-4 × 21-8

seat   seat

DECK
34-8 × 12-0

up

cl

DINING
13-0 × 12-0

KIT.
10-4 × 12-0

BRKFST.
10-8 × 9-8

pd. rm.

UTIL.
dry wash

down

walk-in
closet

master bath

GREAT RM.
13-4 × 19-4

fireplace

cl

MASTER
BED RM.
13-4 × 13-0

up

FOYER

PORCH

© 1991 Donald A. Gardner Architects, Inc.

WIDTH 59'-0"
DEPTH 64'-0"

DESIGN 9645

First Floor: 1,356 square feet
Second Floor: 542 square feet
Total: 1,898 square feet
Bonus Room: 393 square feet

The welcoming charm of this country farmhouse is expressed by its many windows and its covered, wrap-around porch. A two-story entrance foyer is enhanced by a Palladian window in a clerestory dormer above to allow natural lighting. A first-floor master suite allows privacy and accessibility. The master bath includes a whirlpool tub, a shower and double-bowl vanity along with a walk-in closet. The first floor features nine-foot ceilings throughout with the exception of the kitchen area, which features an eight-foot ceiling. The second floor provides two additional bedrooms, a full bath and plenty of storage space. An unfinished basement and bonus room provide room to grow. Please specify basement or crawlspace foundation when ordering.

QUOTE ONE®

Cost to build? See page 434
to order complete cost estimate
to build this house in your area!

down

BONUS
RM.
23-8 × 14-4

© 1991 Donald A. Gardner Architects, Inc.

attic storage   bath   attic storage

down

BED RM.
13-4 × 10-8

BED RM.
17-0 × 10-8

cl   cl   cl   cl

foyer
below

clerestory with palladian window

© 1991 Donald A. Gardner Architects, Inc.

© 1993 Donald A. Gardner Architects, Inc.

DESIGN 9723

First Floor: 2,064 square feet
Second Floor: 594 square feet
Total: 2,658 square feet
Bonus Room: 483 square feet

DESIGN BY
DONALD A. GARDNER
ARCHITECTS, INC.

You'll find country living at its best when meandering through this spacious four-bedroom farmhouse with wraparound porch. A front Palladian window dormer and rear clerestory windows at the great room add exciting visual elements to the exterior while providing natural light to the interior. The large great room boasts a fireplace, bookshelves and a raised cathedral ceiling, allowing a curved balcony overlook above. The great room, master bedroom and breakfast room are accessible to the rear porch for greater circulation and flexibility. Special features such as the large cooktop island in the kitchen, the wet bar, the bedroom/study, the generous bonus room over the garage and ample storage set this plan apart.

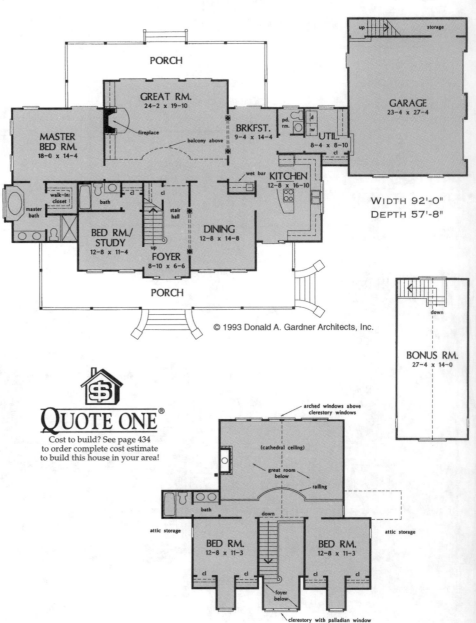

WIDTH 92'-0"
DEPTH 57'-8"

© 1993 Donald A. Gardner Architects, Inc.

Quote One®

Cost to build? See page 434 to order complete cost estimate to build this house in your area!

© 1996 Donald A. Gardner Architects, Inc.

PORCH

PORCH

BRKFST.
9-4 x 9-4

GREAT RM.
22-0 x 19-10
(cathedral ceiling)

shelves

fireplace

MASTER
BED RM.
17-0 x 17-0

up

ste.

balcony above

KITCHEN
18-4 x 14-8

pantry

pd. rm.

walk-in
closet

bath

lin.

master bath

UTIL.
9-10 x
12-0

w
d

DINING
13-2 x 14-0

FOYER
7-0 x 14-0

BED RM./
STUDY
13-6 x 14-0

walk-in
closet

PORCH

© 1996 Donald A Gardner Architects, Inc.

WIDTH 72'-0" (WITHOUT GARAGE)
DEPTH 60'-7" (WITHOUT GARAGE)

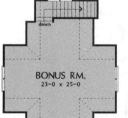

down

BONUS RM.
23-0 x 25-0

storage

up

GARAGE
23-0 x 25-0

GARAGE WIDTH 23'-8"
GARAGE DEPTH 29'-4"

great room
below

railing

down

balcony

walk-in
closet

attic
storage

cl

lin.

BED RM.
11-7 x 13-2

bath

BED RM.
11-7 x 15-6

attic
storage

attic
storage

attic
stor-age

attic
storage

DESIGN 7736

First Floor: 2,516 square feet
Second Floor: 722 square feet
Total: 3,238 square feet
Bonus Room: 513 square feet

With its wide front porch, first-floor nine-foot ceilings and spacious floor plan, this house feels like a Southern plantation. Columns add elegance to the formal dining room, while the generous great room features a cathedral ceiling, fireplace, built-in shelves and back-porch access. The spacious kitchen is open to a sunny breakfast bay and adjacent to a sizable utility room. The first-floor master suite boasts back-porch access, an indulgent bath and a roomy walk-in closet. The bedroom/study has a bath and walk-in closet, while upstairs, two more bedrooms share another full bath. Bonus space is located over the garage and may be developed later into a home office, guest suite or game room.

DESIGN BY
**DONALD A. GARDNER
ARCHITECTS, INC.**

Rear

133

DESIGN Q472

First Floor: 1,099 square feet
Second Floor: 535 square feet
Total: 1,634 square feet

DESIGN BY
SELECT HOME DESIGNS

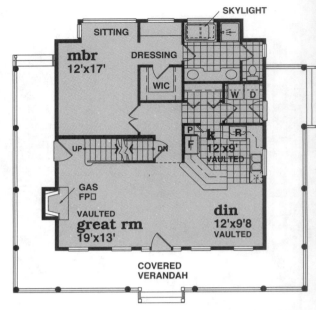

WIDTH 44'-8"
DEPTH 41'-4"

This design offers several different options to make the floor plan exactly as you like it. The exterior is graced by a wrapping veranda, round columns, stone facing with cedar shingled accents and a trio of dormers. Inside, the open plan includes a vaulted great room with fireplace, a vaulted dining room, a vaulted kitchen and three bedrooms. The kitchen has a pass-through to the dining room and large pantry. The master bedroom is found on the first floor for privacy. It contains a walk-in closet with dressing room, sitting area and full skylit bath. Family bedrooms are on the second floor and share a full bath. An optional loft is also available on the second floor. If you choose, you can reconfigure the master bath to allow for a half-bath in the laundry. Plans include details for both a basement and a crawlspace foundation.

Rear Elevation

**Optional Master Bath &
Laundry/ 2 Piece Bath**

134

DESIGN 9608

First Floor: 1,228 square feet
Second Floor: 492 square feet
Total: 1,720 square feet

DESIGN BY
**DONALD A. GARDNER
ARCHITECTS, INC.**

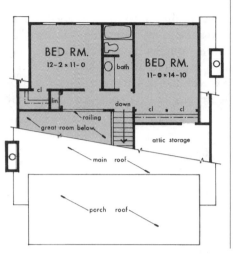

BED RM.
12-2 × 11-0

bath

BED RM.
11-0 × 14-10

cl

lin

railing

great room below

down

cl   cl

attic storage

main roof

porch roof

WIDTH 37'-6"
DEPTH 46'-2"

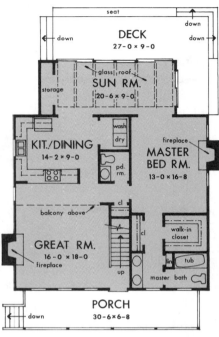

seat

down

DECK
27-0 × 9-0

down

down

glass roof

SUN RM.
20-6 × 9-0

storage

wash
dry

fireplace

KIT./DINING
14-2 × 9-0

pd.
rm.

MASTER
BED RM.
13-0 × 16-8

cl

balcony above

cl

walk-in
closet

GREAT RM.
16-0 × 18-0
fireplace

up

lin

tub

master bath

PORCH
30-6 × 6-8

down

© 1986 Donald A. Gardner Architects, Inc.

Rear

This compact country home lives big on the inside thanks to its simple, open floor plan. The country kitchen opens to dining space in the oversized great room as well as to the sun room which features a bank of six skylights. A powder room in the main hall will be appreciated by visitors. The master suite offers a cozy fireplace, a garden tub and generous closets. It also connects to the sun room. Upstairs, a balcony overlooks the great room with sloped ceiling. Also on this level are two family bedrooms and a full bath. Outside, the covered front porch and rear deck welcome guests and expand living area to the great outdoors.

DESIGN 9663

First Floor: 1,002 square feet
Second Floor: 336 square feet
Total: 1,338 square feet

A mountain retreat, this rustic home features covered porches front and rear. Open living is enjoyed in a great room and kitchen/dining room combination. Here, a fireplace provides the focal point and a warm welcome that continues into the L-shaped island kitchen. The cathedral ceiling that graces the great room gives an open, inviting sense of space. Two bedrooms—one with a walk-in closet—and a full bath on the first level are complemented by a master suite on the second level which includes a walk-in closet and deluxe bath. There is also attic storage on the second level. Please specify basement or crawlspace foundation when ordering.

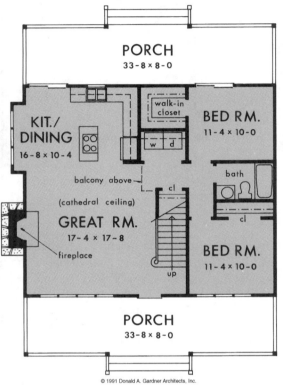

PORCH
33-8 × 8-0

KIT./
DINING
16-8 × 10-4

walk-in
closet

BED RM.
11-4 × 10-0

w | d

balcony above

bath

(cathedral ceiling)

cl

GREAT RM.
17-4 × 17-8

fireplace

up

cl

BED RM.
11-4 × 10-0

PORCH
33-8 × 8-0

© 1991 Donald A. Gardner Architects, Inc.

DESIGN BY
DONALD A. GARDNER
ARCHITECTS, INC.

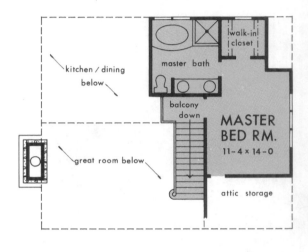

walk-in
closet

master bath

kitchen / dining
below

balcony
down

MASTER
BED RM.
11-4 × 14-0

great room below

attic storage

WIDTH 36'-8"
DEPTH 44'-8"

© 1991 Donald A. Gardner Architects, Inc.

This charming farmhouse design will be economical to build and a pleasure to occupy. Like most vacation homes, this design features an open plan. The large living area includes a living room, a dining room and a massive stone fireplace. A partition separates the kitchen from the living room. The first floor also holds a bedroom, a full bath and a laundry room. Upstairs is a spacious sleeping loft overlooking the living room. Don't miss the large front porch—this will be a favorite spot for relaxing.

DESIGN 4061

First Floor: 1,036 square feet
Second Floor: 273 square feet
Total: 1,309 square feet

D

DESIGN BY
HOME PLANNERS

- WASH | TUB | DRY
- LAUNDRY ROOM
- CLOSET
- D.W. | RANGE
- **KITCHEN & DINING** 20'-0" x 8'-0"
- SINK
- REFRIG
- SHOWER BATH
- CLOSET | CLOSET
- WH | STORAGE
- UP | RAILING
- **BEDROOM** 11'-8" x 13'-0"
- COATS
- **LIVING ROOM** 20'-0" x 19'-0"
- FIREPLACE
- STONE
- DN.
- **PORCH** 36'-0" x 10'-0"
- WOOD POSTS & RAILING

Quote One®

Cost to build? See page 434
to order complete cost estimate
to build this house in your area!

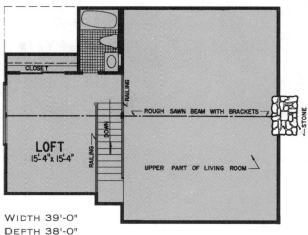

- CLOSET
- RAILING
- DOWN | RAILING
- **LOFT** 15'-4" x 15'-4"
- ROUGH SAWN BEAM WITH BRACKETS
- STONE
- UPPER PART OF LIVING ROOM

WIDTH 39'-0"
DEPTH 38'-0"

© 1992 Donald A. Gardner Architects, Inc.

DESIGN 9697

First Floor: 1,039 square feet
Second Floor: 583 square feet
Total: 1,622 square feet

Charming and compact, this delightful two-story cabin is perfect for the small family or empty-nester. Designed with casual living in mind, the two-story great room is completely open to the dining area and the spacious island kitchen. The master suite is on the first floor for privacy and convenience. It features a roomy bath and a walk-in closet. Upstairs, two comfortable bedrooms—one has a dormer window, the other has a balcony overlooking the great room—share a full hall bath.

DESIGN BY
DONALD A. GARDNER
ARCHITECTS, INC.

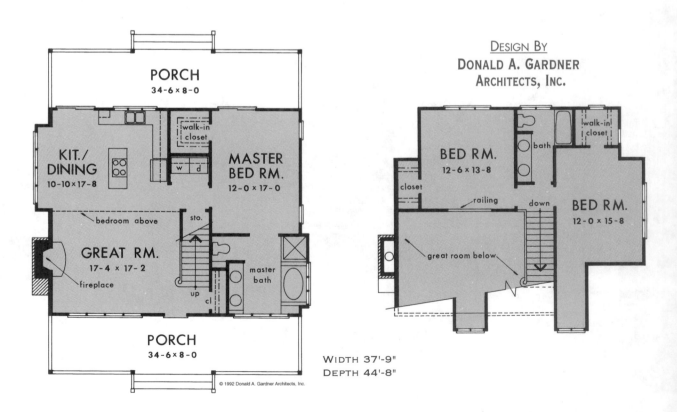

PORCH
34-6 × 8-0

walk-in closet

KIT./DINING
10-10 × 17-8

MASTER BED RM.
12-0 × 17-0

w   d

bedroom above

sto.

GREAT RM.
17-4 × 17-2

fireplace

up   cl

master bath

PORCH
34-6 × 8-0

© 1992 Donald A. Gardner Architects, Inc.

BED RM.
12-6 × 13-8

bath

walk-in closet

closet

railing

down

great room below

BED RM.
12-0 × 15-8

WIDTH 37'-9"
DEPTH 44'-8"

© 1992 Donald A. Gardner Architects, Inc.

This economical, rustic three-bedroom plan sports a relaxing country image with both front and back covered porches. The openness of the expansive great room to kitchen/dining areas and loft/study areas is reinforced with a shared cathedral ceiling for impressive space. The first level allows for two bedrooms, a full bath and a utility area. The master suite on the second level has a walk-in closet and a master bath with whirlpool tub, shower and double-bowl vanity. Please specify basement or crawlspace foundation when ordering.

DESIGN 9666

First Floor: 1,027 square feet
Second Floor: 580 square feet
Total: 1,607 square feet

Quote One®

Cost to build? See page 434 to order complete cost estimate to build this house in your area!

DESIGN BY
DONALD A. GARDNER
ARCHITECTS, INC.

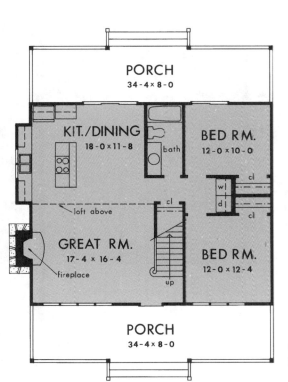

PORCH
34-4 × 8-0

KIT./DINING
18-0 × 11-8

bath

BED RM.
12-0 × 10-0

loft above

cl

w/d

cl

GREAT RM.
17-4 × 16-4

fireplace

BED RM.
12-0 × 12-4

up

PORCH
34-4 × 8-0

WIDTH 37'-4"
DEPTH 44'-8"

LOFT/
STUDY
11-4 × 13-8

STO.
3-4 ×
6-4

master bath

walk-in closet

railing

down

MASTER
BED RM.
12-0 × 14-0

great room below

© 1992 Donald A. Gardner Architects, Inc.

DESIGN 7654

First Floor: 1,055 square feet
Second Floor: 572 square feet
Total: 1,627 square feet

Economical to build, this cozy cottage wastes no space on the inside, while the exterior receives added interest from twin dormers and an arched and gabled entry. Full-length front and back porches expand the home's livable space. A cathedral ceiling adds volume to the great room which is overlooked by a balcony and loft/study, while the staircase shields the great room from noise in the U-shaped kitchen. Two bedrooms on the first floor—one with walk-in closet—share a full bath. The master enjoys privacy, sharing the second floor with the loft/study. The suite features a dormer alcove, walk-in closet and private bath.

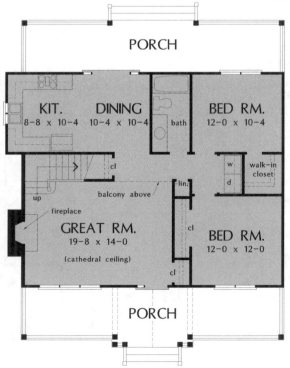

PORCH

KIT.
8-8 x 10-4

DINING
10-4 x 10-4

bath

BED RM.
12-0 x 10-4

cl

balcony above

w
d

walk-in
closet

lin.

up

fireplace

GREAT RM.
19-8 x 14-0
(cathedral ceiling)

cl

cl

BED RM.
12-0 x 12-0

PORCH

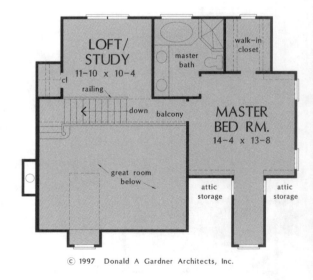

LOFT/
STUDY
11-10 x 10-4

master
bath

walk-in
closet

cl

railing

down

balcony

MASTER
BED RM.
14-4 x 13-8

great room
below

attic
storage

attic
storage

WIDTH 37'-4"
DEPTH 43'-0"

DESIGN BY
DONALD A. GARDNER
ARCHITECTS, INC.

140

DESIGN BY
DONALD A. GARDNER
ARCHITECTS, INC.

DESIGN 7701

First Floor: 1,222 square feet
Second Floor: 521 square feet
Total: 1,743 square feet

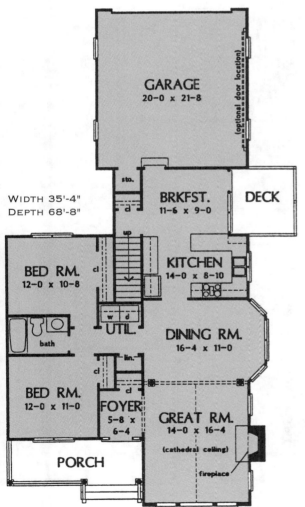

WIDTH 35'-4"
DEPTH 68'-8"

GARAGE
20-0 x 21-8

(optional door location)

sto.

BRKFST.
11-6 x 9-0

DECK

BED RM.
12-0 x 10-8

cl

up

KITCHEN
14-0 x 8-10

w d

UTIL

bath

DINING RM.
16-4 x 11-0

BED RM.
12-0 x 11-0

lin.

cl

cl

FOYER
5-8 x
6-4

GREAT RM.
14-0 x 16-4

(cathedral ceiling)

PORCH

fireplace

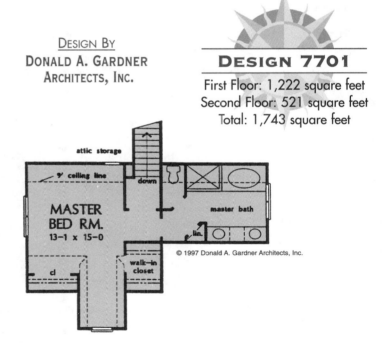

attic storage

9' ceiling line

down

MASTER
BED RM.
13-1 x 15-0

master bath

lin.

cl

walk-in
closet

A splendid Palladian window, a gabled dormer and a cozy front porch provide ample curb appeal for this lovely home. Well-suited for narrow lots, this plan features a rear entry garage and all-over slim design. The vaulted great room is highlighted by the Palladian window and is separated from the bayed dining room by two columns. The U-shaped kitchen opens to a breakfast room with side-deck access. Two first-floor bedrooms share a bath, while, upstairs, the master suite features a dormer alcove, two closets and a private bath with whirlpool tub, separate shower and dual sinks.

141

DESIGN Q219

First Floor: 1,026 square feet
Second Floor: 994 square feet
Total: 2,020 square feet
Bonus Room: 377 square feet

This inviting country home is enhanced by a full-width covered front porch, a fieldstone exterior and a trio of dormers on the second floor. Double doors open to a foyer flanked by a living room on the right and dining room on the left. The living room extends the full depth of the house and has a fireplace and sliding glass doors to the rear patio. A U-shaped kitchen adjoins a breakfast room with sliding glass doors to the patio, also. A laundry and half-bath connect the home to a two-car garage. Second-floor space includes two family bedrooms with shared bath and a master suite with full bath and walk-in closet. A large bonus room adds 377 square feet of living space on the second floor.

DESIGN BY
SELECT HOME DESIGNS

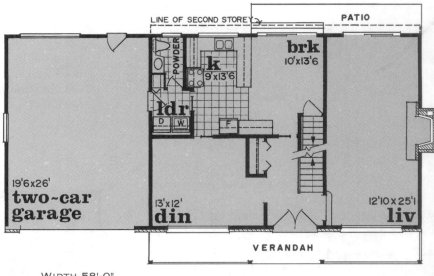

WIDTH 58'-0"
DEPTH 32'-0"

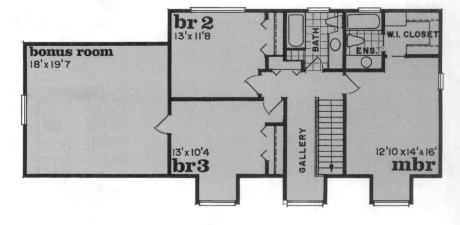

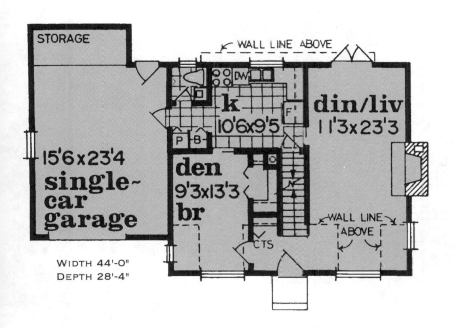

STORAGE

WALL LINE ABOVE

k
10'6x9'5

DW

F

din/liv
11'3x23'3

15'6x23'4
single-
car
garage

den
9'3x13'3
br

P B

CTS

WALL LINE ABOVE

WIDTH 44'-0"
DEPTH 28'-4"

DESIGN Q267

First Floor: 672 square feet
Second Floor: 571 square feet
Total: 1,243 square feet

DESIGN BY
SELECT HOME DESIGNS

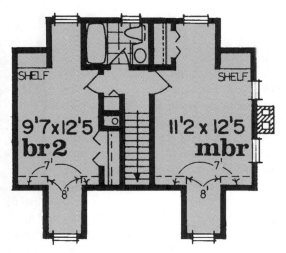

SHELF

SHELF

9'7x12'5
br 2

11'2 x 12'5
mbr

7'

7'

8'

8'

This affordable starter or retirement home is charming with an exterior finished in beveled siding and shutters. The combination living room-dining room sits on the right of the foyer and offers a fireplace and double-door access to the rear yard. A den or third bedroom is on the left of the foyer and has a walk-in closet. The kitchen features an L-shaped work counter, plus space for a breakfast table and leads to the single-car garage through the laundry room and half-bath. Two bedrooms are found on the second floor; each has a dormer window. A full hall bath includes a soaking tub. Note the extra storage space in the garage and the built-in shelves in each of the bedrooms.

143

DESIGN P447

First Floor: 1,189 square feet
Second Floor: 551 square feet
Total: 1,740 square feet
Optional Loft/Bedroom 4:
131 square feet

DESIGN BY
FRANK BETZ
ASSOCIATES, INC.

Put together a high roofline with dormers, a covered front porch and horizontal wood siding and you'll create one wonderful country plan. The floor plan for this one begins with a vaulted foyer with formal vaulted dining room on the left and vaulted great room in the rear. The breakfast room is also vaulted and shares a serving bar with the gourmet kitchen. The master suite is found on the first floor to keep it private from family bedrooms. It features a tray ceiling and large bath with walk-in closet, whirlpool tub and separate shower. The two suites on the second floor (Bedroom 3 is huge!) share a full bath. A loft area could become a fourth bedroom if you choose. Please specify basement or crawlspace foundation when ordering.

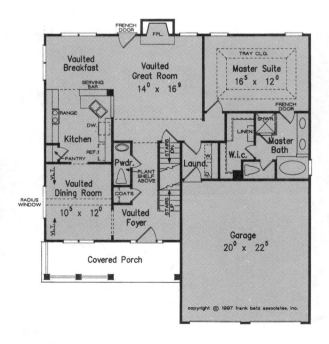

copyright © 1997 frank betz associates, inc.

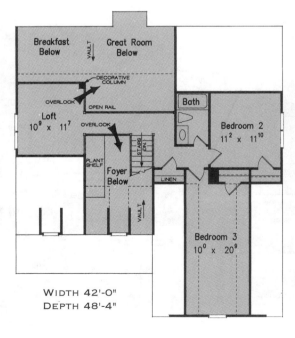

WIDTH 42'-0"
DEPTH 48'-4"

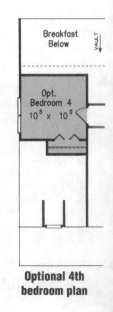

Optional 4th bedroom plan

With much to recommend its exterior style—a covered, railed porch, dormer windows and sidelit entry, this home also has an accommodating floor plan. The entry opens directly into the vaulted family room, which is warmed by a fireplace flanked by radius windows. The dining room shares a serving bar with the open kitchen and has sliding glass doors to the rear yard. No amenity has been forgotten in the first-floor master suite. Decorated with a tray ceiling, the bedroom has the use of a private bath with walk-in closet, spa tub, separate shower and double sink. Family bedrooms are on the second floor and share a full bath.

DESIGN P444

First Floor: 1,061 square feet
Second Floor: 430 square feet
Total: 1,491 square feet

DESIGN BY
FRANK BETZ
ASSOCIATES, INC.

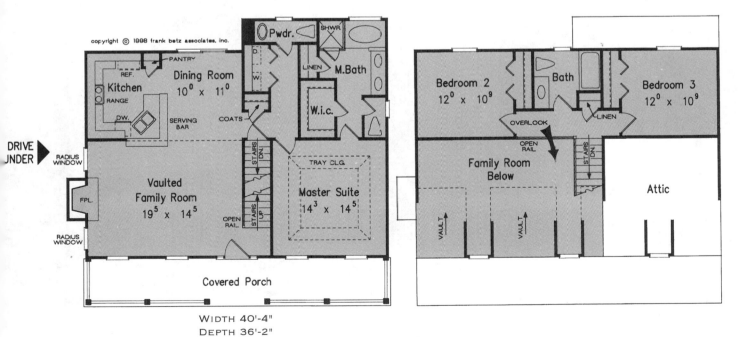

WIDTH 40'-4"
DEPTH 36'-2"

DESIGN Q518

First Floor: 792 square feet
Second Floor: 573 square feet
Total: 1,365 square feet

DESIGN BY
SELECT HOME DESIGNS

This distinctive vacation home is designed ideally for a gently sloping lot, which allows for a daylight basement. It can, however, accommodate a flat lot nicely. An expansive veranda sweeps around two sides of the exterior and is complemented by full-height windows. Decorative wood work and traditional multi-pane windows belie the contemporary interior. An open living/dining room area, with wood stove and two bay windows, is complemented by a galley-style kitchen. A bedroom, or den, on the first floor has the use of a full bath. The second floor holds a master bedroom with balcony and one family bedroom. Both bedrooms have dormer windows and they share a full bath with vaulted ceiling. Choose a basement or a crawlspace foundation—plans include details for both.

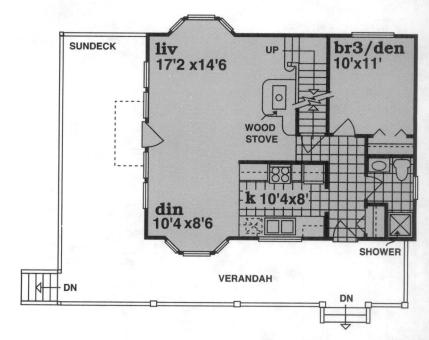

WIDTH 42'-0"
DEPTH 32'-0"

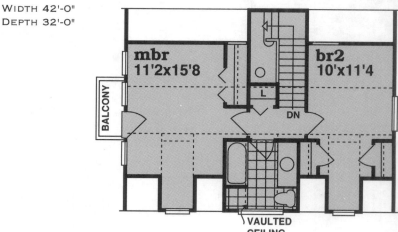

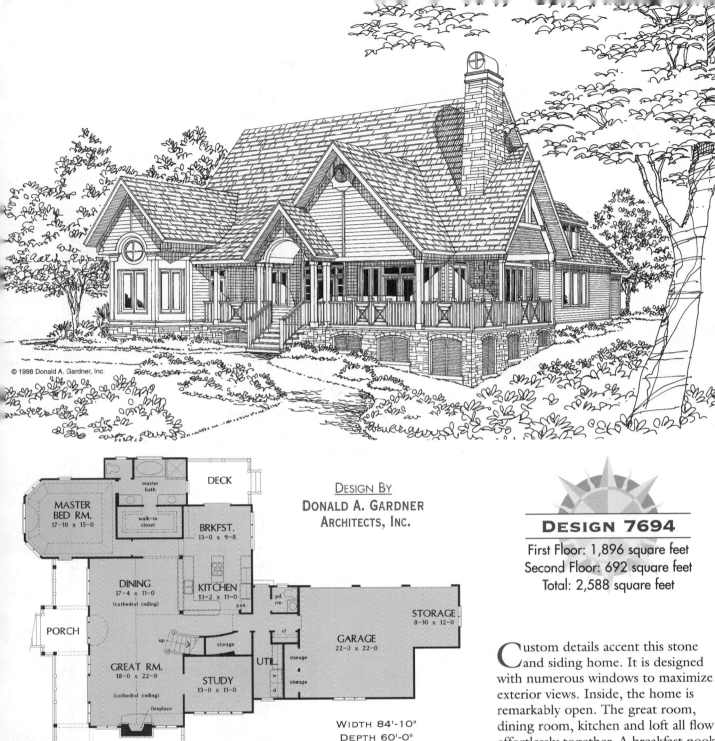

© 1998 Donald A. Gardner, Inc.

master bath

DECK

MASTER BED RM.
17-10 x 15-0

walk-in closet

BRKFST.
13-0 x 9-8

DESIGN BY
DONALD A. GARDNER
ARCHITECTS, INC.

DINING
17-4 x 11-0
(cathedral ceiling)

KITCHEN
13-2 x 11-0

PORCH

up

storage

pd. rm.

cl

STORAGE
8-10 x 12-0

GARAGE
22-0 x 22-0

UTIL.

storage

GREAT RM.
18-0 x 22-0
(cathedral ceiling)

STUDY
13-0 x 11-0

w
d

storage

fireplace

© 1998 Donald A Gardner, Inc.

WIDTH 84'-10"
DEPTH 60'-0"

attic storage

BED RM.
13-0 x 13-0

dining room below

cl

lin.

bath

skylight

up

great room below

down
up

BED RM.
12-8 x 11-4

cl

attic storage

STORAGE
15-8 x 11-4

LOFT/ STUDY
13-0 x 12-0

attic storage

attic storage

DESIGN 7694

First Floor: 1,896 square feet
Second Floor: 692 square feet
Total: 2,588 square feet

Custom details accent this stone and siding home. It is designed with numerous windows to maximize exterior views. Inside, the home is remarkably open. The great room, dining room, kitchen and loft all flow effortlessly together. A breakfast nook offers access to the rear deck, also reached from the first-floor master bath. A cozy study at the front of the plan is a great spot for quiet pursuits. A curved staircase leads up to the two large bedrooms on the second floor. They share a full bath and are joined by a loft/study area and huge storage space. Additional storage space can be found in the two-car garage—perfect for a golf cart or riding mower.

DESIGN Q255

First Floor: 953 square feet
Second Floor: 749 square feet
Total: 1,702 square feet

A railed veranda, providing a protected entry, introduces this compact, cleverly designed home. The entry opens to a central hall leading to formal spaces on the left and the casual areas in the back. The formal living room boasts a fireplace and bay window, while the dining room has a box window overlooking the rear yard. The bayed breakfast room sits between the family room (another fireplace!) and the U-shaped kitchen. A single-car garage is accessed through a service entry at the laundry area. A half-bath graces the front entry. On the second floor are three bedrooms with two full baths. Gable windows, one in the bedroom and one in the bath, adorn the master suite. There is also a walk-in closet here. Plans include details for both a basement and a crawlspace foundation.

DESIGN BY
SELECT HOME DESIGNS

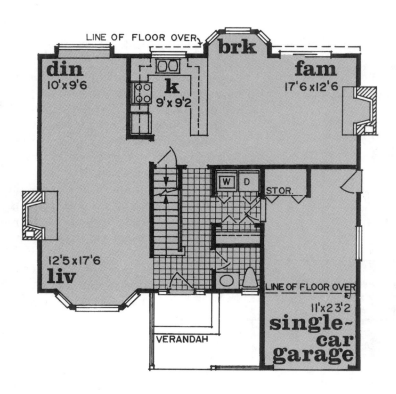

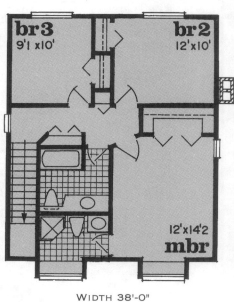

WIDTH 38'-0"
DEPTH 40'-4"

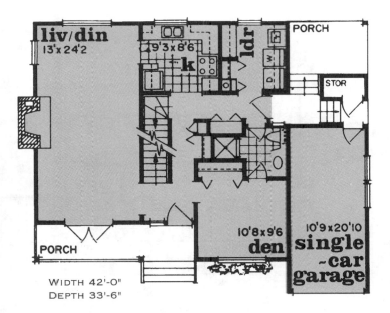

liv/din
13' x 24'2

k
9'3 x 8'6

ldr

PORCH

STOR

PORCH

10'8 x 9'6
den

10'9 x 20'10
single
~car
garage

WIDTH 42'-0"
DEPTH 33'-6"

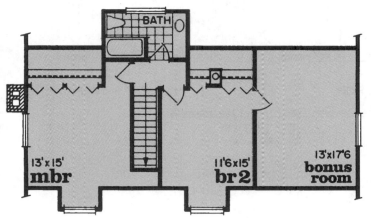

BATH

13'x15'
mbr

11'6 x 15'
br2

13'x17'6
bonus
room

DESIGN Q226

First Floor: 836 square feet
Second Floor: 581 square feet
Total: 1,417 square feet
Bonus Room: 228 square feet

DESIGN BY
SELECT HOME DESIGNS

Charming details add to the rustic appeal of this smaller farmhouse design. The covered porch shelters an entry that opens to a center hall with the living and dining rooms on one side and a cozy den on the other. The living/dining room space is warmed by a fireplace. The den has access to a full bath and can double as a guest room. An L-shaped kitchen is both step-saving and convenient; just beyond is a laundry room and service entrance to the single-car garage. Two bedrooms are on the upper level: a master bedroom with wall closet and a family bedroom. Both share a full bath. Bonus space equal to 228 square feet also is found on the second floor and can be made into another bedroom or a hobby room when needed. Plans include details for both a basement and a crawlspace foundation.

DESIGN Q515

Square Footage: 1,064

This farmhouse design squeezes space-efficient features into its compact design. A cozy front porch opens into a vaulted great room and its adjoining dining room. Twin dormer windows above flood this area with natural light and accentuates the high ceilings. A warm hearth in the great room adds to its coziness. The U-shaped kitchen has a breakfast bar open to the dining room and a sink overlooking a flower box. A nearby side-door access is found in the handy laundry room. Vaulted bedrooms are positioned along the back of the plan. They contain wall closets and share a full bath with soaking tub. An open-rail staircase leads to the basement, which can be developed into living or sleeping space at a later time, if needed. Plans include details for both a basement and a crawlspace foundation.

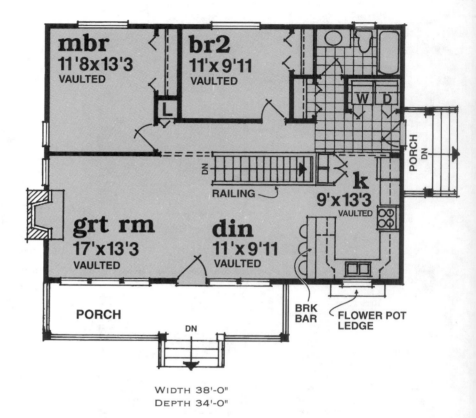

mbr 11'8x13'3 VAULTED

br2 11'x9'11 VAULTED

W D

PORCH DN

DN RAILING

k 9'x13'3 VAULTED

grt rm 17'x13'3 VAULTED

din 11'x9'11 VAULTED

BRK BAR

FLOWER POT LEDGE

PORCH

DN

WIDTH 38'-0"
DEPTH 34'-0"

150

This country-style vacation home is economical to build and offers additional space for future development. A bonus room of 227 square feet may be used as an extra bedroom, a play room or a media center. The front veranda opens to a living room with wood stove and vaulted ceiling. The kitchen and breakfast room are nearby; the kitchen has an L-shaped work counter. The master bedroom is on the first floor for privacy and has its own deck, accessed through sliding glass doors, and a private bath. Note the storage room just beyond the carport. Family bedrooms are on the second floor as is the bonus room.

DESIGN Q490

First Floor: 843 square feet
Second Floor: 340 square feet
Total: 1,183 square feet
Bonus Room: 227 square feet

DESIGN BY
SELECT HOME DESIGNS

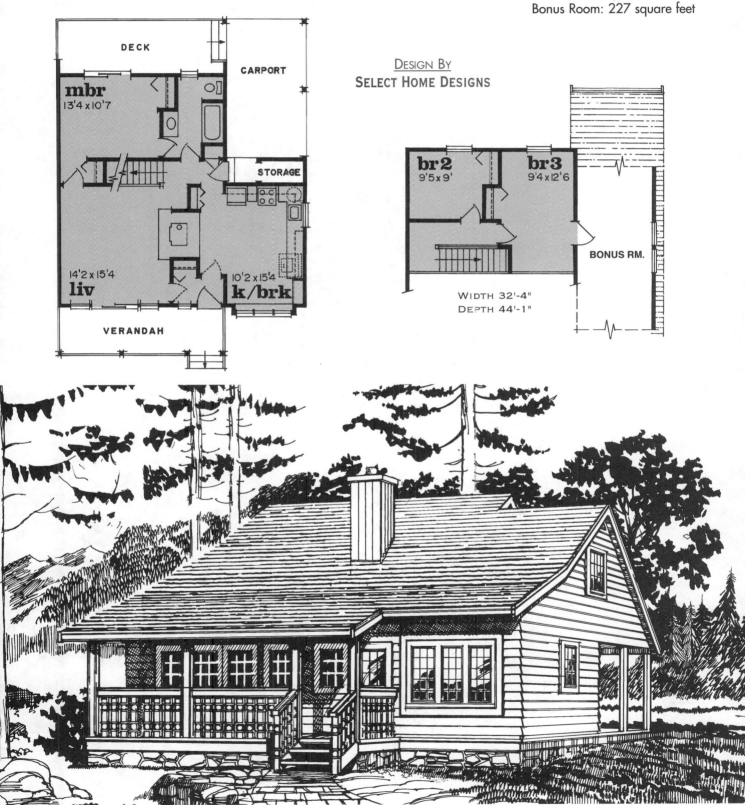

DECK

CARPORT

mbr
13'4 x 10'7

STORAGE

14'2 x 15'4
liv

10'2 x 15'4
k/brk

VERANDAH

br2
9'5 x 9'

br3
9'4 x 12'6

BONUS RM.

WIDTH 32'-4"
DEPTH 44'-1"

DESIGN Q221

Square Footage: 1,360

DESIGN BY
SELECT HOME DESIGNS

This economical-to-build family home features a low-maintenance exterior with stone and horizontal wood siding. A covered front veranda spans the full-width of the home and protects an entry leading to a center hall with living areas on the left and sleeping quarters on the right. The living room is enhanced by a fireplace, the dining room opens to the L-shaped kitchen with breakfast nook. Stairs outside the kitchen offer a landing entry to the single-car garage. The master bedroom is one of three to the right of the plan. It holds separate entry to the bath shared with family bedrooms. Note the double sinks in this bath. One of the family bedrooms could serves as a den or home office.

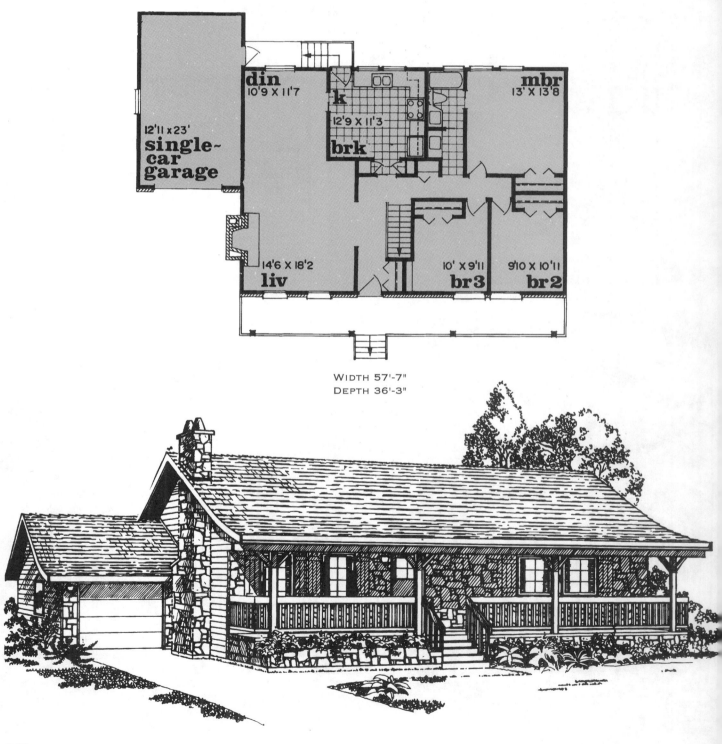

WIDTH 57'-7"
DEPTH 36'-3"

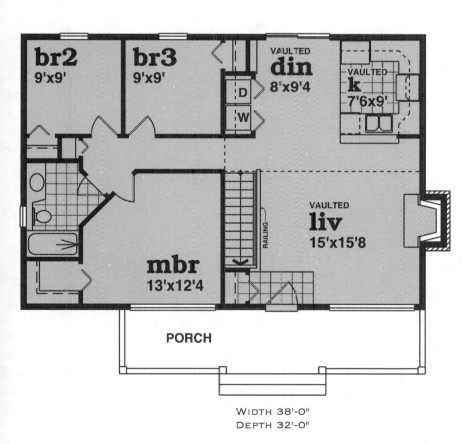

WIDTH 38'-0"
DEPTH 32'-0"

DESIGN Q618

Square Footage: 988

DESIGN BY
SELECT HOME DESIGNS

This economical, compact home is the ultimate in efficient use of space. The central living room features a cozy fireplace and outdoor access to the front porch. A U-shaped kitchen serves both a dining area and a breakfast bar. Sliding glass doors lead from the kitchen/dining area to the rear. The front entry is sheltered by a casual country porch, which also protects the living-room windows. The master bedroom has a walk-in closet and shares a full bath with the secondary bedrooms. A single or double garage may be built to the side or to the rear of the home. An alternative crawlspace foundation is also available.

© 1997 Donald A. Gardner Architects, Inc.

DESIGN 7632

Square Footage: 1,680

DESIGN BY

DONALD A. GARDNER
ARCHITECTS, INC.

Rear

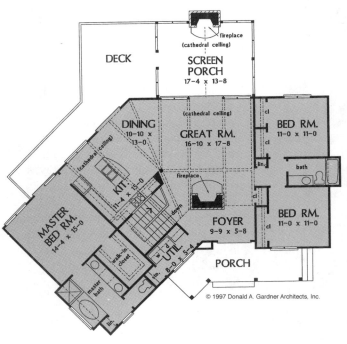

DECK

SCREEN PORCH
17-4 x 13-8

fireplace
(cathedral ceiling)

(cathedral ceiling)

DINING
10-10 x
13-0

GREAT RM.
16-10 x 17-8

BED RM.
11-0 x 11-0

cl

cl

lin.

bath

KIT.
11-4 x 15-0

fireplace

cl

down

MASTER
BED RM.
14-4 x 15-0

walk-in
closet

w   d

UTIL
8-0 x 5-4

FOYER
9-9 x 5-8

BED RM.
11-0 x 11-0

cl

master
bath

sto.

lin.

PORCH

© 1997 Donald A. Gardner Architects, Inc.

With its contemporary exterior and open interior, this plan creates an exciting home designed for sloping lots. Cathedral ceilings grace the great room, dining room, kitchen and screened porch, with exposed wood beams adding rustic charm to the spacious great room. Outdoor living is easy with a porch in front and a deck and screened porch with fireplace in back. Two bedrooms share a bath on one side of the house, while on the other, the master suite boasts rear deck access, a generous walk-in closet and a private bath with separate tub and shower. A two-car garage stands separately from the main house.

GARAGE
22-0 x 22-0

WIDTH 62'-8"
(WITHOUT GARAGE)
DEPTH 59'-10"
(WITHOUT GARAGE)

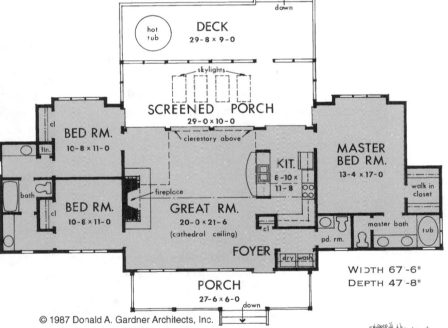

DECK
29-8 × 9-0

hot tub

down

skylights

SCREENED PORCH
29-0 × 10-0

clerestory above

BED RM.
10-8 × 11-0

cl

lin.

bath

BED RM.
10-8 × 11-0

fireplace

KIT.
8-10 ×
11-8

GREAT RM.
20-0 × 21-6
(cathedral ceiling)

MASTER
BED RM.
13-4 × 17-0

walk in closet

master bath

tub

pd. rm.

cl

FOYER

dry | wash

PORCH
27-6 × 6-0

down

DESIGN 9609

Square Footage: 1,426

DESIGN BY
DONALD A. GARDNER
ARCHITECTS, INC.

WIDTH 67-6"
DEPTH 47-8"

Looking for rustic simplicity with all the modern conveniences? This cottage welcomes you to a large central living area that features a cathedral ceiling with exposed wood beams and a clerestory window. This area opens to a long screened porch, made warm and sunny by a bank of skylights. The open kitchen boasts a convenient serving and eating counter. The generous, private master suite also opens to the screened porch and features a walk-in closet, whirlpool tub with separate toilet and dual sinks. Two additional bedrooms share a second bath beyond the great room. Note that each of these two bedrooms enjoys a separate dressing area with sink.

Rear

DESIGN 1472

First Floor: 1,008 square feet
Second Floor: 546 square feet
Total: 1,554 square feet

DESIGN BY
HOME PLANNERS

Wherever built, this smart leisure-time home will surely make your visits memorable ones. The large living area, with its sloped ceiling, dramatic expanses of glass and an attractive fireplace, will certainly offer the proper atmosphere for quiet relaxation. The kitchen is compact and efficient. There is plenty of storage space for all the necessary recreational equipment. There is a full bath and even a stall shower accessible from the outside for use by swimmers. A ladder leads to the second-floor, slope-ceiling dormitory which overlooks the living/dining area.

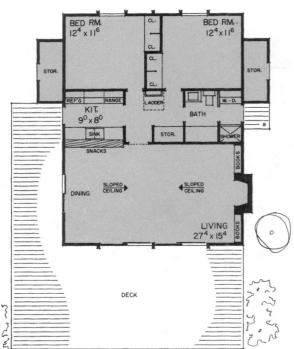

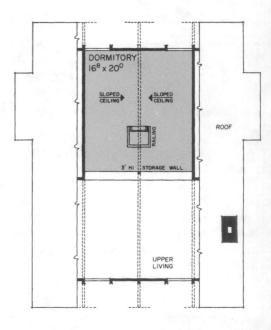

WIDTH 36'-0"
DEPTH 52'-0"

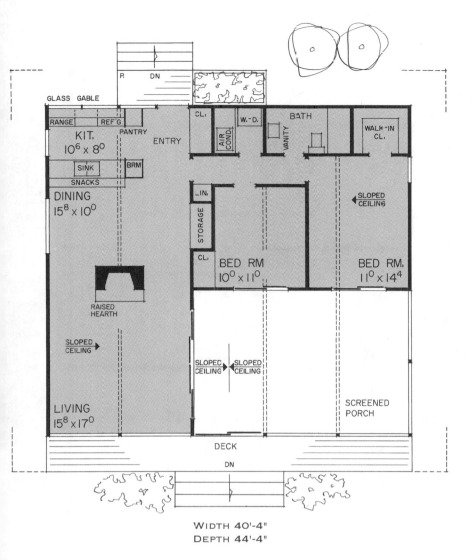

GLASS GABLE

| RANGE | REF'G |
| KIT. $10^6 \times 8^0$ | PANTRY |

ENTRY

CL.

W. D.

BATH

WALK-IN CL.

AIR COND.

VANITY

SINK   BRM

SNACKS

DINING $15^8 \times 10^0$

LIN.

STORAGE

CL.

BED RM. $10^0 \times 11^0$

SLOPED CEILING

BED RM. $11^0 \times 14^4$

RAISED HEARTH

SLOPED CEILING

SLOPED CEILING   SLOPED CEILING

LIVING $15^8 \times 17^0$

SCREENED PORCH

DECK

DN

WIDTH 40'-4"
DEPTH 44'-4"

DESIGN 1471
Square Footage: 1,465

DESIGN BY
HOME PLANNERS

This summer cottage lives up to all its fine potential. Although basically a two-bedroom house, its sleeping and living space is much greater. The large screened porch offers a full measure of flexibility and supplements the living room as an extra informal living area, while also serving as a sleeping porch. Separating the living and dining rooms is an appealing raised-hearth fireplace. A snack bar is handy to the kitchen, which features a glass gable above the wall cabinets. A utility room houses the heating unit and combination washer/dryer. Sloping beamed ceilings help maintain an aura of spaciousness throughout.

DESIGN Q206

Square Footage: 988

DESIGN BY
SELECT HOME DESIGNS

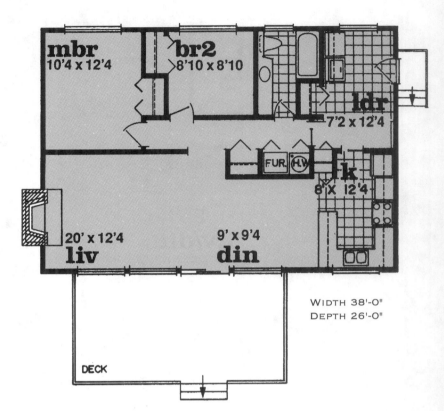

mbr
10'4 x 12'4

br2
8'10 x 8'10

ldr
7'2 x 12'4

FUR HW

k
8' x 12'4

liv
20' x 12'4

din
9' x 9'4

DECK

WIDTH 38'-0"
DEPTH 26'-0"

This cozy design serves nicely as a leisure home for vacations, or as a full-time retirement residence. Horizontal siding and a solid-stone chimney stack are a reminder of a rustic retreat. A spacious living/dining area has a full wall of glass overlooking a deck with views beyond. A masonry fireplace warms the space in the cold months. A U-shaped kitchen is nearby and has a pass-through counter to the dining room. A large laundry/mud room is across the hall and holds storage space. Sleeping quarters are comprised of a large master suite and smaller family bedroom, both with hall closets. A full bath serves both bedrooms.

Design Q210

Square Footage: 950

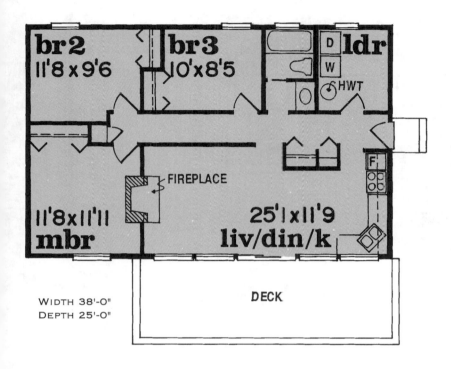

br2
11'8 x 9'6

br3
10'x8'5

ldr

D
W
HWT

FIREPLACE

11'8x11'11
mbr

25'1x11'9
liv/din/k

F

Width 38'-0"
Depth 25'-0"

DECK

This open-plan cottage is perfect for family living—or as a get-away for relaxing vacations. The living area is totally open to act as living room/dining room and corner kitchen. A fireplace at one end adds a warm glow on chilly evenings. Sliding glass doors here open to a wide deck for outdoor enjoyment or alfresco dining. Three bedrooms allow plenty of sleeping space. The master bedroom overlooks views beyond the deck. All three bedrooms share a full bath with soaking tub and separate vanity area. The laundry is large enough to hold a washer and dryer and also to serve as a mud room. There is a side door here.

DESIGN Q422

Square Footage: 817

DESIGN BY
SELECT HOME DESIGNS

This compact, economical cottage is perfect as a get-away retreat or for a cozy retirement home. Abundant windows overlook the sundeck and capture the views beyond for panoramic enjoyment. Vaulted ceilings and an open floor plan throughout the living and dining rooms enhance the feeling of spaciousness on the inside. For colder months, there is a wood stove in the living room. The kitchen is also vaulted and features a U-shaped workspace and countertop open to the dining area. Two bedrooms are to the rear; each has a wall closet. They share a full bath with linen closet.

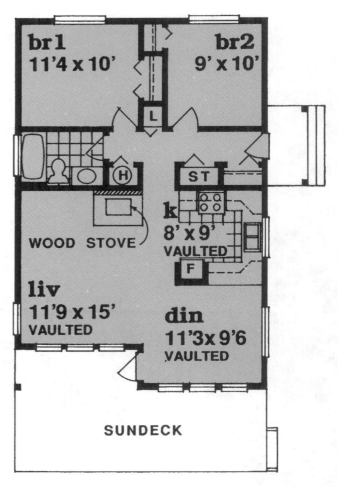

br 1
11'4 x 10'

br 2
9' x 10'

WOOD STOVE

ST

k
8' x 9'
VAULTED

F

liv
11'9 x 15'
VAULTED

din
11'3 x 9'6
VAULTED

SUNDECK

WIDTH 24'-0"
DEPTH 36'-0"

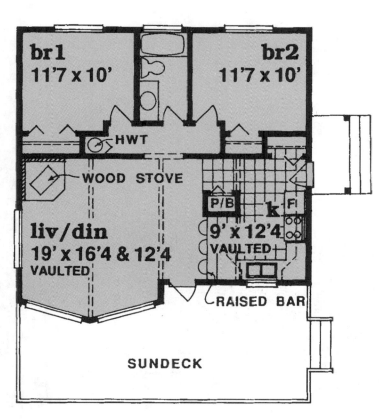

br1	br2
11'7 x 10'	11'7 x 10'

HWT

WOOD STOVE

P/B

k F

liv/din
19' x 16'4 & 12'4
VAULTED

9' x 12'4
VAULTED

RAISED BAR

SUNDECK

WIDTH 30'-0"
DEPTH 30'-0"

DESIGN Q422

Square Footage: 825

DESIGN BY
SELECT HOME DESIGNS

Compact and economical to build, this vacation home is nonetheless quite comfortable. It will fit easily into just about any vacation setting, from seaside to mountainside. A sun deck to the front stretches the width of the home and opens to a vaulted living room/dining room area with corner wood stove and full-height window wall. The kitchen has a raised bar with seating space open to the living area and also features a U-shaped workspace, a window over the sink and a large pantry or broom closet. Two bedrooms are to the back. They have wall closets and share a full bath with soaking tub.

DESIGN 3442

Square Footage: 1,273

L **D**

DESIGN BY
HOME PLANNERS

For those just starting out, or for the empty-nester, this unique one-story plan is sure to delight. A covered porch introduces a dining room with a coffered ceiling and views out two sides of the house. The kitchen is just off this room and is most efficient with a double sink, dishwasher and pantry. The living room gains attention with a volume ceiling, fireplace and access to a covered patio. The master bedroom also features a volume ceiling while enjoying the luxury of a private bath. In it, a walk-in closet, washer/dryer, double-bowl vanity, garden tub, separate shower and compartmented toilet comprise the amenities. Not to be overlooked, a second bedroom may easily convert to a media room or study, the choice is yours.

QUOTE ONE®

Cost to build? See page 434 to order complete cost estimate to build this house in your area!

WIDTH 40'-8"
DEPTH 59'-0"

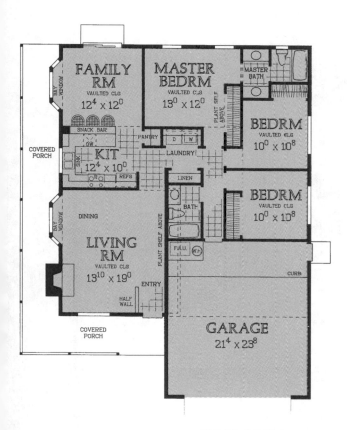

COVERED PORCH

FAMILY RM
vaulted clg
12⁴ x 12⁰

MASTER BEDRM
vaulted clg
13⁰ x 12⁰

MASTER BATH

BEDRM
vaulted clg
10⁰ x 10⁸

SNACK BAR
PANTRY
DW
KIT
12⁴ x 10⁰
SINK
LAUNDRY
D W
REFG
LINEN

PLANT SHELF ABOVE

BEDRM
vaulted clg
10⁰ x 10⁸

BAY WINDOW
DINING

LIVING RM
vaulted clg
13¹⁰ x 19⁰

PLANT SHELF ABOVE
BATH
F.A.U. W.H.

ENTRY
HALF WALL

COVERED PORCH

GARAGE
21⁴ x 23⁸

CURB

WIDTH 44'-8"
DEPTH 54'-6"

DESIGN BY
HOME PLANNERS

DESIGN 3460
Square Footage: 1,389

L

A double dose of charm, this special farmhouse plan offers two elevations in its blueprint package. Though rooflines and porch options are different, the floor plan is basically the same and very livable. A formal living room has a warming fireplace and a delightful bay window. The kitchen separates this area from the more casual family room. Three bedrooms include two family bedrooms served by a full, shared bath and a lovely master suite with its own private bath. Each room has a vaulted ceiling and large windows to let the outdoors in beautifully.

Alternate Exterior

This home, as shown in the photograph, may differ from the actual blueprints.
For more detailed information, please check the floor plans carefully.

Photo by Laszlo Regos

DESIGN 2488

First Floor: 1,113 square feet
Second Floor: 543 square feet
Total: 1,656 square feet

D

A cozy cottage tailor-made for a country lifestyle! This winsome design performs equally well serving active families as a leisure-time retreat or a retirement cottage that provides a quiet haven. As a year-round home, it provides the upstairs with its two sizable bedrooms, full bath and lounge area overlooking the gathering room to comfortably hold family and guests. The second floor may also be used to accommodate a home office, a study, a sewing room, a music area or a hobby room. No matter what the lifestyle, this design functions well.

DESIGN BY
HOME PLANNERS

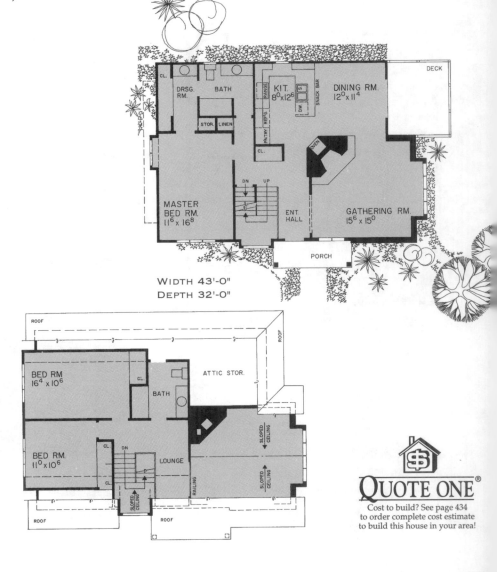

WIDTH 43'-0"
DEPTH 32'-0"

QUOTE ONE®

Cost to build? See page 434
to order complete cost estimate
to build this house in your area!

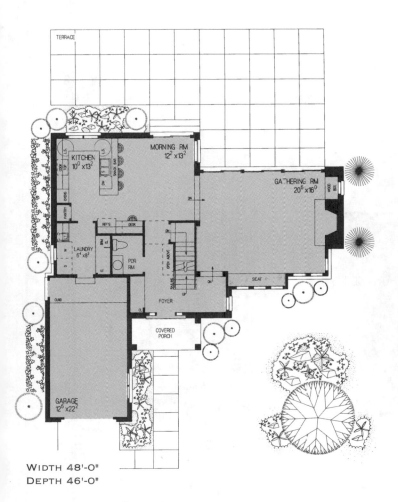

TERRACE

KITCHEN
10⁰ x13²

MORNING RM
12² x13²

GATHERING RM
20⁶ x16⁰

WOOD BOX

LAUNDRY
6⁴ x8²

DESK

REF'S

PDR RM

OPEN ABOVE

SEAT

FOYER

COVERED PORCH

GARAGE
12⁶ x22²

WIDTH 48'-0"
DEPTH 46'-0"

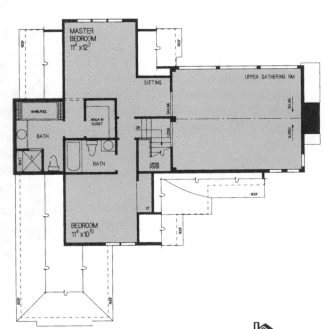

MASTER BEDROOM
11⁴ x12²

SITTING

UPPER GATHERING RM

WHIRLPOOL

WALK-IN CLOSET

BATH

BATH

UPPER FOYER

SEAT

BEDROOM
11⁴ x10¹⁰

ROOF

DESIGN BY
HOME PLANNERS

DESIGN 2491
First Floor: 1,060 square feet
Second Floor: 580 square feet
Total: 1,640 square feet

This modest-looking plan surprises everyone with its wealth of amenities inside. Begin with the central foyer leading right to the huge sunken gathering room with window seat, fireplace and sliding glass doors to the rear terrace. Go straight and you'll find a morning room with terrace access and a snack bar through to the U-shaped kitchen. A desk and pantry further enhance the kitchen. The laundry room holds space for a wash sink, washer and dryer and a huge closet, then leads to the single-car garage. The second floor holds two bedrooms and two full baths. The master suite has a sitting room and bath with whirlpool tub, walk-in closet and shower with seat. Note the overlook in the sitting room to the gathering room below.

QUOTE ONE®
Cost to build? See page 434
to order complete cost estimate
to build this house in your area!

THE ARCHITECTURAL ART

DESIGN 7733

Square Footage: 1,253

DESIGN BY
DONALD A. GARDNER
ARCHITECTS, INC.

This compact home offers gigantic curb appeal and amenities usually found only in larger houses. A continuous cathedral ceiling in the great room, kitchen and dining room gives a spacious feel to an efficient plan. The kitchen, brightened by a skylight, is separated from the great room by a seven-foot wall with a plant shelf above. The master suite opens up with a cathedral ceiling and contains walk-in and linen closets, and a private bath including a garden tub and double-bowl vanity. A cathedral ceiling tops off the front bedroom/study. Connecting the garage to the main house is a lovely screened porch, which also accesses the rear deck.

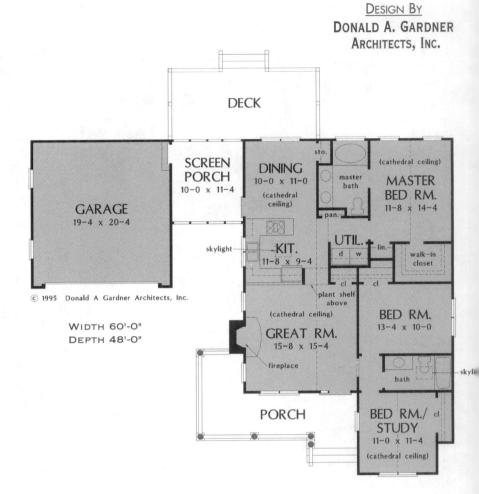

DECK

SCREEN PORCH
10-0 x 11-4

GARAGE
19-4 x 20-4

DINING
10-0 x 11-0
(cathedral ceiling)

sto.

master bath

MASTER BED RM.
11-8 x 14-4
(cathedral ceiling)

pan.

skylight

KIT.
11-8 x 9-4

UTIL.
d   w

lin.

walk-in closet

cl   cl

plant shelf above

(cathedral ceiling)

GREAT RM.
15-8 x 15-4

fireplace

BED RM.
13-4 x 10-0

bath

skyl

BED RM./ STUDY
11-0 x 11-4
(cathedral ceiling)

cl

PORCH

© 1995   Donald A Gardner Architects, Inc.

WIDTH 60'-0"
DEPTH 48'-0"

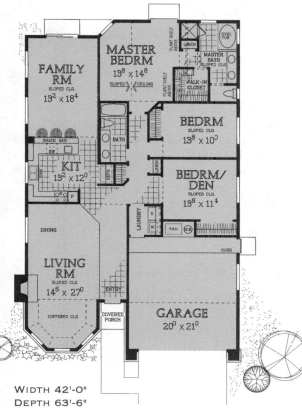

WIDTH 42'-0"
DEPTH 63'-6"

QUOTE ONE®

Cost to build? See page 434
to order complete cost estimate
to build this house in your area!

DESIGN 3481A

Square Footage: 1,901

L

This pleasing one-story home bears all the livability of houses twice its size. A combined living and dining room offers elegance for entertaining; with two elevations to choose from, the living room can either support an octagonal bay or a bumped-out nook. The U-shaped kitchen finds easy access to the breakfast nook and rear family room; sliding glass doors lead from the family room to the back yard. The master bedroom has a quaint potshelf and a private bath with a spa tub, a double-bowl vanity, a walk-in closet and a compartmented toilet. With two additional family bedrooms—one may serve as a den if desired—and a hall bath with dual lavatories, this plan offers the best in accommodations. Both elevations come with the blueprint package.

DESIGN 3481B

Square Footage: 1,908

L

WIDTH 42'-4"
DEPTH 63'-10"

DESIGN 2420

Upper Level: 768 square feet
Lower Level: 768 square feet
Total: 1,536 square feet

Two-level living can be fun anytime. When it comes to two-level living at the lake, at the seashore or in the woods, the experience will be positively delightful. Two huge living areas include a lower-level game room, filled with natural light from two sets of sliding glass doors, with two bedrooms and a full bath nearby, and an upper-level living room, also with two sets of sliding glass doors and a dining area at one end. A small, yet efficient kitchen nearby and easily serves family meals. Two bedrooms and a full bath complete this comfortable vacation home. Note the washer/dryer space with laundry tray and nearby closet in the game room.

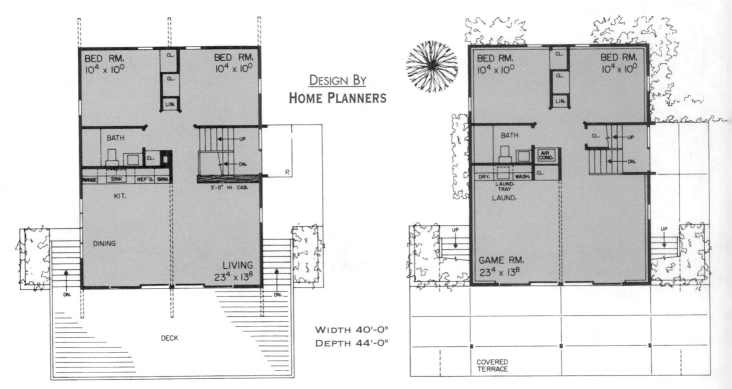

DESIGN BY
HOME PLANNERS

WIDTH 40'-0"
DEPTH 44'-0"

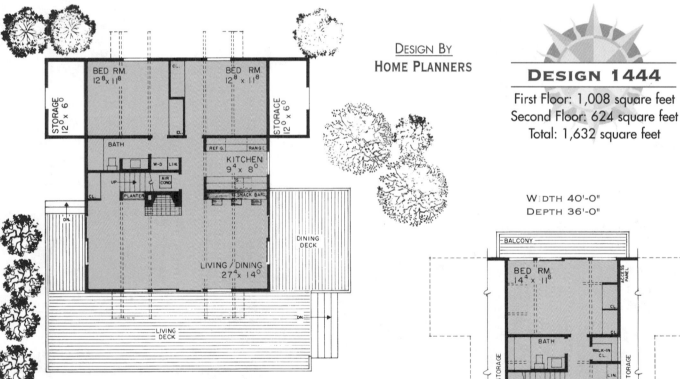

DESIGN BY
HOME PLANNERS

DESIGN 1444

First Floor: 1,008 square feet
Second Floor: 624 square feet
Total: 1,632 square feet

WIDTH 40'-0"
DEPTH 36'-0"

E verybody will enjoy vacations spent at this cottage. The superb quality of the indoor/outdoor relationships is evident by the spaciousness of the living and dining decks, the two balconies off the upstairs bedrooms and the large living area inside, which is warmed by a fireplace. Sliding glass doors are abundant and provide views in three directions. The snack bar in the kitchen makes serving meals a pleasant chore. Two bedrooms and a full bath complete the first floor. Upstairs, two bedrooms, each with its own balcony and walk-in closet, share a full bath and a linen closet. Note the double storage spaces to either side of the main house, accessed from outside.

Design Q202

Square Footage: 680
Unfinished Loft: 419 square feet

DESIGN BY
SELECT HOME DESIGNS

Full window walls flood the living room and the dining room of this rustic vacation home with natural light. A full sun deck with built-in barbecue sits just outside the living area and is accessed by sliding glass doors. The entire large living space has a vaulted ceiling to gain spaciousness and to allow for the full-height windows. The efficient U-shaped kitchen has a pass-through counter to the dining area and a corner sink with windows over it. A master bedroom is on the first floor and has the use of a full bath. A loft on the second floor overlooks the living room. It provides an additional 419 square feet not included in the total. Use it for an additional bedroom or as a studio. It has a vaulted ceiling.

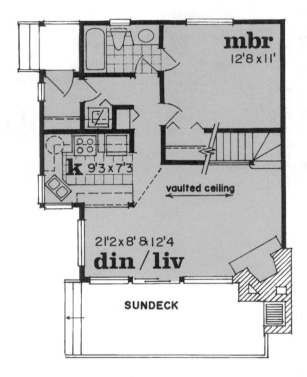

mbr
12'8 x 11'

k 9'3 x 7'3

vaulted ceiling

21'2 x 8' & 12'4
din / liv

SUNDECK

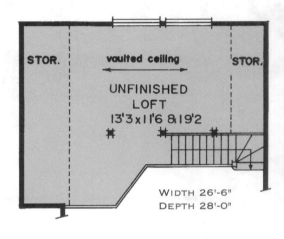

STOR.

vaulted ceiling

STOR.

UNFINISHED LOFT
13'3 x 11'6 & 19'2

WIDTH 26'-6"
DEPTH 28'-0"

A partially covered, wraparound deck on this vacation home allows for outdoor relaxation; a sunken spa adds to the enjoyment. The living room and dining room are vaulted and warmed by a central fireplace between the two. The kitchen offers a breakfast counter as separation from the dining room. The master suite is luxurious and sits to the rear of the first floor. Its bath contains a whirlpool spa. An additional half-bath is found near the entry, just to the left of a laundry/storage area. The second floor holds two additional bedrooms—one with built-in desk—and a full bath. Plans include details for both a basement and a crawlspace foundation.

DESIGN Q325

First Floor: 1,186 square feet
Second Floor: 597 square feet
Total: 1,783 square feet

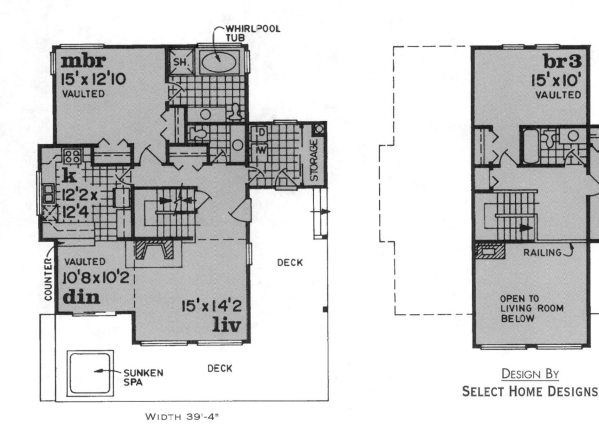

WIDTH 39'-4"
DEPTH 41'-4"

DESIGN BY
SELECT HOME DESIGNS

DESIGN A296

First Floor: 1,661 square feet
Second Floor: 882 square feet
Total: 2,543 square feet

Golf-course lots will welcome this exciting two-story plan. Its interior is spacious yet warm and its exterior is inviting. Note how the interior rooms flow together in an open configuration. The large foyer blends into the gathering room and the dining room. The casual dining room is open to the gathering room and the island kitchen. The more private master suite features terrace access—as does the gathering room—and has His and Hers walk-in closets and a bath fit for a king. The second floor holds a linkside retreat with large windows overlooking the rear yard. Two bedroom suites flank this area—each with a private bath. Suite 3 shares a fairway veranda with the retreat. Note the huge storage area on this level.

WIDTH 59'-0"
DEPTH 58'-11"

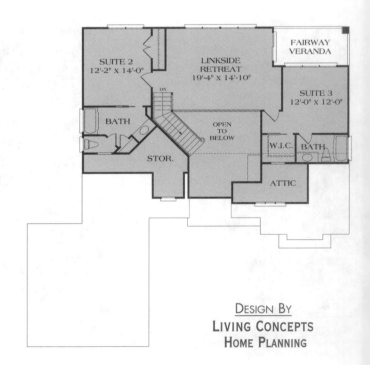

DESIGN BY
LIVING CONCEPTS
HOME PLANNING

Beautiful craftsman accents are evident in this design, perfect for a sloping lot. A double-door entry opens off a covered porch to an impressive vaulted foyer. Living areas are to the back and manifest in vaulted living and dining rooms. The living room boasts a bay window and fireplace. Access to the deck sits between the living and dining rooms. The L-shaped kitchen features an island work space and vaulted breakfast bay with deck access. The laundry area is to the front of the house and contains a half bath. Stairs to the lower level are found in the foyer. Sleeping quarters are found below—two family bedrooms and a master suite. The master suite has a walk-in closet and bath with separate tub and shower. Family bedrooms share a full bath.

DESIGN Q478

Lower Level: 1,092 square feet
Upper Level: 1,128 square feet
Total: 2,220 square feet

DESIGN BY
SELECT HOME DESIGNS

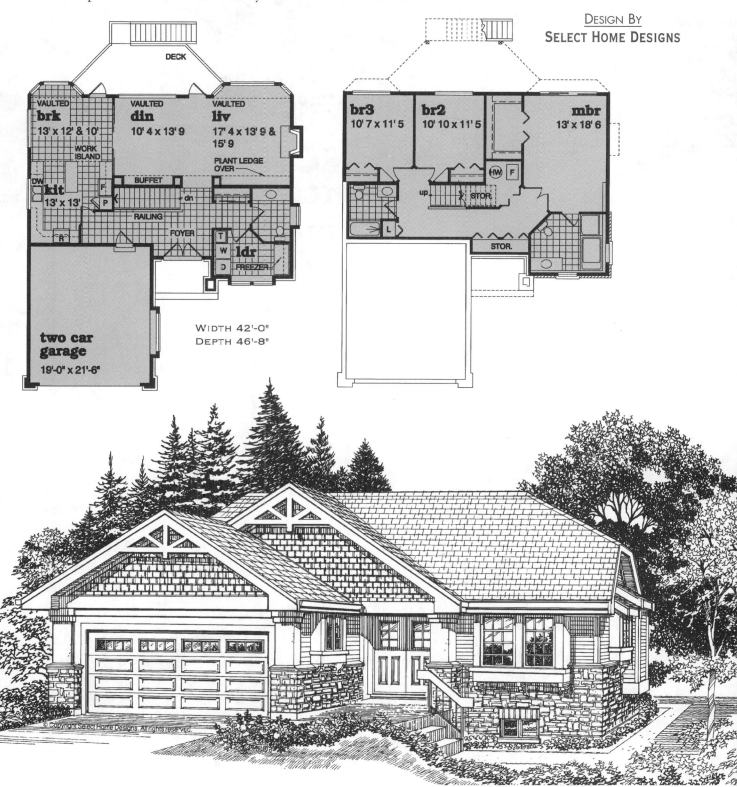

173

DESIGN Q205

First Floor: 1,185 square feet
Second Floor: 497 square feet
Total: 1,682 square feet

A full-length multi-paned window wall adorns the living room of this cottage and is covered on the exterior by a gabled roof. The living room is vaulted and has a masonry fireplace and wood storage bin. Double doors open to the covered patio. The kitchen is open to the dining room and has an L-shaped work area. The rear covered veranda opens to a storage room and the laundry room. The first-floor master bedroom features a walk-through closet to a private bath with corner tub and separate shower. Second-floor bedrooms are separated by a gallery and share a full bath. Note the single-car garage in the back. Plans include details for both a basement and a crawlspace foundation.

DESIGN BY
SELECT HOME DESIGNS

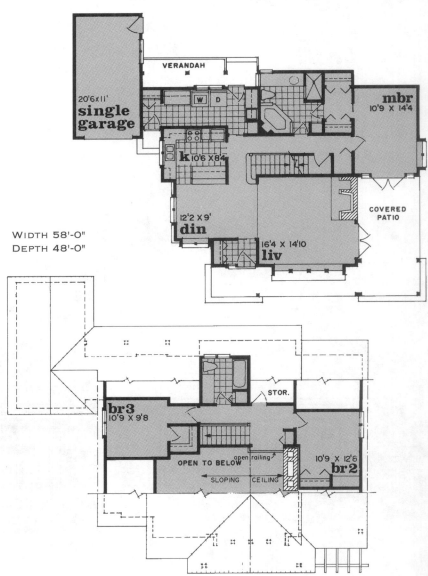

WIDTH 58'-0"
DEPTH 48'-0"

174

Gables, rafter-tails, pillars supporting the shed roof over the porch and window detailing all bring the flavor of Craftsman styling to your neighborhood—with a touch of grace. This spacious home has a place for everyone. The angled kitchen, with a work island, peninsular sink and plenty of counter and cabinet space, will truly please the gourmet of the family. The spacious gathering room offers a warming fireplace, built-ins and access to a rear terrace. Filled with amenities, the first-floor master suite is designed to pamper. Upstairs, two suites, each with a private bath, share an open area known as the linkside retreat. Here, access is available to a small veranda, perfect for watching sunsets.

DESIGN A250

First Floor: 1,662 square feet
Second Floor: 882 square feet
Total: 2,544 square feet

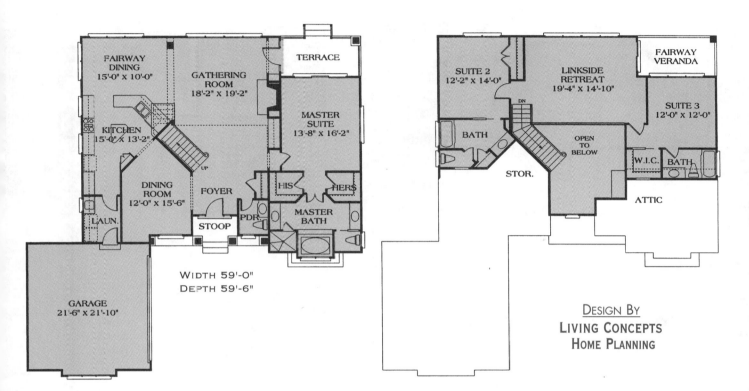

WIDTH 59'-0"
DEPTH 59'-6"

DESIGN BY
LIVING CONCEPTS
HOME PLANNING

175

DESIGN Q545

Square Footage: 1,318
Bonus Space: 629 square feet

This compact design holds a surprise on its lower level—there's bonus space that can be developed later for additional room. The main living level is commodious by itself, however, and includes a living room with fireplace and access to the front veranda, a dining room that connects to the L-shaped kitchen and breakfast room and three bedrooms. Sliding glass doors in the dining room lead to a private patio at the front of the house. Bedrooms 2 and 3 share a full hall bath; Bedroom 3 has a private balcony. The master suite has a private half-bath. Don't miss the covered patio, just off the kitchen, which contains a built-in barbecue. It also accesses the one-car garage to the front of the house.

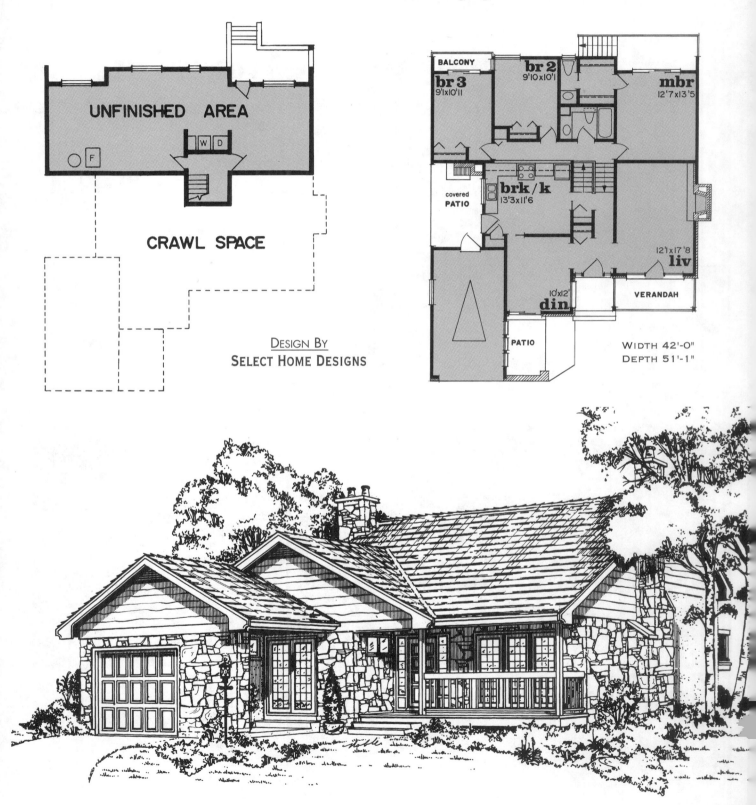

UNFINISHED   AREA

W   D

F

CRAWL SPACE

DESIGN BY
SELECT HOME DESIGNS

BALCONY

br 3
9'1x10'11

br 2
9'10x10'1

mbr
12'7x13'5

covered
PATIO

brk/k
13'3x11'6

din
10x12

PATIO

liv
12'1x17'8

VERANDAH

WIDTH 42'-0"
DEPTH 51'-1"

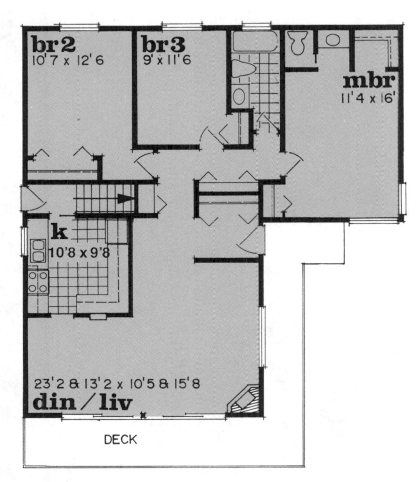

br2
10'7 x 12'6

br3
9' x 11'6

mbr
11'4 x 16'

k
10'8 x 9'8

23'2 & 13'2 x 10'5 & 15'8
din/liv

DECK

WIDTH 38'-0"
DEPTH 40'-0"

DESIGN Q530
Square Footage: 1,244

With a simple floor plan and lovely siding, including vertical siding and brick, this casual ranch is the ideal retirement home. It features an open plan with a living/dining area to the front and bedrooms to the rear. The convenient kitchen connects directly to the dining room and shares its view of the front deck through sliding glass doors. The master suite has His and Hers closets and a private half bath. Family bedrooms share a full hall bath. Make one of them into a den or guest room to fit your lifestyle. If you choose, a full basement could be developed later into livable space—or keep it as a storage area.

DESIGN BY
SELECT HOME DESIGNS

DESIGN Q204

First Floor: 1,022 square feet
Second Floor: 551 square feet
Total: 1,573 square feet

This quaint cottage works equally well in the mountains or at a lake shore. Its entry is sliding glass and opens to a vaulted living room with fireplace tucked into a large windowed bay. The dining room has sliding glass access to the deck. The skylit kitchen features a greenhouse window over the sink and is just across from a handy laundry room. The master bedroom captures views through sliding glass doors and a triangular feature window. It has the use of a full bath. The second floor holds another bedroom and full bath and a loft area that could be used as a bedroom, if you choose.

DESIGN BY
SELECT HOME DESIGNS

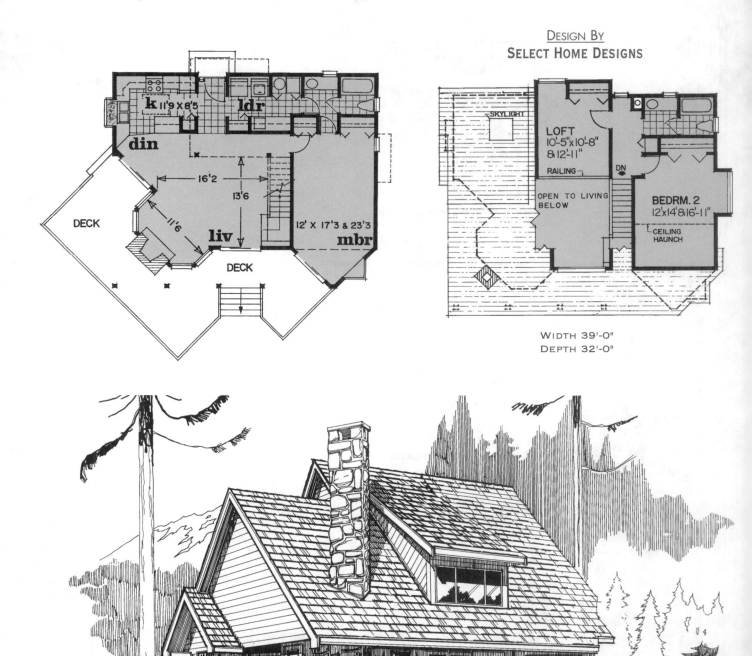

WIDTH 39'-0"
DEPTH 32'-0"

An expansive wall of glass, rising to the roof's peak, adds architectural interest and gives the living room of this home a spectacular view. The living room also boasts a vaulted ceiling and an oversized masonry fireplace and has deck access where there is a wonderful spa tub. The dining room is nearby, directly across from the galley-style kitchen. Two bedrooms sit to the rear of the plan and share a full bath. The master suite is on the second level and caters to comfort with a walk-in closet, spa tub and separate shower. Note how the open-railed staircase winds to the gallery on the second floor and overlooks the living room below.

DESIGN Q281

First Floor: 1,070 square feet
Second Floor: 552 square feet
Total: 1,622 square feet

DESIGN BY
SELECT HOME DESIGNS

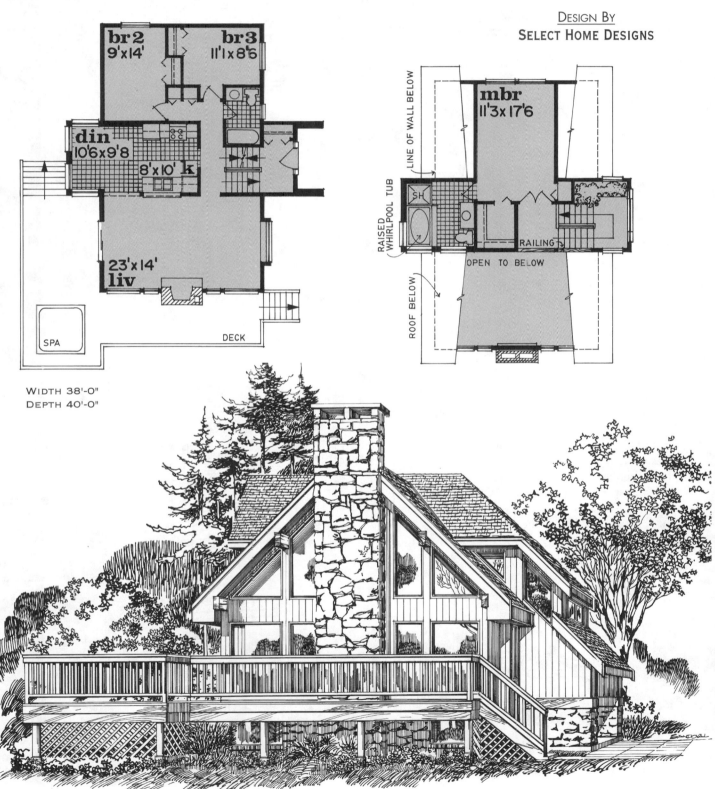

WIDTH 38'-0"
DEPTH 40'-0"

DESIGN Q537

First Floor: 1,283 square feet
Second Floor: 688 square feet
Total: 1,971 square feet

A massive stone chimney stack combines with vertical wood siding on the exterior of this home to provide a rustic feel. The interior opens through an offset entry to the formal living and dining areas, warmed by a corner fireplace. The sunken family room has a fireplace as well and accesses the rear yard through sliding glass doors. The kitchen and breakfast room sit between the two living spaces. A cozy den is tucked in a corner behind the service area with full bath and laundry. Bedrooms are on the second level and include a master bedroom and two family bedrooms circulating around a skylit hall. The master bath is reached via a walk-thru closet. Family bedrooms share a full hall bath.

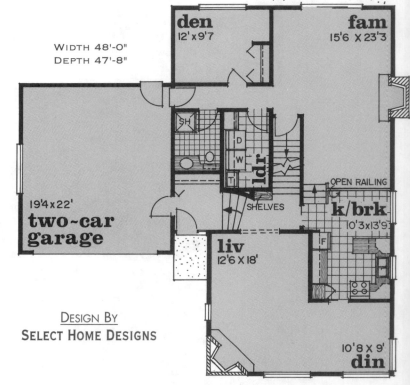

WIDTH 48'-0"
DEPTH 47'-8"

DESIGN BY
SELECT HOME DESIGNS

den
12' x 9'7

fam
15'6 X 23'3

PATIO

two-car garage
19'4x22'

ldr

SH

D
W
T

SHELVES

OPEN RAILING

k/brk
10'3x13'9

liv
12'6 X 18'

F

10'8 X 9'
din

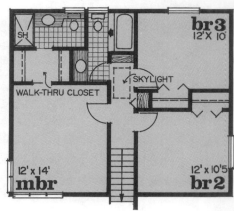

br3
12' X 10'

SH

WALK-THRU CLOSET

SKYLIGHT

12' x 14'
mbr

12' x 10'5
br2

Alternate Exterior

Sided in horizontal wood with a large stone fireplace, this country retreat is the image of a rustic hideaway. A recessed entry opens to a central hall with bedrooms flanking it. A few steps down, the living areas are positioned to take advantage of outdoor views and the long deck with sunken spa that wraps two sides of the design. The living room, dining room and kitchen are all vaulted. The living room is further enhanced by a fireplace. A greenhouse, just beyond the kitchen, can serve as a breakfast room, if desired. Two family bedrooms share the use of a skylit bath and also have box-bay windows. The master suite has double box-bays, a walk-in closet, vaulted ceiling and a private sun deck. Clerestory windows illuminate the main entry and hallway.

DESIGN Q283

Square Footage: 1,679

DESIGN BY
SELECT HOME DESIGNS

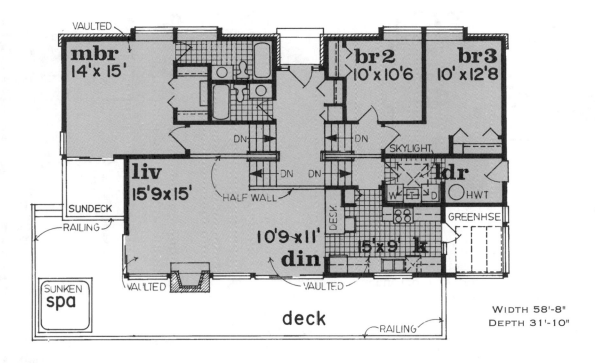

WIDTH 58'-8"
DEPTH 31'-10"

Design 2481

First Floor: 1,160 square feet
Second Floor: 828 square feet
Total: 1,988 square feet

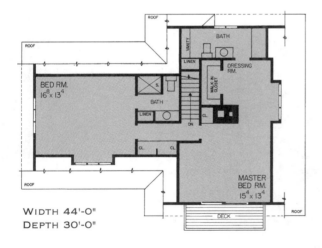

WIDTH 44'-0"
DEPTH 30'-0"

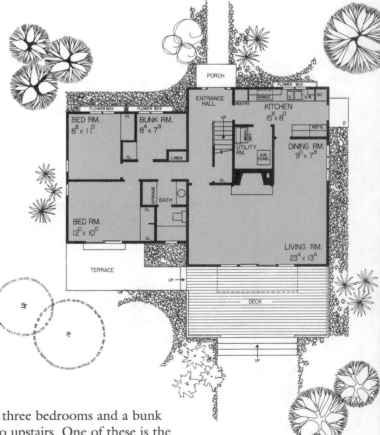

Five rooms for sleeping! A complete master suite plus three bedrooms and a bunk room. Three full baths, one on the first floor and two upstairs. One of these is the master bath, complete with dressing room and walk-in closet. The living room will enjoy easy access to a large deck plus a fireplace. The dining room is conveniently located between the living area and the efficient kitchen which has a pantry and nearby laundry/utility room. Surely a great planned work center for a vacation home. Note the special extras: three flower boxes, a private terrace for one of the family bedrooms, ample linen and storage space and a private deck for the master suite.

DESIGN BY
HOME PLANNERS

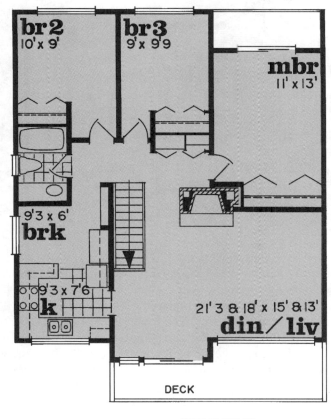

br2
10' x 9'

br3
9' x 9'9

mbr
11' x 13'

9'3 x 6'
brk

9'3 x 7'6
k

21'3 & 18' x 15' & 13'
din / liv

DECK

WIDTH 32'-0"
DEPTH 40'-0"

DESIGN Q217

Entry Level: 113 square feet
Main Level: 1,063 square feet
Total: 1,176 square feet

Site this home to take advantage of views at the front of the lot. A huge window wall and sliding glass doors to the deck in the living/dining area make this possible. The entry—113 square feet—has a staircase leading up to the main living level, but unfinished space on the lower level may be developed for a future family room or extra bedroom. Special features of the plan include a fireplace in the living area, a private deck off the master bedroom and a convenient U-shaped kitchen. Two family bedrooms assure plenty of sleeping space for the whole family.

Rear Elevation

DESIGN 8629

First Floor: 1,782 square feet
Second Floor: 264 square feet
Total: 2,046 square feet

This delightful 1½-story plan has a formal living and dining area for evening entertainment and boasts a huge family gathering space. Designed for efficiency, the two secondary bedrooms have private entrances off the formal living area. The master bedroom has all of the features of a larger home, including a soaking tub, a large walk-in shower and a private toilet area. The kitchen is at the heart of the home with a bay-windowed breakfast area adjacent to the efficient laundry room. A loft area on the second floor provides additional space for the growing family. Included in the blueprints are details for two different exteriors.

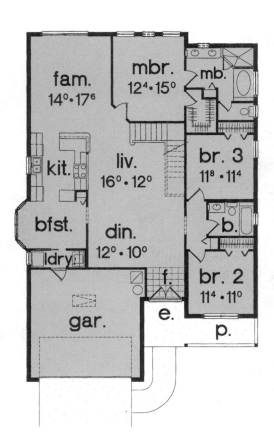

fam.
14⁰·17⁶

mbr.
12⁴·15⁰

mb.

kit.

liv.
16⁰·12⁰

br. 3
11⁸·11⁴

bfst.

din.
12⁰·10⁰

b.

ldry

f.

br. 2
11⁴·11⁰

gar.

e.

p.

loft
11⁸·20⁰

WIDTH 40'-0"
DEPTH 61'-0"

DESIGN BY
HOME DESIGN
SERVICES

Alternate Exterior

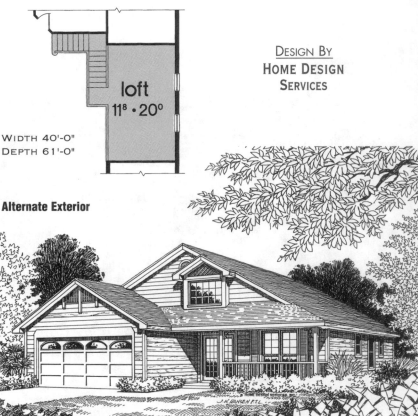

A covered porch introduces this two-story home and complements the horizontal wood siding with vertical siding trim. Inside, an open floor plan reigns. The vaulted living room is to the front where double doors open to the porch. Columns separate the living room from the formal dining room and the family room from the main hall. A corner fireplace and built-in shelves adorn the family room. The nook has sliding glass doors to the rear yard and is open to the kitchen. Three family bedrooms, a master suite and a den are on the second floor. Note the walk-in closet and sumptuous bath in the master suite.

DESIGN 7494

First Floor: 1,072 square feet
Second Floor: 1,108 square feet
Total: 2,180 square feet

DESIGN BY
ALAN MASCORD
DESIGN ASSOCIATES, INC.

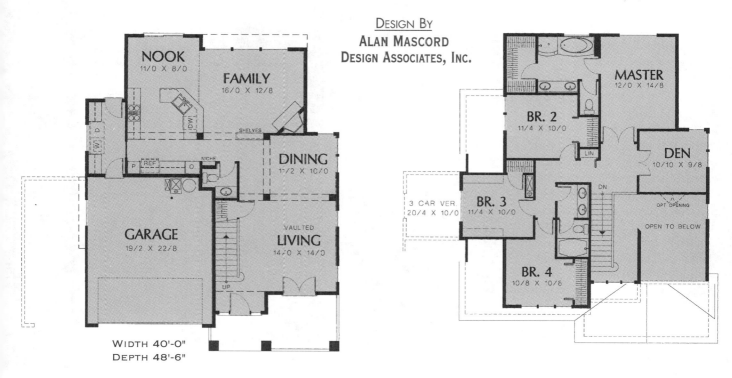

NOOK
11/0 X 8/0

FAMILY
16/0 X 12/8

SHELVES

DINING
11/2 X 10/0

NICHE

REF

P

W D

GARAGE
19/2 X 22/8

VAULTED
LIVING
14/0 X 14/0

UP

WIDTH 40'-0"
DEPTH 48'-6"

MASTER
12/0 X 14/8

BR. 2
11/4 X 10/0

LIN

DEN
10/10 X 9/8

3 CAR VER.
20/4 X 10/0

BR. 3
11/4 X 10/0

DN

OPT OPENING

OPEN TO BELOW

BR. 4
10/8 X 10/8

DESIGN 7631

First Floor: 1,750 square feet
Second Floor: 604 square feet
Total: 2,354 square feet

DESIGN BY
DONALD A. GARDNER
ARCHITECTS, INC.

Front and back covered porches extend living to the outdoors for this unique home. Open and casual, this home includes a generous, two-story great room with exposed beams, while two glass-walled dining areas provide optimum enjoyment in sunlight and dazzling views. The U-shaped kitchen is centrally located for convenience. Upstairs, a loft/study overlooks the great room, while the secluded master suite includes a luxurious bath with walk-in closet. Downstairs, family/guest quarters abound with two options—a bunk room and separate bedroom or three private bedrooms.

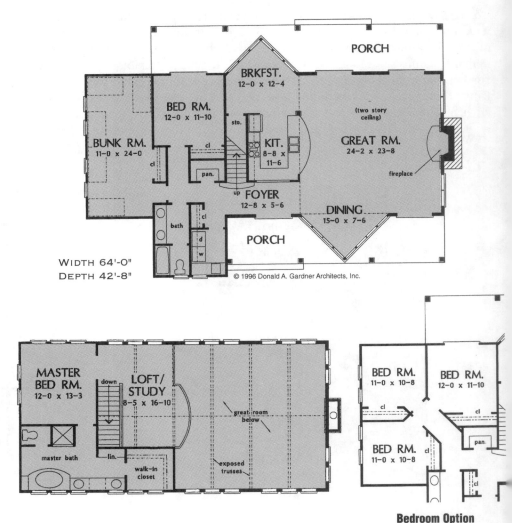

WIDTH 64'-0"
DEPTH 42'-8"

© 1996 Donald A. Gardner Architects, Inc.

Bedroom Option

© 1996 Donald A. Gardner Architects, Inc.

DESIGN 7464

First Floor: 847 square feet
Second Floor: 845 square feet
Total: 1,692 square feet

This diminutive plan is large on details and great livability. From the columned front entry, proceed directly to the vaulted great room on the right (note the media center and fireplace) and vaulted dining room on the left. The U-shaped kitchen is nearby and has an attached nook with side-porch access. Behind it all is a two-car garage reached through the rear service entrance with laundry and powder room. Three bedrooms are on the second floor: two family bedrooms sharing a full bath and the master suite with private bath. The master bedroom features a walk-in closet; the bath has a spa tub and separate shower.

DESIGN BY
**ALAN MASCORD
DESIGN ASSOCIATES, INC.**

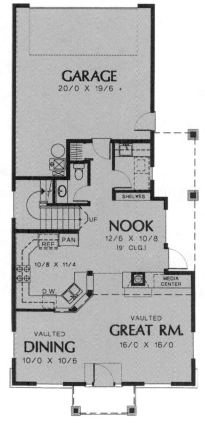

WIDTH 27'-0"
DEPTH 61'-0"

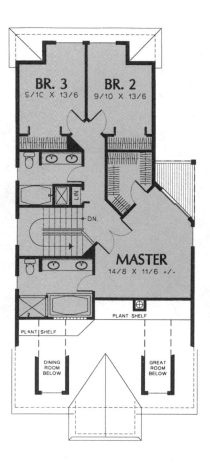

© 1996 Donald A. Gardner Architects, Inc.

B. NATHAN

DESIGN 7680

Square Footage: 1,888
Bonus Room: 358 square feet

Stone, shingle siding and a hip roof add traditional polish to this 1,888 square foot home. It is as stunning on the inside as it is on the outside. Interior columns add a special accent as they anchor and divide the dining room and great room, which also feature twelve-foot ceilings. Nine-foot ceilings throughout the rest of the house create spaciousness. A popular island kitchen is open to the great room and breakfast bay. Homeowners will enjoy the master suite, featuring a tray ceiling, dual facing walk-in closets and a generous master bath with large garden tub. Two additional bedrooms and a generous skylit bonus room complete this plan.

DESIGN BY
DONALD A. GARDNER
ARCHITECTS, INC.

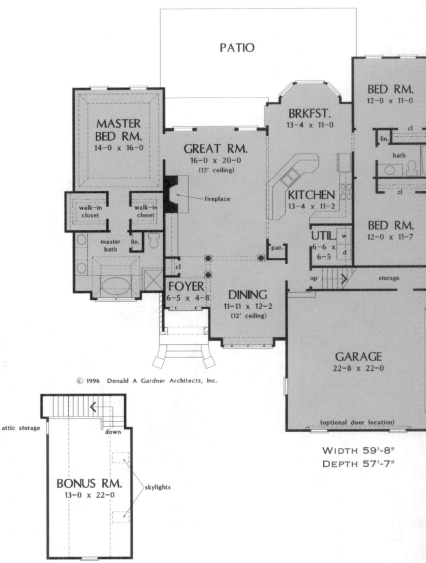

PATIO

MASTER BED RM.
14-0 x 16-0

GREAT RM.
16-0 x 20-0
(12' ceiling)

BRKFST.
13-4 x 11-0

BED RM.
12-0 x 11-0

walk-in closet

walk-in closet

fireplace

KITCHEN
13-4 x 11-2

lin.

cl

bath

cl

master bath

lin.

pan.

UTIL.
6-6 x 6-5

w d

BED RM.
12-0 x 11-7

FOYER
6-5 x 4-8

cl

DINING
11-11 x 12-2
(12' ceiling)

up

storage

GARAGE
22-8 x 22-0

(optional door location)

© 1996   Donald A Gardner Architects, Inc.

WIDTH 59'-8"
DEPTH 57'-7"

attic storage

down

BONUS RM.
13-0 x 22-0

skylights

188

© 1998 Donald A. Gardner Architects, Inc.

B. NATHAN

DECK

KIT.
11-10 x 14-0

BRKFST.
10-0 x 14-0

LIVING RM.
16-4 x 20-0

(cathedral ceiling)

fireplace

MASTER
BED RM.
17-0 x 14-0

down

railing

linen

master
bath

walk-in
closet

DINING
13-0 x 14-4

FOYER
6-8 x
13-2

bath

cl

cl

BED RM.
12-0 x 13-0

UTIL.
7-4 x
9-0

d
w

cl

BED RM./
STUDY
13-0 x 13-0

bath

storage

PORCH

© 1998 Donald A Gardner, Inc.

GARAGE
22-0 x 22-8

storage

WIDTH 70'-10"
DEPTH 69'-0"

COVERED
PATIO

bath

FAMILY RM.
16-4 x 20-0

fireplace

cl

lin.

BED RM.
13-3 x 14-0

cl

cl

pd.
rm.

BED RM.
14-8 x 12-4

bath

storage

up

© 1998 Donald A Gardner, Inc.

STORAGE
(unfinished)

DESIGN 7693

Main Level: 2,297 square feet
Lower Level: 1,212 square feet
Total: 3,509 square feet

Cedar shake, stone and siding embellish the sophisticated exterior of this European-style, sloping lot home, while an expansive deck allows for spectacular rear views. Special ceiling treatments enhance the open living and dining rooms as well as the versatile bedroom/study. The kitchen features a favorable layout with center cooktop island. A nearby open staircase leads to a partial basement with casual family room, two bedrooms, two-and-a-half baths and a large, unfinished storage area. Three bedrooms and three baths are located on the main level and include a lovely master suite with French-door access to the spacious rear deck.

DESIGN BY
DONALD A. GARDNER
ARCHITECTS, INC.

DESIGN A203

First Floor: 2,202 square feet
Second Floor: 1,355 square feet
Total: 3,557 square feet
Bonus Room: 523 square feet

Beautiful cedar shake shingles adorn the facade of this two-story beauty. The floor plan is open and devised for fine family living. A central foyer separates the formal living and dining rooms and leads to the casual gathering room with fireplace at the rear. Double French doors open to a rear deck/terrace. Columns define the bayed breakfast room which shares a snack-bar counter with the L-shaped kitchen. The master suite is on the first floor for convenience. It has a large walk-in closet and bath with separate tub and shower and dual sinks. Three family bedrooms inhabit the second floor—all of which have walk-in closets. Suite 4 has a private bath. You'll also find club quarters here and a large bonus area that can be developed into an additional bedroom in the future.

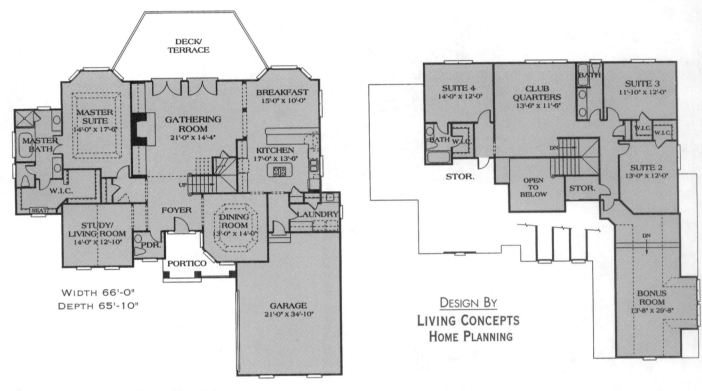

DECK/TERRACE

MASTER SUITE
14'-0" x 17'-6"

MASTER BATH

W.I.C.

SEAT

STUDY/LIVING ROOM
14'-0" x 12'-10"

PDR.

FOYER

PORTICO

GATHERING ROOM
21'-0" x 14'-4"

BREAKFAST
15'-0" x 10'-0"

KITCHEN
17'-0" x 13'-6"

UP

DINING ROOM
13'-0" x 14'-0"

LAUNDRY

GARAGE
21'-0" x 34'-10"

WIDTH 66'-0"
DEPTH 65'-10"

SUITE 4
14'-0" x 12'-0"

BATH

W.I.C.

STOR.

CLUB QUARTERS
13'-6" x 11'-6"

BATH

OPEN TO BELOW

DN

STOR.

SUITE 3
11'-10" x 12'-0"

W.I.C.   W.I.C.

SUITE 2
13'-0" x 12'-0"

DN

BONUS ROOM
13'-8" x 29'-8"

DESIGN BY
LIVING CONCEPTS
HOME PLANNING

© American Home Gallery, Ltd.

QUOTE ONE®

Cost to build? See page 434
to order complete cost estimate
to build this house in your area!

PORCH

BEDROOM/
OFFICE
10'-4" X 11'-0"

BREAKFAST
13'-4" X 9'-0"

MASTER
BATH

MASTER BEDRDOOM
16'-4" X 13'-6"

GREAT ROOM
17'-0" X 17'-8"

BEDROOM NO. 2
10'-4" X 12'-0"

KITCHEN
13'-4" X 10'-6"

BATH

LAUNDRY

BATH

DN.

TWO CAR GARAGE
20'-6" X 19'-6"

DINING ROOM
11'-4" X 12'-10"

FOYER
5'-4" X
12'-10"

BEDROOM/
STUDY
11'-2" X 12'-0"

PORCH

WIDTH 61'-0"
DEPTH 70'-6"

Rear

DESIGN T052

Square Footage: 2,090

This traditional home features board-and-batten and cedar shingles in an attractively proportioned exterior. Finishing touches include a covered entrance and porch with column detailing and an arched transom, flower boxes and shuttered windows. The foyer opens to both the dining room and great room which has French doors opening to the porch. Through the double doors to the right of the foyer is the combination bedroom/study. A short hallway leads to a full bath and a secondary bedroom with ample closet space. The master bedroom is spacious, with walk-in closets on both sides of the entrance to the master bath. With separate vanities, a shower and compartmented toilet, the master bath forms a private retreat at the rear of the home. Convenient to both the great room and dining room, the kitchen opens to an attractive breakfast area featuring a bay window. An additional room is remotely located off the kitchen, providing a retreat for today's at-home office or guest. This home is designed with a basement foundation.

DESIGN BY
DESIGN TRADITIONS

DESIGN 7431

First Floor: 1,389 square feet
Second Floor: 1,049 square feet
Total: 2,438 square feet

Shingles, stone work and skylights all combine to make this country house a delight to live in. The pleasure continues inside with a two-story great room acting as the heart of the home. Here a built-in media center flanks a warming fireplace. The L-shaped island kitchen offers an adjacent bayed nook for casual times, while the formal dining room easily accommodates elegant dinner parties. A den with a window seat finishes out the first floor. Nicely open to the lower floor, the upstairs contains two family bedrooms and a lavish, vaulted master suite. Here, a walk-in closet is reached via a luxurious bath that includes twin vanities and a separate shower and tub.

DESIGN BY
ALAN MASCORD
DESIGN ASSOCIATES, INC.

WIDTH 45'-0"
DEPTH 51'-0"

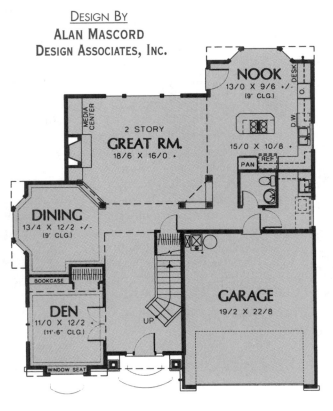

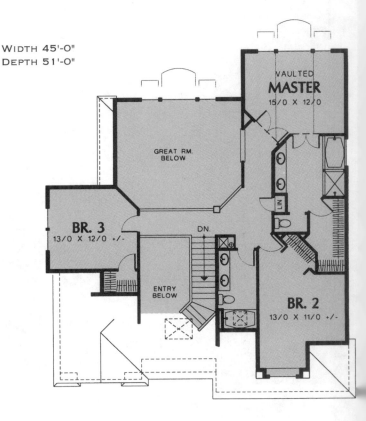

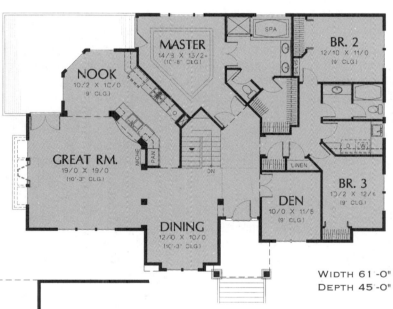

NOOK
10/2 X 10/0
(9' CLG.)

MASTER
14/3 X 13/2+
(10'-8" CLG.)

SPA

BR. 2
12/10 X 11/0
(9' CLG.)

GREAT RM.
19/0 X 19/0
(10'-3" CLG.)

NICHE
PAN

DN

LINEN

DEN
10/0 X 11/5
(9' CLG.)

DW

BR. 3
13/2 X 12/4
(9' CLG.)

DINING
12/0 X 10/0
(10'-3" CLG.)

WIDTH 61'-0"
DEPTH 45'-0"

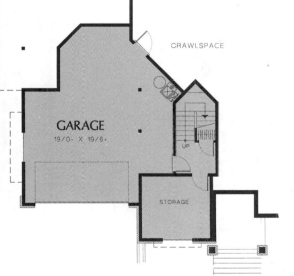

CRAWLSPACE

GARAGE
19/0- X 19/6+

UP

STORAGE

DESIGN 7508

Main Level: 2,124 square feet
Lower Level: 112 square feet
Total: 2,236 square feet

DESIGN BY
**ALAN MASCORD
DESIGN ASSOCIATES, INC.**

This lovely hillside home is perfect for a lot that slopes to the side. The garage is on the lower level, as well as storage space. The main level holds a hearth-warmed great room, formal dining room, sunny nook, galley-style kitchen, private den and three bedrooms. The master suite is particularly worthy of note with a huge walk-in closet and bath with spa tub, separate shower, dual sinks and compartmented toilet. Two family bedrooms share a full bath. A large terrace area is accessed from the great room and the master bedroom. A laundry that separates the two family bedrooms has sufficient space for a laundry sink.

DESIGN 7535

First Floor: 1,026 square feet
Second Floor: 936 square feet
Total: 1,962 square feet

Shingle siding, a recessed entry and multi-pane windows are some of the many architectural details that enhance the exterior of this home. Inside, the floor plan is simple and elegant and caters to casual living. The entry foyer connects a cozy den with double doors to a half-bath and then to the large great room with corner fireplace. The dining area and U-shaped island kitchen are just beyond. Double doors in the dining room lead outside. A three-car garage is reached through a service entrance near the laundry room. The second floor holds three bedrooms—two family bedrooms and a master suite. The master bedroom is vaulted and has a walk-in closet. Family bedrooms share a full hall bath.

WIDTH 48'-0"
DEPTH 45'-0"

DESIGN BY
ALAN MASCORD
DESIGN ASSOCIATES, INC.

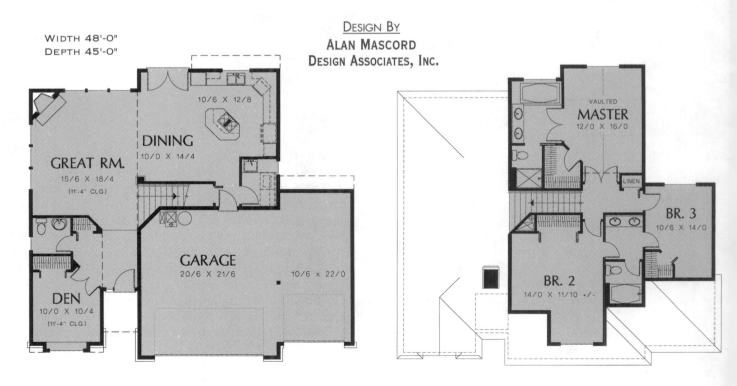

GREAT RM.
15/6 X 18/4
(11'-4" CLG.)

DINING
10/0 X 14/4

10/6 X 12/8

GARAGE
20/6 X 21/6

10/6 x 22/0

DEN
10/0 X 10/4
(11'-4" CLG.)

VAULTED
MASTER
12/0 X 16/0

LINEN

BR. 3
10/6 X 14/0

BR. 2
14/0 X 11/10 +/-

Unique details make the most of this shingle-sided two-story: a covered front porch with circle window and side-lit entry, two Palladian windows and a second-story dormer. The interior is also filled with delightful surprises. The entry foyer shows an angled staircase to the second floor and a den (or parlor) opening through double doors on the right. The formal dining room is defined by columns, as is the family room. A corner hearth and built-in media center further enhance the family room. A sun-filled nook adjoins the island kitchen and gives access to a covered side porch. On the second floor are two family bedrooms, sharing a full bath, and a master suite with tray ceiling, walk-in closet and grand bath. Don't miss the grand spa-style bathtub in the master bath. A vaulted bonus room adds future space for an additional bedroom.

DESIGN 7534

First Floor: 1,308 square feet
Second Floor: 1,078 square feet
Total: 2,386 square feet
Bonus Room: 227 square feet

NOOK
11/0 X 11/0 +/-
(9' CLG.)

FAMILY
16/6 X 16/0
(9' CLG.)

11/6 X 13/2

D.W.

PANTRY

MEDIA CENTER

10/0 X 12/6

GARAGE
20/0 X 24/6

DINING
13/0 X 10/4
(9' CLG.)

REF.

BUILT-IN

UP

DEN/
PARLOR
11/0 X 14/2
(10'-6' CLG.)

WIDTH 47'-0"
DEPTH 56'-0"

DESIGN BY
ALAN MASCORD
DESIGN ASSOCIATES, INC.

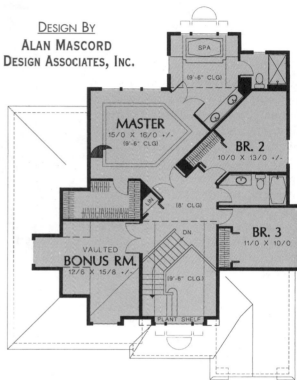

SPA
(9'-6' CLG.)

MASTER
15/0 X 16/0 +/-
(9'-6' CLG)

BR. 2
10/0 X 13/0 +/-

LIN

(8' CLG)

DN.

VAULTED
BONUS RM.
12/6 X 15/8 +/-

(9'-6' CLG.)

BR. 3
11/0 X 10/0

PLANT SHELF

DESIGN 7495

First Floor: 860 square feet
Second Floor: 845 square feet
Total: 1,705 square feet

DESIGN BY
ALAN MASCORD
DESIGN ASSOCIATES, INC.

From the symmetrical, shingle-sided exterior, to the well-planned interior, this home is a master of fine design. Though smaller in square footage, it offers all the amenities of much larger homes. The two-story great room and dining room sit togther in the front of the home and share the warmth of a fireplace with built-in media center. The modified U-shaped kitchen is nearby and has an attached nook with access to a side terrace. The two-car garage is to the back. It features extra storage or work space. Bedrooms are on the second floor and include a master suite and two family bedrooms. A large walk-in closet graces the master bedroom.

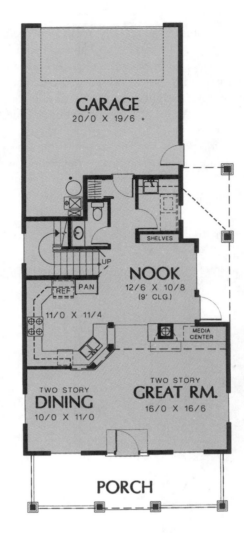

GARAGE
20/0 X 19/6 +

SHELVES

NOOK
12/6 X 10/8
(9' CLG.)

UP

REF PAN

11/0 X 11/4

MEDIA CENTER

TWO STORY
DINING
10/0 X 11/0

TWO STORY
GREAT RM.
16/0 X 16/6

PORCH

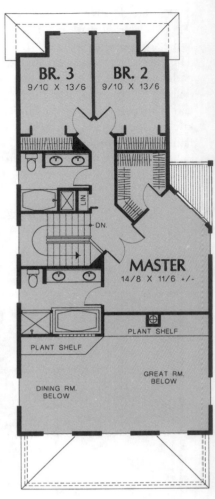

BR. 3
9/10 X 13/6

BR. 2
9/10 X 13/6

LIN

DN.

MASTER
14/8 X 11/6 +/-

PLANT SHELF

PLANT SHELF

DINING RM. BELOW

GREAT RM. BELOW

WIDTH 27'-0"
DEPTH 64'-0"

As a starter or vacation home, this two-story design functions well. An attractive traditional exterior introduces the interior by way of a covered front porch. The living room opens directly off the foyer and features a fireplace and an expansive window seat. Sharing space with this area is the gourmet kitchen. It delights with an island cooktop, a sunny sink and a pantry. Room for a dinette set is right near a side door. Accommodations for a washer and dryer, a rear deck and a powder room complete the first floor. Upstairs, three bedrooms all include vaulted ceilings. The master bedroom enjoys its own private bath and deck.

DESIGN 9534

First Floor: 762 square feet
Second Floor: 738 square feet
Total: 1,500 square feet

DESIGN BY
ALAN MASCORD
DESIGN ASSOCIATES, INC.

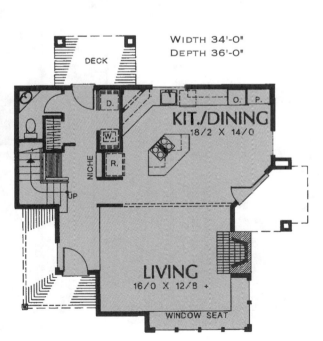

WIDTH 34'-0"
DEPTH 36'-0"

DECK

KIT./DINING
18/2 X 14/0

NICHE

UP

LIVING
16/0 X 12/8 +

WINDOW SEAT

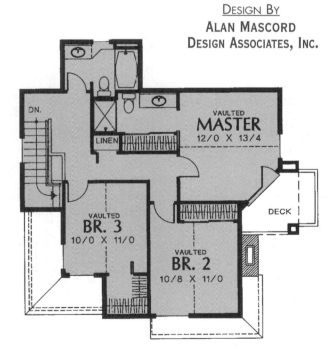

DN.

LINEN

VAULTED
MASTER
12/0 X 13/4

VAULTED
BR. 3
10/0 X 11/0

DECK

VAULTED
BR. 2
10/8 X 11/0

Design 8263

First Floor: 2,055 square feet
Second Floor: 1,229 square feet
Total: 3,284 square feet

Stately elegance prevails throughout this two-story manor. Formal areas are defined by high ceilings and open areas. The living room is especially grand with double French doors to the rear yard. A large combination kitchen, breakfast room, and family room will become the favorite gathering spot at day's end. The secluded main-level master bedroom features a sumptuous bath with separate walk-in closets and sinks, a shower with built-in seating, and a corner whirlpool tub. Three bedrooms, two baths, and a game room reside on the upper level. Both Bedroom 3 and Bedroom 4 feature walk-in closets. Please specify crawlspace or slab foundation when ordering.

<u>Design By</u>
Larry E. Belk
Designs

Width 65'-0"
Depth 60'-10"

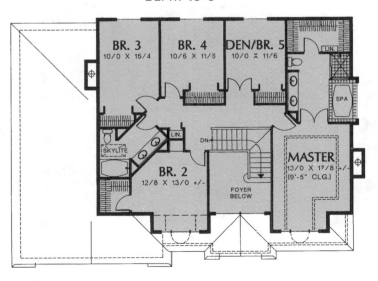

FAMILY
14/6 X 15/8

12/8 X 16/4

NOOK
8/0 X 15/8 +/-

D.W.

DINING
10/6 X 13/10

REF.

9/0 X 15/8

DESK PAN.

LIVING
13/0 X 16/2

UP

GARAGE
23/4 X 21/0

D W.

WIDTH 56'-0"
DEPTH 40'-0"

BR. 3
10/0 X 15/4

BR. 4
10/6 X 11/6

DEN/BR. 5
10/0 X 11/6

LIN.

SPA

LIN.

SKYLITE

DN.

BR. 2
12/8 X 13/0 +/-

FOYER
BELOW

MASTER
13/0 X 17/8
(9'-5" CLG.)

DESIGN 9536

First Floor: 1,200 square feet
Second Floor: 1,339 square feet
Total: 2,539 square feet

DESIGN BY
**ALAN MASCORD
DESIGN ASSOCIATES, INC.**

A covered front porch introduces this home's comfortable living patterns. The two-story foyer opens to a living room with a fireplace and lots of natural light. The formal dining room looks out over the living room. In the kitchen, an island cooktop, a pantry, a built-in planning desk and a nook with double doors to outside livability aim to please. A spacious family room with another fireplace will accommodate casual living. Upstairs, five bedrooms—or four and a den—make room for all family members and guests. The master bedroom suite is superb with an elegant ceiling and a pampering spa bath. A full hall bath with a skylight and dual lavatories serves the secondary bedrooms.

DESIGN 9587

First Floor: 822 square feet
Second Floor: 1,175 square feet
Total: 1,997 square feet

The wraparound porch surrounding this shingled home provides a front row seat to enjoy the soothing sounds of the country—literally. At the entrance to the front porch, a built-in bench has been thoughtfully placed for convenience. Inside, an open floor plan makes the most of the first-floor living area. Enhanced with built-ins, the great room also features a warming fireplace. Here, a wall of windows provides plenty of natural light and unobstructed views of the backyard. A bay window fills the adjacent nook with sunlight and brightens the adjoining U-shaped kitchen. Located near the garage for convenience, a laundry room and powder room complete the first floor. The second floor contains a restful master suite, two family bedrooms that share a full bath, and a game room.

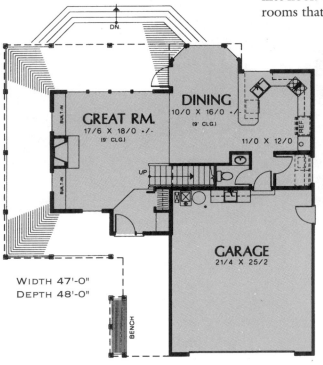

GREAT RM.
17/6 X 18/0 +/-
(9' CLG.)

DINING
10/0 X 16/0 +/-
(9' CLG.)

11/0 X 12/0

GARAGE
21/4 X 25/2

WIDTH 47'-0"
DEPTH 48'-0"

BENCH

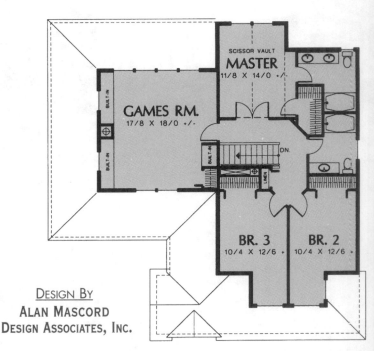

GAMES RM.
17/8 X 18/0 +/-

SCISSOR VAULT
MASTER
11/8 X 14/0 +/-

BR. 3
10/4 X 12/6

BR. 2
10/4 X 12/6

DESIGN BY
ALAN MASCORD
DESIGN ASSOCIATES, INC.

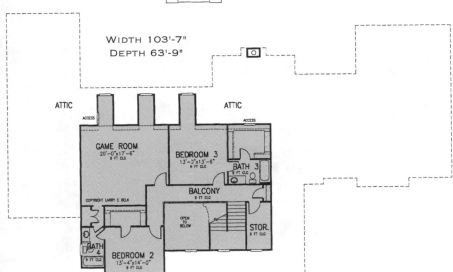

MSTR. BATH
10 FT CLG

MASTER BEDROOM
16'-4"x19'-0"
10 FT CLG

PORCH

LIVING ROOM
17'-8"x16'-8"
10 FT CLG

PAN

FAMILY ROOM
18'-6"x15'-2"
10 FT CLG

BREAKFAST
12'-8"x11'-6"
10 FT CLG

GARAGE
21'-6"x36'-6"

COPYRIGHT LARRY E. BELK

DINING
15'-6"x12'-2"
10 FT CLG

KITCHEN
21'-4"x13'-0"
10 FT CLG

UTL.
10 FT CLG

PORCH

BATH 2

BEDROOM 2
13'-4"x13'-4"
10 FT CLG

FOYER
2 STORY CLG

PWD.
10 FT

PORCH
10'-6" CLG

COPYRIGHT LARRY E. BELK

WIDTH 103'-7"
DEPTH 63'-9"

ATTIC ACCESS

ATTIC ACCESS

GAME ROOM
20'-0"x17'-6"
9 FT CLG

BEDROOM 3
13'-3"x13'-6"
9 FT CLG

BATH 3
9 FT CLG

BALCONY
9 FT CLG

COPYRIGHT LARRY E. BELK

OPEN TO BELOW

STOR.
9 FT CLG

BATH 4
9 FT CLG

BEDROOM 2
13'-4"x14'-0"
9 FT CLG

DESIGN BY
LARRY E. BELK
DESIGNS

DESIGN 8251
First Floor: 2,931 square feet
Second Floor: 1,319 square feet
Total: 4,250 square feet

Beautiful stonework, a gabled roof and attractive shutters combine to give this four-bedroom home plenty of curb appeal. From the covered front porch, enter a large foyer which leads to the formal areas of the living room and dining room. At the rear of the home, the spacious family room waits to entertain with a warming fireplace and access to the rear covered porch. An angled, island kitchen easily serves the sunny breakfast room and offers a walk-in pantry. Located on the far left side of the home, the master suite is full of amenities, including two large walk-in closets, a lavish bath and a private covered porch. A secondary bedroom, with its own bath, makes a great guest suite. Upstairs, two more family bedrooms pamper with private baths and walk-in closets. A large game room and an extra storage closet complete this level.

DESIGN 9590

First Floor: 1,205 square feet
Second Floor: 1,123 square feet
Total: 2,328 square feet

A covered porch, multi-pane windows and shingle-and-stone siding combine to give this home plenty of curb appeal. Inside, the foyer is flanked by the formal living room and an angled staircase. The formal dining room shares space with the living room, and the kitchen is accessible through double doors. A large family room is graced by a fireplace and opens off a cozy eating nook. The second level presents many attractive angles. The master suite has a spacious walk-in closet and a sumptuous bath complete with a garden tub and separate shower. Three family bedrooms share a full hall bath.

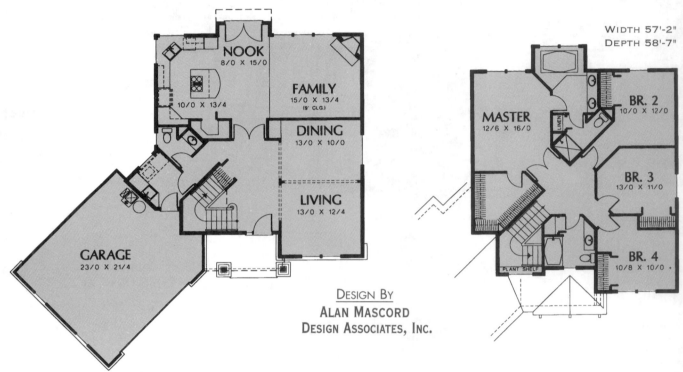

WIDTH 57'-2"
DEPTH 58'-7"

NOOK
8/0 X 15/0

FAMILY
15/0 X 13/4
(9' CLG.)

10/0 X 13/4

DINING
13/0 X 10/0

LIVING
13/0 X 12/4

GARAGE
23/0 X 21/4

MASTER
12/6 X 16/0

BR. 2
10/0 X 12/0

LINEN

BR. 3
13/0 X 11/0

BR. 4
10/8 X 10/0

PLANT SHELF

DESIGN BY
ALAN MASCORD
DESIGN ASSOCIATES, INC.

Wood shingles, a double-door glass entry and varying roof lines add a special twist to this otherwise traditional home. The plan is designed for easy living. To the right of the foyer are the formal living and dining rooms. Adjacent to the dining area is an efficient, step-saving kitchen featuring a cooktop island and a walk-in pantry. The nearby breakfast nook offers dual access to the terrace and combines well with the family room for family gatherings. The second floor contains three bedrooms, a bath and the master suite. Two walk-in closets lead to the unique and luxurious master bath. A den, with a detailed ceiling and access to a private deck, and a bonus room complete the upstairs.

DESIGN 9551

First Floor: 1,682 square feet
Second Floor: 1,589 square feet
Total: 3,271 square feet
Bonus Room: 287 square feet

DESIGN BY
**ALAN MASCORD
DESIGN ASSOCIATES, INC.**

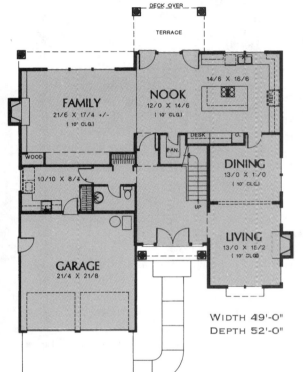

WIDTH 49'-0"
DEPTH 52'-0"

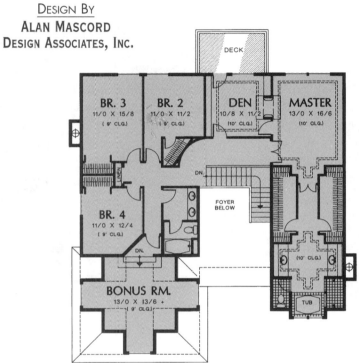

203

DESIGN 7515

First Floor: 898 square feet
Second Floor: 777 square feet
Total: 1,675 square feet

DESIGN BY
ALAN MASCORD
DESIGN ASSOCIATES, INC.

This unusual design is a model for great casual living. The garage level has additional shop and storage space and is the perfect foundation for the two levels above. An open floor plan on the main level includes a dining room and a living room with deck, fireplace and built-ins and a nearby dining room. The island kitchen is open to the dining room and also has access to a quaint side porch. The second floor has sleeping accommodations in two family bedrooms and a master suite. A walk-in closet and full bath grace the master bedroom; family bedrooms share a full bath. Notice that the laundry is on the second floor, close to bedrooms.

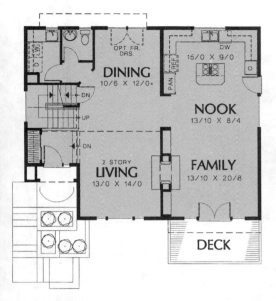

DINING
10/6 X 12/0+

OPT. FR. DRS.

DW
15/0 X 9/0

NOOK
13/10 X 8/4

2 STORY
LIVING
13/0 X 14/0

FAMILY
13/10 X 20/8

DECK

BR. 3
11/0 X 10/8

BR. 2
11/0 X 10/0

SHELVES

LOFT

FOYER
BELOW

LIVING
BELOW

LIN

VAULTED
MASTER
15/2 X 12/0

WIDTH 38'-0"
DEPTH 35'-0"

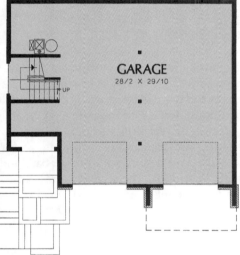

GARAGE
28/2 X 29/10

DESIGN 7469

First Floor: 1,106 square feet
Second Floor: 872 square feet
Total: 1,978 square feet

DESIGN BY
ALAN MASCORD
DESIGN ASSOCIATES, INC.

What an interesting design—full of lovely levels, roof planes and large window areas. The lower level is devoted to garage space and serves as the foundation for main-level living above. Besides a formal living and dining room on the main level, there is a family room, nook and island kitchen. The family room and living room share a through-fireplace. If you choose, install double doors in the dining room for rear-yard access. The second-floor bedrooms are connected by a loft overlooking the living room below. Bedrooms 2 and 3 share a full bath that separates them; the vaulted master suite has a private bath and walk-in closet.

DESIGN A263

First Floor: 2,122 square feet
Second Floor: 719 square feet
Total: 2,841 square feet
Storage Area: 535 square feet

DESIGN BY
LIVING CONCEPTS
HOME PLANNING

In grand style, this shingle-sided design cuts an impressive swath through any neighborhood. The two-car garage is separate from the main house, but reached easily via a breezeway that connects the two. Space above it can be used for storage or as guest quarters. The main house features a large great room at its center, warmed by a fireplace and accessing the rear deck through double French doors. A dining room also connects to the deck and is open to the kitchen. A guest room with private bath and a master suite with private bath and attached hearth-warmed study complete the first floor. The second floor holds two bedroom suites with private baths and a large loft area with walk-in closet. A balcony separates the two areas and overlooks the great room below.

WIDTH 117'-0"
DEPTH 57'-2"

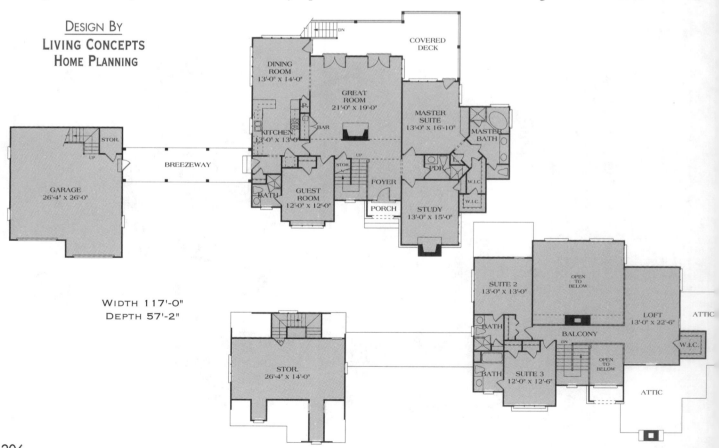

This wonderful plan has more to offer than just a gorgeous shingle-sided facade. It also contains living space fit for a king. The great room dominates the first floor and separates the breakfast room and kitchen from the grand master suite. A portico just off the service entrance opens to the portico connecting the main house to the two-car garage. A rear deck is accessed from the master bedroom and the great room and is complemented by a screened porch reached via the breakfast room. Three bedroom suites on the second floor are joined by a balcony overlooking the great room. Suite 4 has a private bath. Note the space above the garage which can be used for storage or guest quarters.

DESIGN A264

First Floor: 1,793 square feet
Second Floor: 1,115 square feet
Total: 2,908 square feet
Storage Area: 266 square feet

DESIGN BY
LIVING CONCEPTS
HOME PLANNING

WIDTH 103'-8"
DEPTH 57'-6"

Front

Rear

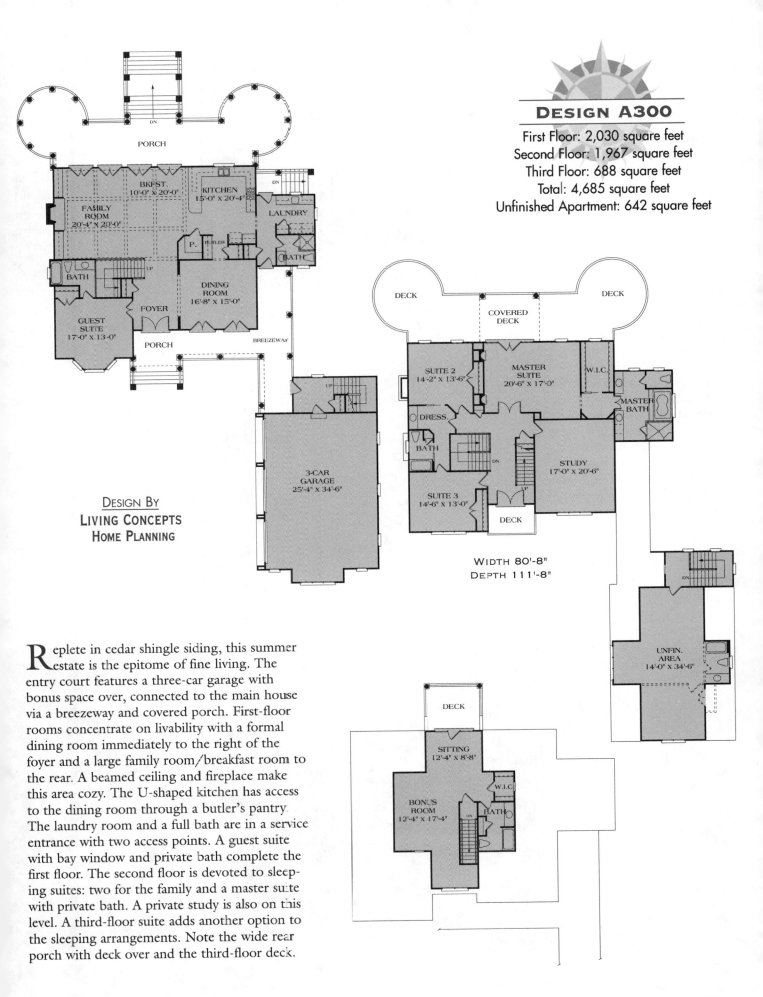

PORCH

BKFST.
10'-0" x 20'-0"

KITCHEN
15'-0" x 20'-4"

DN

LAUNDRY

FAMILY
ROOM
20'-4" x 20'-0"

P. BUTLER

BATH

BATH

UP

DINING
ROOM
16'-8" x 15'-0"

FOYER

GUEST
SUITE
17'-0" x 13'-0"

PORCH

BREEZEWAY

UP

3-CAR
GARAGE
25'-4" x 34'-6"

DESIGN BY
LIVING CONCEPTS
HOME PLANNING

DESIGN A300

First Floor: 2,030 square feet
Second Floor: 1,967 square feet
Third Floor: 688 square feet
Total: 4,685 square feet
Unfinished Apartment: 642 square feet

DECK

COVERED
DECK

DECK

SUITE 2
14'-2" x 13'-6"

MASTER
SUITE
20'-6" x 17'-0"

W.I.C.

MASTER
BATH

DRESS.

BATH

DN

STUDY
17'-0" x 20'-6"

UP

SUITE 3
14'-6" x 13'-0"

DECK

WIDTH 80'-8"
DEPTH 111'-8"

DN

UNFIN.
AREA
14'-0" x 34'-6"

DECK

SITTING
12'-4" x 8'-8"

W.I.C.

BATH

BONUS
ROOM
12'-4" x 17'-4"

DN

Replete in cedar shingle siding, this summer estate is the epitome of fine living. The entry court features a three-car garage with bonus space over, connected to the main house via a breezeway and covered porch. First-floor rooms concentrate on livability with a formal dining room immediately to the right of the foyer and a large family room/breakfast room to the rear. A beamed ceiling and fireplace make this area cozy. The U-shaped kitchen has access to the dining room through a butler's pantry. The laundry room and a full bath are in a service entrance with two access points. A guest suite with bay window and private bath complete the first floor. The second floor is devoted to sleeping suites: two for the family and a master suite with private bath. A private study is also on this level. A third-floor suite adds another option to the sleeping arrangements. Note the wide rear porch with deck over and the third-floor deck.

DESIGN A138

First Floor: 2,253 square feet
Second Floor: 792 square feet
Total: 3,045 square feet

This rambling, three-bedroom country design features a breezeway to the two-car garage, two fireplaces and the ultimate in master bedroom suites. The imposing living room, open to the second floor, features a fireplace flanked by built-in bookshelves and double doors to the curved rear terrace. A second fireplace in the family room backs to the terrace barbecue. The island kitchen is open to both the family room and the dining room. The master bedroom suite is centered between a study in the front and a private screened porch in the back, and includes a separate bath with His and Hers walk-in closets and vanities.

DESIGN BY
LIVING CONCEPTS
HOME PLANNING

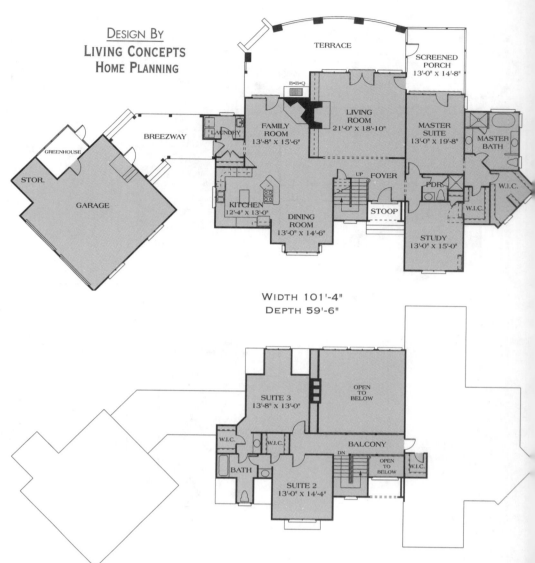

WIDTH 101'-4"
DEPTH 59'-6"

Nothing is left undone in this country estate, from shingle-siding to lovely stone accents. The interior is equally thoughtful. The grand room sits at the heart of the home around which revolve a formal dining room, the breakfast nook, the island kitchen and the first-floor master suite. Luxury amenities include a covered rear porch, a study with fireplace, a corner fireplace in the grand room, rear patio access at five points and a breezeway that connects the three-car garage to the main house. The second floor holds two bedroom suites, each with a walk-in closet and private bath. A balcony overlooking the grand room connects these suites. Unfinished bonus space over the garage can be developed later.

DESIGN A268

First Floor: 2,689 square feet
Second Floor: 1,180 square feet
Total: 3,869 square feet
Bonus Room: 723 square feet

DESIGN BY
LIVING CONCEPTS
HOME PLANNING

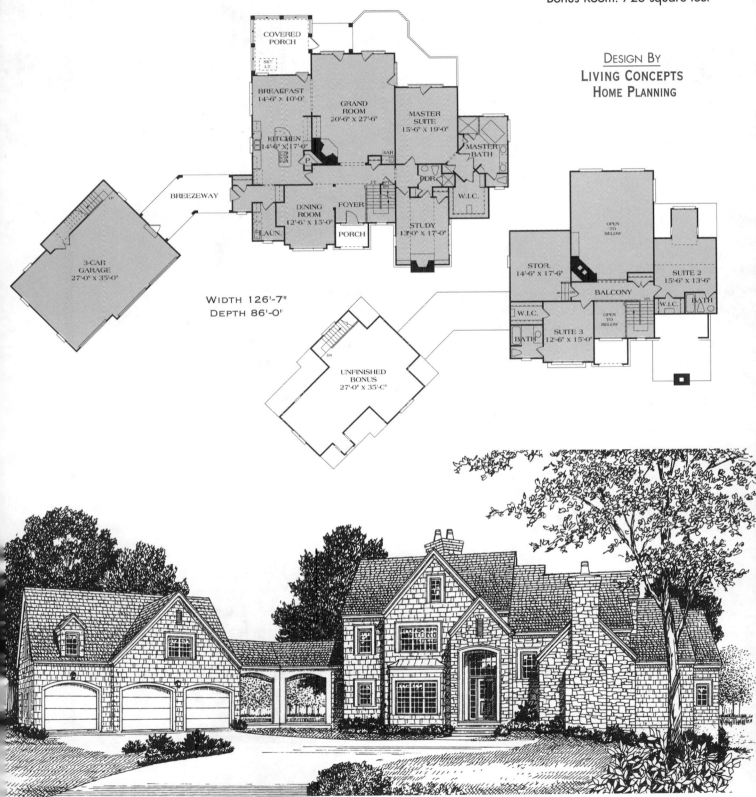

COVERED PORCH

SK' LT.

BREAKFAST
14'-6" x 10'-0"

GRAND ROOM
20'-6" x 27'-6"

MASTER SUITE
15'-6" x 19'-0"

KITCHEN
14'-6" X 17'-0"

MASTER BATH

3AR

P.

W.I.C.

BREEZEWAY

DINING ROOM
12'-6" x 15'-0"

FOYER

PDR.

STUDY
13'-0" x 17'-0"

PORCH

LAUN.

3-CAR GARAGE
27'-0" x 35'-0"

WIDTH 126'-7"
DEPTH 86'-0"

OPEN TO BELOW

STOR.
14'-6" x 17'-6"

SUITE 2
15'-6" x 13'-6"

BALCONY

W.I.C.

BATH

W.I.C.

BATH

SUITE 3
12'-6" x 15'-0"

OPEN TO BELOW

UNFINISHED BONUS
27'-0" x 35'-0"

DN

DESIGN A269

First Floor: 2,696 square feet
Second Floor: 1,374 square feet
Total: 4,070 square feet

This stone-and-shingle cottage brings to mind mild summer evenings on the lake, watching the fireflies spin their magic on the air. The covered porch is responsible for these summer dreams, of course. It wraps around the house on two sides and allows for two gazebo extensions. On the inside are rooms fit for a summer away: a music room, large family room with fireplace and built-ins, formal dining room, breakfast room and island kitchen. The master suite with two walk-in closets and private bath is on the first floor. The second floor holds three family suites—one with a private bath—and a home theater. The three-car garage juts at an angle and connects to the main house at the laundry room and home office.

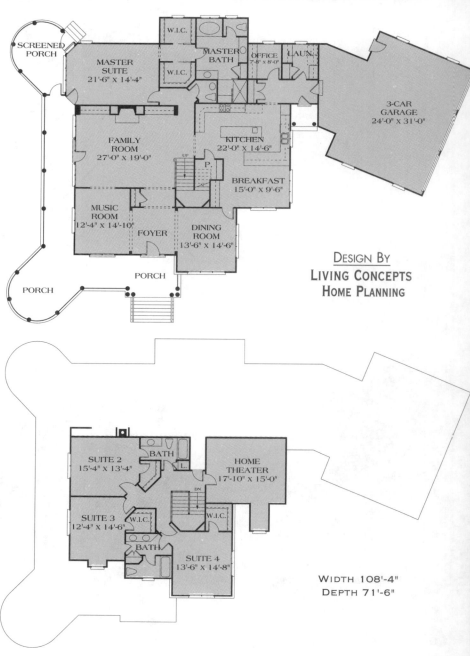

DESIGN BY
LIVING CONCEPTS
HOME PLANNING

WIDTH 108'-4"
DEPTH 71'-6"

Though it appears as a two-story plan, this home is really a one-story with walk-out basement that includes unfinished space for later expansion. The main living areas are on the first floor: a formal dining room, a family room with fireplace, built-ins and terrace access, an island kitchen and a breakfast room with attached sun room. The master suite is also on the first floor and reached through a rotunda in the hall. It has a private deck. The two-car garage has a one-car extension for a boat or golf cart, if you choose. The lower level holds three bedroom suites—one with private bath. A rec room in the center has a fireplace, built-ins and access to the lower terrace.

DESIGN A274

Main Level: 3,054 square feet
Lower Level: 1,539 square feet
Total: 4,593 square feet
Unfinished Space: 553 square feet

DESIGN BY
**LIVING CONCEPTS
HOME PLANNING**

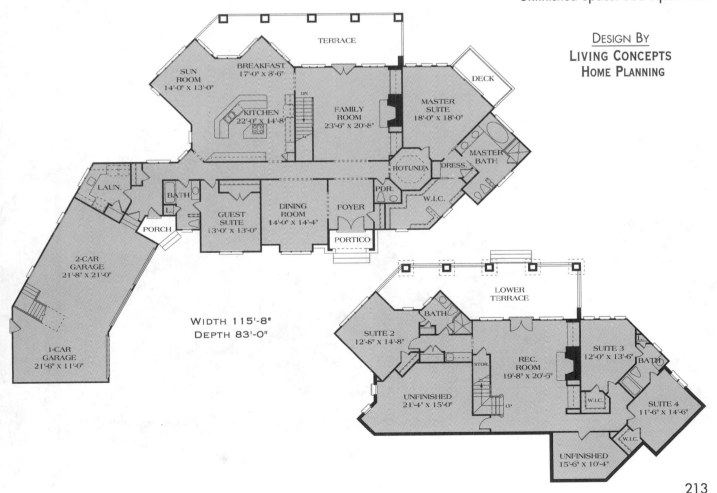

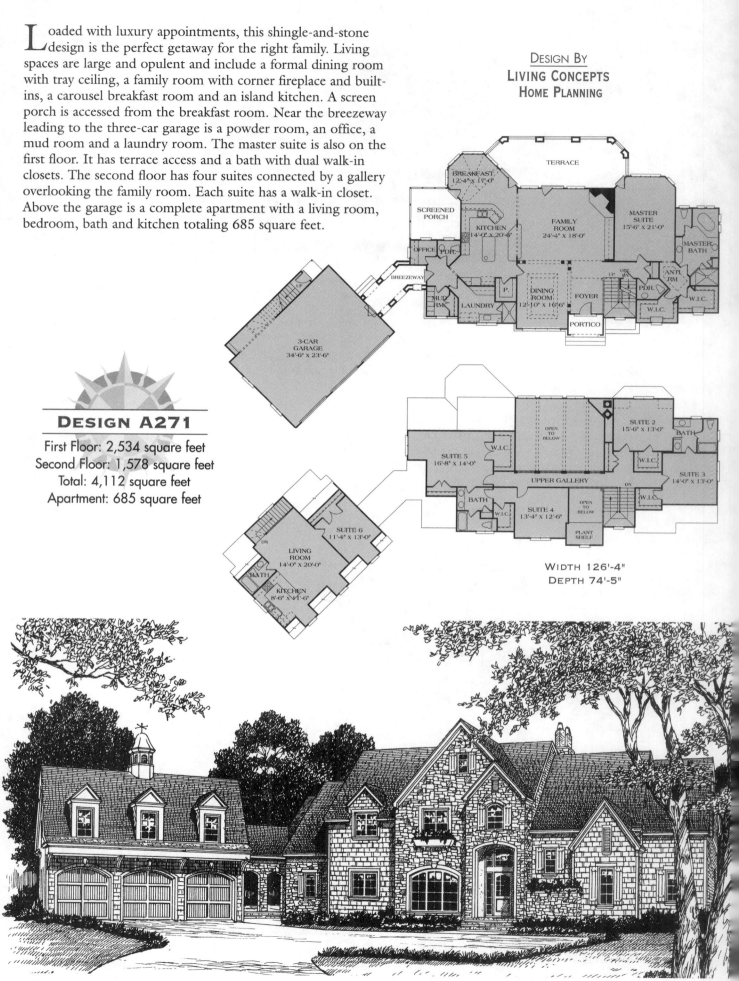

oaded with luxury appointments, this shingle-and-stone design is the perfect getaway for the right family. Living spaces are large and opulent and include a formal dining room with tray ceiling, a family room with corner fireplace and built-ins, a carousel breakfast room and an island kitchen. A screen porch is accessed from the breakfast room. Near the breezeway leading to the three-car garage is a powder room, an office, a mud room and a laundry room. The master suite is also on the first floor. It has terrace access and a bath with dual walk-in closets. The second floor has four suites connected by a gallery overlooking the family room. Each suite has a walk-in closet. Above the garage is a complete apartment with a living room, bedroom, bath and kitchen totaling 685 square feet.

DESIGN BY
LIVING CONCEPTS
HOME PLANNING

DESIGN A271

First Floor: 2,534 square feet
Second Floor: 1,578 square feet
Total: 4,112 square feet
Apartment: 685 square feet

WIDTH 126'-4"
DEPTH 74'-5"

214

Stone-and-shingle siding, gables and columns framing the front entry all combine to give this home plenty of curb appeal. A two-story ceiling that starts in the foyer and runs through the great room gives a feeling of spaciousness. The great room is further enhanced by a built-in media center, a fireplace and direct access to the kitchen. Double doors lead into a vaulted den which also offers built-ins. Located on the first floor for privacy, the master bedroom suite is designed to pamper the homeowner. Here, amenities such as a huge walk-in closet, separate tub and shower and sliding glass doors to a rear porch make sure the homeowner is comfortable. Upstairs, two secondary bedrooms share a full hall bath.

DESIGN 7445

First Floor: 2,943 square feet
Second Floor: 597 square feet
Total: 3,540 square feet

DESIGN BY
**ALAN MASCORD
DESIGN ASSOCIATES, INC.**

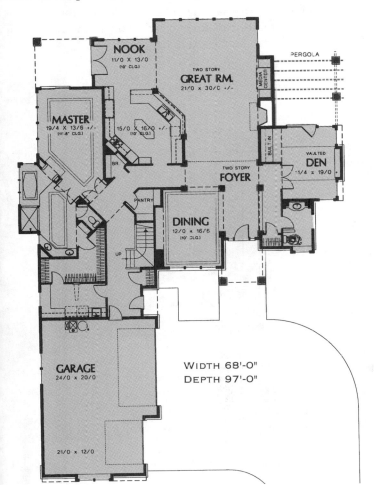

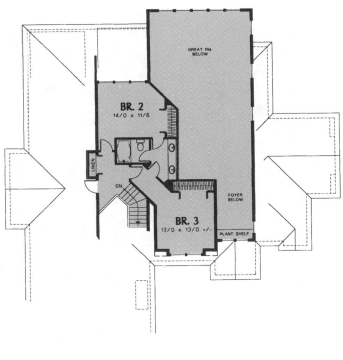

DESIGN A297

First Floor: 1,758 square feet
Second Floor: 685 square feet
Total: 2,443 square feet
Bonus Room: 260 square feet

Full of delights, this tidy stone-and-shingle cottage makes the most of its floor plan. The double-door entry opens to a foyer with dining room on the right and family room to the back. Double doors in the family room lead out to a rear patio. The island kitchen with bayed breakfast nook is nearby. In a service entrance to the garage are a half-bath and the laundry. The master suite dominates the left side of the first floor. It is graced by a tray ceiling, dual walk-in closets and a grand master bath. Two family suites on the second floor have private baths. A huge unfinished storage area and a bonus room that can be finished later are also on the second floor.

PATIO

BREAKFAST
11'-8" X 9'-4"

MASTER SUITE
14'-6" X 14'-0"

FAMILY ROOM
20'-6" X 15'-4"

KITCHEN
13'-0" X 15'-2"

W.I.C.

W.I.C.

MASTER BATH

FOYER

UP

P.

DINING ROOM
12'-6" X 12'-6"

PDR.

LAUNDRY

DESIGN BY
LIVING CONCEPTS
HOME PLANNING

GARAGE
20'-10" X 22'-6"

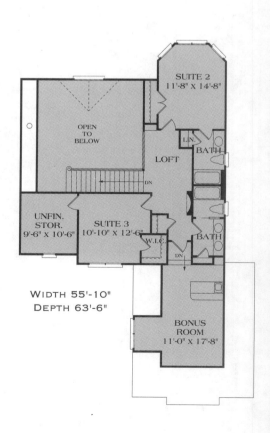

SUITE 2
11'-8" X 14'-8"

OPEN TO BELOW

LIN.

BATH

LOFT

DN

UNFIN. STOR.
9'-6" X 10'-6"

SUITE 3
10'-10" X 12'-6"

W.I.C.

BATH

DN

WIDTH 55'-10"
DEPTH 63'-6"

BONUS ROOM
11'-0" X 17'-8"

Quaint is the byword for this stone-and-shingle cottage. Convenience is the hall-mark of its floor plan. The main level holds the bulk of the livability with a large family room with fireplace and a formal dining room. The island kitchen has an attached breakfast room with a screened porch nearby for outdoor dining. A covered deck off the family room adds to outdoor livability. Down the service hall to the two-car garage are a half-bath, laundry room and office. The master suite sits on the left side of the plan and holds two walk-in closets and a master bath with whirlpool tub and dual sinks. Family suites and a guest suite are on the lower level along with a rec room and giant storage room. A lower terrace is reached from the rec room and from Suites 2 and 3.

DESIGN A267

Main Level: 2,213 square feet
Lower Level: 1,333 square feet
Total: 3,546 square feet
Bonus Room: 430 square feet

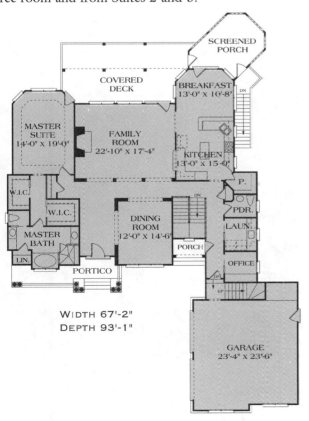

WIDTH 67'-2"
DEPTH 93'-1"

DESIGN BY
LIVING CONCEPTS
HOME PLANNING

DESIGN 2425

Square Footage: 1,106

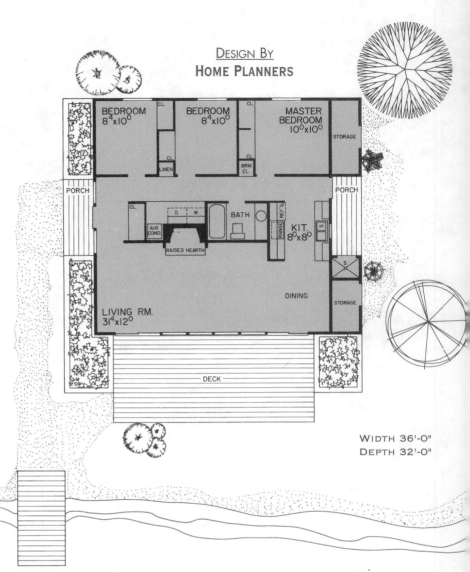

DESIGN BY
HOME PLANNERS

BEDROOM
8⁴x10⁰

BEDROOM
8⁴x10⁰

MASTER
BEDROOM
10⁰x10⁰

CL.

CL.

CL.

STORAGE

LINEN

BRM.
CL.

CL.

PORCH

PORCH

CL.

AIR
COND.

D.

W.

BATH

RANGE

REF'G.

KIT.
8⁰x8⁰

S

RAISED HEARTH

S.

LIVING RM.
31⁴x12⁰

DINING

STORAGE

DECK

WIDTH 36'-0"
DEPTH 32'-0"

Y ou'll adjust to living in this vacation cottage with the greatest of ease. The indoor/outdoor relationships are abundant. Outside are two small side porches and a huge deck to lounge or dine out on. Inside, a spacious living/dining area is bordered on one side by a wall of windows and warmed by a raised-hearth fireplace. The galley-style kitchen easily serves the dining area and is enhanced by its own mini-porch. Three bedrooms share a full bath and have access to a washer/dryer. There is plenty of storage capability. Note the hall broom closet and the linen closet.

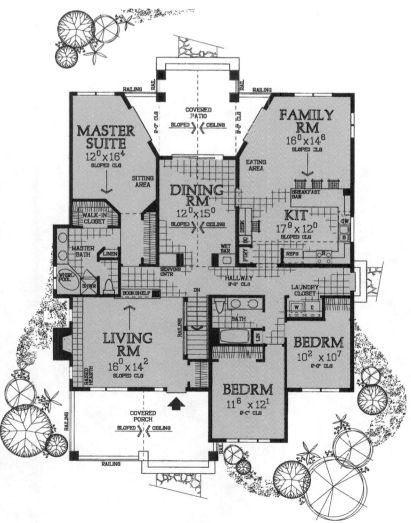

WIDTH 47'-6"
DEPTH 61'-6"

DESIGN 3496

Square Footage: 2,033

L

DESIGN BY
HOME PLANNERS

Get more out of your homebuilding dollars with this unique one-story bungalow. A covered front porch provides sheltered entry into a spacious living room. A bookshelf and a column are special touches. The dining room enjoys a sloped ceiling, a wet bar and direct access to the rear covered patio. In the nearby kitchen, a breakfast bar accommodates quick meals. The adjacent family room rounds out this casual living area. The large master suite pampers with a sitting area, patio access and a luxurious bath which features a corner tub, a separate shower and dual lavatories. Two secondary bedrooms share a full hall bath.

QUOTE ONE®

Cost to build? See page 434
to order complete cost estimate
to build this house in your area!

DESIGN 1486

Square Footage: 480

DESIGN BY
HOME PLANNERS

For that prime piece of property, this little vacation house will delight all vacationers. Two sets of sliding glass doors open to the living and dining area. A kitchen with a double sink, closet and porch door is just a step away. Two bedrooms share the same dimensions while utilizing a full hall bath. Whether you decide to build this house on your own or with the aid of a professional, you will not have to wait long for its completion.

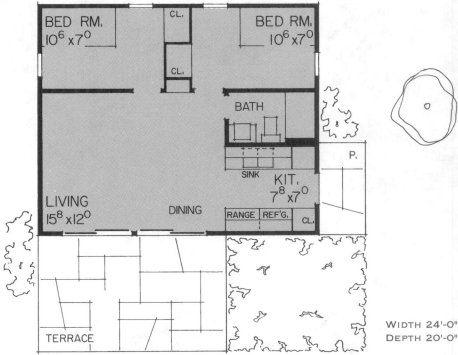

BED RM.
10^6 x 7^0

CL.

BED RM.
10^6 x 7^0

CL.

CL.

BATH

P.

SINK

KIT.
7^8 x 7^0

LIVING
15^8 x 12^0

DINING

RANGE | REF'G. | CL.

TERRACE

WIDTH 24'-0"
DEPTH 20'-0"

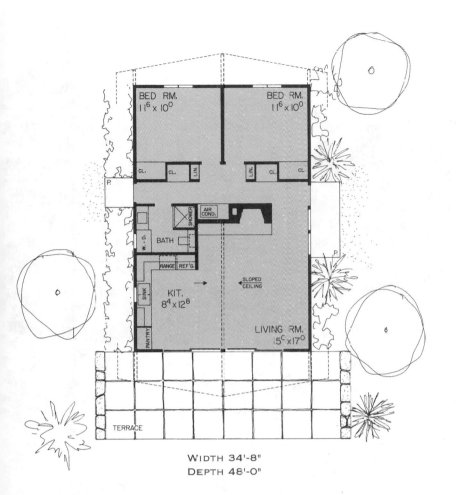

WIDTH 34'-8"
DEPTH 48'-0"

DESIGN 2423

Square Footage: 864

A true vacationer's delight, this two-bedroom home extends the finest contemporary livability. Two sets of sliding glass doors open off the kitchen and living room where a sloped ceiling lends added dimension. In the kitchen, full counter space and cabinetry assure ease in meal preparation. A pantry stores all of your canned and boxed goods. In the living room, a fireplace serves as a nice design as well as a practical feature. The rear of the plan is comprised of two bedrooms of identical size. A nearby full bath holds a washer/dryer unit. Two additional closets, as well as two linen closets, add to storage capabilities.

DESIGN BY
HOME PLANNERS

DESIGN 2439

Square Footage: 1,312

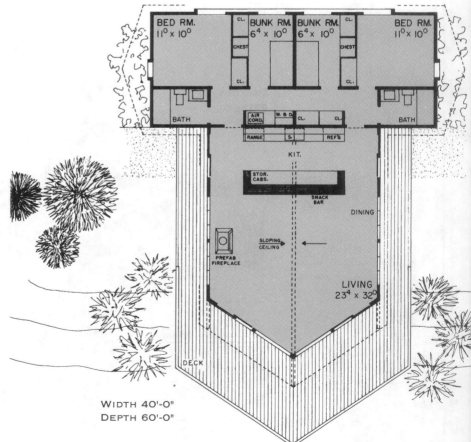

WIDTH 40'-0"
DEPTH 60'-0"

Here is a wonderfully organized plan with an architectural design that commands attention, both inside and out. The dramatic roof lines, pointed glass and gable-end wall bring the outdoors in with beautiful views. The delightful deck echoes the roof line and invites outdoor entertainment. Inside, the spacious living room is crowned by a sloping ceiling with an exposed ridge beam. A free-standing fireplace will make its contribution to a cheerful atmosphere. The sleeping zone has two bedrooms, two bunk rooms, two full baths, two built-in chests and lots of closet space.

DESIGN BY
HOME PLANNERS

DESIGN Q426

Entry Level: 72 square feet
Main Level: 1,253 square feet
Total: 1,325 square feet
Unfinished Lower Level: 1,272 square feet

DESIGN BY
SELECT HOME DESIGNS

A lovely bay window and a recessed entry, complemented by vertical wood siding, enhance the exterior of this split level. Skylights brighten the entry foyer and staircase to the main level. A half-wall separates the staircase and the living room—note the fireplace in the living room. The dining area connects to an L-shaped kitchen with breakfast bay and access to the rear sundeck. Three bedrooms line the left side of the plan. The master suite has a full bath and walk-in closet. Family bedrooms share a full bath just off a skylit hall. The lower level contains 1,272 square feet of unfinished space that can be developed into two additional bedrooms, a full bath, a den and a recreation room. The laundry is also on this level and offers access to a sunken patio.

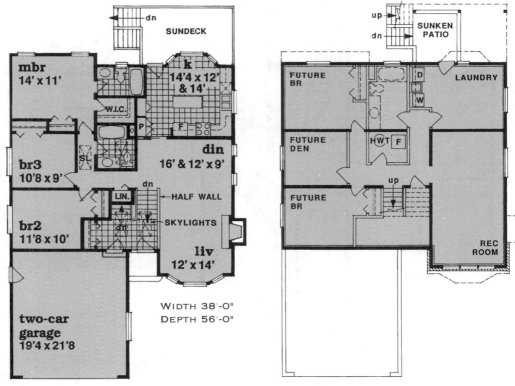

DESIGN Q289

Square Footage: 1,299
Unfinished Lower Level: 514
square feet

DESIGN BY
SELECT HOME DESIGNS

This elegant split-level home is made even more so with columns at the front entry, further adorned by a half-circular transom window. Railings in the living room overlook the cathedral entry. The living room connects to a formal dining room and is warmed by a fireplace. Look for handy buffet space in the dining room. Sliding glass doors lead out to a deck in the dining room and the breakfast room. The kitchen is U-shaped and holds abundant counter space. Two family bedrooms with box-bay windows join a master suite on the left side of the plan. The master has a private bath, while family bedrooms share a full bath. Space on the lower level—514 square feet—can be developed into a family room with fireplace and sliding glass doors to a covered patio. The laundry is also found on this level and includes a full bath. Note the great storage area in the two-car garage.

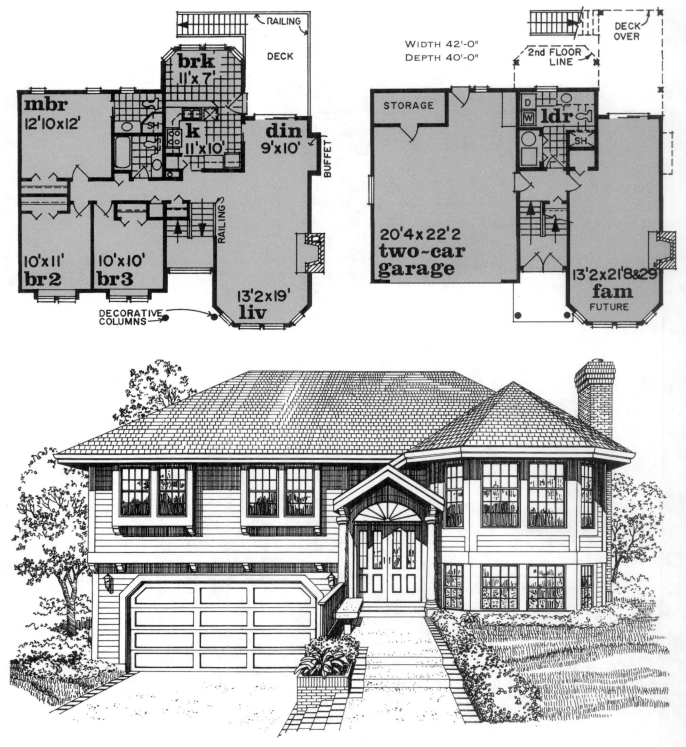

This delightful wood-sided design offers bonus space on the lower level that can be finished later to include a recreation room with patio access and full bath besides the laundry room and single-car garage. The main level holds a living room with fireplace, formal dining room, L-shaped kitchen with bayed breakfast nook and three bedrooms. A sun deck can be reached through sliding glass doors in the nook. The master suite has a walk-in closet and full, private bath, while family bedrooms share a hall bath.

DESIGN Q247

Square Footage: 1,116
Unfinished Lower Level: 765
square feet

DESIGN BY
SELECT HOME DESIGNS

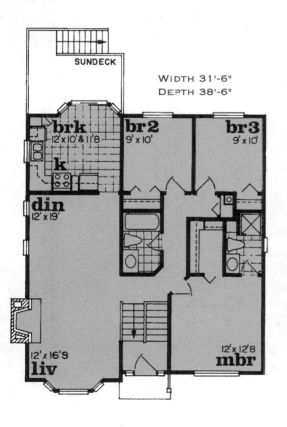

SUNDECK

WIDTH 31'-6"
DEPTH 38'-6"

brk
12' x 10' & 11'8"

k

din
12' x 19'

br2
9' x 10'

br3
9' x 10'

liv
12' x 16'8"

mbr
12' x 12'8"

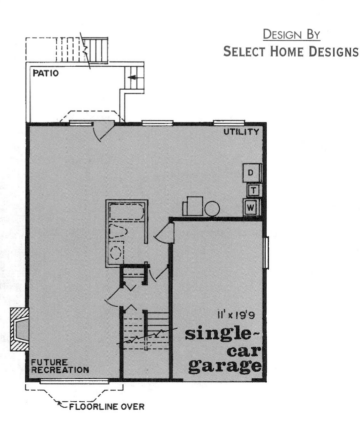

PATIO

UTILITY

D
T
W

FUTURE
RECREATION

single-
car
garage
11' x 19'9"

FLOORLINE OVER

DESIGN Q223

Square Footage: 1,530
Unfinished Lower Level: 1,440
square feet

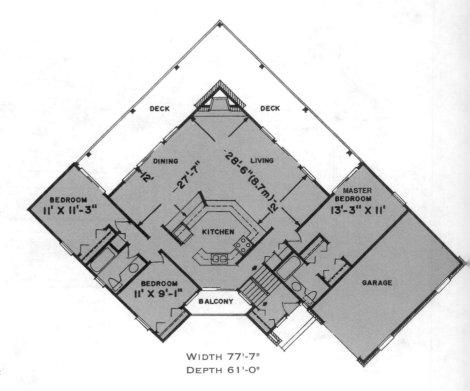

WIDTH 77'-7"
DEPTH 61'-0"

Rustic in nature, this hillside home offers a surrounding deck and upper-level balcony on the exterior to complement its horizontal siding and stone detailing. The entry opens to a staircase leading up to the main level or down to finish-later space in the basement. The kitchen is at the heart of the home and has miles of counter space and a pass-through bar to the dining room. Both the living and dining rooms have sliding glass doors to the deck. A corner fireplace warms and lights both areas. One large bedroom sits to the right of the plan and has a private bath and deck access. Two additional bedrooms with a shared bath sit to the left of the plan. One of these bedrooms has deck access. Unfinished lower-level space adds 1,440 square feet to the total for future development.

DESIGN BY
SELECT HOME DESIGNS

Rear

Craftsman styling and a welcoming porch create marvelous curb appeal for this design. A compact footprint allows economy in construction. A volume ceiling in the living and dining rooms and the kitchen make this home live larger than its modest square footage. The kitchen features generous cabinet space and flows directly into the dining room (note optional buffet) to create a casual country feeling. The master bedroom offers a walk-in closet, full bath and a bumped-out window overlooking the rear yard. Two additional bedrooms also boast bumped-out windows and share a full bath. The lower level provides room for an additional bedroom, a den, a family room and a full bath. Choose the unfinished basement or a crawlspace foundation under the living area. Details for both are included in the plans.

DESIGN Q527

Square Footage: 1,108
Unfinished Lower Level:
620 square feet
Alternative Unfinished Basement:
468 square feet

DESIGN BY
SELECT HOME DESIGNS

DECK

mbr
13'8x11'4

din
9'x11'4
VAULTED

VAULTED
K
8'6x11'4

OPTIONAL
BUFFET

DN

DN

VAULTED
liv
15'2x13'4

SKYLIGHT

br2
9'4x11'

br3
9'4x12'8

PORCH

DN

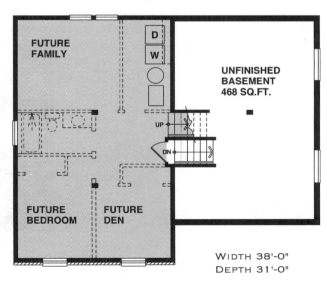

FUTURE FAMILY

D
W

UP

DN

UNFINISHED
BASEMENT
468 SQ.FT.

FUTURE BEDROOM

FUTURE DEN

WIDTH 38'-0"
DEPTH 31'-0"

DESIGN Q432

Square Footage: 2,572
Unfinished Lower Level: 1,607
square feet

California stucco, keystone window details and an open floor plan distinguish this design. The foyer splits to a tray-ceiling living room with fireplace and an arched, floor-to-ceiling window wall—an elegant and formal entertaining area. Stepping up from the foyer is a colonaded hall, which introduces a vaulted family room with built-in media center. French doors beyond open to an expansive railed deck. The gourmet kitchen features a preparation island with salad sink, pantry and a sink under corner windows. The breakfast bay is nearby. The vaulted master bedroom boasts a walk-in closet, access to the rear deck and a sumptuous bath. Two family bedrooms share a full bath. Lower-level space can be developed later.

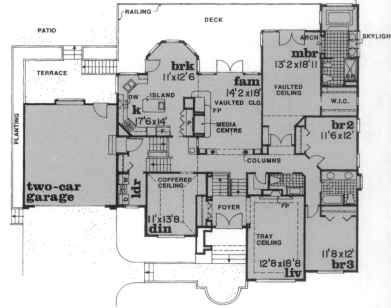

WIDTH 76'-0"
DEPTH 63'-4"

Rear

DESIGN BY
SELECT HOME DESIGNS

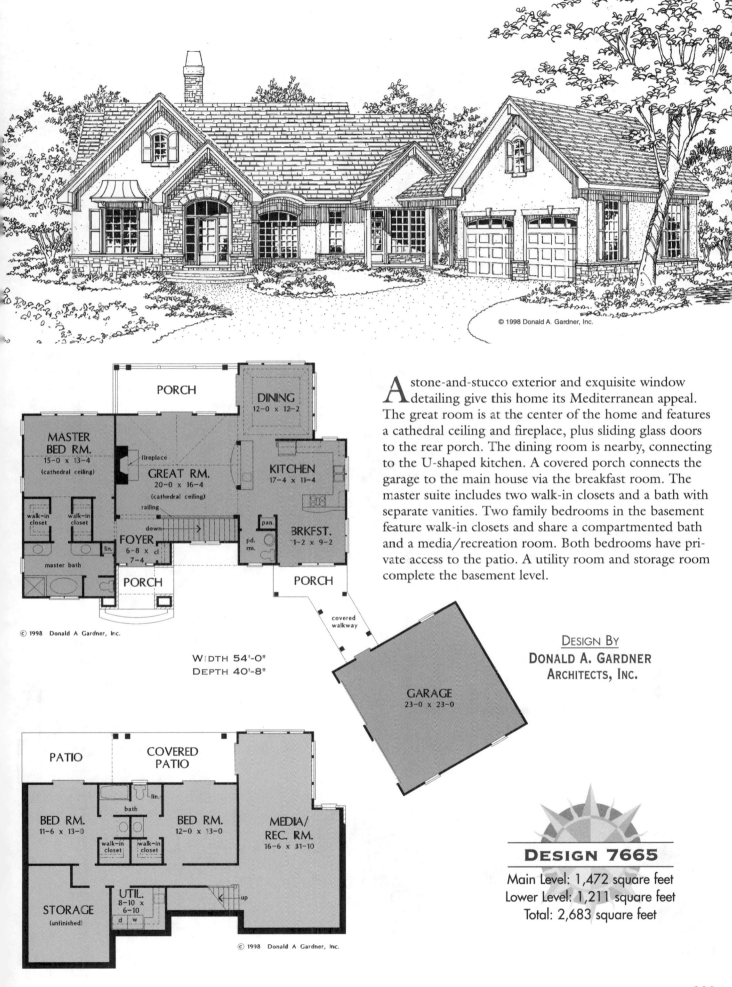

© 1998 Donald A. Gardner, Inc.

PORCH

DINING
12-0 x 12-2

MASTER BED RM.
15-0 x 13-4
(cathedral ceiling)

fireplace

GREAT RM.
20-0 x 16-4
(cathedral ceiling)

railing

KITCHEN
17-4 x 11-4

walk-in closet

walk-in closet

lin.

down

pan.

FOYER
6-8 x cl
7-4

pd. rm.

BRKFST.
?-2 x 9-2

master bath

PORCH

PORCH

© 1998 Donald A Gardner, Inc.

WIDTH 54'-0"
DEPTH 40'-8"

covered walkway

GARAGE
23-0 x 23-0

A stone-and-stucco exterior and exquisite window detailing give this home its Mediterranean appeal. The great room is at the center of the home and features a cathedral ceiling and fireplace, plus sliding glass doors to the rear porch. The dining room is nearby, connecting to the U-shaped kitchen. A covered porch connects the garage to the main house via the breakfast room. The master suite includes two walk-in closets and a bath with separate vanities. Two family bedrooms in the basement feature walk-in closets and share a compartmented bath and a media/recreation room. Both bedrooms have private access to the patio. A utility room and storage room complete the basement level.

DESIGN BY
DONALD A. GARDNER
ARCHITECTS, INC.

PATIO

COVERED PATIO

lin.

bath

BED RM.
11-6 x 13-0

walk-in closet

walk-in closet

BED RM.
12-0 x 13-0

MEDIA/ REC. RM.
16-6 x 31-10

STORAGE
(unfinished)

UTIL.
8-10 x 6-10

d w

up

© 1998 Donald A Gardner, Inc.

DESIGN 7665
Main Level: 1,472 square feet
Lower Level: 1,211 square feet
Total: 2,683 square feet

DESIGN 2761

Main Level: 1,242 square feet
Lower Level: 1,242 square feet
Total: 2,484 square feet

L

This one-story home doubles its livability by exposing the lowest level at the rear. Formal living on the main level and informal living in an activity room and study on the lower level create the best of floor plans. Decks and terraces provide wonderful outdoor livability. The master suite is on the main level for complete privacy. Two family bedrooms reside on the lower level and share a bath with dual sinks.

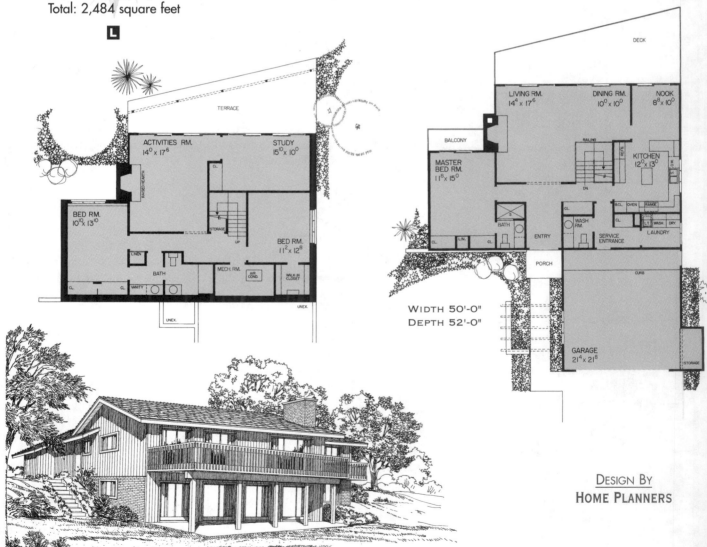

WIDTH 50'-0"
DEPTH 52'-0"

DESIGN BY
HOME PLANNERS

Rear

DESIGN BY
HOME PLANNERS

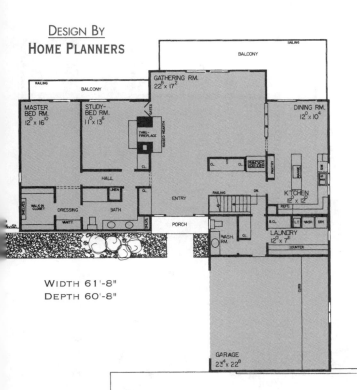

BALCONY RAILING

BALCONY

GATHERING RM.
22⁸ x 17²

MASTER
BED RM.
12⁰ x 16¹⁰

STUDY-
BED RM.
11⁰ x 13⁶

DINING RM.
12⁰ x 10⁴

THRU-
FIREPLACE

HALL

CL

CL

PANTRY

RANGE

ENTRY

RAILING

KITCHEN
12⁰ x 12

WALK-IN
CLOSET

DRESSING

BATH

CL

REF.

VANITY

WASH.
RM.

CL

LAUNDRY
12⁰ x 7⁰

COUNTER

WIDTH 61'-8"
DEPTH 60'-8"

GARAGE
23⁴ x 22⁸

DESIGN 2583

Main Level: 1,838 square feet
Lower Level: 1,558 square feet
Total: 3,396 square feet

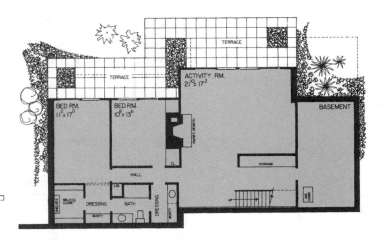

TERRACE

TERRACE

ACTIVITY RM.
21¹⁰ x 17²

BED RM.
11⁰ x 17⁰

BED RM.
10⁸ x 13⁶

BASEMENT

HALL

STORAGE

WALK-IN
CLOSET

DRESSING

BATH

DRESSING

VANITY

UP

AIR
COND.

Rear

Four bedrooms! Or three plus a study, it's your choice. A fireplace in the study/bedroom guarantees a cozy atmosphere. The warmth of a fireplace also will be enjoyed in the gathering room and activities room. Lots of living space, too. An exceptionally large gathering room with sliding glass doors that open onto the main terrace to enjoy the scenic outdoors. A formal dining room, too. And a kitchen that promises to turn a novice cook into a pro. Check out the counter space, the pantry and the island range. Bedrooms include a master suite with dressing area and walk-in closet. Two family bedrooms share a full bath on the lower level. This house is designed to make living pleasant.

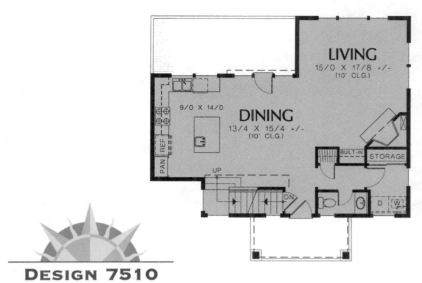

LIVING
15/0 X 17/8 +/-
(10' CLG.)

DINING
13/4 X 15/4 +/-
(10' CLG.)

9/0 X 14/0

PAN | REF

UP

DN

BUILT-IN | STORAGE

D | W

DESIGN 7510

First Floor: 813 square feet
Second Floor: 726 square feet
Total: 1,539 square feet

Wood siding, both vertical and horizontal, works to bring a Craftsman flavor to the exterior of this home. Its wonderful plan has two large storage areas at the garage level—which only add to the spaces above. The first floor includes a living room and dining room open to one another and to the L-shaped island kitchen. A corner fireplace in the living room and deck access in the dining room are extra special accents. A half-bath at the entry sits in front of the laundry and a storage closet. The second floor is devoted to bedrooms: a master suite with private bath and two family bedrooms sharing a full bath.

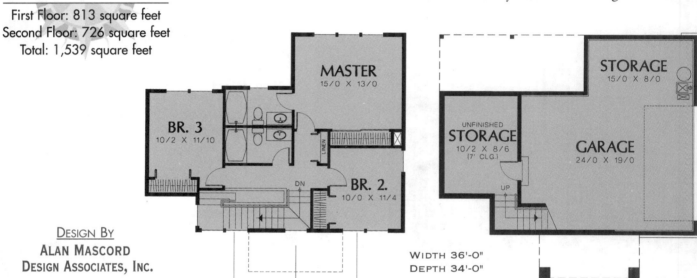

MASTER
15/0 X 13/0

BR. 3
10/2 X 11/10

LINEN

DN

BR. 2.
10/0 X 11/4

STORAGE
15/0 X 8/0

UNFINISHED
STORAGE
10/2 X 8/6
(7' CLG.)

GARAGE
24/0 X 19/0

UP

DESIGN BY
ALAN MASCORD
DESIGN ASSOCIATES, INC.

WIDTH 36'-0"
DEPTH 34'-0"

HOLZHALER
INC.

LIVING
13/0 x 17/0
(10' CLG.)

DINING
10/0 x 15/0
(10' CLG.)

BR. 2
14/0 x 10/0
(8' CLG.)

BUILT-IN   BUILT-IN

UP   DN

DN

REF.

PAN

WIDTH 30'-0"
DEPTH 40'-0"

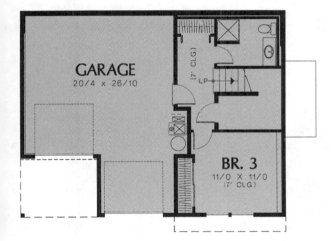

GARAGE
20/4 x 26/10

(7' CLG.)

LP

BR. 3
11/0 x 11/0
(7' CLG.)

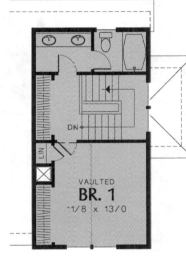

DN

LIN

VAULTED
BR. 1
11/8 x 13/0

DESIGN 7509

First Floor: 954 square feet
Second Floor: 348 square feet
Lower Level: 409 square feet
Total: 1,711 square feet

DESIGN BY
ALAN MASCORD
DESIGN ASSOCIATES, INC.

Just right for a sloping lot, this home has a double garage at the lower level, along with a bedroom and full bath. The main level contains living and dining space, graced by ten-foot ceilings. The living room has a fireplace surrounded by built-ins. The L-shaped kitchen is defined and separated from the living areas by its island work space. A second bedroom and full bath are on the right side of the main level. The second floor contains a private, vaulted bedroom with a long wall closet and a compartmented bath with dual sinks. Note the open deck space just off the living room and facing to the front.

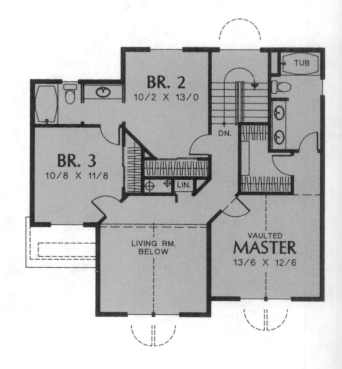

DESIGN 9509

First Floor: 1,022 square feet
Second Floor: 813 square feet
Total: 1,835 square feet

DESIGN BY
ALAN MASCORD
DESIGN ASSOCIATES, INC.

This house not only accommodates a narrow lot, but it also fits a sloping site. Notice how the two-car garage is tucked away under the first level of the house. The angled corner entry gives way to a two-story living room with a tiled hearth. The dining room shares an interesting angled space with this area and enjoys easy service from the efficient kitchen. A large pantry and an angled corner sink add character to this area. The family room offers double doors to a refreshing balcony. A powder room and a laundry room complete the main level. Upstairs, three bedrooms include a vaulted master suite with a private bath. Bedrooms 2 and 3 each take advantage of direct access to a full bath.

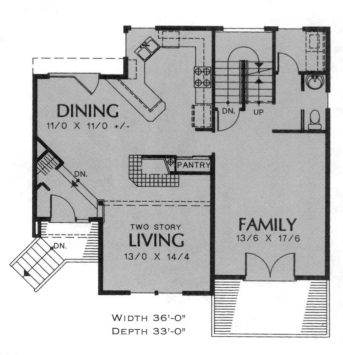

DINING
11/0 X 11/0 +/-

DN.

PANTRY

TWO STORY
LIVING
13/0 X 14/4

DN.

FAMILY
13/6 X 17/6

DN. UP

WIDTH 36'-0"
DEPTH 33'-0"

BR. 2
10/2 X 13/0

TUB

BR. 3
10/8 X 11/8

LIN.

DN.

LIVING RM.
BELOW

VAULTED
MASTER
13/6 X 12/6

This design works best on a lot that slopes to the front, allowing room for the two-car garage and two extra-large storage areas on the lower level. The main level has room for a living room with bay window and deck access, a dining room and an L-shaped island kitchen. Both the living and dining rooms have ten-foot ceilings; the living room also sports a fireplace flanked by built-ins. A large laundry room, half-bath and walk-in pantry are at the back of the plan. The bedrooms are on the second level. Two family rooms share a full bath, while the master suite has a private bath with walk-in closet, spa tub and separate shower.

DESIGN 7516

First Floor: 913 square feet
Second Floor: 811 square feet
Total: 1,724 square feet

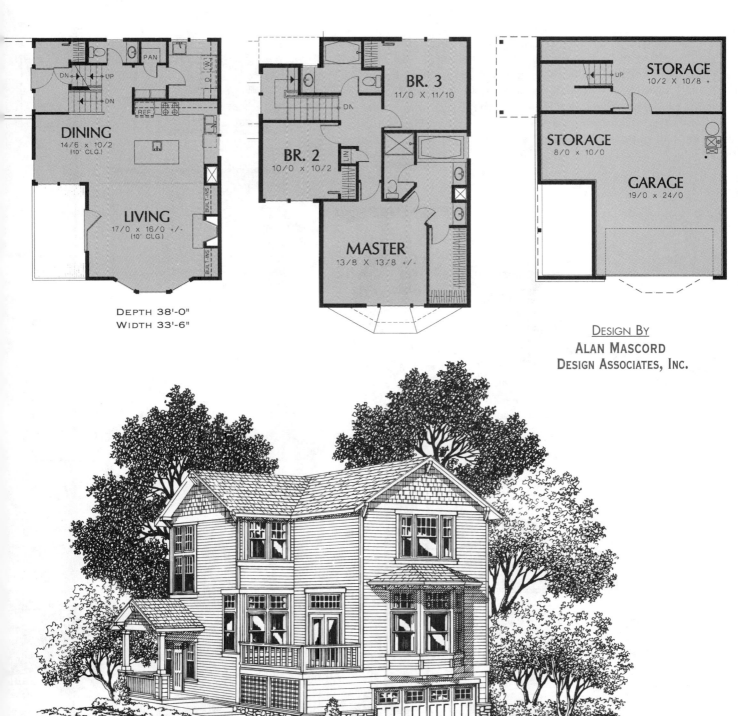

DINING
14/6 x 10/2
(10' CLG.)

LIVING
17/0 x 16/0 +/-
(10' CLG.)

PAN

REF

DEPTH 38'-0"
WIDTH 33'-6"

BR. 3
11/0 X 11/10

BR. 2
10/0 x 10/2

LIN

MASTER
13/8 X 13/8 +/-

STORAGE
10/2 X 10/8 +

STORAGE
8/0 x 10/0

GARAGE
19/0 x 24/0

DESIGN BY
ALAN MASCORD
DESIGN ASSOCIATES, INC.

DESIGN Q224

Square Footage: 1,018
Unfinished Lower Level: 1,018
square feet

DESIGN BY
SELECT HOME DESIGNS

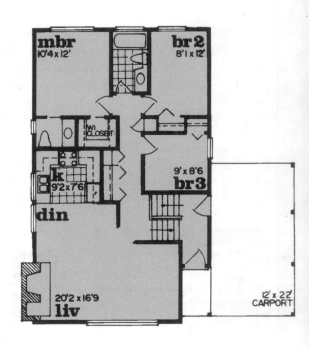

Not only is this compact split-level plan conducive to a narrow lot, but the plans include details for two different exteriors. The floor plan offers a living/dining room with a beautiful view of the front yard and a warming fireplace in the corner. An open kitchen adjoins the dining room and is U-shaped for convenience. A master bedroom with walk-in closet and two family bedrooms share a full bath. The lower level has a fireplace and rough-in plumbing so that it can be developed in the future to a family room, bedroom and bath—or make it a complete in-law suite.

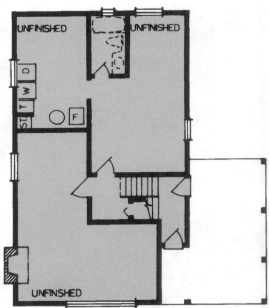

WIDTH 37'-0"
DEPTH 42'-0"

Alternate Exterior

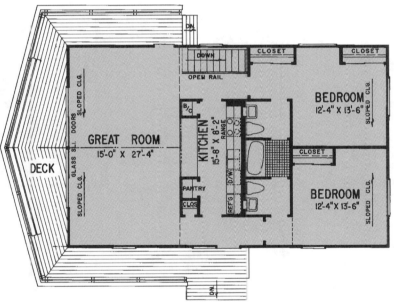

WIDTH 52'-0"
DEPTH 36'-0"

Main Level Floor Plan

DN

DOWN

CLOSET   CLOSET

OPEN RAIL

GREAT ROOM
15'-0" X 27'-4"

KITCHEN
15'-8" X 8'-2"
RANGE

B/C

BEDROOM
12'-4" X 13'-6"

SLOPED CLG.

SLOPED CLG.

SLOPED GLASS DOORS

DECK

SLOPED CLG.

CLOSET

D/W

PANTRY

CLOS.

REF'G

BEDROOM
12'-4" X 13'-6"

SLOPED CLG.

DN.

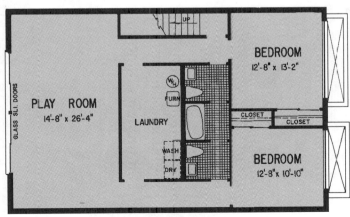

GLASS SLI. DOORS

PLAY ROOM
14'-8" x 26'-4"

UP

W.I.

FURN

LAUNDRY

CLOSET   CLOSET

WASH

DRY

BEDROOM
12'-8" x 13'-2"

BEDROOM
12'-8" x 10'-10"

Optional Basement

DESIGN 4027

Square Footage: 1,320
Unfinished Lower Level: 1,320
square feet

DESIGN BY
HOME PLANNERS

Good things come in small packages! The size and shape of this design will help hold down construction costs without sacrificing livability. The enormous great room is a multi-purpose living space with room for a dining area and several seating areas. Also notice the sloped ceilings. Sliding glass doors provide access to the wraparound deck and sweeping views of the outdoors. The well-equipped kitchen includes a pass-through and pantry. Two bedrooms, each with sloped ceilings and compartmented bath, round out the plan. The unfinished area on the lower level can be developed as needs arise.

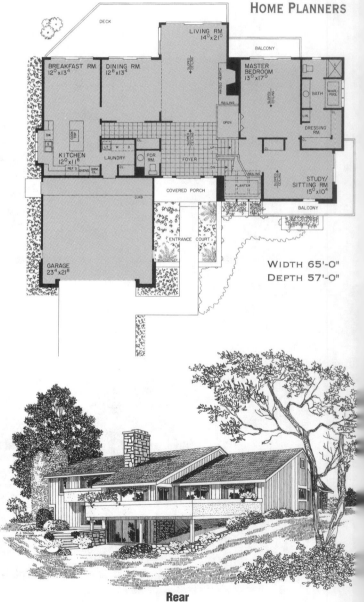

DESIGN 2679

Main Level: 1,179 square feet
Upper Level: 681 square feet
Lower Level: 680 square feet
Family Room Level: 643 square feet
Total: 3,183 square feet

This spacious contemporary home offers plenty of livability on many levels. The central living room features a sloped ceiling and a raised-hearth fireplace. The formal dining room is open to this area and adjacent to the breakfast room and island kitchen. The isolated master bedroom enjoys an adjacent sitting room. Two bedrooms reside on the lower level as does a family room with a wet bar. Note the deck, terraces and balconies for outdoor enjoyment. A two-car garage sits to the front of the plan to save space and to shield the plan from street noise.

WIDTH 65'-0"
DEPTH 57'-0"

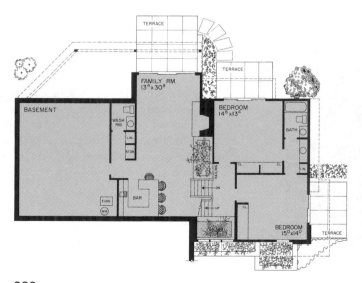

Rear

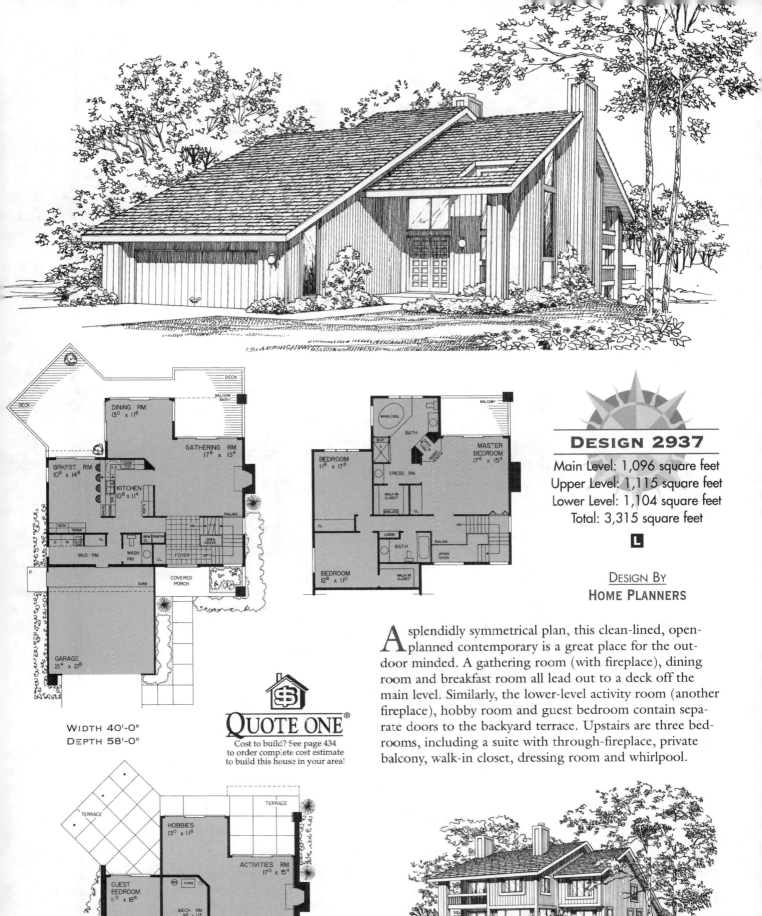

DECK

DINING RM.
13⁰ x 11⁸

GATHERING RM.
17⁸ x 15⁴

BRKFST. RM.
10⁸ x 14⁸

KITCHEN
10⁸ x 11⁵

MUD RM.

WASH RM.

FOYER

COVERED PORCH

GARAGE
21⁴ x 21⁸

WIDTH 40'-0"
DEPTH 58'-0"

BEDROOM
11⁸ x 13⁸

WHIRLPOOL

BATH

DRESS. RM.

MASTER BEDROOM
17⁸ x 15⁴

WALK-IN CLOSET

LINEN

BATH

BEDROOM
12⁸ x 11⁰

WALK-IN CLOSET

DESIGN 2937

Main Level: 1,096 square feet
Upper Level: 1,115 square feet
Lower Level: 1,104 square feet
Total: 3,315 square feet

L

DESIGN BY
HOME PLANNERS

A splendidly symmetrical plan, this clean-lined, open-planned contemporary is a great place for the outdoor minded. A gathering room (with fireplace), dining room and breakfast room all lead out to a deck off the main level. Similarly, the lower-level activity room (another fireplace), hobby room and guest bedroom contain separate doors to the backyard terrace. Upstairs are three bedrooms, including a suite with through-fireplace, private balcony, walk-in closet, dressing room and whirlpool.

QUOTE ONE®
Cost to build? See page 434
to order complete cost estimate
to build this house in your area!

TERRACE

HOBBIES
13⁰ x 11⁸

TERRACE

ACTIVITIES RM.
17⁰ x 15⁴

GUEST BEDROOM
11⁰ x 18⁸

MECH. RM.
9⁰ x 11⁴

LINEN

BATH

Rear

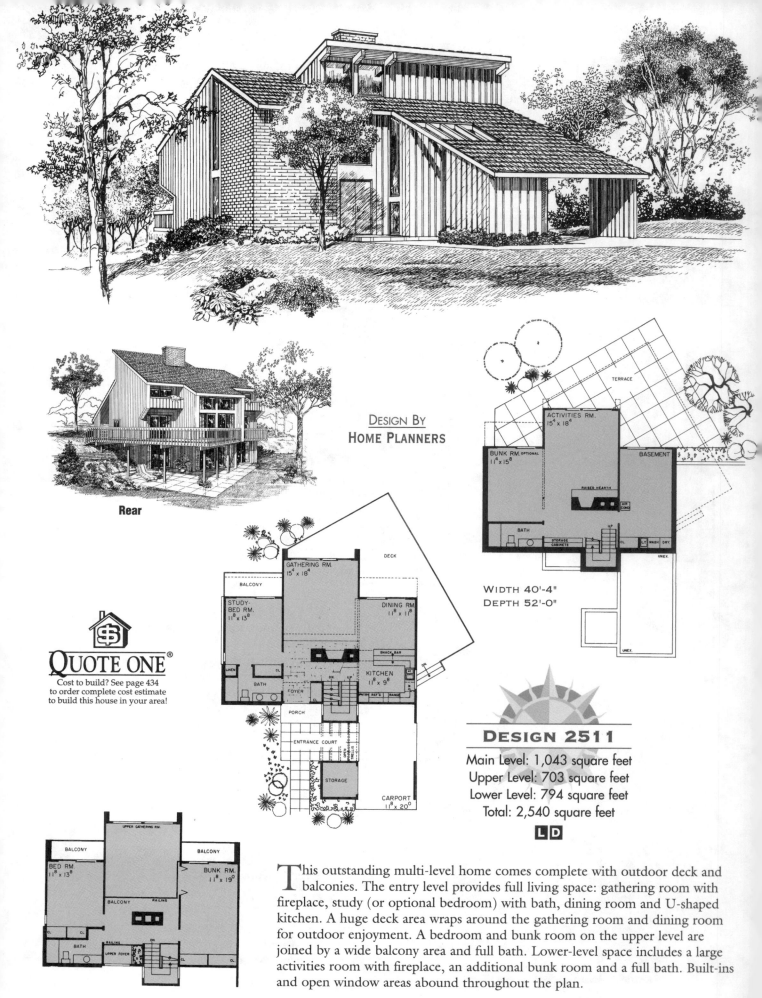

Rear

DESIGN BY
HOME PLANNERS

TERRACE

ACTIVITIES RM.
15⁴ x 18⁴

BUNK RM. OPTIONAL
11⁴ x 15⁸

BASEMENT

RAISED HEARTH

AIR COND.

BATH

STORAGE CABINETS

UP

CL

LT WASH DRY

UNEX.

UNEX.

WIDTH 40'-4"
DEPTH 52'-0"

DECK

GATHERING RM.
15⁴ x 18⁴

BALCONY

STUDY-
BED RM.
11⁸ x 13⁸

DINING RM.
11⁸ x 11⁸

SNACK BAR

LINEN

CL

KITCHEN
11⁸ x 9⁸

BATH

DN UP

PTRY REF G RANGE

FOYER

CL

PORCH

ENTRANCE COURT

OPEN TRELLIS

STORAGE

CARPORT
11⁸ x 20⁰

Quote One®

Cost to build? See page 434
to order complete cost estimate
to build this house in your area!

UPPER GATHERING RM.

BALCONY

BALCONY

BED RM.
11⁸ x 13⁸

BUNK RM.
11⁸ x 19⁰

BALCONY

RAILING

CL CL

RAILING

BATH

UPPER FOYER

DN

CL

CL CL

DESIGN 2511

Main Level: 1,043 square feet
Upper Level: 703 square feet
Lower Level: 794 square feet
Total: 2,540 square feet

L D

This outstanding multi-level home comes complete with outdoor deck and balconies. The entry level provides full living space: gathering room with fireplace, study (or optional bedroom) with bath, dining room and U-shaped kitchen. A huge deck area wraps around the gathering room and dining room for outdoor enjoyment. A bedroom and bunk room on the upper level are joined by a wide balcony area and full bath. Lower-level space includes a large activities room with fireplace, an additional bunk room and a full bath. Built-ins and open window areas abound throughout the plan.

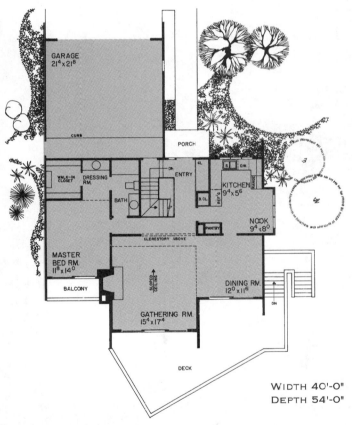

GARAGE
21⁴ x 21⁸

PORCH

WALK-IN CLOSET | DRESSING RM. | ENTRY | KITCHEN 9⁴ x 5⁶

BATH

NOOK 9⁴ x 8⁰

PANTRY

CLERESTORY ABOVE

MASTER BED RM. 11⁸ x 14⁰

BALCONY

SLOPED CEILING

DINING RM. 12⁰ x 11⁶

GATHERING RM. 15⁴ x 17⁴

DECK

WIDTH 40'-0"
DEPTH 54'-0"

DESIGN 2485

Main Level: 1,108 square feet
Lower Level: 983 square feet
Total: 2,091 square feet

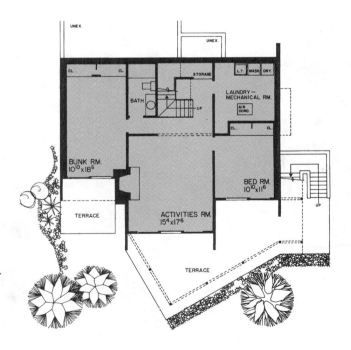

UNEX.

UNEX.

CL. | CL. | STORAGE | L.T. WASH. DRY.

BATH | UP | LAUNDRY — MECHANICAL RM.

AIR COND.

CL. | CL.

BUNK RM. 10¹⁰ x 18⁵

BED RM. 10¹⁰ x 11⁶

TERRACE

ACTIVITIES RM. 15⁴ x 17⁶

UP

TERRACE

This hillside vacation home contains lots of livability. Notice the projecting deck and how it shelters the terrace. Each of the generous glassed areas is protected from the summer sun by overhangs and extended walls. The gathering room is sure to please with its fireplace. The U-shaped kitchen easily serves an adjacent nook as well as the formal dining room. The master suite is on the first floor and features a dressing room and walk-in closet. A secondary bedroom and bunk room are on the lower level and share a full hall bath. Note the rear-facing garage which connects to the main house at the entry.

DESIGN BY
HOME PLANNERS

DESIGN 4115

Entry Level: 1,494 square feet
Upper Level: 597 square feet
Total: 2,091 square feet

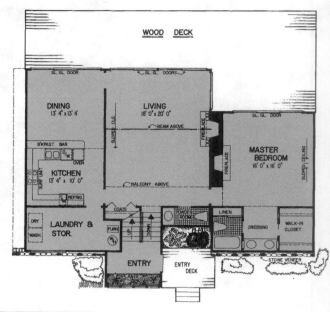

I nterior spaces are dramatically pro-portioned because of the long and varied rooflines of this contemporary. The two-story living area has a sloped ceiling, as does the master bedroom and two upper-level bedrooms. Two fireplaces, a huge wooden deck, a small upstairs sitting room and a liberal number of windows—including sliding glass doors to the deck—make this a most comfortable residence. The kitchen is U-shaped for convenience and has a breakfast bar through to the dining room. Note the large convenient laundry room.

DESIGN BY
HOME PLANNERS

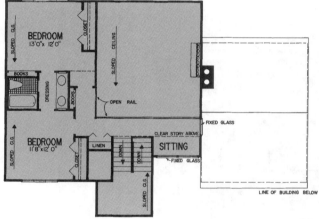

WIDTH 50'-8"
DEPTH 47'-8"

242

Design 2431

First Floor: 1,057 square feet
Second Floor: 406 square feet
Total: 1,463 square feet

Dramatic use of glass and sweeping lines characterize a class favorite—the A-frame. The sloped ceiling and exposed beams in this one's living room are gorgeous touches complemented by a wide deck for enjoying the fresh air. Two additional decks adorn the entry and the kitchen entrance. The convenience of a central bath with attached powder room is accentuated by space here for a washer and dryer. The truly outstanding feature of this plan, however, is its magnificent master suite. There's a private balcony outside and a balcony lounge inside—the scenery is splendid from every angle.

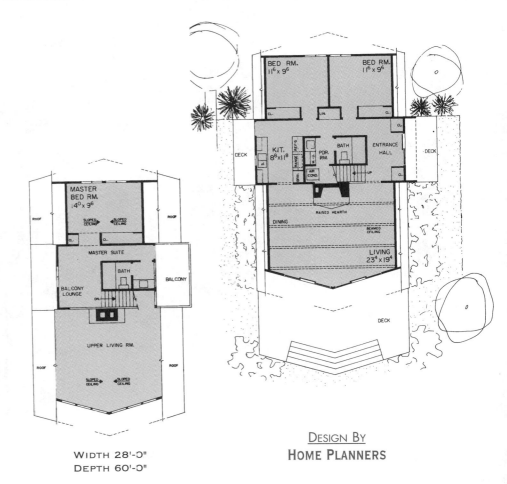

WIDTH 28'-0"
DEPTH 60'-0"

Design By
Home Planners

DESIGN 1432

First Floor: 1,512 square feet
Second Floor: 678 square feet
Total: 2,190 square feet

DESIGN BY
HOME PLANNERS

Perhaps more than any other design in recent years, the A-frame has captured the imagination of the prospective vacation home builder. There is a gala air about its shape that fosters a holiday spirit whether the house be a summer retreat or a structure for year 'round living. This particular A-frame offers a lot of living with five bedrooms, two baths, an efficient kitchen, a family/dining area and outstanding storage. As in most designs of this type, the living room with its great height and large glass area is extremely dramatic at first sight. It opens to a huge sun deck that wraps around two sides of the design.

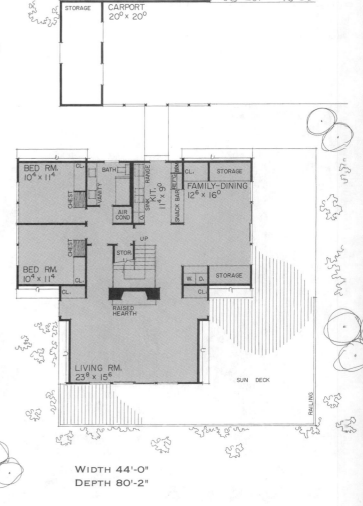

WIDTH 44'-0"
DEPTH 80'-2"

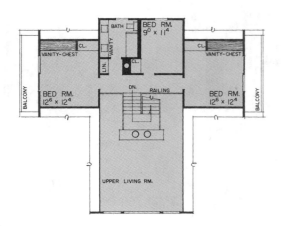

Three-level living results in family living patterns which will foster a delightful feeling of informality. Upon arrival at this charming second home, each family member will enthusiastically welcome the change in environment—both indoors and out. Whether looking down into the living room from the dormitory balcony, or walking through the sliding doors onto the huge deck, or participating in some family activity in the game room, everyone will count the hours spent here as relaxing ones. Study the plan carefully. Note the sleeping facilities on each of the three levels. Two bedrooms and a dormitory in all to sleep the family and friends comfortably. There are two full baths, a separate laundry room and plenty of storage. Don't miss the efficient U-shaped kitchen.

DESIGN 1499

Main Level: 896 square feet
Upper Level: 298 square feet
Lower Level: 896 square feet
Total: 2,090 square feet

DESIGN BY
HOME PLANNERS

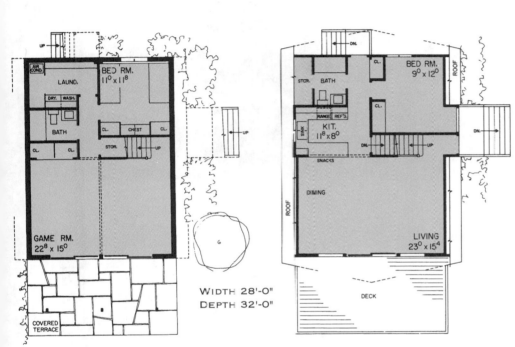

WIDTH 28'-0"
DEPTH 32'-0"

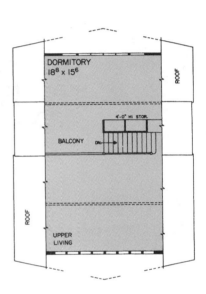

DESIGN 2459

First Floor: 1,264 square feet
Second Floor: 556 square feet
Total: 1,820 square feet

The look of this A-frame is dramatic. The soaring roof projections highlight the slanted glass gable end. The expanse of the roof is broken to provide access to the side deck from the dining room. Above is the balcony of the second-floor lounge. This room with its high sloping ceiling looks down into the spacious first-floor living room where a fireplace waits to warm cool evenings and a wall of windows provides glorious views. The master bedroom also has an outdoor balcony. There are two large bedrooms and a kitchen rounding out this wonderful vacation home.

DESIGN BY
HOME PLANNERS

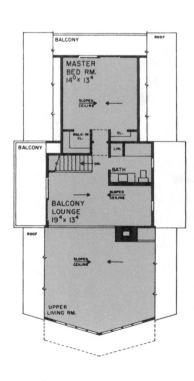

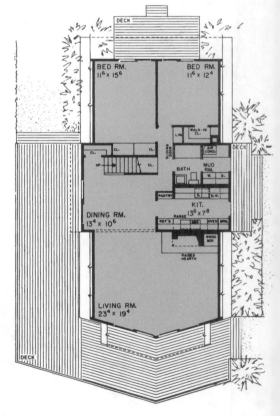

WIDTH 40'-0"
DEPTH 72'-0"

The level, A-frame living can be dramatic and, also, offer your family living patterns that will be a lot of fun throughout the year. The ceiling of the living room soars upward to an apex of approximately twenty-four feet. Both the second floor and the upper-level loft overlook the living room below. The wall of glass permits a fine view of the outdoors from each of these levels. With all those sleeping facilities, even the largest family will have space left over for friends. Note two baths, efficient kitchen, snack bar and deck, which are available to serve your everyday needs.

DESIGN 1470

First Floor: 1,000 square feet
Second Floor: 482 square feet
Loft: 243 square feet
Total: 1,725 square feet

DESIGN BY
HOME PLANNERS

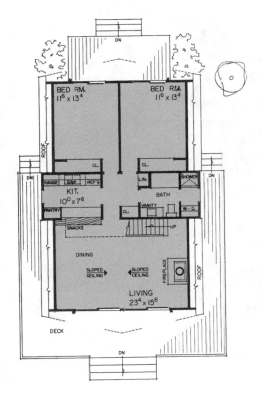

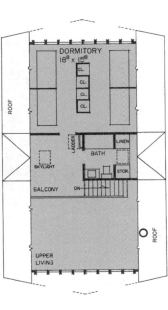

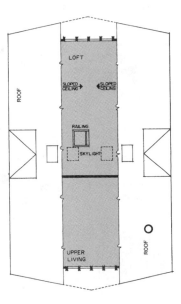

WIDTH 36'-4"
DEPTH 56'-4"

DESIGN 1491

First Floor: 576 square feet
Second Floor: 234 square feet
Total: 810 square feet

DESIGN BY
HOME PLANNERS

Whether situated in the north-ern woods or on the southern coast, this enchanting A-frame will function as a perfect retreat. Whether called upon to serve as a ski lodge or a summer haven, it will perform admirably. The large liv-ing/dining room area offers direct access to a huge outdoor deck and an efficient kitchen fulfills all family meal needs. A bedroom and full bath complete this floor. Upstairs is a large loft perfect for bunks or use as a game room.

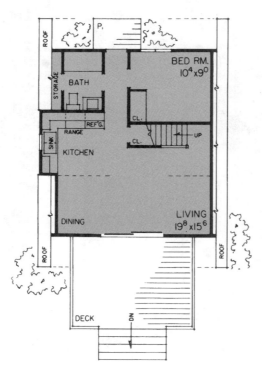

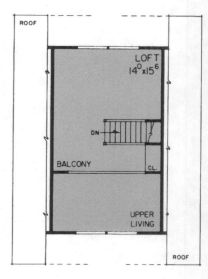

WIDTH 24'-0"
DEPTH 36'-0"

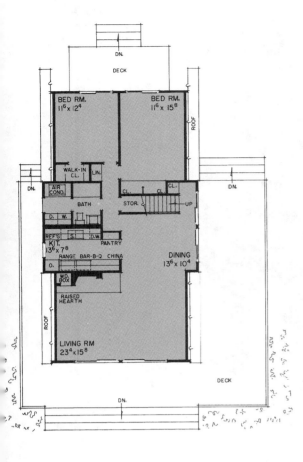

BED RM.
11⁶ x 12⁴

BED RM.
11⁶ x 15⁸

DECK
DN.
ROOF
DN.
DN.

WALK-IN CL.   LIN.
AIR COND.
BATH   STOR.   CL.   CL.   CL.   UP
D.   W.
REF'G   S.   D.W.
KIT.
13⁶ x 7⁸   PANTRY
RANGE   BAR-B-Q   CHINA
O.
W.D. BOX
RAISED HEARTH

DINING
13⁶ x 10⁴

ROOF

LIVING RM
23⁴ x 15⁸

DECK
DN.

DESIGN BY
HOME PLANNERS

WIDTH 44'-0"
DEPTH 48'-4"

ROOF   BALCONY
MASTER BED RM.
14⁰ x 13⁴

CL.
WALK-IN CL.
BATH   DN.

ROOF
LOUNGE
ROOF
RAIL

UPPER LIVING RM.

DESIGN 1451

First Floor: 1,224 square feet
Second Floor: 464 square feet
Total: 1,688 square feet

This dramatic A-frame will surely command its share of attention wherever located. Its soaring roof and large glass areas put this design in a class all on its own. Raised wood decks on all sides provide delightful outdoor living areas. In addition, there is a balcony outside the second floor master bedroom. The living room is the focal point of the interior. The attractive raised-hearth fireplace is a favorite feature. Another favored highlight is the lounge area of the second floor overlooking the living room. The kitchen work center has all the conveniences of home. Note the barbecue unit, pantry and china cabinet, which are sure to make living easy. Two secondary bedrooms complete this plan.

A. J. YOUNG
FUQUAY VARINA N.C.

DESIGN 1406

First Floor: 776 square feet
Second Floor: 300 square feet
Total: 1,076 square feet

A spacious living room is really a plus in a vacation home—especially when it has a high, vaulted ceiling and a complete wall of windows. Because of the wonderful glass area, the livability of the living room seems to spill right out onto the huge wood deck. In addition to the bedrooms downstairs, there is a sizable dormitory upstairs for sleeping quite a crew. Sliding glass doors open onto the outdoor balcony from the dormitory. Don't miss the fireplace, the efficient kitchen and the numerous storage facilities. The outside storage units are accessible from just below the roofline and are great for stowing recreational equipment.

DESIGN BY
HOME PLANNERS

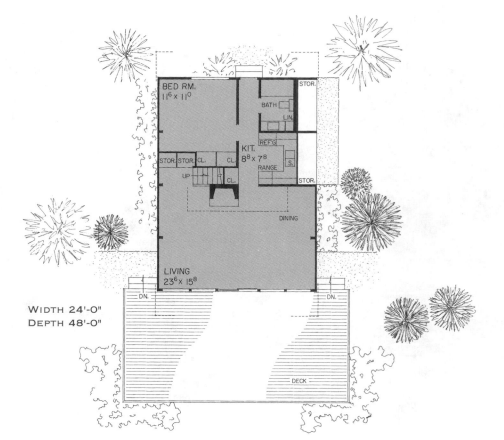

WIDTH 24'-0"
DEPTH 48'-0"

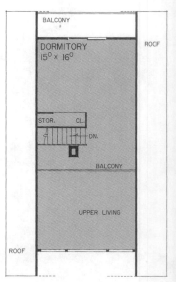

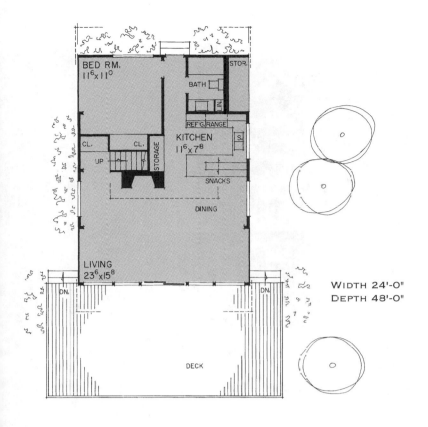

BED RM.
11⁶x11⁰

STOR.

BATH

REF'G. RANGE

KITCHEN
11⁶x7⁸

CL. CL.

UP

STORAGE

S.

SNACKS

DINING

LIVING
23⁶x15⁸

DN.

DN.

DECK

DESIGN 1448

First Floor: 776 square feet
Second Floor: 300 square feet
Total: 1,076 square feet

DESIGN BY
HOME PLANNERS

WIDTH 24'-0"
DEPTH 48'-0"

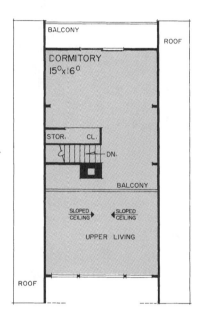

BALCONY

ROOF

DORMITORY
15⁰x16⁰

STOR. CL.

DN.

BALCONY

SLOPED CEILING → ← SLOPED CEILING

UPPER LIVING

ROOF

If you've got a smaller crew and prefer a low-maintenance vacation home, this plan is perfect for you. Its A-frame configuration allows for a roomy dormitory loft on the second level where kids or guests can stay and even enjoy a private balcony. The first level has a private bedroom and full bath. The efficient kitchen has a snack bar for easy dining. The large front deck offers outdoor options. For winter vacationing, enjoy the cozy hearth in the living room, which has a full wall of windows overlooking the deck. A large storage space on the outside works well for stowing equipment and little-used items.

DESIGN Q200

First Floor: 1,094 square feet
Second Floor: 576 square feet
Total: 1,670 square feet

DESIGN BY
SELECT HOME DESIGNS

A covered veranda with covered patio above opens through French doors to the living/dining area of this vacation cottage. A masonry fireplace with wood storage bin warms this area. A modified U-shaped kitchen serves the dining room; a laundry is just across the hall with access to a side veranda. The master bedroom is on the first floor and has the use of a full bath. Sliding glass doors in the master bedroom and the living room lead to still another veranda. The second floor has two family bedrooms, a full bath and a family room with a balcony overlooking the living room and dining room, a fireplace and double doors to a patio. A large storage area on this level adds convenience.

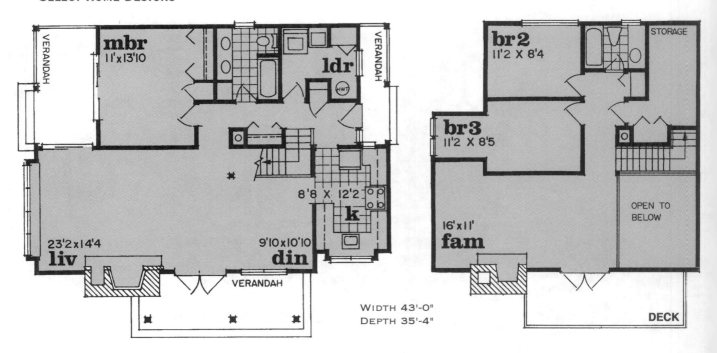

WIDTH 43'-0"
DEPTH 35'-4"

S tone and siding complement this cozy design, with chalet features. The vaulted living and dining rooms, with exposed beam ceilings, are open to the loft above. A spacious wood storage area is found off the living room to feed the warm hearth inside. The kitchen features a pass-through counter to the dining area and leads to a laundry room with work bench. The master suite is on the first floor and has a private patio and bath. An additional half-bath is located in the main hall. The second floor holds a family room with a deck and two family bedrooms with shared bath.

DESIGN Q292

First Floor: 1,036 square feet
Second Floor: 630 square feet
Total: 1,666 square feet

DESIGN BY
SELECT HOME DESIGNS

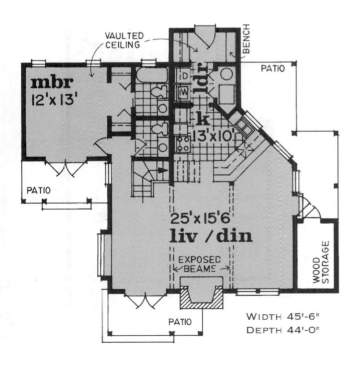

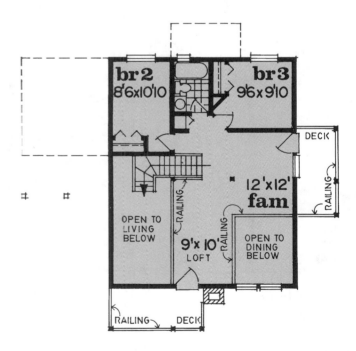

Design Q208

First Floor: 780 square feet
Second Floor: 601 square feet
Total: 1,381 square feet

This A-frame cottage takes advantage of a front view from a deck and a balcony. The side entrance has direct access to the laundry/mud room, which connects directly into the galley kitchen. The open living and dining rooms are warmed by a wood stove and stretch out to enjoy the deck. The master bedroom is to the rear and has a walk-in closet and a bath nearby. Two bedrooms upstairs have large wall closets and share a full bath. Bedroom 3 has double doors to the balcony.

Design By
Select Home Designs

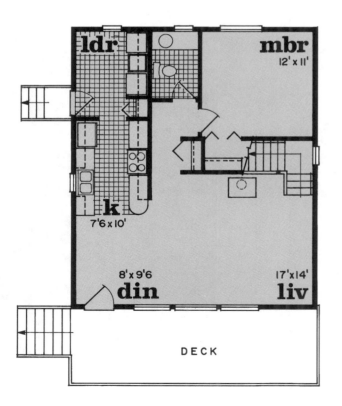

ldr

mbr
12' x 11'

k
7'6 x 10'

8' x 9'6
din

17'x14'
liv

DECK

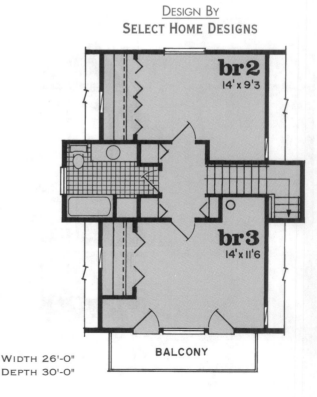

br2
14' x 9'3

br3
14' x 11'6

BALCONY

Width 26'-0"
Depth 30'-0"

A surrounding sun deck and expansive window wall capitalize on vacation-home views in this design. The full-height windows flood the living and dining rooms with abundant natural light and bring attention to the high vaulted ceilings. A wood stove in the living area warms cold winter nights. The efficient U-shaped kitchen has ample counter and cupboard space. Behind it is a laundry room and rear entrance. The master bedroom sits on this floor and has a large wall closet and full bath. Two family bedrooms are on the second floor and have use of a half-bath.

DESIGN Q424

First Floor: 898 square feet
Second Floor: 358 square feet
Total: 1,256 square feet

DESIGN BY
SELECT HOME DESIGNS

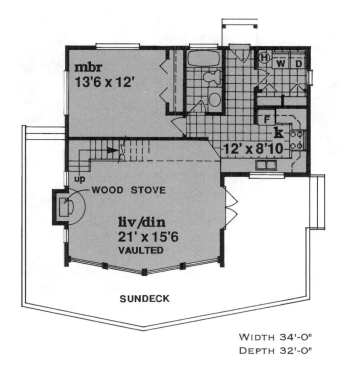

mbr
13'6 x 12'

H W D

F

k
12' x 8'10

up

WOOD STOVE

liv/din
21' x 15'6
VAULTED

SUNDECK

WIDTH 34'-0"
DEPTH 32'-0"

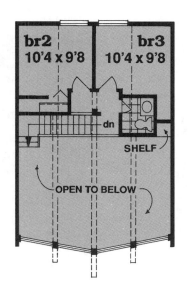

br2
10'4 x 9'8

br3
10'4 x 9'8

dn

SHELF

OPEN TO BELOW

255

DESIGN Q491

Square Footage: 1,197
Vaulted Loft: 497 square feet

DESIGN BY
SELECT HOME DESIGNS

A fieldstone fireplace and wrapping deck add much to the rustic beauty of this design. An expansive window wall highlights the living and dining room's vaulted ceiling and fills the area with natural light. An oversized masonry fireplace is flanked by a set of sliding glass doors opening to the deck. The U-shaped kitchen has great counter and shelf space. Pocket doors seclude it from the dining room and the laundry room at the back. Behind the laundry room is a bedroom with wall closet. It shares a bath with the master bedroom, which has a walk-in closet. A vaulted loft can serve as additional sleeping space. Plans include details for both a basement and a crawlspace foundation.

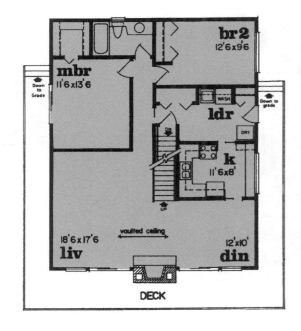

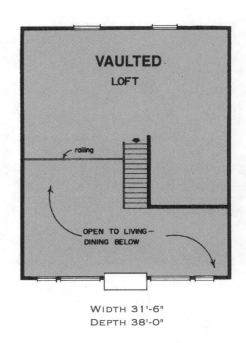

WIDTH 31'-6"
DEPTH 38'-0"

An expansive sun deck with optional spa wraps around this design to highlight outdoor living. Tall windows accent the living and dining rooms' vaulted ceiling. Both areas are warmed by a central fireplace flanked by doors to the deck. A U-shaped kitchen is open to the dining room. Two bedrooms with walk-in closets sit to the back of the first floor. They share the use of a full bath. The master suite dominates the upper level and has a full bath and large wall closet. Note the laundry room and side entries. Plans include details for both a basement and a crawlspace foundation.

DESIGN Q295

First Floor: 1,235 square feet
Second Floor: 543 square feet
Total: 1,778 square feet

DESIGN BY
SELECT HOME DESIGNS

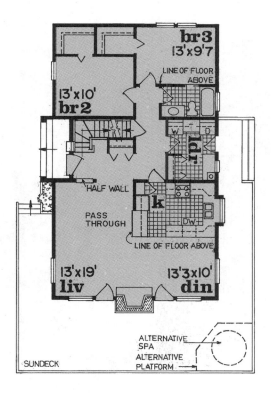

br3
13'x9'7

LINE OF FLOOR ABOVE

13'x10'
br2

lpr.

HALF WALL

PASS THROUGH

k

Dw

LINE OF FLOOR ABOVE

13'x19'
liv

13'3x10'
din

SUNDECK

ALTERNATIVE SPA

ALTERNATIVE PLATFORM

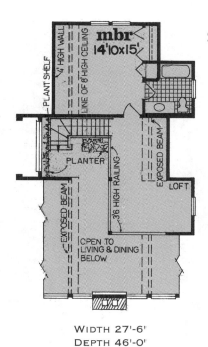

PLANT SHELF

4' HIGH WALL
LINE OF 8' HIGH CEILING

mbr
14'10x15'

EXPOSED BEAM

PLANTER

36' HIGH RAILING

EXPOSED BEAM

EXPOSED BEAM

LOFT

OPEN TO LIVING & DINING BELOW

WIDTH 27'-6'
DEPTH 46'-0'

257

DESIGN Q430

First Floor: 1,061 square feet
Second Floor: 482 square feet
Total: 1,543 square feet

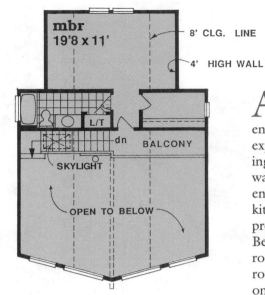

mbr
19'8 x 11'

8' CLG. LINE

4' HIGH WALL

L/T

dn

BALCONY

SKYLIGHT

OPEN TO BELOW

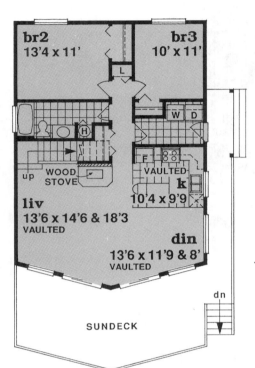

br2
13'4 x 11'

br3
10' x 11'

L

W D

up WOOD STOVE

F

VAULTED

k
10'4 x 9'9

liv
13'6 x 14'6 & 18'3
VAULTED

din
13'6 x 11'9 & 8'
VAULTED

dn

SUNDECK

WIDTH 28'-0"
DEPTH 39'-9"

A sun deck makes this design popular, but it is enhanced by views through an expansive wall of glass in the living and dining rooms. They are warmed by a wood stove and enjoy vaulted ceilings, as well. The kitchen is also vaulted and has a prep island and breakfast bar. Behind the kitchen is a laundry room with side access. Two bedrooms and a full bath are found on the first floor. A skylit staircase leads up to the master bedroom and its walk-in closet and private bath on the second floor.

DESIGN BY
SELECT HOME DESIGNS

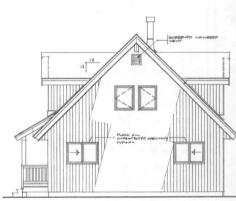

SCREENED LOUVERED VENT

12
12

FLASH ALL UNPROTECTED OPENINGS TYPICAL

Rear Elevation

This leisure home is perfect for outdoor living with French doors opening to a large sun deck and sunken spa. The open-beam, vaulted ceiling and high window wall provide views for the living and dining rooms, which are decorated with wood columns and warmed by a fireplace. The step-saving U-shaped kitchen has ample counter space and a bar counter to the dining room. The master bedroom on the first floor features a walk-in closet and bath with twin vanity, shower and soaking tub. A convenient mud room with adjoining laundry accesses a rear deck. Two bedrooms are on the second floor and share a full bath. Bedroom 3 sports a vaulted ceiling. Plans include details for both a basement and a crawlspace foundation.

DESIGN Q499

First Floor: 1,157 square feet
Second Floor: 638 square feet
Total: 1,795 square feet

DESIGN BY
SELECT HOME DESIGNS

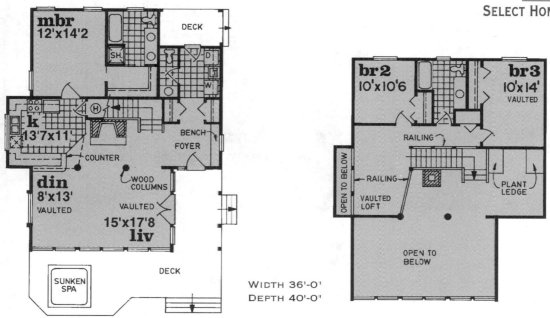

WIDTH 36'-0"
DEPTH 40'-0"

259

Design Q492

First Floor: 974 square feet
Second Floor: 322 square feet
Total: 1,296 square feet

With a striking roofline and impressive stone chimney, this cottage is the essence of rustic design. Walls of glass fill the living/dining room and the kitchen with sunlight. A corner hearth serves both the living and dining areas and allows for a built-in barbecue on the wide wrapping deck. The U-shaped kitchen has a built-in breakfast bar. Two bedrooms sit to the rear of the home and share the use of a full bath. A third bedroom on the second level has a balcony overlook to the living area below. Note the extra large storage areas on the second floor.

Design By
SELECT HOME DESIGNS

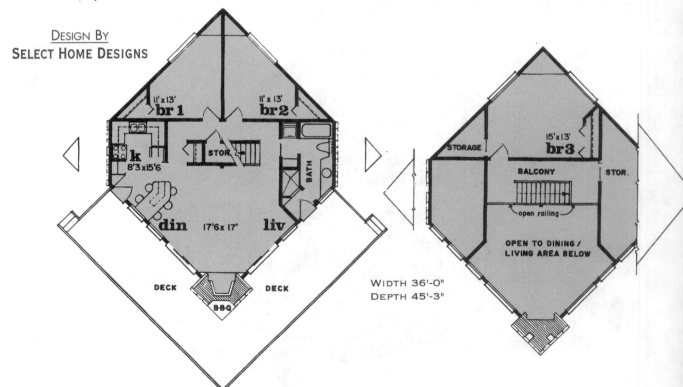

WIDTH 36'-0"
DEPTH 45'-3"

With a deck to the front, this vacation home can't miss out on any outdoor fun. The living and dining rooms are dominated by a window wall to take advantage of the view. A high vaulted ceiling and wood-burning fireplace create a warm atmosphere. The U-shaped kitchen, with adjoining laundry room, is open to the dining room with a pass-through counter. Note the deck beyond the kitchen and full wall closet. The master bedroom is to the rear and has the use of a full bath with large linen closet. Two family bedrooms are upstairs and share a full bath with skylight. Plans include details for both a basement and a crawlspace foundation.

DESIGN Q439

First Floor: 1,042 square feet
Second Floor: 456 square feet
Total: 1,498 square feet

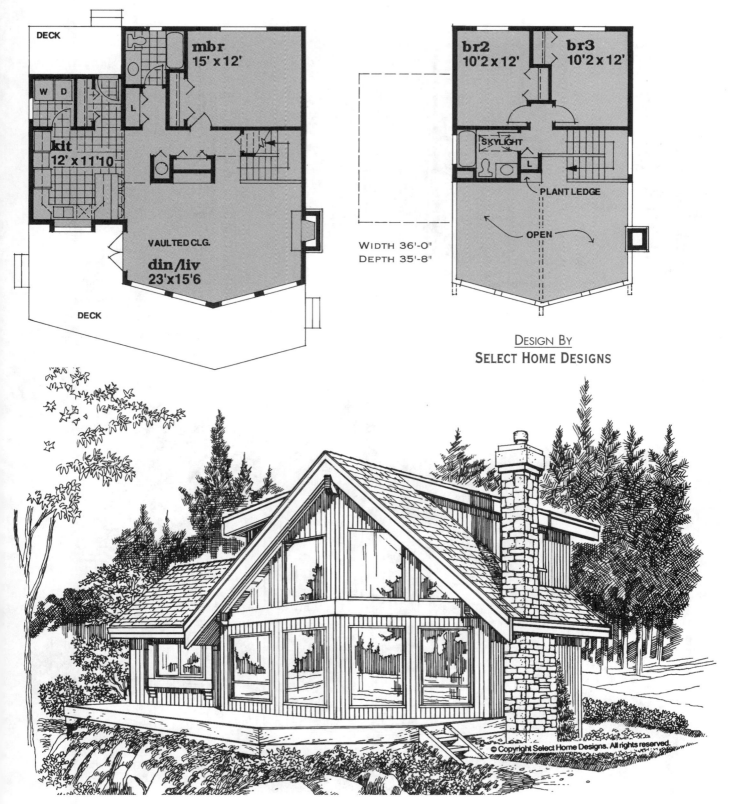

DECK

mbr
15' x 12'

W   D

L

kit
12' x 11'10

VAULTED CLG.

din/liv
23' x 15'6

DECK

br2
10'2 x 12'

br3
10'2 x 12'

SKYLIGHT

L

PLANT LEDGE

OPEN

WIDTH 36'-0"
DEPTH 35'-8"

DESIGN BY
SELECT HOME DESIGNS

Design Q428

First Floor: 878 square feet
Second Floor: 262 square feet
Total: 1,140 square feet

Windows galore and sliding glass doors take advantage of views in this vacation home. A full deck wraps around to the side to a covered side entry. Vaulted ceilings throughout the living and dining rooms and the large upstairs bedroom give a feeling of spaciousness to the plan and allow for tall, bright windows. The kitchen is open to the dining room and is galley-style. Two bedrooms line the rear of the plan—a master bedroom and a secondary bedroom. They share the full bath, along with Bedroom 3. Convenient storage is found under the stairs.

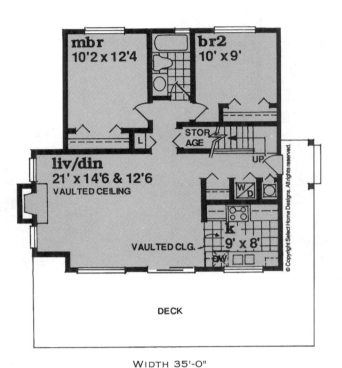

WIDTH 35'-0"
DEPTH 30'-6"

DESIGN BY
SELECT HOME DESIGNS

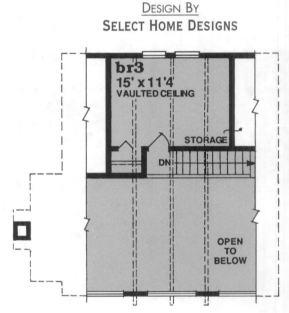

Rear

DESIGN Q493

First Floor: 922 square feet
Second Floor: 683 square feet
Total: 1,605 square feet

DESIGN BY
SELECT HOME DESIGNS

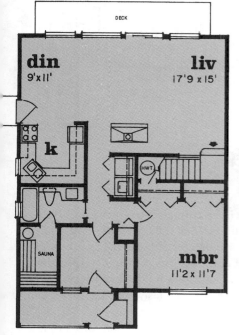

DECK

din
9'x11'

liv
17'9 x 15'

k

HWT

SAUNA

mbr
11'2 x 11'7

WIDTH 27'-7"
DEPTH 39'-5"

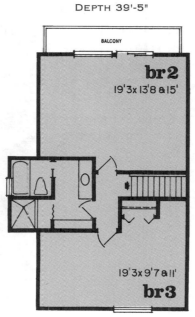

BALCONY

br2
19'3x 13'8 &15'

19'3x 9'7 &11'
br3

This charming cottage is the perfect size and configuration for a leisure-time home. A weather-protected entry opens to a mud room and serves as a storage space and air lock. The gathering area is comprised of a living room and a dining room and is warmed by a wood-burning stove. An entire wall of glass with sliding doors opens to a rear deck. The master bedroom is on the first floor and features a main-floor bath with attached sauna. Two bedrooms and a full bath are on the second floor. Bedroom 2 has a private balcony.

DESIGN Q209

First Floor: 900 square feet
Second Floor: 780 square feet
Total: 1,680 square feet

DESIGN BY
SELECT HOME DESIGNS

This leisure cottage offers spacious living within a chalet-style exterior. The front entry opens directly into the living room/dining room combination, which is warmed by a hearth and features a full wall of windows. The nearby galley kitchen leads to a laundry room in the rear. One bedroom and a full bath sit in the opposite corner. The second level holds a master bedroom with double closets and fireplace and two family bedrooms. There is an additional full bathroom on this level. Note the wide balcony that graces the master bedroom and the single-car garage to the rear.

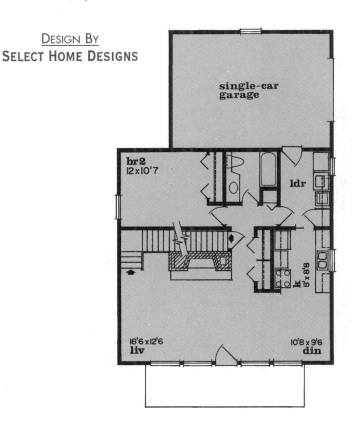

single-car garage

br2
12 x 10'7

ldr

k
8 x 8'8

18'6 x 12'6
liv

10'8 x 9'6
din

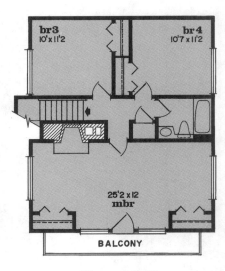

br3
10' x 11'2

br 4
10'7 x 11'2

25'2 x 12
mbr

BALCONY

WIDTH 30'-0"
DEPTH 46'-5"

This charming four-bedroom home is dramatic on the outside and comfortable on the inside. Large sliding glass doors and floor-to-ceiling windows flood the interior with natural light. A vaulted living room has an oversize fireplace and connects to the dining area. A galley kitchen features a sink overlooking the deck. The master bedroom and a secondary bedroom are to the rear and share the use of a full bath. The second floor holds two additional bedrooms and a gallery area with front and side decks. Use this area as a playroom or studio.

DESIGN Q203

First Floor: 986 square feet
Second Floor: 722 square feet
Total: 1,708 square feet

DESIGN BY
SELECT HOME DESIGNS

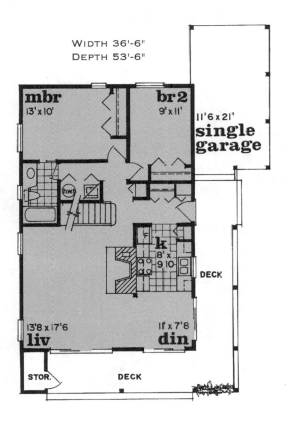

WIDTH 36'-6"
DEPTH 53'-6"

mbr
13' x 10'

br 2
9' x 11'

11'6 x 21'
single garage

hw

k
8' x 9'10

DECK

13'8 x 17'6
liv

If x 7'8
din

STOR.

DECK

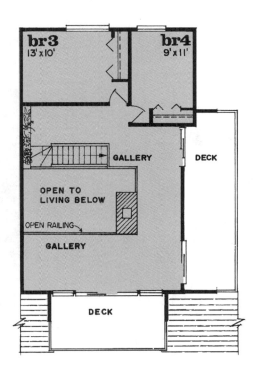

br3
13' x 10'

br4
9' x 11'

GALLERY

DECK

OPEN TO
LIVING BELOW

OPEN RAILING

GALLERY

DECK

DESIGN Q546

Square Footage: 1,102
Unfinished Lower Level: 986 square feet

DESIGN BY
SELECT HOME DESIGNS

This affordable chalet design has additional space for future expansion. The unfinished lower level, with fireplace and rough-in plumbing, provides 986 square feet for a family room, bedrooms, or whatever your family needs. The entry steps up to a living room with balcony and fireplace and back to the dining area and U-shaped kitchen. Sliding glass doors in the dining room open to the rear deck. Three bedrooms sit on the left side of the plan and include a master bedroom with private bath and two family bedrooms sharing a full bath.

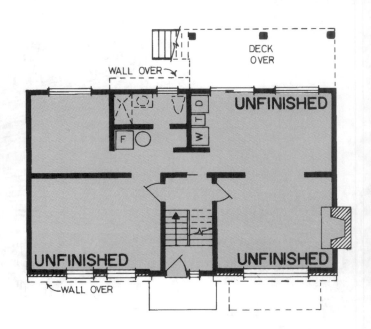

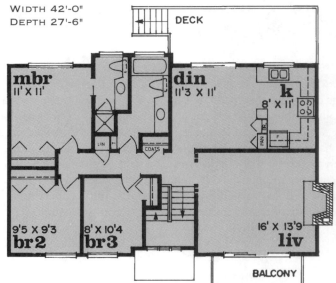

WIDTH 42'-0"
DEPTH 27'-6"

Make your vacation dreams a reality with this fabulous chalet. The most carefree characteristic is the second-floor master bedroom balcony which looks down onto the wood deck. Also on the second floor is the three-bunk dormitory. Panels through the knee walls give access to an abundant storage area—perfect for all of your seasonal storage needs. Downstairs, the kitchen utilizes a dining area and an efficient layout and has direct access to the outside. A large living room offers a grand view to a fantastic deck and has a warming fireplace. A first-floor bedroom enjoys the use of a full hall bath.

DESIGN 2427

First Floor: 784 square feet
Second Floor: 504 square feet
Total: 1,288 square feet

DESIGN BY
HOME PLANNERS

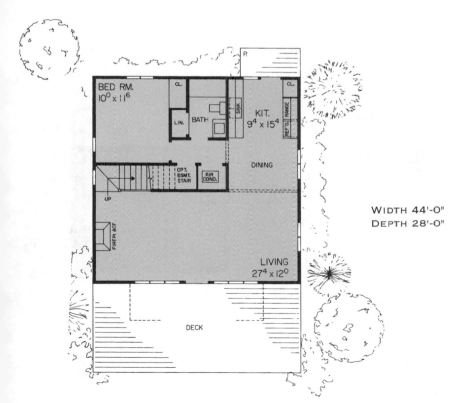

WIDTH 44'-0"
DEPTH 28'-0"

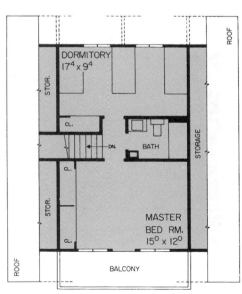

DESIGN 1475

First Floor: 1,120 square feet
Second Floor: 522 square feet
Lower Level: 616 square feet
Total: 2,258 square feet

If ever a design had "vacation home" written all over it, this one does. Built to accommodate the slopes, this hillside design with an exposed lower level meets winter vacation needs without a second thought. The covered lower terrace is the ideal entrance to a ski lounge with a raised-hearth fireplace and a walk-in ski storage area. The main floor holds slope-ceilinged dining and living areas (with yet another raised-hearth fireplace), a kitchen with a patio, two bedrooms and a full bath. The most carefree characteristic is the second-floor balcony which looks down onto the living room. Also on the second floor are two additional bedrooms and a bath.

DESIGN BY
HOME PLANNERS

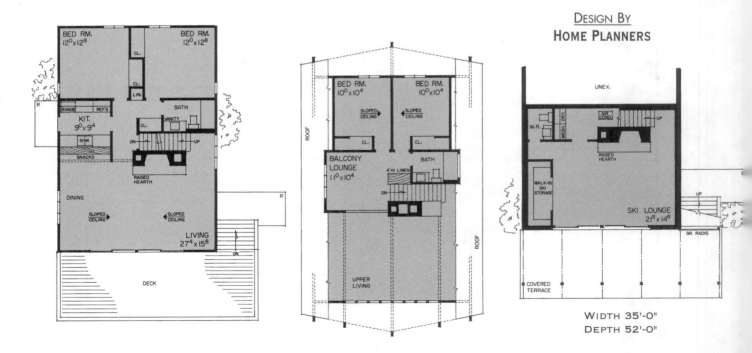

WIDTH 35'-0"
DEPTH 52'-0"

This cozy chalet design begins with a railed veranda opening to a living room with warm fireplace and a dining room with snack-bar counter through to the kitchen. The kitchen itself is U-shaped and has a sink with window over. A full bath and large storage area sit just beyond the kitchen. One bedroom with roomy wall closet is on the first floor. The second floor holds two additional bedrooms—one a master suite with private balcony—and a full bath. Additional storage is found on the second floor, as well.

DESIGN Q212

First Floor: 725 square feet
Second Floor: 561 square feet
Total: 1,286 square feet

DESIGN BY
SELECT HOME DESIGNS

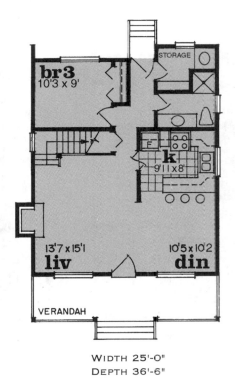

br3
10'3 x 9'

STORAGE

k
9'11 x 8'

liv
13'7 x 15'1

din
10'5 x 10'2

VERANDAH

WIDTH 25'-0"
DEPTH 36'-6"

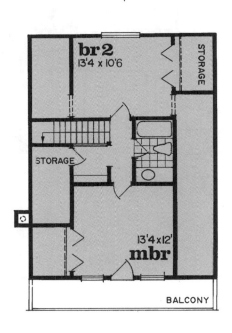

br2
13'4 x 10'6

STORAGE

STORAGE

mbr
13'4 x 12'

BALCONY

DESIGN 3658

First Floor: 784 square feet
Second Floor: 275 square feet
Total: 1,059 square feet

LD

This chalet-type vacation home with its steep, overhanging roof, will catch the eye of even the most casual onlooker. It is designed to be completely livable whether the season be for swimming or skiing. The dormitory on the upper level will sleep many vacationers, while the two bedrooms on the first floor provide the more convenient and conventional sleeping facilities. The upper level overlooks the beam-ceilinged living and dining area. With a wraparound terrace and plenty of storage space, what more could you ask for?

DESIGN BY
HOME PLANNERS

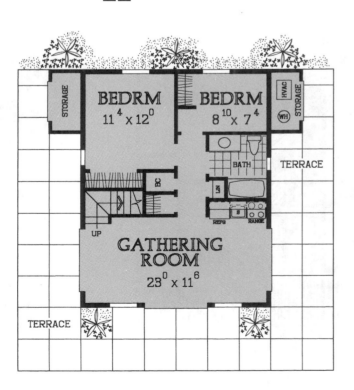

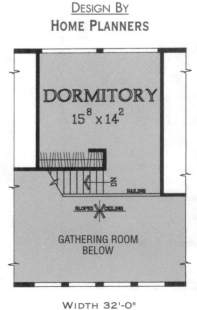

STORAGE

BEDRM
11⁴ x 12⁰

BEDRM
8¹⁰ x 7⁴

HVAC
WH
STORAGE

BATH

TERRACE

BC

LIN

UP

REFG   RANGE

GATHERING
ROOM
23⁰ x 11⁶

TERRACE

DORMITORY
15⁸ x 14²

DN

RAILING

SLOPED CEILING

GATHERING ROOM
BELOW

WIDTH 32'-0"
DEPTH 30'-0"

QUOTE ONE®

Cost to build? See page 434
to order complete cost estimate
to build this house in your area!

Rustic details such as a stone fireplace work well for a country cottage such as this. A floor-to-ceiling window wall accents the living and dining rooms and provides an expansive view past a wide deck on this design. Twin sliding glass doors access the deck from the living space. The U-shaped kitchen offers roomy counters and is open to the dining room. Behind it is a laundry room and then a full bath serving the master bedroom. An additional bedroom sits on the second floor and may be used as a studio, if you wish.

DESIGN Q211

First Floor: 616 square feet
Second Floor: 300 square feet
Total: 916 square feet

DESIGN BY
SELECT HOME DESIGNS

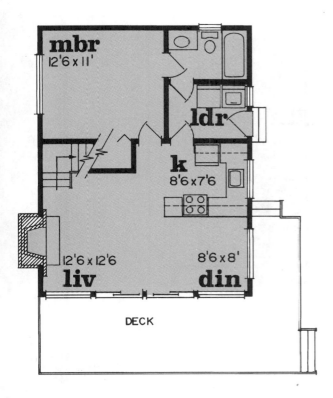

mbr
12'6 x 11'

ldr

k
8'6 x 7'6

liv
12'6 x 12'6

din
8'6 x 8'

DECK

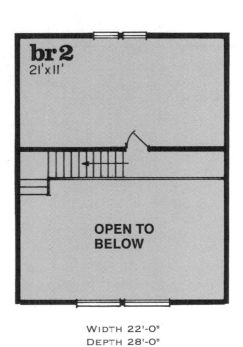

br2
21' x 11'

OPEN TO
BELOW

WIDTH 22'-0"
DEPTH 28'-0"

DESIGN 1482

First Floor: 1,008 square feet
Second Floor: 637 square feet
Total: 1,645 square feet

Here is a chalet right from the pages of travel folders. In addition to the big bedrooms on the first floor, there are three more upstairs. The large master bedroom has a balcony which overlooks the lower wood deck. There are two full baths. The first-floor bath is directly accessible from the outdoors. Note the snack bar and the pantry. A laundry area is adjacent to the side door. Beyond the living room, with warming fireplace, is a wide deck for enjoying the outdoors. The galley kitchen and a dining area are nearby.

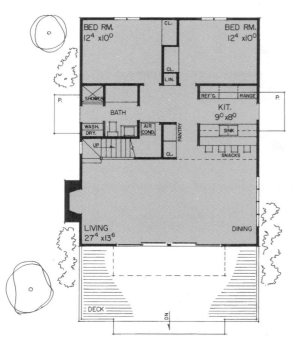

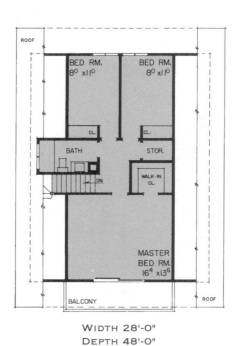

DESIGN BY
HOME PLANNERS

WIDTH 28'-0"
DEPTH 48'-0"

This chalet plan is enhanced by a steep gable roof, scalloped fascia boards and fieldstone chimney detail. The front facing deck and covered balcony add to outdoor living spaces. The fireplace is the main focus in the living room, separating it from the dining room, which is near the U-shaped kitchen. One bedroom is found on the first floor. It has the use of a full hall bath. A storage/mud room is at the back for keeping skis and boots. Two additional bedrooms and a full bath are upstairs. The master bedroom has a full bath and walk-in closet. Three large storage areas are also found on the second floor. Plans include details for both a basement and a crawlspace foundation.

DESIGN Q207

First Floor: 672 square feet
Second Floor: 401 square feet
Total: 1,073 square feet

DESIGN BY
SELECT HOME DESIGNS

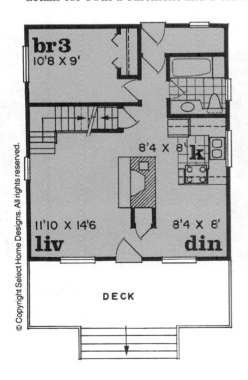

br3
10'8 X 9'

8'4 X 8' **k**

11'10 X 14'6
liv

8'4 X 8'
din

DECK

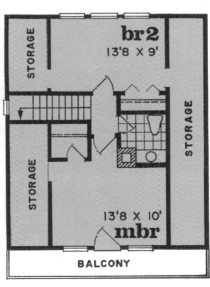

STORAGE

br2
13'8 X 9'

STORAGE

STORAGE

13'8 X 10'
mbr

BALCONY

WIDTH 24'-0"
DEPTH 36'-0"

Rear Elevation

273

DESIGN 2456

First Floor: 1,160 square feet
Second Floor: 840 square feet
Total: 2,000 square feet

Certainly an appealing design whatever the season, this Swiss chalet adaptation is a delightful haven for skiers, fishermen and hunters alike. The clever design of sleeping facilities allows for the whole gang to join in the fun! The first floor has two private bedrooms, a compartmented bath plus a unique room which will take a double bunk. A disappearing stair unit leads to the upstairs bunk room with a full bath. The placement of single bunks or cots here will allow for the sleeping of three or four more—a perfect kid's room. The master suite is up the main stairs and is complete with a walk-in closet, dressing room, full bath and private balcony. Warm up or just relax around the old-fashioned fireplace in the spacious living room.

DESIGN BY
HOME PLANNERS

WIDTH 44'-0"
DEPTH 30'-0"

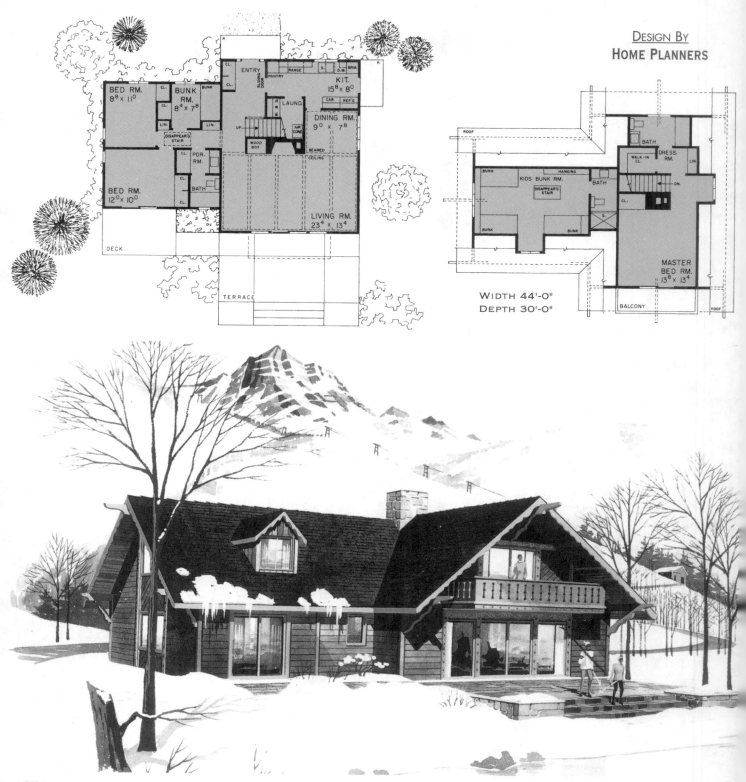

DESIGN Q240

Square Footage: 1,608

DESIGN BY
SELECT HOME DESIGNS

The plans for this cute bungalow offer choices of exterior finishes. The recessed entry is weather-protected and opens to a skylit, tiled foyer. The living room is sunken a few steps and enjoys a bay window and focal-point fireplace. Adjoining is the formal dining room, separated from the living room by an open railing. The kitchen takes on a modified U-shape and has a bright window box over the sink. The connecting breakfast bay/family room has a corner fireplace and sliding glass door to the patio. Bedrooms are positioned away from noisy traffic areas and include a master suite with full bath (note the plant shelf and skylight). Two family bedrooms and a shared bath are nearby. The laundry room connects the main house to the two-car garage. Plans include details for both a basement and a crawlspace foundation.

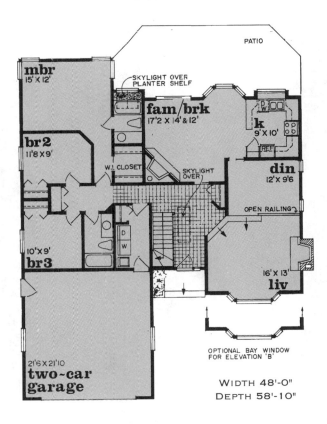

WIDTH 48'-0"
DEPTH 58'-10"

DESIGN 1404

Square Footage: 1,336

Here is an exciting design, unusual in character, yet fun to live in. This design, with its frame exterior and large glass areas, has as its dramatic focal point a hexagonal living area which gives way to interesting angles. The spacious living area features sliding glass doors through which traffic may pass to the terrace stretching across the entire length of the house. The wide overhanging roof projects over the terraces, thus providing partial protection from the weather. The sloping ceilings converge above the unique, open fireplace. The sleeping areas are located in each wing from the hexagonal center.

DESIGN BY
HOME PLANNERS

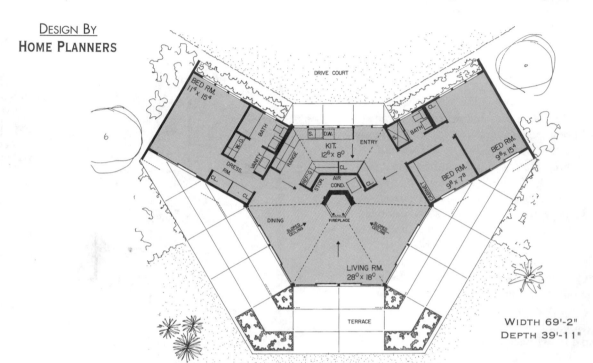

WIDTH 69'-2"
DEPTH 39'-11"

If you have the urge to make your vacation home one that has a distinctive flair of individuality, this design is it. Not only will you love the unique exterior appeal of your new home, but you'll also love the exceptional living patterns offered by the interior. The basic living area is a hexagon. To this space-conscious shape is added the sleeping wings with baths. The master bedroom has a bath with separate powder room. Family bedrooms share a bath with powder room. The center of the sloped-ceiling living area has as its focal point a dramatic fireplace. The kitchen sits behind it and features a sloped ceiling. A wide terrace wraps around the entire front of the design.

DESIGN 2461
Square Footage: 1,400

DESIGN BY
HOME PLANNERS

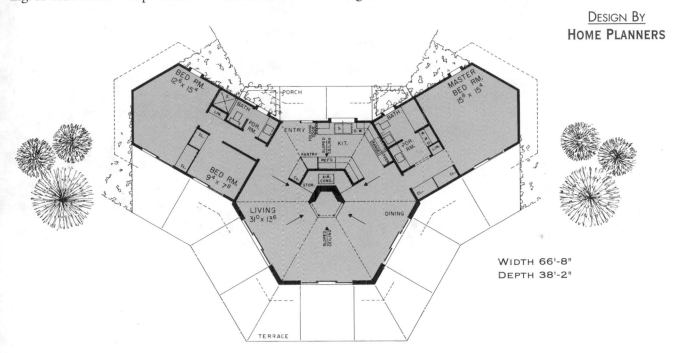

WIDTH 66'-8"
DEPTH 38'-2"

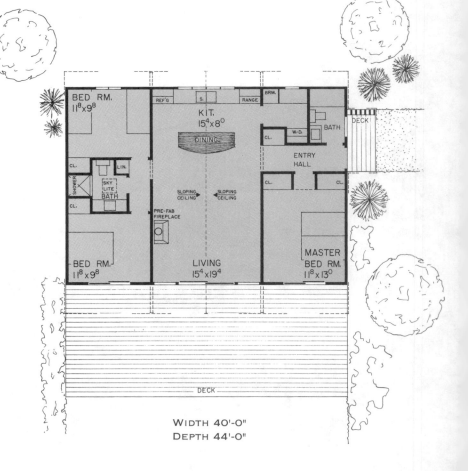

Design 2428

Square Footage: 1,120

Design By
Home Planners

This delightfully different vacation home will provide a wonderful getaway for you and your family. The wood deck allows views and outdoor enjoyment and is accessed directly from the living room and two of the bedrooms. The living space is open and features a sloped ceiling and dining area that separates the living room from the kitchen. The master bedroom is on the right and has the use of a bath across the side entry. Family bedrooms are on the left and share a full skylit bath. A fireplace in the living room keeps things warm and cozy in the colder winter months. Note the smaller deck at the side entrance.

Width 40'-0"
Depth 44'-0"

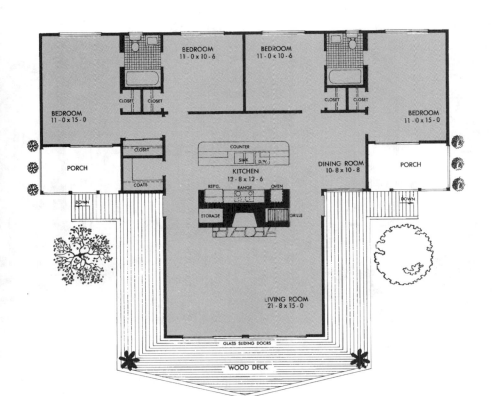

BEDROOM
11-0 x 10-6

BEDROOM
11-0 x 10-6

CLOSET CLOSET

CLOSET CLOSET

BEDROOM
11-0 x 15-0

BEDROOM
11-0 x 15-0

CLOSET

PORCH

COATS

COUNTER

SINK   D.W.

KITCHEN
12-8 x 12-6

REFG.   RANGE   OVEN

STORAGE

GRILLE

DINING ROOM
10-8 x 10-8

PORCH

DOWN

DOWN

LIVING ROOM
21-8 x 15-0

GLASS SLIDING DOORS

WOOD DECK

WIDTH 57'-0"
DEPTH 50'-8"

DESIGN 4015

Square Footage: 1,420

DESIGN BY
HOME PLANNERS

The perfect vacation home combines open, informal living spaces with lots of sleeping space. The spacious living room has a warming fireplace and sliding glass doors onto the deck. Convenient to the dining room, the efficient kitchen is carefully placed so as not to interfere with the living room. Notice the four spacious bedrooms—there's plenty of room for accommodating guests. Two of the bedrooms boast private porches.

Design Q516

Square Footage: 1,405

DESIGN BY
SELECT HOME DESIGNS

This three-bedroom leisure home is perfect for the family that spends casual time out of doors. An expansive wall of glass gives a spectacular view to the great room and accentuates the high vaulted ceilings throughout the design. The great room is also warmed by a hearth and is open to the dining room and L-shaped kitchen. A triangular snack bar graces the kitchen and provides space for casual meals. Bedrooms are split, with the master bedroom on the right side of the plan and family bedrooms on the left. The master has exposed beams in the ceiling, a walk-in closet and a full bath with soaking tub. Family bedrooms share a full bath; Bedroom 2 features a walk-in closet. Plans include details for both a basement and a crawlspace foundation.

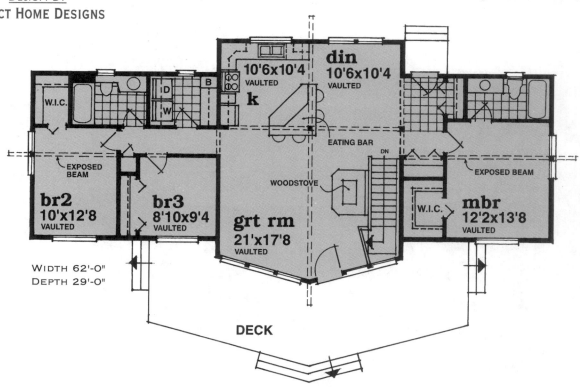

An expansive window wall across the great room of this home adds a spectacular view and accentuates the high ceiling. A corner wood stove warms the room in winter months. The open kitchen shares an eating bar with the dining room and features a convenient U-shape. Sliding glass doors in the dining room lead to the deck. Three bedrooms sit to the back of the plan and share the use of a full bath. The master suite is on the left and has a walk-in closet and private bath. The loft on the upper level adds living or sleeping space and offers a wealth of storage space as well. Plans include both a basement and a crawlspace foundation.

DESIGN Q519

First Floor: 1,375 square feet
Loft: 284 square feet
Total: 1,659 square feet

DESIGN BY
SELECT HOME DESIGNS

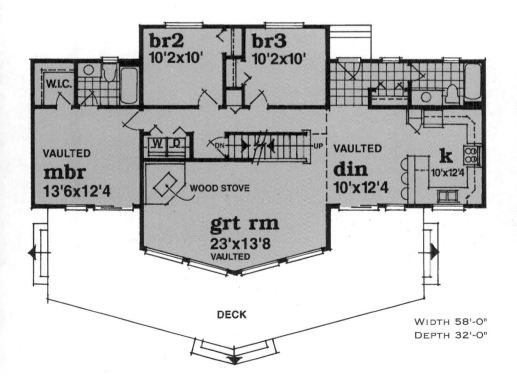

WIDTH 58'-0"
DEPTH 32'-0"

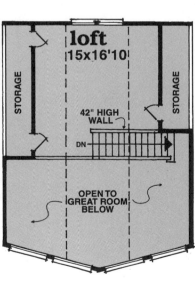

DESIGN 4210

First Floor: 768 square feet
Second Floor: 288 square feet
Total: 1,056 square feet

This unusual contemporary design is not just another pretty face. The floor plan is amazingly simple and accommodating for casual living. Three decks—one at the kitchen, one at the secondary bedroom and one large one at the living room—provide plenty of outdoor living space. The main deck has a built-in bench seat at its outer edge. The interior consists of a large living area warmed by a fireplace, an L-shaped kitchen with pantry and two bedrooms with baths. The master bedroom sits on the second floor and has sliding glass doors to the outdoors. Note the washer and dryer space in the center hall.

DESIGN BY
HOME PLANNERS

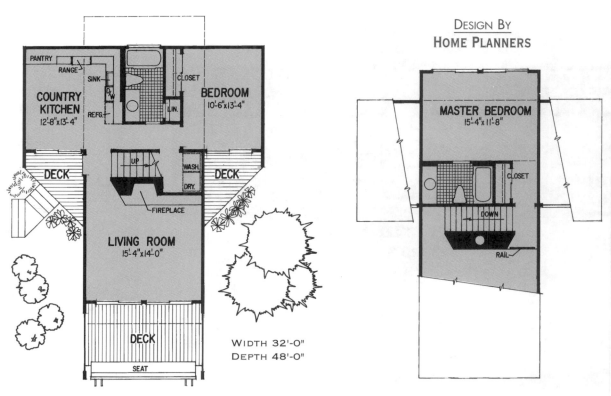

Vacations begin with this unique house. The angled terrace is echoed throughout the floor plan—with this orientation, no view is missed. The living room features a sloped ceiling and large dimensions. In the kitchen, a built-in table accommodates a feast. Three bedrooms sleep all. Two of these include built-in chests. Another bedroom located on the other side of the house will make a nice master retreat. Two full baths and storage space round out the amenities.

DESIGN 1433
Square Footage: 1,160

DESIGN BY
HOME PLANNERS

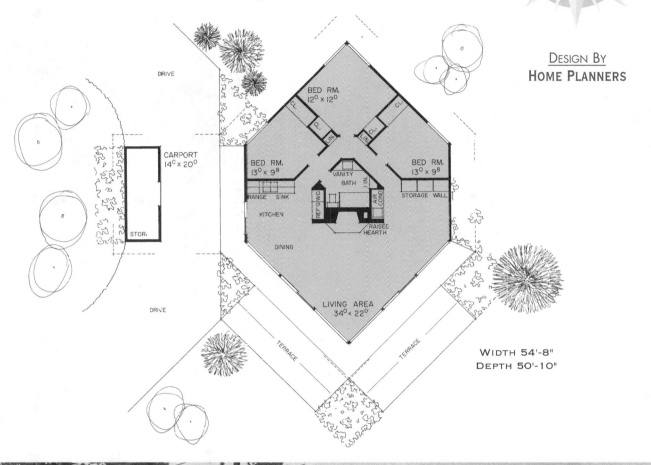

WIDTH 54'-8"
DEPTH 50'-10"

DESIGN Q437

First Floor: 1,084 square feet
Second Floor: 343 square feet
Total: 1,427 square feet

Vertical siding and a wide deck grace the exterior of this plan. Inside, the floor plan features a secluded second-floor master suite with private bath and walk-in closet. Extra-high vaulted ceilings and a wall of windows make the living/dining room a comfortable gathering area. It is warmed by a fireplace and open to the U-shaped kitchen. A laundry room is just beyond. The back entrance has a closet and opens to a rear deck. Two family bedrooms are on the first floor and share a full bath.

DESIGN BY
SELECT HOME DESIGNS

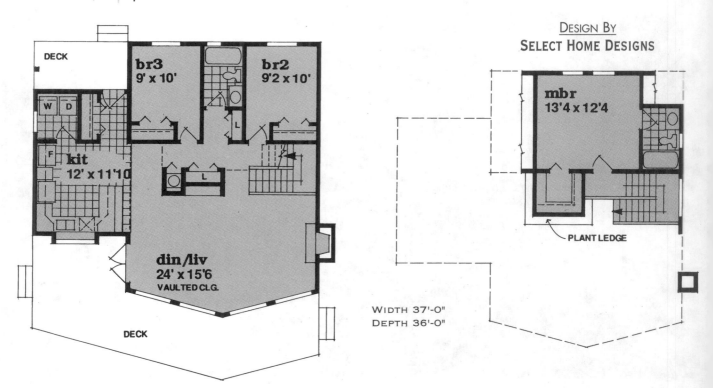

DECK

br3
9' x 10'

br2
9'2 x 10'

W   D

F   kit
12' x 11'10

din/liv
24' x 15'6
VAULTED CLG.

DECK

mbr
13'4 x 12'4

PLANT LEDGE

WIDTH 37'-0"
DEPTH 36'-0"

This three-bedroom cottage is cozy and comfortable, yet has room enough for the whole family. Its vertical wood siding and massive chimney grace the facade. Inside, a wall of windows in the living area allows for wonderful views; a vaulted ceiling and a wood stove further enhance its appeal. Double glass doors lead to a full-width deck that surrounds the living/dining area. The U-shaped kitchen features a box-bay window over the double sink and a pass-through counter to the dining area. Just beyond is the laundry. The master bedroom leaves nothing to chance, with deck access, a walk-in closet and full private bath. Family bedrooms share a full bath that separates them.

DESIGN Q436

Square Footage: 1,292

DESIGN BY
SELECT HOME DESIGNS

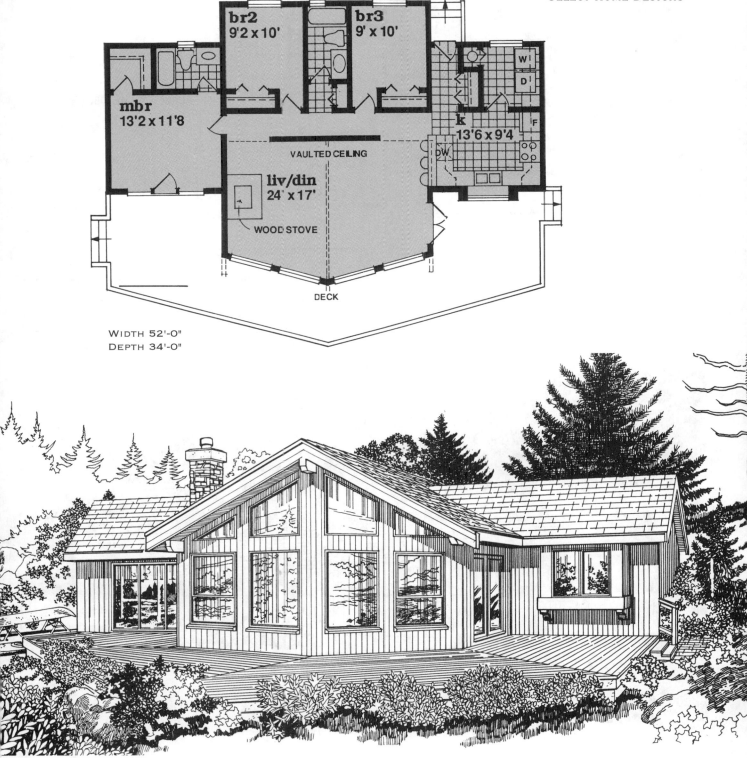

br2
9'2 x 10'

br3
9' x 10'

W
D

mbr
13'2 x 11'8

k
13'6 x 9'4

F

VAULTED CEILING

DW

liv/din
24' x 17'

WOOD STOVE

DECK

WIDTH 52'-0"
DEPTH 34'-0"

DESIGN Q494

Square Footage: 1,089

Brick and wood siding work in combination on the exterior of this cozy one-story home. The entry is protected by a covered porch and opens to a foyer with half-wall separating it from the living room, which features a large window overlooking the front porch. A fireplace warms this gathering space in cold weather. The U-shaped kitchen has abundant counter space and is adjacent to the dining room for convenience. Down a few steps is the handy laundry area with stairs to the basement and access to the single-car garage. Three bedrooms with wall closets share a main bath with soaking tub. The basement may be developed in the future to add more bedrooms or to create additional gathering space.

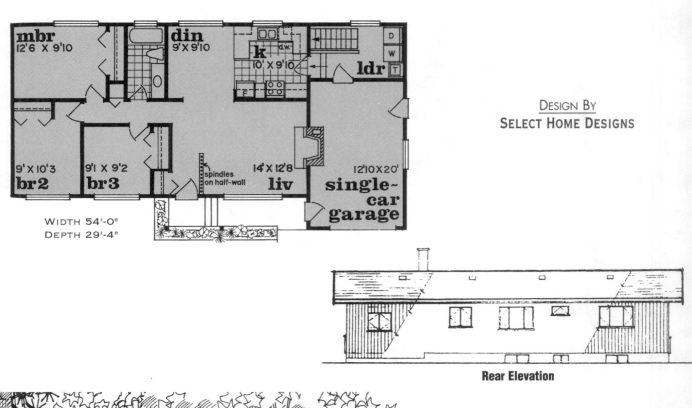

mbr
12'6 X 9'10

din
9' X 9'10

k
10' X 9'10

d.w.

ldr

D
W
T

F

br2
9' X 10'3

br3
9'1 X 9'2

spindles on half-wall

liv
14' X 12'8

single-car garage
12'10 X 20'

WIDTH 54'-0"
DEPTH 29'-4"

DESIGN BY
SELECT HOME DESIGNS

Rear Elevation

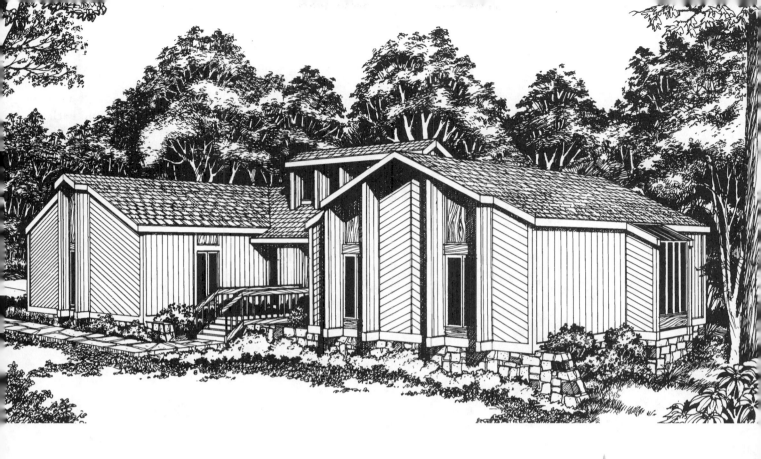

DESIGN BY
HOME PLANNERS

DESIGN 4293

Square Footage: 1,873

D

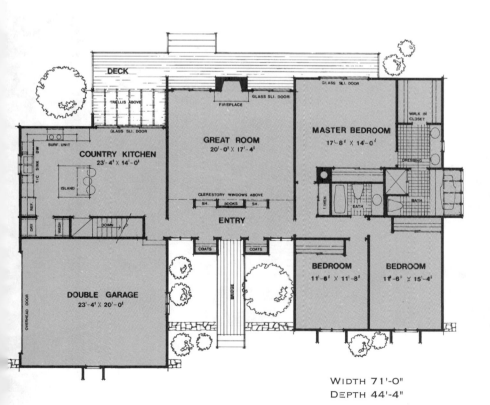

WIDTH 71'-0"
DEPTH 44'-4"

Simple lines and a balanced sense of proportion dominate the look of this compact design. The open great room with clerestory windows, the country kitchen with island work area and the master bedroom all overlook a rear deck. The master bedroom is further enhanced with a private bath with garden tub, walk-in closet and dressing area with double sinks. Two family bedrooms share a full hall bath. Special features of this design include a fireplace in the great room, built-in shelves in the entry, and a trellised area on the rear deck. The double side-facing garage connects to the main house at the laundry room.

DESIGN 1425

Basic Unit: 576 square feet;
Expanded Unit: 1,152 square feet

Here is a vacation home that can be easily built in three stages. This procedure will stretch your building budget and enable you to continue as your finances permit. Blueprints show details for the construction of the basic unit first. This features the kitchen, the bath, a bedroom and the living room. The second stage can be either the addition of the two extra bedrooms or the screened porch. Each addition is a modular 12 x 24 foot unit. The ceilings are sloping, thus contributing to the feeling of spaciousness. The finished home has excellent storage facilities. If desired, the screened porch could be modified to be built as a family room addition. Such a move would permit year round use. Note the perfectly rectangular shape of this home which will result in economical construction costs.

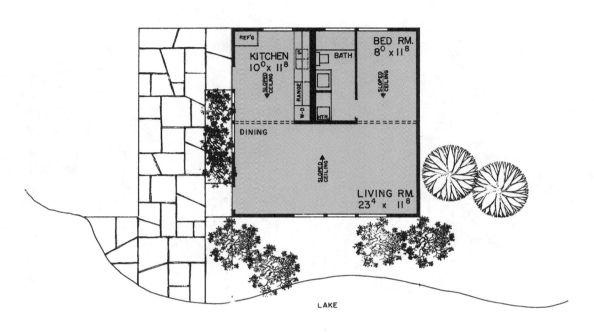

KITCHEN
10⁰ x 11⁸

REF'G

BATH

BED RM.
8⁰ x 11⁸

SLOPED CEILING

SLOPED CEILING

W-D RANGE

HTR.

DINING

SLOPED CEILING

LIVING RM.
23⁴ x 11⁸

LAKE

WIDTH 48'-0"
DEPTH 24'-0"

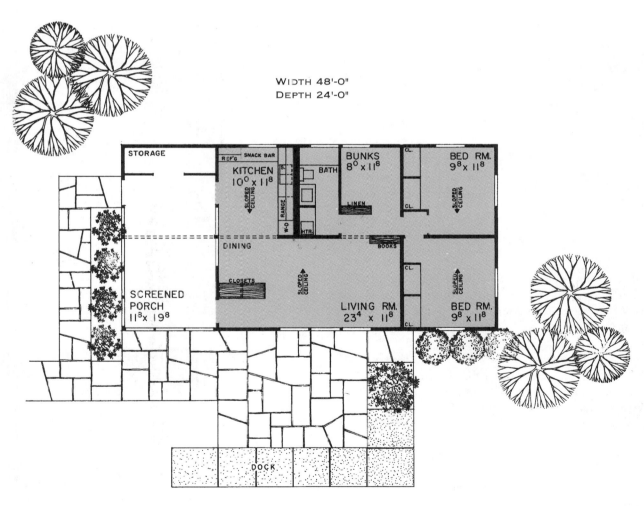

STORAGE

REF'G SNACK BAR

KITCHEN
10⁰ x 11⁸

BATH

BUNKS
8⁰ x 11⁸

CL.

BED RM.
9⁸ x 11⁸

SLOPED CEILING

LINEN

SLOPED CEILING

CL.

W-D RANGE

HTR.

DINING

BOOKS

CL.

SCREENED
PORCH
11⁸ x 19⁸

CLOSETS

SLOPED CEILING

SLOPED CEILING

LIVING RM.
23⁴ x 11⁸

BED RM.
9⁸ x 11⁸

CL.

DOCK

DESIGN 1427

First Floor: 1,008 square feet
Second Floor: 688 square feet
Total: 1,696 square feet

DESIGN BY
HOME PLANNERS

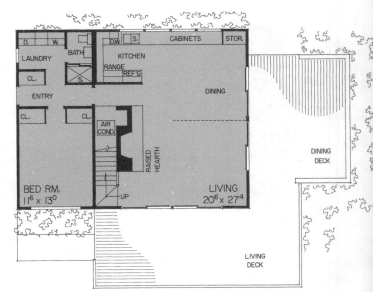

CARPORT
13⁰ x 22⁰

STORAGE

D. W. BATH DW. S. CABINETS STOR.

LAUNDRY KITCHEN
RANGE REF'G

CL. S.

ENTRY DINING

CL. CL.

AIR
COND.

BED RM.
11⁶ x 13⁰

RAISED
HEARTH

UP

LIVING
20⁶ x 27⁴

DINING
DECK

LIVING
DECK

WIDTH 69'-0"
DEPTH 40'-0"

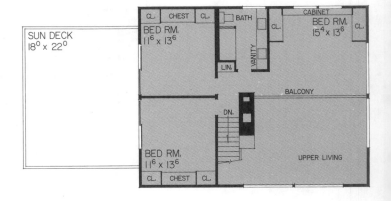

SUN DECK
18⁰ x 22⁰

CL. CHEST CL. BATH CABINET

BED RM.
11⁶ x 13⁶

CL.

BED RM.
15⁴ x 13⁶

CL.

LIN.

VANITY

BALCONY

DN.

BED RM.
11⁶ x 13⁶

UPPER LIVING

CL. CHEST CL.

This wonderful vacation cottage for seashore or mountain glade offers many of the special features you want in a second home. Begin with the wraparound deck that covers two sides of the home on the first floor. It is complemented by a sun deck on the second floor that serves two of the three bedrooms. The living and dining areas are open and expansive and connect directly to a U-shaped kitchen. The living room is further graced by a warm hearth. One bedroom with full bath is on the first floor and a large laundry area is nearby. Built-ins dominate the three second-floor bedrooms, with built-in chests in the two smaller bedrooms and a built-in cabinet in the larger one. A balcony overlook gives views of the living area.

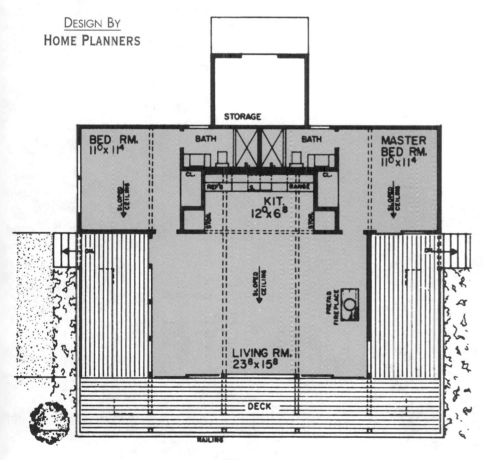

STORAGE

BED RM.
11⁰ x 11⁴

BATH

BATH

MASTER
BED RM.
11⁰ x 11⁴

CL.

CL.

SLOPED CEILING

SLOPED CEILING

REF'S

RANGE

KIT.
12⁰ x 6⁸

SLOPED CEILING

PREFAB FIRE PLACE

LIVING RM.
23⁸ x 15⁸

DECK

RAILING

WIDTH 40'-0'
DEPTH 42'-0'

DESIGN 1435

Square Footage: 864

An abundance of windows, a fireplace, two full baths and a spacious deck all combine to create a wonderful vacation home in this design. The deck wraps around three sides of the home, to allow access from the master bedroom and from the main living area in two places. The kitchen is centrally placed and holds two large storage closets. Both bedrooms have sloped ceilings and private baths. A huge storage area at the back is accessed from outside and allows plenty of room for sports equipment and other items.

DESIGN Q201

Square Footage: 936
Bonus Space: 358 square feet

This space-efficient leisure home offers many extras. Adding the optional carport adds an extra 12 feet to the width of the home. The sun deck wraps around two sides and features a built-in barbecue and hot tub. The living room boasts a soaring vaulted ceiling, a large fireplace and sliding glass doors to the sun deck. The galley-style kitchen has a breakfast bar that connects it to the living area. Two bedrooms on the first level share the use of a full bath. A ladder to the second level reaches to a loft area that works as additional bedroom space.

DESIGN BY
SELECT HOME DESIGNS

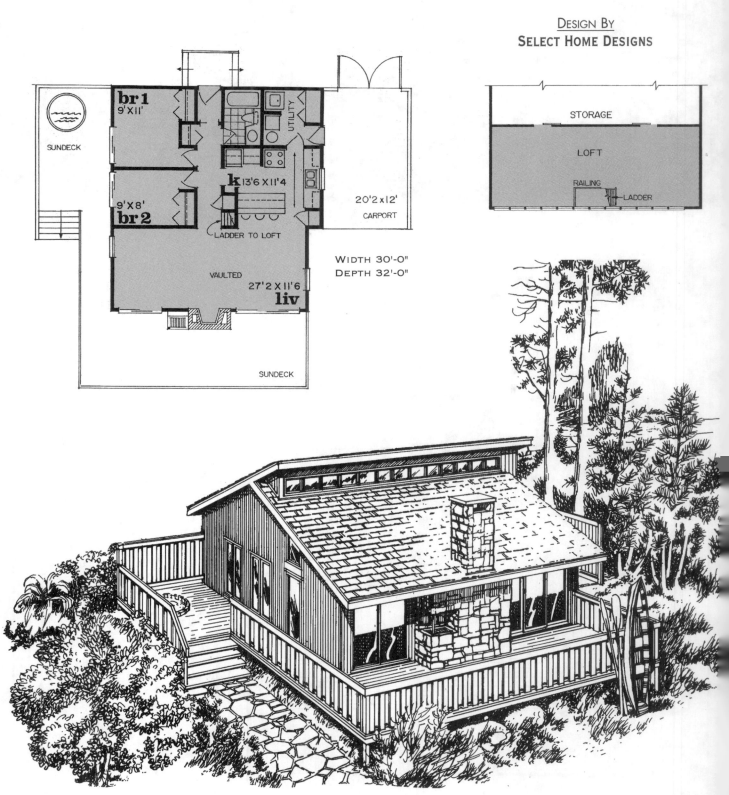

SUNDECK

br 1
9'X11'

UTILITY

br 2
9'X8'

k 13'6 X 11'4

LADDER TO LOFT

VAULTED

liv
27'2 X 11'6

SUNDECK

20'2 x 12'
CARPORT

WIDTH 30'-0"
DEPTH 32'-0"

STORAGE

LOFT

RAILING
LADDER

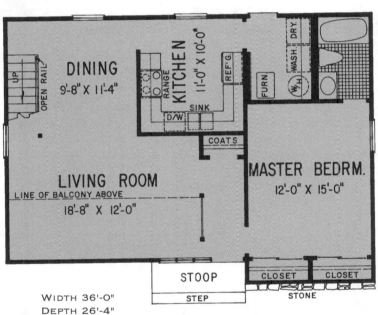

DINING
9'-8" X 11'-4"

KITCHEN
11'-0" X 10'-0"

RANGE

REF'G.

SINK

D/W

FURN.

W.H.

WASH

DRY.

UP

OPEN RAIL

COATS

LIVING ROOM
LINE OF BALCONY ABOVE
18'-8" X 12'-0"

MASTER BEDRM.
12'-0" X 15'-0"

STOOP

STEP

CLOSET

CLOSET

STONE

WIDTH 36'-0"
DEPTH 26'-4"

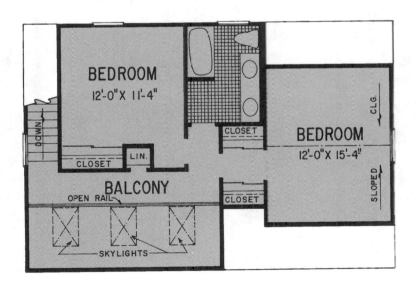

BEDROOM
12'-0" X 11'-4"

CLOSET

LIN.

CLOSET

CLG.

BEDROOM
12'-0" X 15'-4"

DOWN

BALCONY

OPEN RAIL

CLOSET

SLOPED

SKYLIGHTS

Design 4153

Square Footage: 1,442

L D

Design By
Home Planners

The rectangular shape of this design will make it an economical and easy-to-build choice for those wary of high construction costs. The first floor benefits from the informality of open planning: the living room and dining room combine to make one large living space. The partitioned kitchen is conveniently adjacent yet keeps the cooking process out of the living area. Also downstairs is the master bedroom and bath. The second floor houses two large bedrooms, a full bath and a balcony over the living room.

DESIGN Q238

Square Footage: 1,276
Unfinished Lower Level: 967 square feet

If you'd like to start small and expand later as your family grows, this plan offers that option. The basement is unfinished but can be developed into a family room, bedroom and full bath in addition to the laundry room and two-car garage at this level. A large living/dining area is found on the main level. It is graced by a fireplace, buffet space and sliding glass doors to the rear deck. The L-shaped kitchen is efficiently designed and holds space for a breakfast table. Three bedrooms and two full baths include a master suite with walk-in closet.

DESIGN BY
SELECT HOME DESIGNS

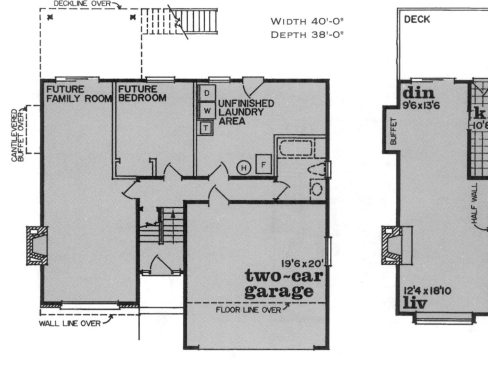

WIDTH 40'-0"
DEPTH 38'-0"

DECKLINE OVER

CANTILEVERED BUFFET OVER

FUTURE FAMILY ROOM   FUTURE BEDROOM   D W T   UNFINISHED LAUNDRY AREA

H   F

two-car garage
19'6 x 20'

FLOOR LINE OVER

WALL LINE OVER

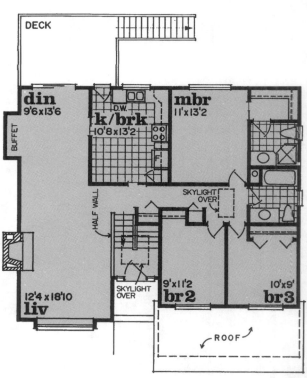

DECK

din
9'6x13'6

BUFFET

k/brk
10'8x13'2
D.W.

mbr
11'x13'2

HALF WALL

SKYLIGHT OVER

SKYLIGHT OVER

12'4 x 18'10
liv

9'x11'2
br2

10'x9'
br3

ROOF

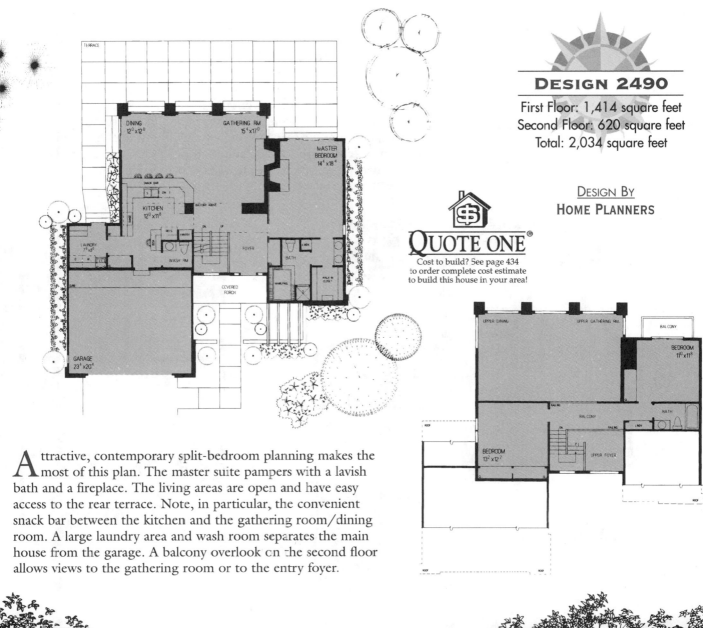

DESIGN 2490

First Floor: 1,414 square feet
Second Floor: 620 square feet
Total: 2,034 square feet

DESIGN BY
HOME PLANNERS

QUOTE ONE®
Cost to build? See page 434
to order complete cost estimate
to build this house in your area!

A ttractive, contemporary split-bedroom planning makes the most of this plan. The master suite pampers with a lavish bath and a fireplace. The living areas are open and have easy access to the rear terrace. Note, in particular, the convenient snack bar between the kitchen and the gathering room/dining room. A large laundry area and wash room separates the main house from the garage. A balcony overlook on the second floor allows views to the gathering room or to the entry foyer.

DESIGN Q241

First Floor: 1,016 square feet
Second Floor: 766 square feet
Total: 1,782 square feet

This delightful contemporary design features vertical wood siding and large windows in the living room and dining room. Both the living room and family room have warming fireplaces. The family room also features sliding glass doors to the rear patio. The U-shaped kitchen and the breakfast nook combine their space to provide an open casual working and eating area. A railed gallery overlooks the foyer from the second floor. It leads to a master suite with walk-in closet and full bath and two family bedrooms with wall closets. Of special note in this design: the powder room in the entry hall, a large laundry room and a two-car garage. Plans include details for both a basement and a crawlspace foundation.

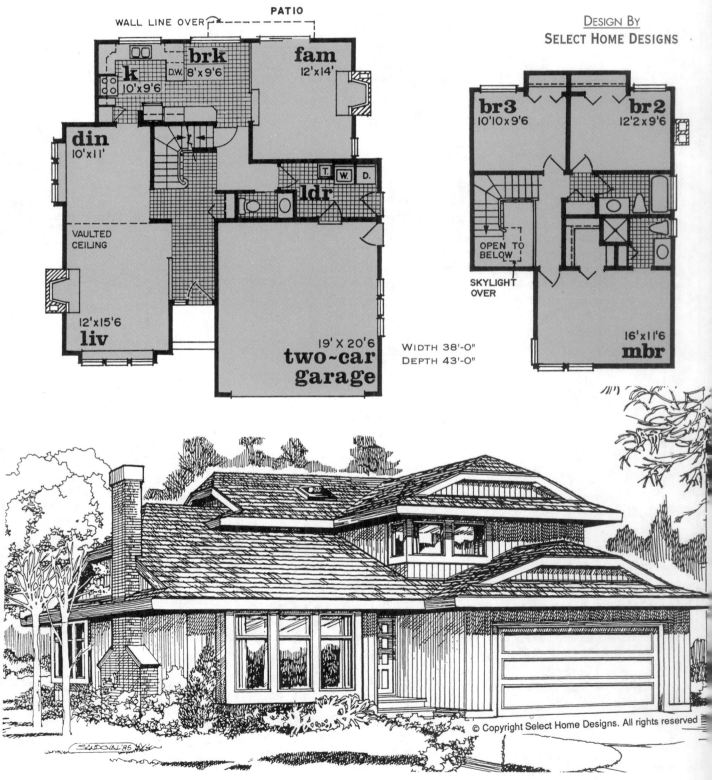

DESIGN BY
SELECT HOME DESIGNS

WALL LINE OVER

PATIO

brk
8'x9'6

fam
12'x14'

k
10'x9'6

din
10'x11'

ldr

VAULTED CEILING

liv
12'x15'6

two-car garage
19' X 20'6

WIDTH 38'-0"
DEPTH 43'-0"

br3
10'10x9'6

br2
12'2x9'6

OPEN TO BELOW

SKYLIGHT OVER

mbr
16'x11'6

Vacation living patterns, because of the very nature of things, are different than the everyday living of the city or suburban America. However, they can be made to be even more delightfully so, when called upon to function in harmony with such a distinctive two-level design as this. The upper level is the pleasantly open and spacious living level. The ceilings are sloped and converge at the skylight. Outside the glass sliding doors is the large deck which looks down onto the surrounding countryside. The lower level is the sleeping level with three bedrooms and a full bath. The covered terrace is just outside two of the bedrooms through sliding glass doors.

DESIGN 1468

Upper Level: 676 square feet
Lower Level: 676 square feet
Total: 1,352 square feet

DESIGN BY
HOME PLANNERS

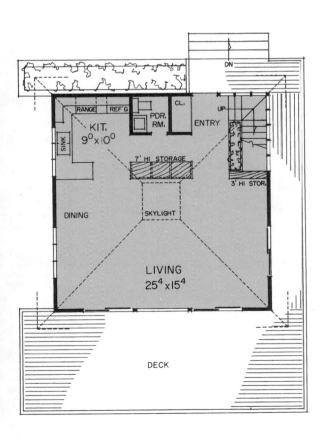

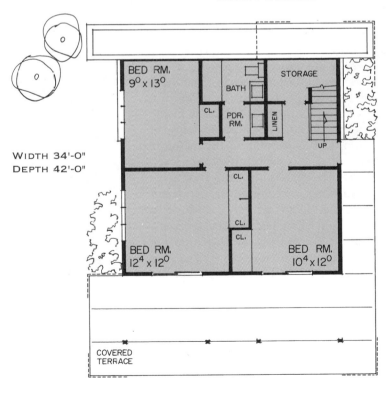

WIDTH 34'-0"
DEPTH 42'-0"

DESIGN Q508

First Floor: 1,296 square feet
Second Floor: 396 square feet
Total: 1,692 square feet

DESIGN BY
SELECT HOME DESIGNS

If your lot slopes to the front and enjoys a view in that direction, this may be the perfect plan for you. The prow front features a wall of windows extending a full two stories, to ensure a view from both the loft and the living room. The huge deck can be accessed from the dining room or the master bedroom and also shelters the lower level entry. The master bedroom is on the main living level along with two family bedrooms. The master has a private bath, while the family bedrooms share a full bath. A loft area provides additional sleeping space if you need it. The plan calls for the lower-level foyer to be finished, with a complete unfinished basement available for future growth.

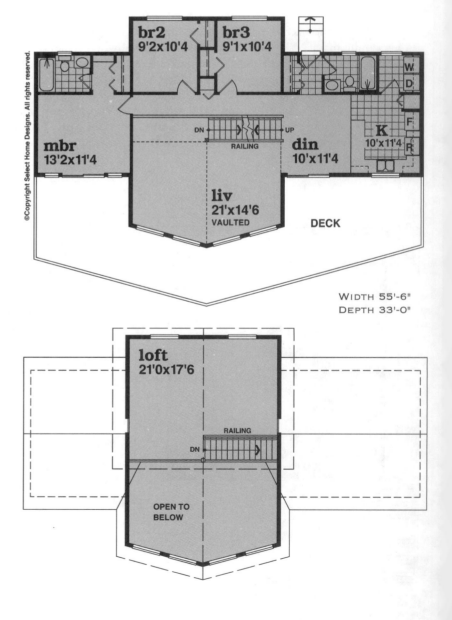

br2
9'2x10'4

br3
9'1x10'4

W
D

mbr
13'2x11'4

DN   UP
RAILING

din
10'x11'4

K
10'x11'4

F
R

liv
21'x14'6
VAULTED

DECK

WIDTH 55'-6"
DEPTH 33'-0"

loft
21'0x17'6

RAILING

DN

OPEN TO
BELOW

This is a grand vacation or retirement home, designed for views and the outdoor lifestyle. The full-width deck complements the abundant windows in rooms facing its way. The living room is made for gathering. It features a vaulted ceiling, a fireplace and full-height windows overlooking the deck. Open to this living space is the dining room with sliding glass doors to the outdoors and a pass-through counter to the U-shaped kitchen. The kitchen connects to a laundry area and has a window over the sink for more outdoor views. Two family bedrooms sit in the middle of the plan. They share a full bath. The master suite has a private bath and deck views. The basement option for this plan adds 1,296 square feet to its total and extends the depth to 33'.

DESIGN Q429

Square Footage: 1,230

DESIGN BY
SELECT HOME DESIGNS

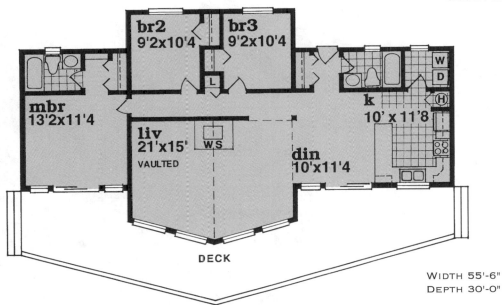

br2
9'2x10'4

br3
9'2x10'4

L

W
D

H

mbr
13'2x11'4

k
10' x 11'8

liv
21'x15'
VAULTED

W S

din
10'x11'4

DECK

WIDTH 55'-6"
DEPTH 30'-0"

Design Q438

Square Footage: 1,495

DESIGN BY
SELECT HOME DESIGNS

This three-bedroom cottage has just the right rustic mix of vertical wood siding and stone accents. Inside, the living is pure resort-style comfort. High vaulted ceilings are featured throughout the living room and master bedroom. The living room also has a fireplace and full-height windows overlooking the deck. The dining room has double door access to the deck; the master bedroom has a single door that opens to the deck. A convenient kitchen has a U-shaped work area with a large storage space beyond. A laundry room with closet is also nearby. Two family bedrooms share a bath that is situated between them. The master suite features a walk-in closet and private bath.

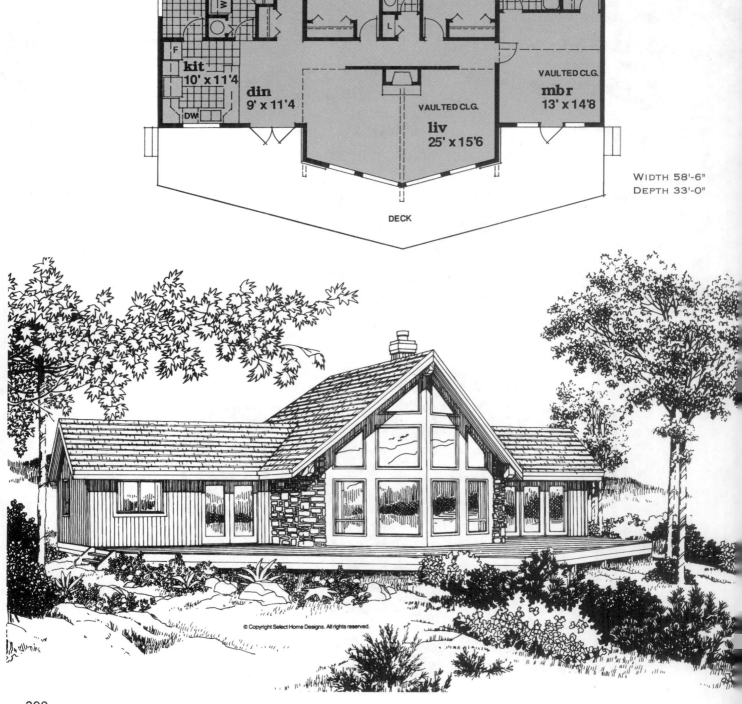

300

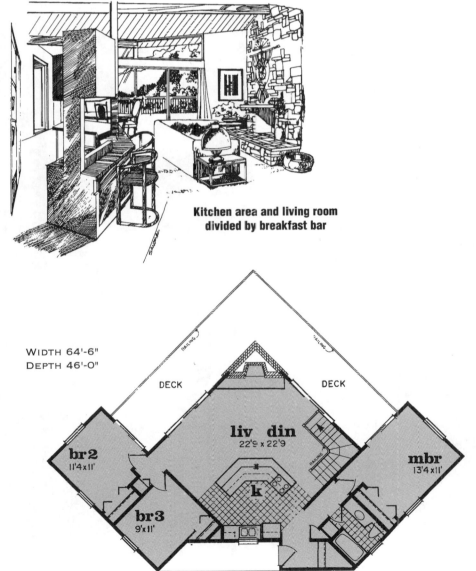

**Kitchen area and living room
divided by breakfast bar**

WIDTH 64'-6"
DEPTH 46'-0"

DECK   DECK

liv din
22'9 x 22'9

br2
11'4 x 11'

br3
9' x 11'

k

mbr
13'4 x 11'

DESIGN Q214
Square Footage: 1,180

Designed to capture views to the rear of the lot, this home can easily accommodate a narrower lot by angling the plan on the site. Wide sliding glass doors in the living room and dining room open to a wrapping deck that maximizes outdoor living. Note the focal-point fireplace in this open living space. The kitchen sits to the front and offers a large breakfast bar to the living space. The master bedroom is split from family bedrooms and has deck access. Bedroom 2 also has deck access. When finished, the lower level offers a fourth bedroom, games room and full bath.

DESIGN BY
SELECT HOME DESIGNS

DESIGN 9614

First Floor: 1,345 square feet
Second Floor: 536 square feet
Total: 1,881 square feet

DESIGN BY
DONALD A. GARDNER
ARCHITECTS, INC.

An elegant exterior combines with a functional interior to offer an exciting design for the contemporary-minded. Notice the cheery sun room that captures the heat of the sun. The master suite and great room both have access to this bright space through sliding glass doors. A U-shaped kitchen has a window garden, a breakfast bar and ample cabinet space. Note how the great room ceiling, with exposed wood beams, slopes from the deck up to operable clerestory windows at the study/play area on the second level. Also notice the bonus storage space in the attic over the garage. Please specify crawlspace or basement foundation when ordering.

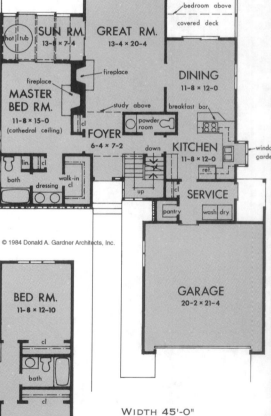

DECK
40-0 × 12-0

bedroom above
covered deck

hot tub | SUN RM. 13-8 × 7-4 | GREAT RM. 13-4 × 20-4

fireplace

fireplace
MASTER BED RM. 11-8 × 15-0 (cathedral ceiling)

study above

DINING 11-8 × 12-0

breakfast bar

FOYER 6-4 × 7-2

powder room

KITCHEN 11-8 × 12-0

window garden

ref.

SERVICE

lin. | cl
bath
dressing
walk-in cl

down
up
cl

pantry | wash | dry

GARAGE 20-2 × 21-4

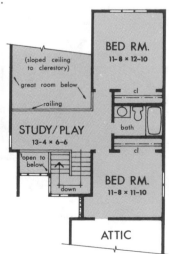

(sloped ceiling to clerestory)
great room below
railing

BED RM. 11-8 × 12-10

cl

bath

STUDY/PLAY 13-4 × 6-6

open to below
down

BED RM. 11-8 × 11-10

ATTIC

WIDTH 45'-0"
DEPTH 69'-4"

Rear

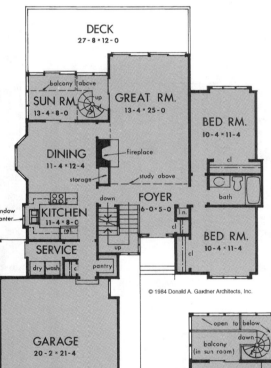

DECK
27-8 × 12-0

balcony | above

SUN RM.
13-4 × 8-0

GREAT RM.
13-4 × 25-0

up

BED RM.
10-4 × 11-4

cl

DINING
11-4 × 12-4

fireplace

study above

storage

bath

window planter

KITCHEN
11-4 × 8-0

ref.

down

FOYER
6-0 × 5-0

ln.

up

BED RM.
10-4 × 11-4

cl

cl

SERVICE

dry | wash | c

pantry

GARAGE
20-2 × 21-4

WIDTH 45'-4"
DEPTH 60'-0"

DESIGN 9613

First Floor: 1,340 square feet
Second Floor: 504 square feet
Total: 1,844 square feet

DESIGN BY
**DONALD A. GARDNER
ARCHITECTS, INC.**

Because this home's sun room is a full two stories high, it acts as a solar collector when oriented to the south. Enjoying the benefits of this warmth are the dining room and great room on the first floor and the master suite on the second floor. A spacious deck further extends the outdoor living potential. Special features to be found in this house include: a sloped ceiling with exposed wood beams and a fireplace in the great room; a cathedral ceiling, a fireplace, built-in shelves and ample closet space in the master bedroom; clerestory windows and a balcony overlook in the upstairs study; and convenient storage space in the attic over the garage. Please specify basement or crawlspace foundation when ordering.

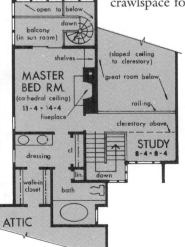

open to below

balcony
(in sun room)

down

shelves

(sloped ceiling to clerestory)

great room below

**MASTER
BED RM.**
(cathedral ceiling)
11-4 × 14-4

fireplace

railing

clerestory above

dressing

cl

lin.

up

STUDY
8-4 × 8-4

down

walk-in closet

bath

ATTIC

Rear

DESIGN 2782

First Floor: 2,060 square feet
Second Floor: 897 square feet
Total: 2,957 square feet

D

DESIGN BY
HOME PLANNERS

What makes this such a distinctive four-bedroom design? This plan includes great formal and informal living space for the family at home or when entertaining guests. The formal gathering room and informal family room share a dramatic raised-hearth fireplace. Other features of the sunken gathering room include high sloped ceilings, a built-in planter and sliding glass doors to the front entrance court. The kitchen has a snack bar, many built-ins, a pass-through to the dining room and easy access to the large laundry/washroom. The master bedroom suite is located on the main level for added privacy and convenience. There's even a study with a built-in bar. The upper level has three more bedrooms, a bath and a lounge looking down into the gathering room.

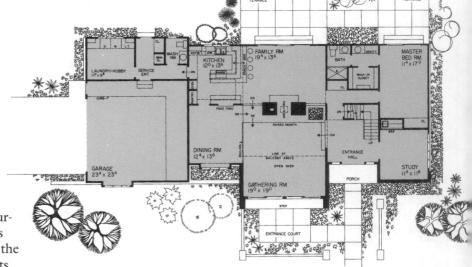

WIDTH 80'-8"
DEPTH 40'-4"

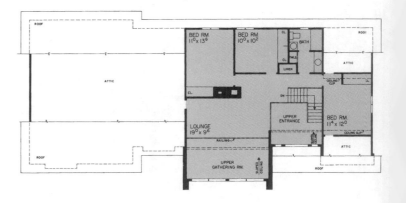

DESIGN 6644

Square Footage: 2,387

DESIGN BY
**THE SATER
DESIGN COLLECTION**

This sunny design opens through double doors into the great room. A rounded dining area contributes a sense of the dramatic and is easily served by the roomy kitchen. A relaxing study also provides outdoor access. Two secondary bedrooms enjoy ample closet space and share a bath with dual vanities. In the master suite, a tiered ceiling and lots of windows gain attention. A luxury bath with a compartmented toilet, a garden tub, dual vanities and a separate shower also includes a walk-in closet. A bath with a stall shower serves the outdoor living areas.

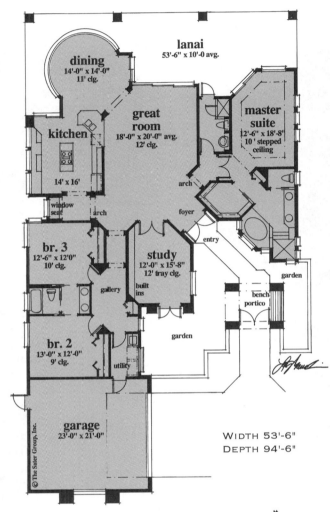

WIDTH 53'-6"
DEPTH 94'-6"

Rear

DESIGN 8603

Square Footage: 2,656

DESIGN BY
HOME DESIGN
SERVICES

A graceful design sets this charming home apart from the ordinary and transcends the commonplace. From the foyer, the dining room branches off the sunny living room, setting a lovely backdrop for entertaining. Casual living is the focus in the oversized family room, where sliding doors open to the patio and the eat-in, gourmet kitchen is open for easy conversation. Two family bedrooms and a cabana bath are just off the family room. The master suite has a cozy fireplace in the sitting area, twin closets and a compartmented bath. A large covered patio adds to the living area.

WIDTH 92'-0"
DEPTH 69'-0"

© HOME DESIGN SERVICES, INC.

J.N. HANSEN P.T.L.

DESIGN BY
HOME DESIGN
SERVICES

DESIGN BY
HOME DESIGN
SERVICES

Master Bedroom 18⁰ • 16⁰

see-thru fireplace

tray ceiling

Master Bath

linen

Breakfast Nook vaulted ceiling

dw

Kitchen

mg

ref

pantry

w.i.c.

Utility w d

wh

ac

ac

Covered Patio

summer kitchen

Family Room vaulted ceiling 16⁰ • 23⁰

fireplace

shelves

shelves

linen

Bedroom 2 14⁰ • 11⁰

Bath 2

lin

Bedroom 3 11⁰ • 12⁰

linen

Bath 3

ac

3 Car Garage

shelves

Dining vaulted ceiling 11⁰ • 12⁰

Foyer

Entry

Living Room vaulted ceiling 12⁰ • 13⁰

Bedroom 4 12⁰ • 11⁰

planter

planter

WIDTH 70'-0"
DEPTH 76'-0"

DESIGN 8653
Square Footage: 2,962

Enter the formal foyer of this home and you are greeted with a traditional split living and dining room layout. The family room is where the real living takes place—whether gathered around the fireplace or expanding the space with the help of sliding glass to include the outside patio and summer kitchen. The ultimate master suite contains coffered ceilings, a "boomerang" vanity and angular mirrors that reflect the bayed soaking tub and shower. Efficient use of space creates a huge closet with little dead center space. Two family bedrooms are situated to share a hall bath. Another bedroom has a semi-private bath, offering guests luxurious comfort.

DESIGN 8732

Square Footage: 2,311
Bonus Room: 279 square feet

A niche becomes the focal point as the tiled foyer flows to the heart of the home. The gourmet kitchen invites all occasions—planned events and casual gatherings—with an island counter, a sizable pantry and angled counters. A wall of sliding glass doors in the living room offers wide views of the back property. Two walk-in closets introduce a spacious bath in the master suite. Tucked out of the way near the master suite's entry vestibule is a convenient powder room. Three family bedrooms are placed at the opposite end of the plan, with a full bath. A cabana bath serves traffic from the back covered patio.

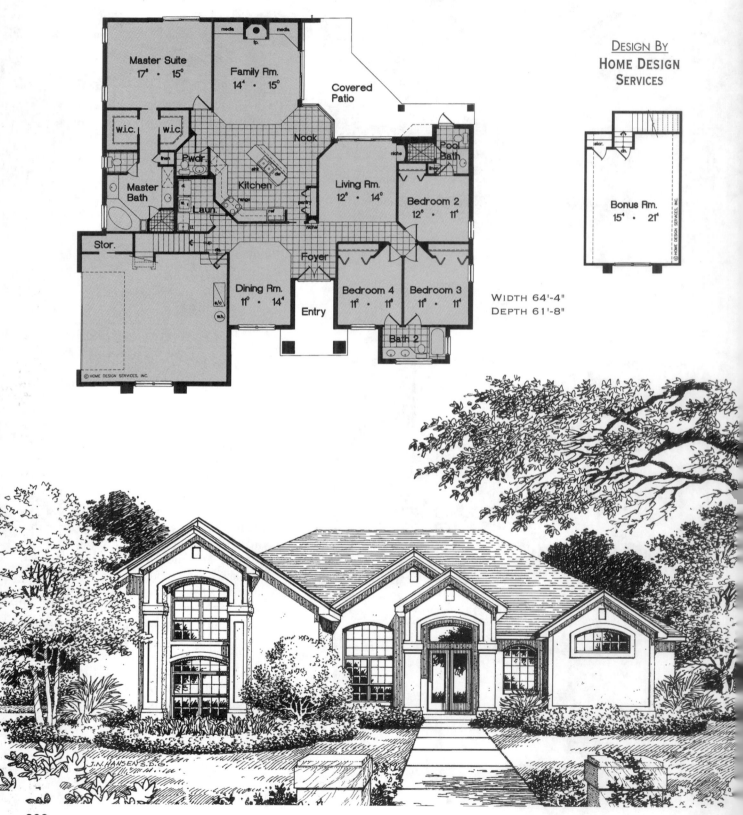

DESIGN BY
HOME DESIGN
SERVICES

WIDTH 64'-4"
DEPTH 61'-8"

DESIGN 8682

Square Footage: 2,551
Bonus Room: 287 square feet

DESIGN BY
HOME DESIGN
SERVICES

Family Room
vaulted ceiling
16⁰ · 19⁶

Covered Patio

Breakfast

fireplace

Kitchen

dw

ref

pantry

Bedroom 3
volume ceiling
12⁴ · 11⁰

Bath

desk

lin

desk

Bedroom 4
volume ceiling
11⁰ · 11⁰

up

Utility

w

d

down

Living Room
volume ceiling
14⁴ · 13⁶

wet bar

Bath

linen

w.i.c.

w.i.c.

Master Bedroom
19⁰ · 18⁰

Dining
volume ceiling
10⁸ · 13⁰

Foyer

Study
volume ceiling
10⁰ · 14⁰

Bath

Entry

up

Double Garage

WIDTH 69'-8"
DEPTH 71'-4"

ac

Bonus
11⁰ · 20⁴

Shutters and multi-pane windows dress up the exterior of this lovely stucco home. Formal and informal areas flow easily, beginning with the dining room sized to accommodate large parties and function with the adjacent living room. A gourmet kitchen is complete with a walk-in pantry and a cozy breakfast nook. Double doors lead to the spacious master suite. The lavish master bath features His and Hers walk-in closets, a tub framed by a columned archway and an oversized shower. Off the angular hallway are two bedrooms that share a pullman-style bath and a study desk. A bonus room over the garage provides additional space.

DESIGN 8644

Square Footage: 1,831

DESIGN BY
HOME DESIGN
SERVICES

A two-story entry, varying rooflines and multi-pane windows add to the spectacular street appeal of this three-bedroom home. To the right, off the foyer, is the dining room surrounded by elegant columns. Adjacent is the angular kitchen, which opens to the bayed breakfast nook. The family room includes plans for an optional fireplace and accesses the covered porch. The master bedroom is tucked in the back of the home and features a walk-in closet and full bath with a dual vanity, spa tub and oversized shower. Two additional bedrooms share a full bath.

WIDTH 59'-0"
DEPTH 55'-4"

This sunny home offers a wealth of livability in less than 2,300 square feet. The covered entry gives way to living and dining rooms. The kitchen is well equipped with a pantry and a breakfast room. The family room is a few steps away and delights with a fireplace. Two family bedrooms reside on this side of the plan. The master bedroom offers large proportions and an expansive bath with dual walk-in closets, a double-bowl vanity, a whirlpool tub, a separate shower and a compartmented toilet. A den is located off the entry and can also serve as another bedroom.

DESIGN 8669

Square Footage: 2,287

DESIGN BY
HOME DESIGN
SERVICES

WIDTH 63'-4"
DEPTH 62'-4"

DESIGN 8600

Square Footage: 2,041

DESIGN BY
HOME DESIGN
SERVICES

The striking facade of this house is only the beginning to a very livable design. A dramatic foyer with columns branches off into the living room on one side and the dining room on the other. A spacious family room graces the center of the house—a true focal point. Beyond the kitchen and breakfast nook you'll find the master bedroom with private access to the covered patio. The bath here is grand with a corner whirlpool tub, large shower, double sinks and walk-in closet. Three family bedrooms occupy the other side of the house. Note the two-car garage which connects to the main house at the laundry room.

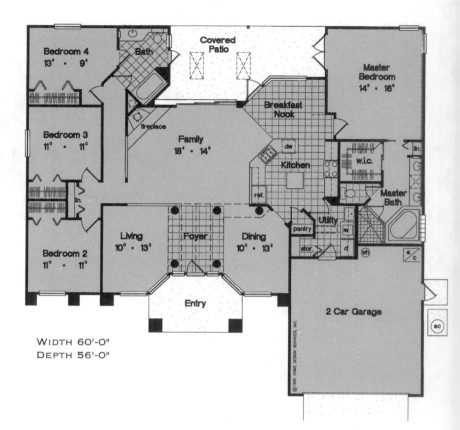

WIDTH 60'-0"
DEPTH 56'-0"

R. BRADSHAW

DESIGN BY
**HOME DESIGN
SERVICES**

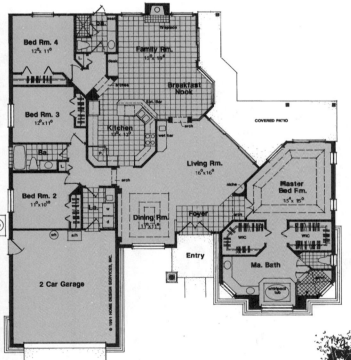

WIDTH 61'-8"
DEPTH 64'-8"

DESIGN 8646
Square Footage: 2,352

An array of varied, arched windows sets off this striking Italianate home. Double doors reveal the foyer, which announces the living room accented by a wet bar, niche and patio access. The coffered dining room combines with the living room to create a perfect space for formal entertaining. An arched entry to the informal living area presents a bayed breakfast nook and adjoining family room warmed by a fireplace. A pass-through kitchen comes with a deep pantry and informal eating bar. Double doors open to the coffered master bedroom. Its sumptuous bath has two walk-in closets, a dual vanity and spa tub. Arched entries lead to three additional bedrooms: two share a full bath and the third boasts a private bath with yard access. Blueprints include an alternate elevation at no extra charge.

Alternate Exterior

313

DESIGN 8662

Square Footage: 2,005

DESIGN BY
HOME DESIGN
SERVICES

Vaulted and volume ceilings soar above well-designed living areas in this spectacular move-up home. Open spaces create interior vistas and invite both formal and informal gatherings. An elegant dining room, defined by columns, offers views to the front property through multi-level muntin windows. To the left of the foyer, an extensive living room offers plans for an optional fireplace as well as privacy for quiet gatherings. The great room offers a vaulted ceiling and views to outdoor areas, and opens to the breakfast room with patio access and the kitchen with angled counter. Two family bedrooms, each with a volume ceiling, and a bath with twin lavatories complete the right side of the plan. The master bedroom enjoys its own bath with a whirlpool tub, separate shower, dual vanity and compartmented toilet.

WIDTH 58'-0"
DEPTH 60'-0"

A luxurious master suite is yours with this lovely plan—and it comes with two different options—one has a wet bar and fireplace. An over-sized great room with a grand fireplace is the heart of casual living in this relaxed plan. A formal dining room lies just off the foyer and offers easy access to the gourmet kitchen. Family bedrooms are split from the living area, perfect for a guest's comfort and privacy. A hall bath is shared by the two bedrooms as is a private door to the covered patio.

DESIGN 8601

Square Footage: 2,125

DESIGN BY
HOME DESIGN
SERVICES

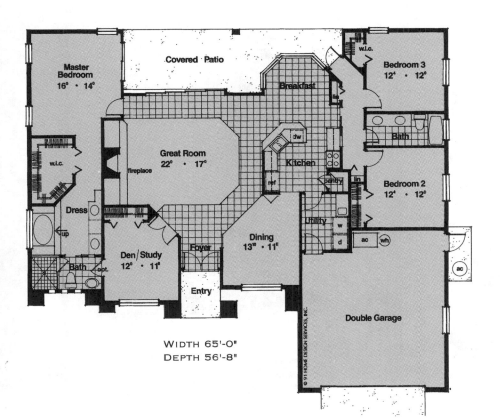

WIDTH 65'-0"
DEPTH 56'-8"

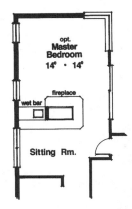

Optional Master Bedroom

DESIGN BY
HOME DESIGN
SERVICES

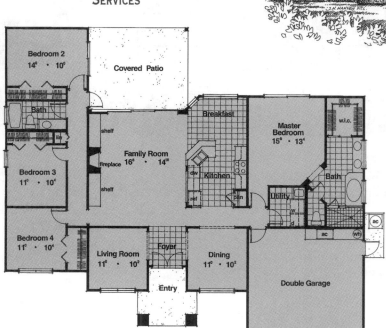

WIDTH 62'-8"
DEPTH 56'-0"

Alternate Exterior

The contemporary use of glass defines this dramatic exterior, but the real excitement begins with the interior design. A private living room offers a quiet place for formal entertaining and important conversations. The dining room, just across the foyer, offers views and light from graceful, arch-topped, muntin windows and opens to a gallery hall, with the kitchen just steps away. For informal gatherings, the family room offers a warming fireplace, built-in shelves for an entertainment center or library, and views and access to a covered patio. The family area opens to a tiled kitchen and breakfast area with views to the rear yard. Bedrooms are positioned to provide a private retreat for the homeowners in a secluded master suite, which offers a generous bath with garden tub, oversized shower, compartmented toilet and walk-in closet. Three family bedrooms share a full bath and access to the covered patio. Plans for this home include a choice of two exterior elevations.

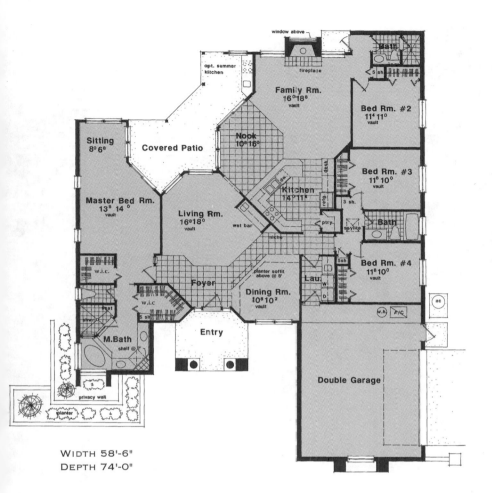

Sitting
8⁰ 6⁸

Covered Patio

Family Rm.
16⁰ 18⁸
vault

apt. summer kitchen

window above

fireplace

Bath

5 sh.

Bed Rm. #2
11⁴ 11⁰
vault

Nook
10⁰ 16⁰

Master Bed Rm.
13⁸ 14⁰
vault

Living Rm.
16⁰ 18⁰
vault

Kitchen
14⁰ 11⁸

desk

Bed Rm. #3
11⁸ 10⁰
vault

3 sh.

wet bar

niche

ref/g.

ptry.

skylite

Bath

w.i.c.

Foyer

planter soffit above @ 8'

Lau.

Bed Rm. #4
11⁸ 10⁰
vault

5 sh.

w.i.c.

seat

shwr

5 sh.

Dining Rm.
10⁸ 10²
vault

W

D

w.h.

F/C

ac

M.Bath

shelf @ 7'

Entry

Double Garage

privacy wall

planter

WIDTH 58'-6"
DEPTH 74'-0"

DESIGN 8645

Square Footage: 2,224

DESIGN BY
HOME DESIGN
SERVICES

Arches crowned by a gentle, hipped roof provide Italianate charm in this bright and spacious, family-oriented plan. A covered entry leads to the foyer that presents the angular, vaulted living and dining rooms. A kitchen with V-shape counter includes a walk-in pantry and looks out over the breakfast nook and family room with fireplace. The master suite features a sitting area, two walk-in closets and a full bath with garden tub. A roomy bedroom, with an adjacent cabana bath, opens off the family room and works perfectly as a guest room. Two additional bedrooms share a full bath located between them.

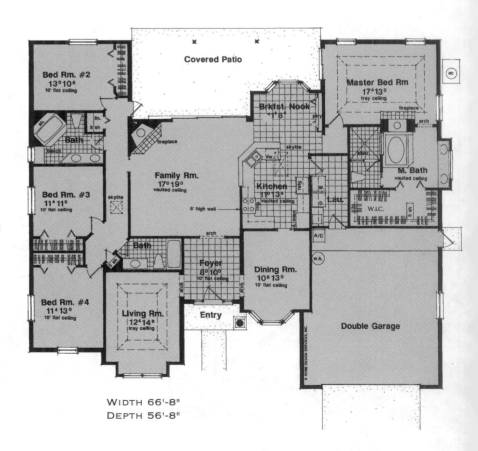

DESIGN 8620

Square Footage: 2,454

This one-story sports many well-chosen, distinctive exterior details including a cameo window and hipped rooflines. The dining and living rooms flank the foyer. A tray ceiling in the living room adds further enhancement. The bayed breakfast area admits light softened by the patio. Secluded from the main portion of the house, the master bedroom features a tray ceiling and fireplace through to the master bath. A raised tub, double vanity and immense walk-in closet highlight the bath.

DESIGN BY
HOME DESIGN
SERVICES

WIDTH 66'-8"
DEPTH 56'-8"

Covered Patio

Bed Rm. #2
13⁰10⁸
10' flat ceiling

Master Bed Rm
17⁴13⁰
tray ceiling

Brkfst. Nook
11⁴8⁰

Family Rm.
17⁰19⁰
vaulted ceiling

Kitchen
11⁰13⁴
vaulted ceiling

M. Bath
vaulted ceiling

Bath

Bed Rm. #3
11⁴11⁸
10' flat ceiling

skylite

Lau.

W.I.C.

8' high wall

A/C

w.h.

Bath

Foyer
8⁰10⁰
10' flat ceiling

Dining Rm.
10⁸13⁰
10' flat ceiling

Bed Rm. #4
11⁴13⁰
10' flat ceiling

Living Rm.
12⁴14⁸
tray ceiling

Entry

Double Garage

DESIGN 8639

Square Footage: 2,149

sh
fireplace
Family Room
16⁰ · 14⁰
sh

Covered Patio

Nook

dw

Kitchen

ref

pantry

Bedroom 2
11² · 10⁰

Living Room
13⁰ · 12⁰

Bath

Master Bedroom
16⁰ · 13⁴

Bath

Bath
lin

w.i.c.

Bath

niche

Foyer

Dining
11⁴ · 11⁰

Den/Study
14ᶜ · 11⁰

Entry

Bedroom 3
11⁴ · 10⁰

Utility

w

d

wh   ac

© 91 HOME DESIGN SERVICES, INC.

Double Garage

WIDTH 60'-8"
DEPTH 62'-3"

T his impressive plan creates views which make this house look much larger than it really is. Upon entry into this four-bedroom, three-bath home, the formal living room overflows to outdoor living space. The formal dining room is designed with open wall areas for an air of spaciousness. A decorative arch leads to the family spaces of the home. The two bedrooms share a pullman bath, accessible only from the rooms themselves for total privacy. The kitchen/family room/nook area is large and inviting, all with beautiful views of the outdoor living spaces. The master wing of the home is off the den/study and the pool bath. Double doors welcome you into the master suite with a glass bed wall and angled sliding glass doors to the patio. The efficient use of space makes the bath as functional as it is beautiful.

J.N.HANSEN P.T.L.

DESIGN 8612

Square Footage: 1,576

Though modest in size, this home boasts an interior courtyard with solarium. The master suite surrounds the solarium and opens with double doors to the large open family room. The dining room shares a volume ceiling with this space and connects via a serving bar to the kitchen. Besides the fireplace in the family room, there is also a sliding glass door to a covered patio. Family bedrooms are to the rear of the plan. They share a full bath. Note the utility area just off the foyer and breakfast nook with bright multi-paned windows. Plans include three different elevation choices!

Alternate Exterior

Alternate Exterior

DESIGN BY
HOME DESIGN
SERVICES

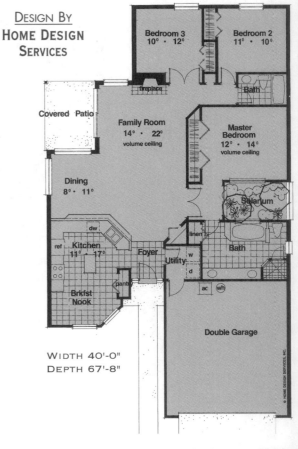

WIDTH 40'-0"
DEPTH 67'-8"

This home, as shown in the photograph, may differ from the actual blueprints. For more detailed information, please check the floor plans carefully.

Photo by Home Design Services

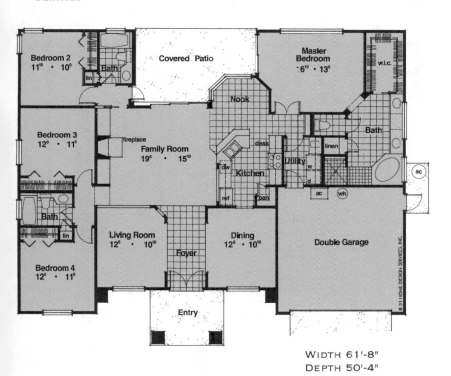

WIDTH 61'-8"
DEPTH 50'-4"

DESIGN 8637

Square Footage; 2,089

This four-bedroom, three-bath home offers the finest in modern amenities. The formal living spaces have a classic split design, perfect for quiet time and conversation. The huge family room, which opens up to the patio with twelve-foot, pocket sliding doors, has space for a fireplace and media equipment. Two family bedrooms share their own bath while one bedroom has a private bath with patio access, making it the perfect guest room. The master suite, located just off the kitchen and nook, is private yet easily accessible. It has a double-door entry and a bed wall with glass above. The angled entry to the bath makes for a luxurious view of the corner tub. The step-down shower and private toilet room, walk-in linen closet, lavish vanity and closet make this a super bath!

DESIGN Q272

Square Footage: 1,375

DESIGN BY
SELECT HOME DESIGNS

This compact, affordable plan offers a choice of exteriors. The stucco version has box windows and a weather-protected entry. The heritage version offers a covered veranda and circle-top window. Plans include details for both. Off the foyer, the living room boasts a vaulted ceiling and a wood-burning fireplace with wood bin. The dining room has an optional buffet nook and sliding glass doors to the patio. The kitchen and attached breakfast room enjoy views of the garden and are directly in line with the entry hall. A master bedroom and two family bedrooms sit to the left of the plan. The family bedrooms share a full hall bath, while the master has a private bath. A stairway just off the breakfast room leads to a basement which can be developed into living or sleeping space at a later time.

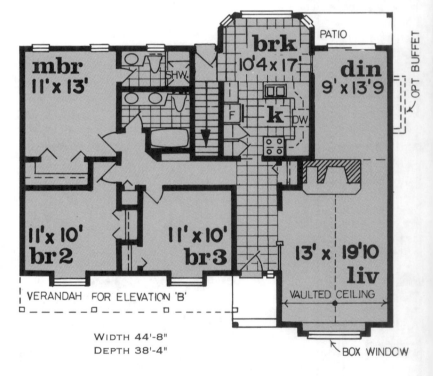

mbr 11' x 13'

brk 10'4 x 17'

PATIO

OPT BUFFET

din 9' x 13'9

SHW.

F

k DW

br 2 11' x 10'

br3 11' x 10'

liv 13' x 19'10

VAULTED CEILING

VERANDAH FOR ELEVATION 'B'

BOX WINDOW

WIDTH 44'-8"
DEPTH 38'-4"

Plans include all exteriors shown

DESIGN Q334
Square Footage: 2,966

Alternate Exterior

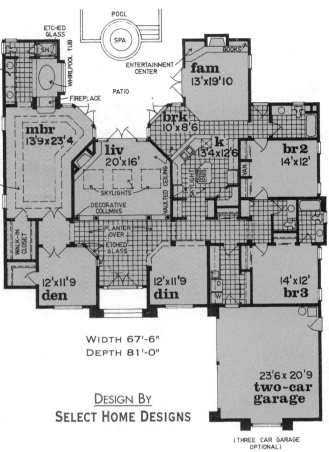

WIDTH 67'-6"
DEPTH 81'-0"

DESIGN BY
SELECT HOME DESIGNS

(THREE CAR GARAGE OPTIONAL)

Wrapping around a patio courtyard, this three- or four-bedroom home works perfectly in sunny climes. Decorative quoins adorn the exterior, including a wide entry with double doors opening to the foyer. Columns introduce the living room and separate the dining room from the central hall. The living room is further enhanced by skylights, a vaulted ceiling, a fireplace and French doors to the patio beyond. An island kitchen features a peninsular counter overlooking the breakfast room and a roomy pantry. The breakfast room also has double doors to the patio. A nearby family room sports built-ins, another fireplace and more patio access. Bedrooms are split with the family bedrooms—each with its own bath—on the right and the master suite on the left. The master bedroom has a tray ceiling, walk-in closet, patio access and a through-fireplace to the master bath. Look for a spa tub and separate shower here. A cozy den opens through double doors in the master suite entry. The two-car garage is accessed through the service entrance. Plans include details for both a basement and a crawlspace foundation. Details for both elevations are also included.

Rear Elevation

DESIGN Q599
Square Footage: 2,804

An angled entry allows for privacy in this three-bedroom bungalow. The foyer is a hub which leads to all of the main living spaces, which are defined by columns. The living room is sunken and has a fireplace. The nearby dining room overlooks the front of the house. The family room is also sunken and features a fireplace and double doors to the rear covered lanai. The master bedroom also opens off the main foyer through double doors. It has a sitting area with lanai access, double walk-in closets and a grand bath with whirlpool tub. The kitchen and breakfast nook are just beyond the family room, just across the hall from a cozy den. Two family bedrooms and a full bath are on the left side of the plan.

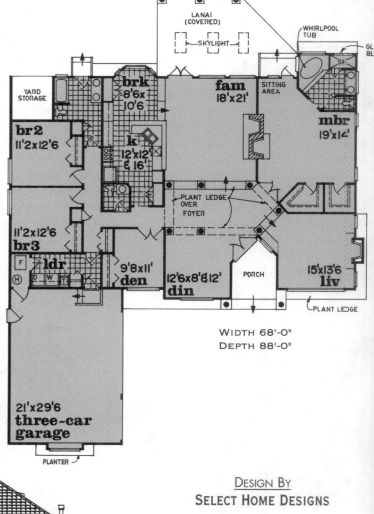

LANAI (COVERED)
SKYLIGHT
WHIRLPOOL TUB
GLA BLO
YARD STORAGE
brk 8'6x 10'6
fam 18'x21'
SITTING AREA
br2 11'2x12'6
k 12'x12' & 16'
mbr 19'x1c'
11'2x12'6
br3
ldr
D W T
9'8x11' den
PLANT LEDGE OVER FOYER
12'6x8'&12' din
PORCH
15'x13'6 liv
PLANT LEDGE
21'x29'6
three-car garage
PLANTER

WIDTH 68'-0"
DEPTH 88'-0"

DESIGN BY
SELECT HOME DESIGNS

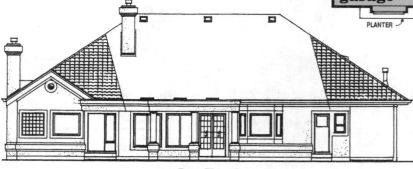

Rear Elevation

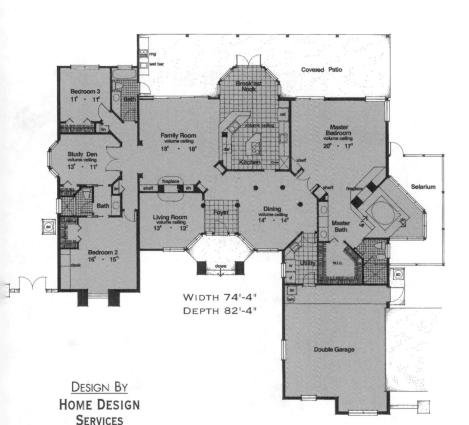

DESIGN 8624

Square Footage: 2,987

Covered Patio

Breakfast Nook

Bedroom 3
11⁰ · 11⁴

Bath

mg
wet bar

Family Room
volume ceiling
18⁴ · 18²

volume ceiling

Kitchen

ref

shelf

Master Bedroom
volume ceiling
20⁰ · 17⁰

Study Den
volume ceiling
13⁴ · 11⁰

Bath

fireplace

shelf

sh

dw

oven

shelf

fireplace

Solarium

Living Room
volume ceiling
13⁴ · 12²

Foyer

Dining
volume ceiling
14⁴ · 14⁵

Master Bath

up

dn

Bedroom 2
16⁶ · 15⁴

desk

Utility

w.i.c.

w

d

ac

(wh)

downs

dn

WIDTH 74'-4"
DEPTH 82'-4"

Double Garage

DESIGN BY
HOME DESIGN
SERVICES

Classic columns, a tiled roof and beautiful arched windows herald a gracious interior for this fine home. Arched windows also mark the entrance into the vaulted living room with a tiled fireplace. The dining room opens off the foyer with vaulted ceiling. Filled with light from a wall of sliding glass doors, the family room leads to the covered patio (note the wet bar and range that enhance outdoor living). The kitchen features a vaulted ceiling and unfolds into the roomy nook which boasts French doors onto the patio. The master bedroom also has patio access and shares a dual fireplace with the master bath. A solarium lights this space. A vaulted study/bedroom sits between two additional bedrooms—all share a full bath.

This home, as shown in the photograph, may differ from the actual blueprints. For more detailed information, please check the floor plans carefully.

Photo by Peter A. Burg

DESIGN Q319

Square Footage: 1,501

DESIGN BY
SELECT HOME DESIGNS

Alternate Exterior

Choose either the California stucco option or the version with horizontal siding and brick for the facade of this home. Details for both are included in the plans. An interesting floor plan awaits inside. A kitchen and breakfast room reside just beyond the entry and are open to a long living room/dining room combination. This area has a vaulted ceiling, a fireplace and access to the rear patio. A plant ledge decorates the hall entry and is lit by a centered skylight. Three bedrooms line the right side of the plan. Family bedrooms share a full hall bath. The master suite is to the rear and has a plant ledge at its entry, a vaulted ceiling and a bath with whirlpool tub. A door to the rear yard brightens the master bedroom. A laundry alcove sits in a service entrance to the two-car garage. If you choose, you may build this plan with a basement that can be expanded at a later time. Plans include details for both a basement and a crawlspace foundation.

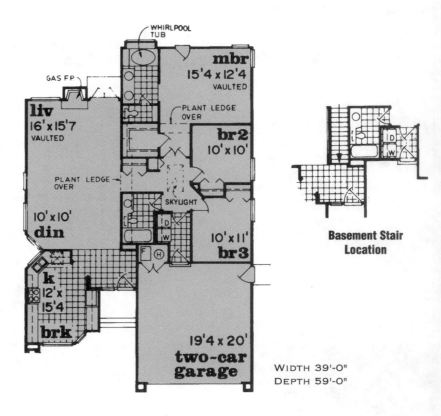

Basement Stair Location

WIDTH 39'-0"
DEPTH 59'-0"

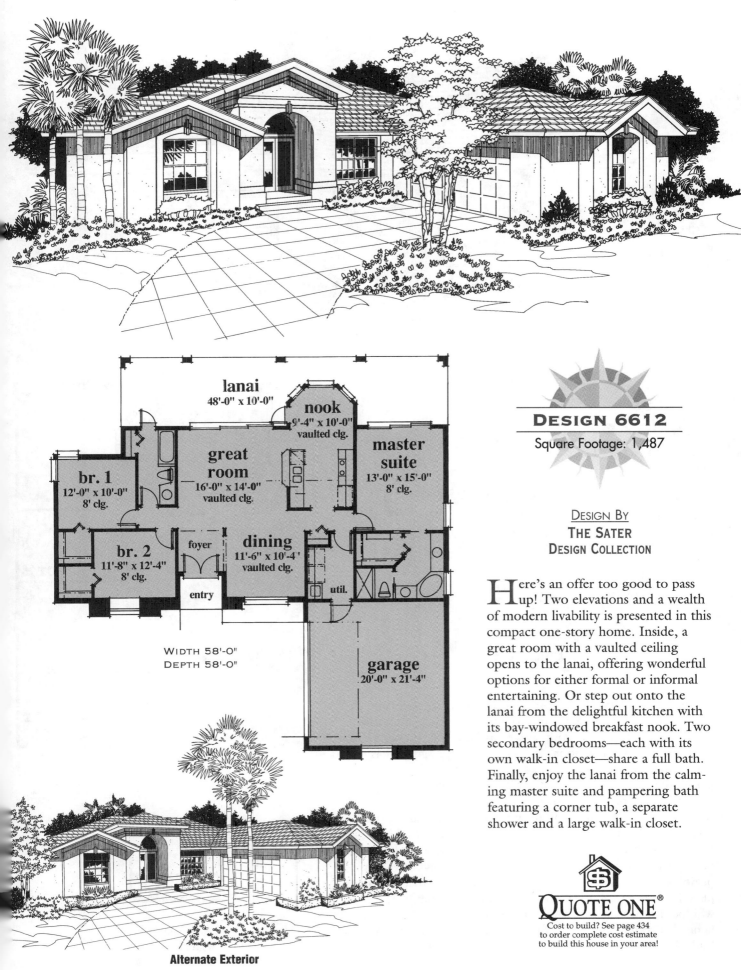

lanai
48'-0" x 10'-0"

nook
9'-4" x 10'-0"
vaulted clg.

great room
16'-0" x 14'-0"
vaulted clg.

master suite
13'-0" x 15'-0"
8' clg.

br. 1
12'-0" x 10'-0"
8' clg.

br. 2
11'-8" x 12'-4"
8' clg.

foyer

dining
11'-6" x 10'-4'
vaulted clg.

entry

util.

WIDTH 58'-0"
DEPTH 58'-0"

garage
20'-0" x 21'-4"

Alternate Exterior

DESIGN 6612

Square Footage: 1,487

DESIGN BY
**THE SATER
DESIGN COLLECTION**

Here's an offer too good to pass up! Two elevations and a wealth of modern livability is presented in this compact one-story home. Inside, a great room with a vaulted ceiling opens to the lanai, offering wonderful options for either formal or informal entertaining. Or step out onto the lanai from the delightful kitchen with its bay-windowed breakfast nook. Two secondary bedrooms—each with its own walk-in closet—share a full bath. Finally, enjoy the lanai from the calming master suite and pampering bath featuring a corner tub, a separate shower and a large walk-in closet.

QUOTE ONE®
Cost to build? See page 434
to order complete cost estimate
to build this house in your area!

DESIGN Q316

Square Footage: 1,328

Alternate Exterior

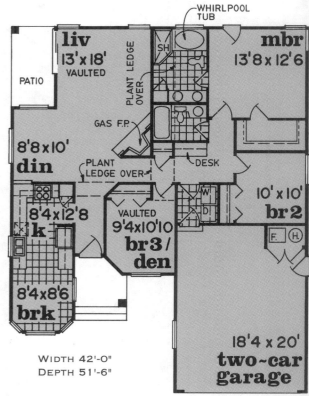

WHIRLPOOL TUB

liv 13'x18' VAULTED

PATIO

PLANT LEDGE OVER

mbr 13'8 x 12'6

SH

GAS F.P.

8'8x10' **din**

PLANT LEDGE OVER

DESK

k 8'4x12'8

br3/ den 9'4x10'10 VAULTED

W D

10' x 10' **br2**

F. H

8'4x8'6 **brk**

WIDTH 42'-0"
DEPTH 51'-6"

18'4 x 20' **two~car garage**

DESIGN BY
SELECT HOME DESIGNS

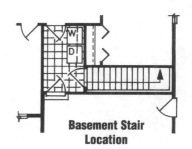

W
D

Basement Stair Location

The choice is yours: California stucco or horizontal wood siding. Both are appealing and true to their classic traditions. Plans include details for both, as well as for a crawlspace or basement foundation. The floor plan is designed for living areas to the rear of the plan, to capture views and take advantage of a rear patio. The living room is vaulted and has a corner fireplace and sliding glass doors. The L-shaped kitchen and breakfast room sit to the front. The kitchen has abundant counter space and a pass-through to the dining room. A vaulted ceiling graces the den (or third bedroom) which is also brightened by a transom window. A handy hall desk can serve the student in the family or work as a planning desk. A great master retreat awaits at the back of the plan. It holds a walk-in closet, rear access and a bath with whirlpool tub, separate shower and double vanities. The additional family bedroom has use of a full bath in the hall. A laundry alcove leads the way through a service entrance to the two-car garage.

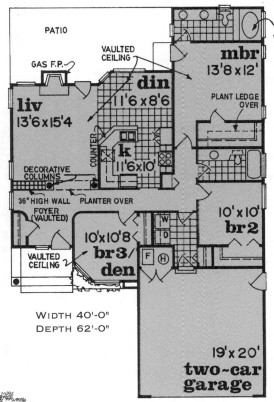

PATIO

GAS F.P.

VAULTED CEILING

din
11'6 x 8'6

mbr
13'8 x 12'

PLANT LEDGE OVER

liv
13'6 x 15'4

COUNTER

k
11'6 x 10'

DECORATIVE COLUMNS

36" HIGH WALL   PLANTER OVER

FOYER (VAULTED)

10'x10'8
br3/ den

VAULTED CEILING

W   D

F   H

10' x 10'
br2

WIDTH 40'-0"
DEPTH 62'-0"

19'x 20'
two-car garage

DESIGN Q314

Square Footage: 1,365

This design offers the option of a traditional wood-sided plan or a cool, stucco version. Details for both facades are included in the plans. The interior offers a very comfortable floor plan in a smaller footprint. The off-set entry is covered and opens to a vaulted foyer with coat closet. Decorative columns and a three-foot high wall mark the boundary of the living room, which is vaulted and warmed by a gas fireplace. The dining area is nearby and connects to a U-shaped kitchen with peninsular counter. Both have cathedral ceilings. A den in the hall might be used as a third bedroom, if you choose. An additional family bedroom has a walk-in closet and full bath nearby. A vaulted ceiling highlights the master bedroom. Additional features here include a walk-in closet and a fully appointed bath. A two-car garage remains in the front of the plan and acts as a shield for the bedrooms. Plans include details for both a basement and a crawlspace foundation.

DESIGN BY
SELECT HOME DESIGNS

Alternate Exterior

DESIGN 8611

Square Footage: 1,413

DESIGN BY
HOME DESIGN
SERVICES

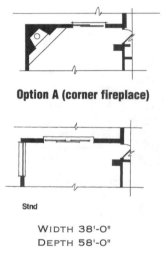

Option A (corner fireplace)

Stnd

WIDTH 38'-0"
DEPTH 58'-0"

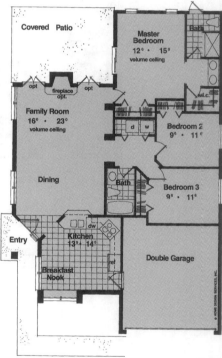

An angled side entry to this home allows for a majestic, arched window that dominates its facade. The interior, though small in square footage, holds an interesting and efficient floor plan. Because the breakfast room is placed to the front of the plan, it benefits from two large, multipane windows. The dining and family rooms form a single space enhanced by a volume ceiling and an optional fireplace, which is flanked by sets of optional double doors. Both the family room and master bedroom boast access to the covered patio. A volume ceiling further enhances the master bedroom, which also has a dressing area, walk-in closet and full bath. The plans include options for a family room with corner fireplace with French doors or a sliding glass door instead of a fireplace. The package includes plans for three different elevations.

Alternate Exterior

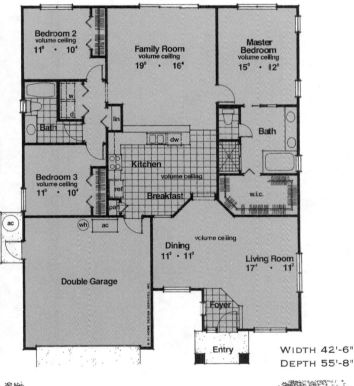

Bedroom 2
volume ceiling
11⁰ · 10⁴

Family Room
volume ceiling
19⁰ · 16⁴

Master
Bedroom
volume ceiling
15⁰ · 12⁰

Bath

w

d

lin

Bath

Kitchen
volume ceiling

dw

Bedroom 3
volume ceiling
11⁰ · 10⁴

ref

Breakfast

w.i.c.

pan

ac

wh

ac

volume ceiling

Double Garage

Dining
11² · 11⁰

Living Room
17⁴ · 11²

Foyer

Entry

WIDTH 42'-6"
DEPTH 55'-8"

Alternate Exterior

DESIGN 8632
Square Footage: 1,750

This dapper design boasts two exterior elevation choices—both with true good looks. Inside, a volume ceiling enlivens the combined living and dining rooms. Interestingly, the kitchen acts as the heart of the home, both in location and style. A tiled floor and a volume ceiling set the mood of the room, while ample counterspace lends to its practicality. Casual living takes precedence in the spacious family room. In the master bedroom, you'll find a private bath that includes dual lavatories, a private commode and an expansive walk-in closet. The secondary bedrooms find privacy by design as well as convenience in the full bath that separates them. Also noteworthy, the washer and dryer location rests in a tidy alcove by these bedrooms.

DESIGN BY
HOME DESIGN
SERVICES

DESIGN 8630

Square Footage: 1,550

DESIGN BY
**HOME DESIGN
SERVICES**

Enjoy resort-style living in this striking sun-country home. Guests will always feel welcome when entertained in the formal living and dining areas, but the eat-in country kitchen overlooking the family room will be the center of attention. Casual living will be enjoyed in the large family room and out on the patio with the help of an optional summer kitchen and view of the fairway. Built-in shelves and an optional media center give you decorating options. The master suite features a volume ceiling and oversized master bath. Two secondary bedrooms accommodate guests or family and share a full hall bath. Plans for this home include a choice of two exterior elevations.

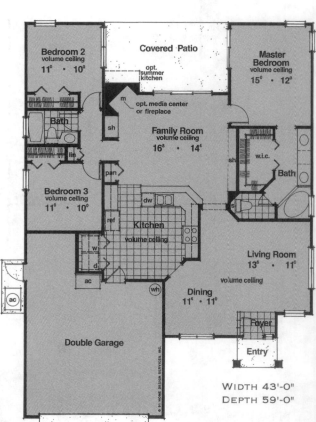

WIDTH 43'-0"
DEPTH 59'-0"

Alternate Exterior

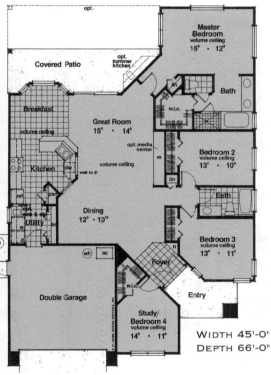

Covered Patio

opt. summer kitchen

Master Bedroom
volume ceiling
16⁸ · 12⁸

Breakfast
volume ceiling

Great Room
15⁸ · 14⁹

opt. media center

Bath

w.i.c.

Kitchen

wall to 8'

m

Bedroom 2
volume ceiling
13⁸ · 10⁹

lin

ref

opt. sink & ste

Utility

Dining
12⁹ · 10¹⁰

Bath

Bedroom 3
volume ceiling
13⁴ · 11⁴

n

ac

wh

ac

Double Garage

Foyer

w.i.c.

Entry

Study/Bedroom 4
volume ceiling
14⁹ · 11⁹

WIDTH 45'-0"
DEPTH 66'-0"

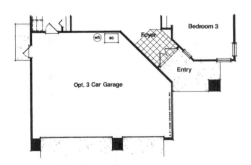

wh   ac

Foyer

Bedroom 3

Entry

Opt. 3 Car Garage

Optional 3-Car Garage

DESIGN 8633
Square Footage: 1,865

DESIGN BY
HOME DESIGN
SERVICES

This innovative plan features an angled entry into the home, lending visual impact to the facade and giving the interior floor plan space for a fourth bedroom. A fabulous central living area with volume ceiling includes a dining area with kitchen access, a great room with built-in media center and access to the rear covered patio. The tiled kitchen shares natural light from the bayed breakfast area with volume ceiling. The kitchen and breakfast nook overlook the outdoor living space which even offers an optional summer kitchen—great for entertaining. A plush master suite opens from the great room through a privacy door and offers vistas to the rear and side grounds. The traditional feel of the exterior and the up-to-date interior make this home a perfect design for the nineties.

Alternate Exterior

333

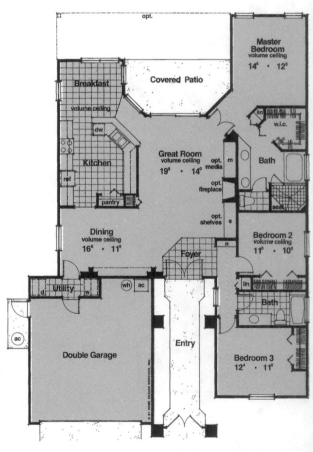

DESIGN 8631
Square Footage: 1,697

DESIGN BY
HOME DESIGN
SERVICES

Great great-room design! This exciting plan features a main gathering area bordered on the left by the formal dining area with a decorative built-in wall for a custom touch. The unobstructed view of the rear outdoor space is maximized from the gathering space as well as the kitchen and breakfast room. The placement of secondary bedrooms toward the front of the home gives a sense of privacy. The master suite compares favorably to much larger homes, boasting a huge shower, compartmented toilet and oversized vanity and closet. Space for a media center and fireplace are also allowed for in the design. The blueprints for this design include options for two different exteriors.

WIDTH 45'-0"
DEPTH 68'-4"

Dining

Optional Kitchen Plan

Alternate Exterior

334

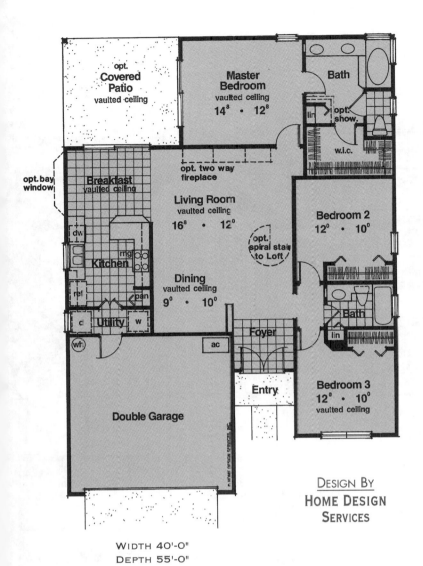

opt.
Covered Patio
vaulted ceiling

Master Bedroom
vaulted ceiling
14⁸ • 12⁸

Bath

opt. show.

lin

w.i.c.

opt. bay window

Breakfast
vaulted ceiling

opt. two way fireplace

Living Room
vaulted ceiling
16⁸ • 12⁰

Bedroom 2
12⁰ • 10⁰

dw

rng

Kitchen

opt. spiral stair to Loft

Dining
vaulted ceiling
9⁰ • 10⁰

ref

pan

c

Utility

w

Bath

lin

wh.

ac

Foyer

Double Garage

Entry

Bedroom 3
12⁰ • 10⁰
vaulted ceiling

WIDTH 40'-0"
DEPTH 55'-0"

DESIGN BY
HOME DESIGN SERVICES

A volume entry and open planning give this house a feeling of spaciousness that goes far beyond its modest square footage. The foyer opens to a large living and dining area that combines for flexible entertaining needs. The kitchen is planned to fulfill a gourmet's dream and merges with the breakfast area for informal dining. Located to the rear for privacy, the master suite opens onto the patio and features a lush bath with a huge walk-in closet. Two secondary bedrooms share a full hall bath. The covered rear patio has a dramatic vaulted ceiling, giving an extra touch of elegance to casual living.

© HOME DESIGN SERVICES, INC.

DESIGN 8610

Square Footage: 1,280

DESIGN BY
HOME DESIGN
SERVICES

This plan is ideal for the young family looking for a house that's small but smart. As in larger plans, this home boasts a private master's retreat with lots of closet space, dual vanities and a shower. The living area embraces the outdoor living space. The family eat-in kitchen design allows for efficient food preparation. Note the interior laundry closet included in the home. This plan comes with three options for Bedroom 2 and one option for the master bath. It also includes blueprints for three elevation choices!

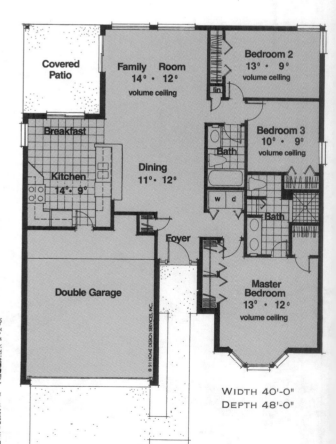

WIDTH 40'-0"
DEPTH 48'-0"

Alternate Exterior

A recessed entry with double doors introduces this lovely plan. Vaulted ceilings throughout the foyer, living room, dining room and kitchen add a sense of spaciousness and allow for plant ledges. A peninsula fireplace separates the dining room and living room. The family room has another fireplace, flanked by shelves to serve as an entertainment center. A private den sits just beyond the family room. Note the deck that sits outside the dining room and breakfast room. Bedrooms are on the second floor: a master suite and two family bedrooms. The master bedroom has a walk-in closet and private bath with raised whirlpool tub. Family bedrooms share a full hall bath and a built-in desk on the landing. Plans include details for both a basement and a crawlspace foundation.

DESIGN Q330

First Floor: 1,520 square feet
Second Floor: 929 square feet
Total: 2,449 square feet

DESIGN BY
SELECT HOME DESIGNS

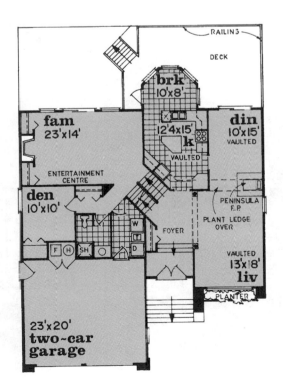

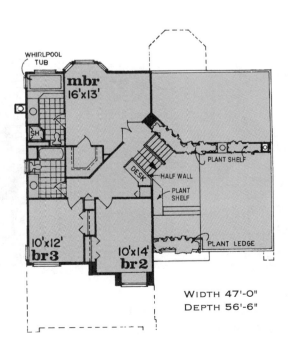

WIDTH 47'-0"
DEPTH 56'-6"

DESIGN Q294

Square Footage: 1,692

DESIGN BY
SELECT HOME DESIGNS

A dormer window brightens the foyer of this smaller Floridian home. A sunken living room to the left of the foyer takes advantage of a coffered ceiling and full-width window wall. The attached dining room connects to the U-shaped kitchen and bayed breakfast room. An open family room with gas fireplace completes the living spaces. Sleeping quarters are located to the right of the plan. The master suite has double doors to the rear yard and a pampering bath with separate whirlpool tub and shower and double vanities. Family bedrooms share a full hall bath. The two-car garage is accessed through a service entrance past the laundry alcove. Plans include details for a crawlspace and a basement foundation.

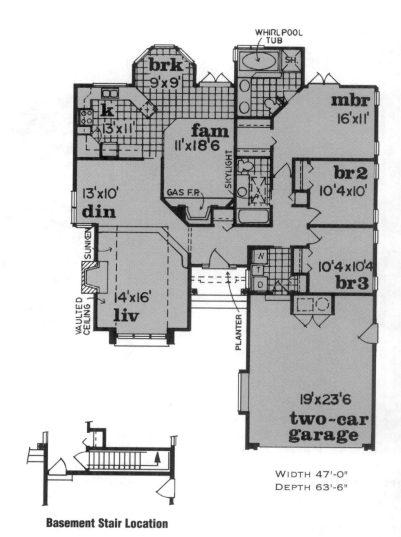

WIDTH 47'-0"
DEPTH 63'-6"

Basement Stair Location

DESIGN BY
SELECT HOME DESIGNS

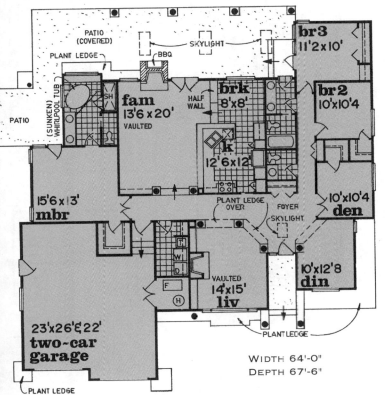

PATIO (COVERED)

PLANT LEDGE

SKYLIGHT

BBQ

br3
11'2 x 10'

(SUNKEN) WHIRLPOOL TUB

SH

fam
13'6 x 20'
VAULTED

HALF WALL

brk
8'x8'

br2
10'x10'4

PATIO

k
12'6 x 12

15'6 x 13'
mbr

PLANT LEDGE OVER

FOYER
SKYLIGHT

10'x10'4
den

VAULTED
14'x15'
liv

10'x12'8
din

23'x26'&22'
two-car
garage

PLANT LEDGE

PLANT LEDGE

WIDTH 64'-0"
DEPTH 67'-6"

DESIGN Q607

Square Footage: 2,257

A covered and skylit rear patio, graced by an array of columns and a built-in barbecue, is the highlight of this casual design. The interior is open and lives easily. The breakfast room and efficient kitchen overlook the sunken family room, which is warmed by a hearth. Columns separate the family room from the central hall and also define the formal living and dining rooms. The master suite boasts a walk-in closet, private patio and luxurious bath with sunken whirlpool tub, His and Hers vanities, a private shower and compartmented toilet. A den, with walk-in closet, can be used as a fourth bedroom. Additional bedrooms share a full bath with patio access.

Rear Elevation

DESIGN Q372

Square Footage: 1,883

DESIGN BY
SELECT HOME DESIGNS

Finish this home in either California stucco or horizontal siding, with the garage opening to the front or the side of the home. Rooflines vary depending on your choice. The interior retains the same great floor plan. From a skylit, covered porch, the plan begins with a large entry opening to the living room with fireplace and den—or Bedroom 2—which can be accessed through double doors in the entry or a single door in the hall. Decorative columns line the hall and define the family room space. A fireplace, flanked by windows is a focal point in this casual living area. The nearby breakfast room opens to the patio and connects the family room to the U-shaped kitchen. The master bedroom is huge—and amenity filled. It also has patio access and features a bath with whirlpool tub and separate shower. An additional bedroom is served by a full bath. A large laundry room connects the two-car garage to the main house. Plans include details for both a basement and a crawlspace foundation.

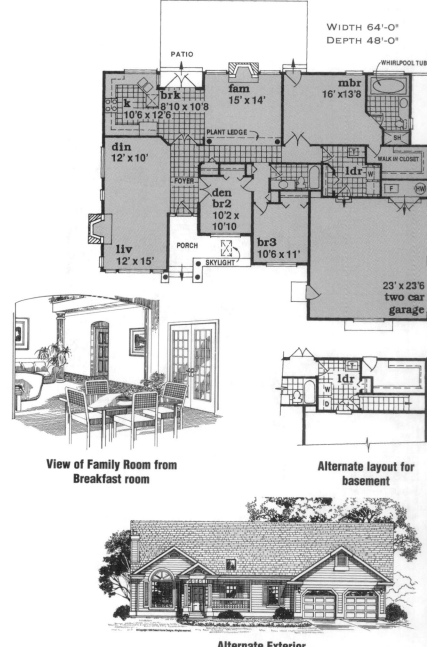

View of Family Room from Breakfast room

Alternate layout for basement

Alternate Exterior

340

DESIGN Q417

Square Footage: 2,657

DESIGN BY
SELECT HOME DESIGNS

WIDTH 68'-0"
DEPTH 71'-6"

Alternate Bedroom Layout

Rear Elevation

Elegant arched windows, a portico entry and low-maintenance stucco distinguish this California design. The interior is well-appointed and thoughtfully planned. Flanking the foyer are the formal living and dining rooms—defined by decorative columns and plant shelves. The living room boasts a tray ceiling and fireplace. A sunken family room sits in the center of the plan and is graced by double doors to the patio, a fireplace, a vaulted ceiling and a skylight. Two steps up is the U-shaped kitchen with island and attached breakfast room, separated by a snack-bar counter. Family bedrooms and a full bath are on the left side of the plan. The master suite and a den with full bath sit on the right. The master suite contains access to the patio and a bath with whirlpool tub, double vanities and a separate shower. An alternate bedroom layout is included in the plans. Plans also include details for both a basement and a crawlspace foundation.

DESIGN Q418

Square Footage: 2,761

DESIGN BY
SELECT HOME DESIGNS

Dramatic rooflines dominate this three-bedroom sun-country design. Interior space begins with a double-door entrance leading directly through the vaulted foyer to a sunken living room with vaulted ceiling and fireplace. A fully glazed wall at one end of the living room allows views to the covered, skylit lanai. A built-in barbecue adds to the fun on the lanai. Decorative columns separate the living room, dining room and Bedroom 3 from the foyer. If you choose, Bedroom 3 could be used as a den. The dining room reaches to the kitchen through a butler's pantry. In the kitchen are snack counters and an attached breakfast room with bay window. A sunken family room is just beyond. It is warmed by a fireplace and has double-door access to a rear patio. Bedrooms include a master suite with hearth-warmed sitting room, lanai access and bath with walk-in closet and whirlpool tub. Plans include details for both a basement and a crawlspace foundation.

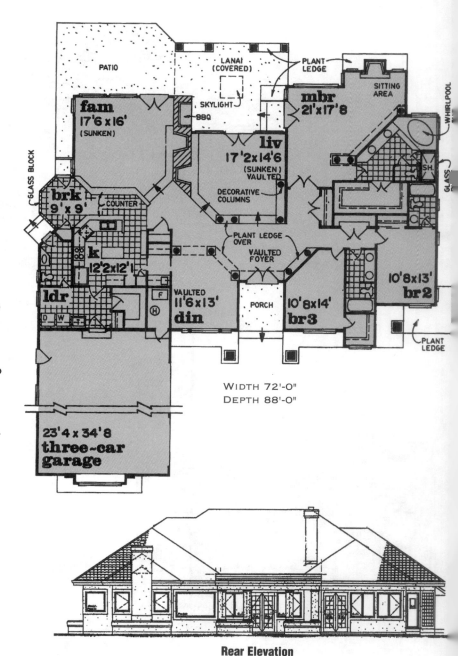

WIDTH 72'-0"
DEPTH 88'-0"

Rear Elevation

Alternate Exterior

This compact plan may be built with a Floridian facade in stucco, or a more traditional siding-and-brick facade. Details for both exteriors are included in the plans. You also have the option of two or three bedrooms. One of the bedrooms could be used as a family room. A half wall separates the foyer from the living room, which is highlighted by a window seat in its box window, a fireplace and an attached dining room. A U-shaped kitchen features abundant counter space, an angled sink under a corner plant shelf and a sunny breakfast area with access to the rear patio. The family room—or third bedroom—has a bright window seat, also. The master bedroom has no rival for luxury. It has a bay-window seating area, large wall closet and private bath. Access the two-car garage through the service entrance at the laundry alcove. Plans include optional basement foundation details.

DESIGN BY
SELECT HOME DESIGNS

PATIO
OPTIONAL WALL
SEAT
PLANT LEDGE
brk
k 16'x10'8
din 12'10'6
br3/ fam 9'6 x 10'8
mbr 11'x14'
ART NICHE
FOYER
WALL
liv 12'15'2
SEAT
D W
br2 10'x9'
two-car garage 19'x20'6

WIDTH 40'-0"
DEPTH 54'-6"
STOR.
FOYER
D W
br2 9'x10'6
two-car garage 19'x20'

Basement stair location

DESIGN Q354
Square Footage: 1,336

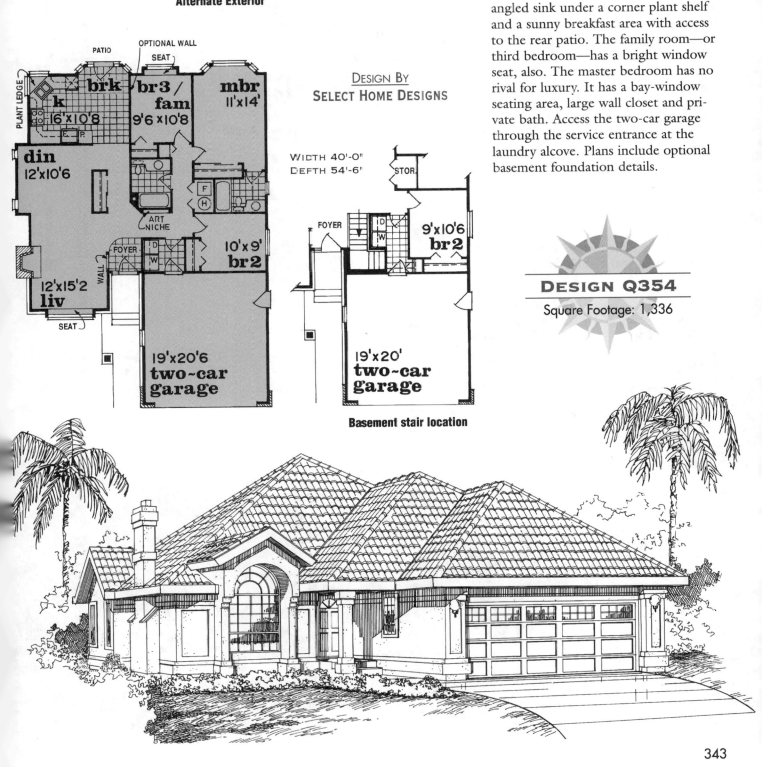

343

DESIGN 8672

Square Footage: 2,397

DESIGN BY
HOME DESIGN SERVICES

WIDTH 60'-0"
DEPTH 71'-8"

Low-slung, hipped rooflines and an abundance of glass enhance the unique exterior of this sunny, one-story home. Inside, the use of soffits and tray ceilings heighten the distinctive style of the floor plan. To the left, double doors lead to the private master suite, which is bathed in natural light—compliments of an abundant use of glass—and enjoys a garden setting from the corner tub. Convenient planning of the gourmet kitchen places everything at minimum distances and serves the outdoor summer kitchen, breakfast nook and family room with equal ease. Completing the plan are two family bedrooms that share a full bath.

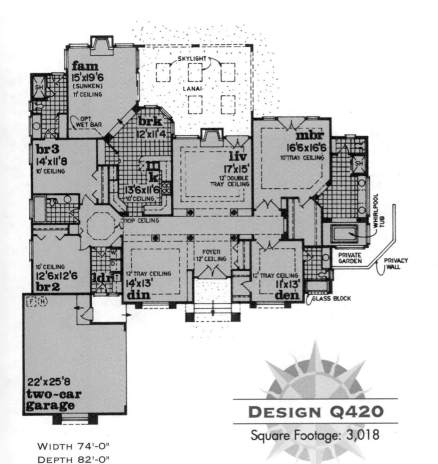

fam
15'x19'6
(SUNKEN)
11' CEILING

SKYLIGHT

LANAI

OPT.
WET BAR

brk
12'x11'4

mbr
16'6x16'6
10' TRAY CEILING

br3
14'x11'8
10' CEILING

k
13'6x11'6
10' CEILING

liv
17'x15'
12' DOUBLE
TRAY CEILING

WHIRLPOOL
TUB

TOP CEILING

10' CEILING
12'6x12'6
br2

ldr

12' TRAY CEILING
din
14'x13'

FOYER
12' CEILING

12' TRAY CEILING
den
11'x13'

PRIVATE
GARDEN

PRIVACY
WALL

GLASS BLOCK

22'x25'8
**two-car
garage**

WIDTH 74'-0"
DEPTH 82'-0"

DESIGN Q420
Square Footage: 3,018

Two distinct exteriors can be built from the details for this plan—both are perfect as sun-country designs. The entry is grand and allows for a twelve-foot ceiling in the entry foyer. Open planning calls for columns to separate the formal living room and the formal dining room from the foyer and central hall. Both rooms have tray ceilings, and the living room has a fireplace and double door access to the skylit lanai. The modified U-shaped kitchen has an attached breakfast room and steps down to the family room with fireplace and optional wet bar. A lovely octagonal foyer introduces family bedrooms and their private baths. A den with tray ceiling and full bath sits to the right of the foyer and doubles as guest room space when needed. The master suite is separated from family bedrooms. It has double-door access to the rear yard, a walk-in closet and a full bath with whirlpool tub, double vanity, compartmented toilet and separate shower. The whirlpool overlooks a private garden outside. Note the two-car garage just beyond the laundry area. Plans include details for both a basement and a crawlspace foundation.

DESIGN BY
SELECT HOME DESIGNS

Alternate Exterior

Rear

DESIGN Q329

First Floor: 1,199 square feet
Second Floor: 921 square feet
Total: 2,120 square feet

DESIGN BY
SELECT HOME DESIGNS

An angled entry gives a new slant to this cool California design. The two-story foyer is lighted by a multi-paned window and leads down two steps to a sunken foyer. A pair of decorative columns separates the living room and formal dining room. A U-shaped kitchen, with walk-in pantry, serves the breakfast room. Just beyond is the family room with fireplace and rear-yard access. A den is tucked in between the laundry room and two-car garage (note storage). On the second floor, the master suite has a walk-in closet and private bath with corner whirlpool and separate shower. Two additional bedrooms share a full bath. A laundry chute in the hall sends clothes to the laundry room for washing. Plans include details for both a basement and a crawlspace foundation.

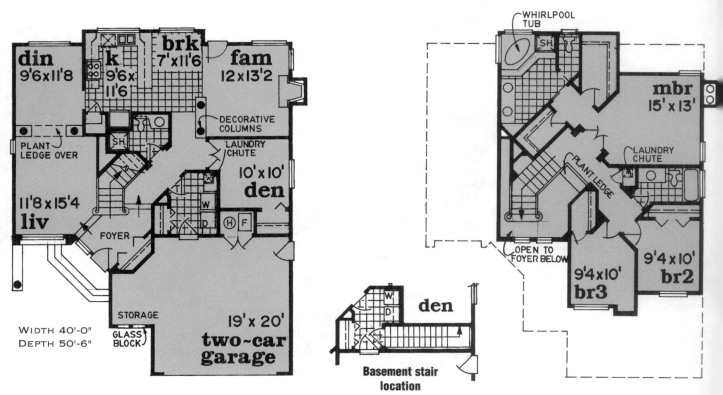

F inish this design in stucco, horizontal siding or brick. Whichever you choose, you'll have a lovely lasting home with a most livable floor plan. The vaulted foyer introduces the interior plan and is brightened by clerestory windows. The breakfast bay sits between the hearth-warmed sunken family room and the U-shaped kitchen and accesses a rear patio for alfresco dining. Formal spaces are on the extreme left side of the plan and include a living room with fireplace and a formal dining room. A den is tucked behind the two-car garage. Bedrooms are on the second floor and include a master suite with private deck and grand bath. Family bedrooms share a full bath. Plans include details for both a basement and a crawlspace foundation.

DESIGN Q285

First Floor: 1,267 square feet
Second Floor: 1,010 square feet
Total: 2,277 square feet

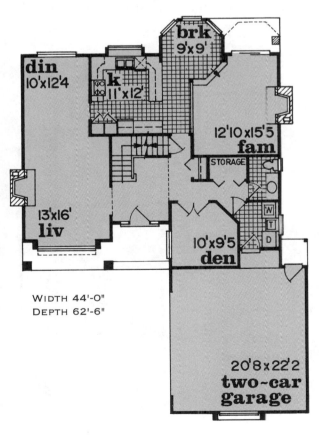

din
10'x12'4

k
11'x12'

brk
9'x9'

12'10x15'5
fam

STORAGE

13'x16'
liv

10'x9'5
den

W
T
D

WIDTH 44'-0"
DEPTH 62'-6"

20'8x22'2
two-car
garage

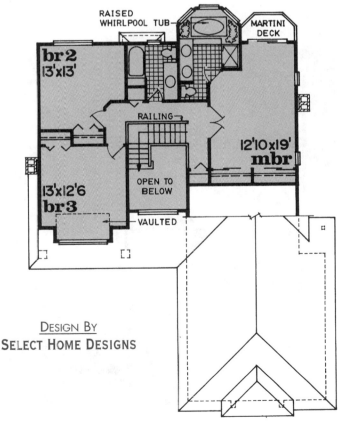

RAISED
WHIRLPOOL TUB

MARTINI
DECK

br2
13'x13'

RAILING

12'10x19'
mbr

13'x12'6
br3

OPEN TO
BELOW

VAULTED

DESIGN BY
SELECT HOME DESIGNS

DESIGN Q326

First Floor: 1,237 square feet
Second Floor: 794 square feet
Total: 2,031 square feet

A weather-protected entry with decorative columns introduces this innovative design. The foyer spills into an open-plan living and dining room. A pair of columns and a planter bridge visually zone the two rooms. The family room has a fireplace and sliding glass doors to the rear patio. It is separated from formal living and dining areas by the island kitchen and light-filled breakfast room. A cozy den opens through double doors just off the foyer. The master bedroom is on the second floor with two family bedrooms. It features a walk-in closet and bath with whirlpool tub and separate shower. The family bedrooms share a full bath with soaking tub. Note the two-car garage and the half-bath in the foyer. Plans include details for both a basement and a crawlspace foundation.

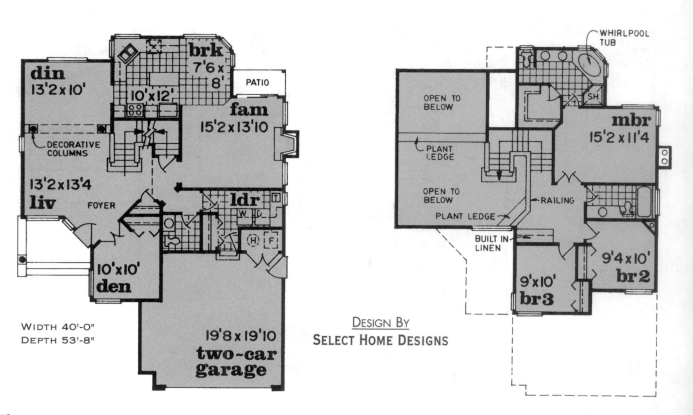

DESIGN BY
SELECT HOME DESIGNS

L ooking for drama and spaciousness? This design has volume rooflines to allow for vaulted ceilings in the living room, dining room and foyer. The gourmet kitchen, hearth-warmed family room and bumped-out breakfast nook form a large casual area for gatherings. Note the sliding glass doors in the family room leading to the rear yard. A den is positioned close to a full bath so it can double easily as a guest room. Three second-floor bedrooms include a master suite with private bath, vaulted ceiling and window seat. If you like, choose the three-car garage option. Plans include details for both a basement and a crawlspace foundation.

DESIGN Q327

First Floor: 1,195 square feet
Second Floor: 893 square feet
Total: 2,088 square feet

DESIGN BY
SELECT HOME DESIGNS

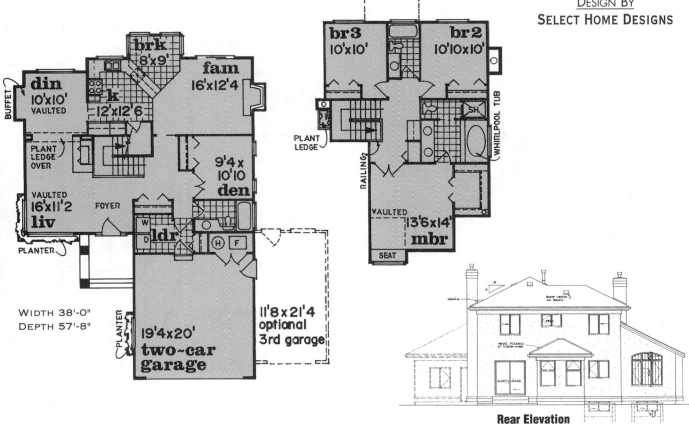

WIDTH 38'-0"
DEPTH 57'-8"

Rear Elevation

DESIGN Q297

First Floor: 1,776 square feet
Second Floor: 483 square feet
Total: 2,259 square feet

Two circle-top windows—one over the entry and one in the living room—echo the gentle arch over the recessed entry of this home. Double doors open to a center hall with staircase to the second floor. Formal living and dining rooms are on the left. Both have vaulted ceilings. The living room is sunken and boasts a gas fireplace. The family room also has a vaulted ceiling and a gas fireplace and is brightened by skylights. In between sits the island kitchen with attached breakfast bay. A deck is accessed through sliding glass doors in the family room. The master bedroom is on the first floor for privacy. It holds a private deck, a through-fireplace to its well-appointed bath and a walk-in closet. An additional bedroom with full bath and a den with private deck are found on the second floor. Plans include details for both a basement and a crawlspace foundation.

DESIGN BY
SELECT HOME DESIGNS

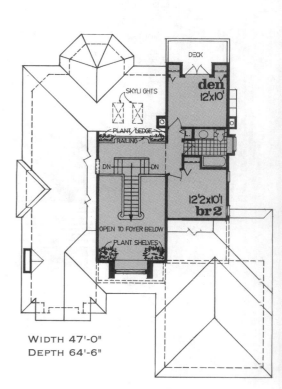

WIDTH 47'-0"
DEPTH 64'-6"

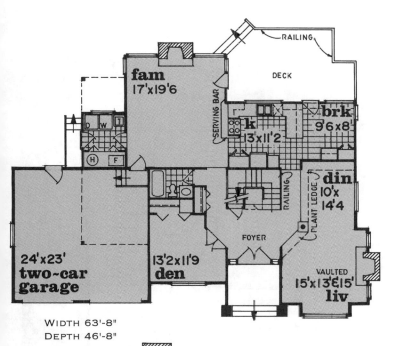

fam
17'x19'6

DECK

RAILING

SERVING BAR

brk
9'6x8'

k
13'x11'2

D W

H F

din
10'x
14'4

PLANT LEDGE

RAILING

FOYER

24'x23'
two-car
garage

13'2x11'9
den

vaulted
15'x13'&15'
liv

WIDTH 63'-8"
DEPTH 46'-8"

DESIGN Q598

First Floor: 1,583 square feet
Second Floor: 1,086 square feet
Total: 2,669 square feet

This exciting three-bedroom home can be finished in either California stucco or traditional brick with horizontal siding accents. Vaulted ceilings extend from the foyer to the living room and add a sense of spaciousness to the interior. A plant ledge lines the living and dining rooms and provides visual separation from the foyer. The den, with wall closet and private access to a full bath, can double as an extra guest suite or bedroom. The family room has a masonry fireplace and joins the U-shaped kitchen and breakfast room in the rear of the house. Three bedrooms form the upper level of the house. The master bedroom has a vaulted ceiling and sitting room with fireplace. The master bath is well appointed.

SITTING

WHIRLPOOL TUB

SH

mbr
15'x15'6 & 19'6
VAULTED

br 2
11'6x10'
& 15'

RAILING

OPEN
BELOW

VAULTED
10'8x10'9
br 3

VAULTED

DESIGN BY
SELECT HOME DESIGNS

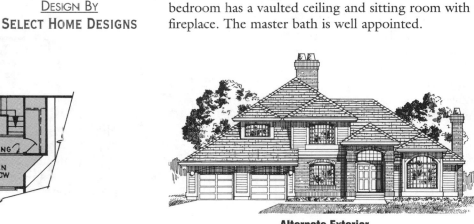

Alternate Exterior

DESIGN Q243

First Floor: 1,224 square feet
Second Floor: 866 square feet
Total: 2,090 square feet

Completed in sunny stucco, this design has the flavor of the Mediterranean. The entry is angled and leads to an expansive living room with raised-hearth fireplace. The dining room is attached and has double doors to the family room (note the vaulted ceiling and fireplace) and breakfast room. The den is at the other end of the plan; it can double as a guest room. The kitchen is U-shaped and has a lovely window sink. The second floor holds two family bedrooms sharing a full bath, plus a master suite with His and Hers closets and bath with whirlpool tub and separate corner shower. A two-car garage holds the family fleet easily.

DESIGN BY
SELECT HOME DESIGNS

WIDTH 43'-3"
DEPTH 66'-0"

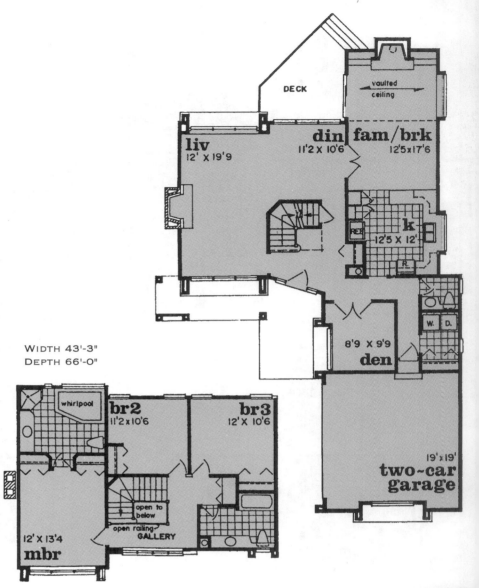

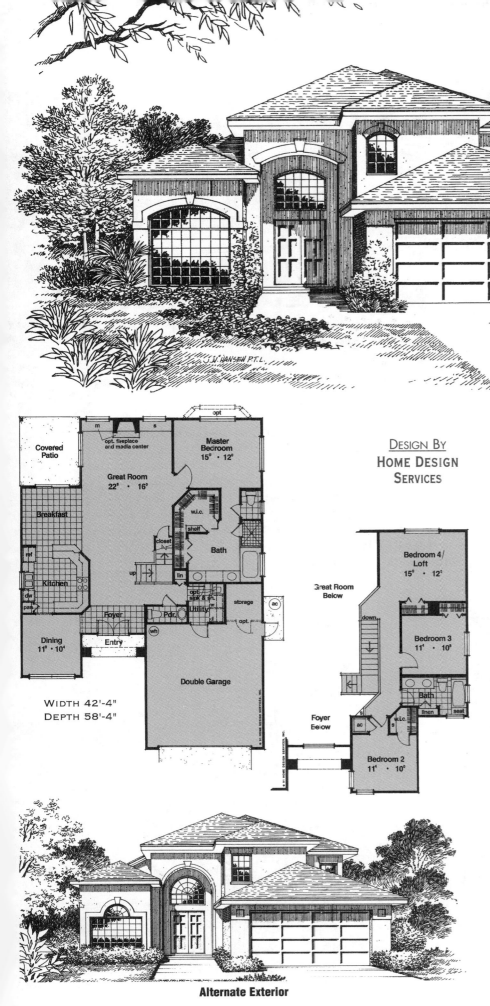

WIDTH 42'-4"
DEPTH 58'-4"

Alternate Exterior

DESIGN BY
HOME DESIGN
SERVICES

DESIGN 8640

First Floor: 1,485 square feet
Second Floor: 697 square feet
Total: 2,182 square feet

This two-story home has everything for the young family or empty-nester. The double-door entry foyer has a seemingly unlimited view of the huge great room. This living area comes complete with fireplace and media center. The formal dining room, tucked away in the front of the home, is perfect for quiet candlelight dinners. The kitchen and nook areas overlook the outdoor living space and the great room. The master suite on the first floor features a California closet plan for the best use of space. Other amenities include a soaking tub, adjacent shower and private toilet. The stairs to the second floor have a free-floating design with open rails. Bedrooms on the second floor are ample; Bedroom 4 can be used as a loft area or activity room for the kids. Blueprints come with options for two different exteriors.

DESIGN 8635

First Floor: 982 square feet
Second Floor: 982 square feet
Total: 1,964 square feet

This two-story has it all! Remarkable views as you enter this home are only the beginning. Every major living area on the first floor has a view of the rear yard. The formal living and dining area is the perfect place for entertaining and special candlelight dinners. The island kitchen has a commanding view of the breakfast and family areas, as well as the rear yard. The second floor boasts four bedrooms, with the master suite overlooking the rear yard. The California closet layout in the master bath makes efficient use of space and maximizes storage. Bedroom 4 can double as a master sitting room or den. Blueprints come with options for two different exteriors.

DESIGN BY
**HOME DESIGN
SERVICES**

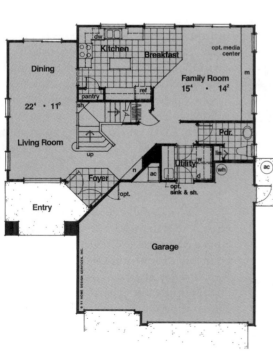

WIDTH 40'-0"
DEPTH 48'-10"

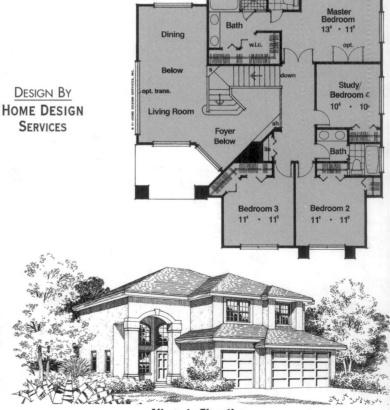

Alternate Elevation

The tiled foyer of this two-story home opens to a living/dining space with a soaring ceiling, a fireplace in the living room and access to a covered patio that invites outdoor livability. The kitchen has an oversized, sunny breakfast area with a volume ceiling. The first-floor master bedroom offers privacy with its sumptuous bath; a corner soaking tub, dual lavatories and a compartmented toilet lend character to the room. Upstairs, a loft overlooking the living spaces could become a third bedroom. One of the family bedrooms features a walk-in closet. Both bedrooms share a generous hall bath.

DESIGN 8659

First Floor: 1,230 square feet
Second Floor: 649 square feet
Total: 1,879 square feet

DESIGN BY
HOME DESIGN
SERVICES

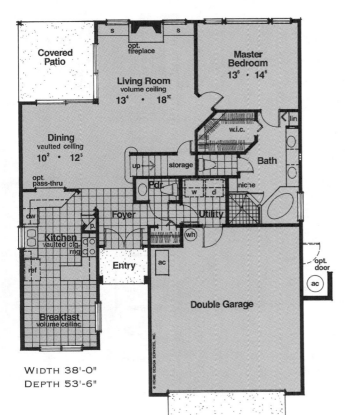

WIDTH 38'-0"
DEPTH 53'-6"

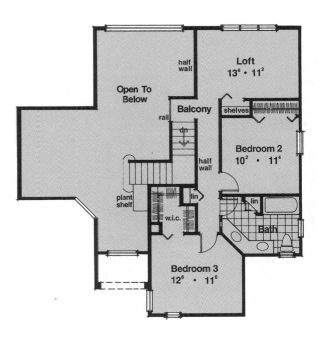

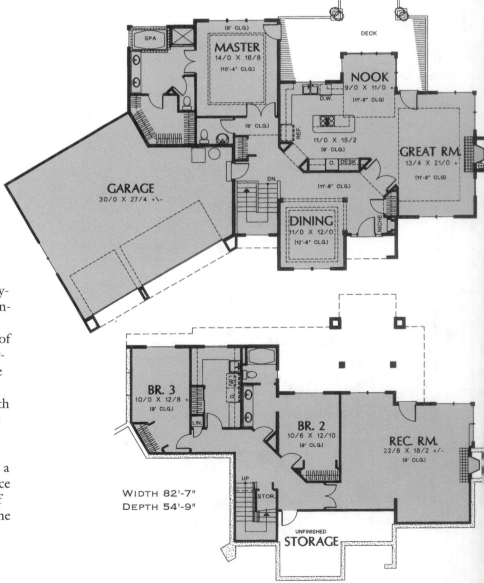

DESIGN 9537

Main Level: 1,687 square feet
Lower Level: 1,251 square feet
Total: 2,938 square feet

DESIGN BY
ALAN MASCORD
DESIGN ASSOCIATES, INC.

This striking home is perfect for daylight basement lots. An elegant dining room fronts the plan. It is near an expansive kitchen that features plenty of cabinet and counter space. A nook surrounded by a deck adds character. The comfortable great room, with a raised ceiling and a fireplace, shares space with these areas. The master bedroom suite includes private deck access and a superb bath with a spa tub and dual lavatories. Downstairs, two bedrooms, a laundry room with lots of counter space and a rec room with a fireplace cap off the plan. A three-car garage furthers the custom feel of this home.

Grand design, in stucco with keystone arches over the windows and entry, makes the most of this two-story. For entertaining, there is the grand room with fireplace, built-ins and double-door access to the rear covered terrace. It is complemented by the dining hall and living room (or study) at the front of the plan. The peninsula kitchen and attached morning room occupy space on the right side of the plan. The master suite is on the left—don't miss its outstanding master bath and walk-in closet. The second floor has three family suites—one with a private bath. A balcony overlooks the grand room below. Bonus space over the garage can become an additional bedroom if you choose.

DESIGN A205

First Floor: 2,417 square feet
Second Floor: 1,238 square feet
Total: 3,655 square feet
Bonus Room: 413 square feet

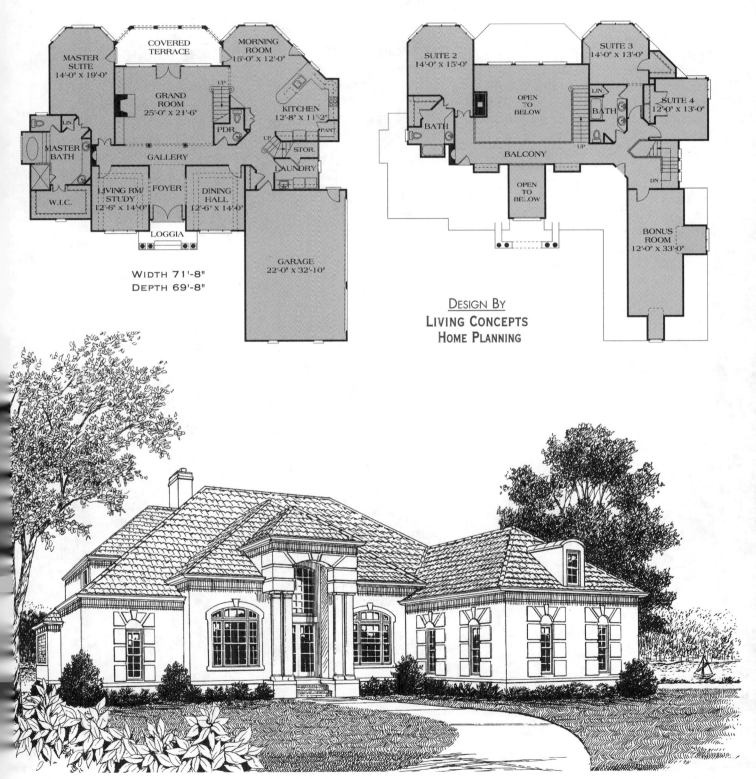

MASTER SUITE
14'-0" x 19'-0"

COVERED TERRACE

MORNING ROOM
15'-0" x 12'-0"

GRAND ROOM
25'-0" x 21'-6"

KITCHEN
12'-8" x 11'-2"

MASTER BATH

GALLERY

W.I.C.

LIVING RM/STUDY
12'-6" x 14'-0"

FOYER

DINING HALL
12'-6" x 14'-0"

LOGGIA

STOR.

LAUNDRY

GARAGE
22'-0" x 32'-10"

WIDTH 71'-8"
DEPTH 69'-8"

SUITE 2
14'-0" x 15'-0"

SUITE 3
14'-0" x 13'-0"

OPEN TO BELOW

SUITE 4
12'-0" x 13'-0"

BATH

BATH

BALCONY

OPEN TO BELOW

BONUS ROOM
12'-0" x 33'-0"

DESIGN BY
LIVING CONCEPTS
HOME PLANNING

DESIGN 8690

Square Footage: 3,556

DESIGN BY
**HOME DESIGN
SERVICES**

A beautiful curved portico provides a majestic entrance to this one-story home. Curved ceilings in the formal living and dining rooms continue the extraordinary style. To the left of the foyer is a den/bedroom with a private bath, ideal for use as a guest suite. The exquisite master suite features a see-through fireplace and an exercise area with a wet bar. A sumptuous soaking tub and island shower in the master bath invite relaxation. The family wing is geared for casual living with a powder room/patio bath, a huge island kitchen with a walk-in pantry, a glass-walled breakfast nook and a grand family room with a fireplace and media wall. Two family bedrooms share a private bath.

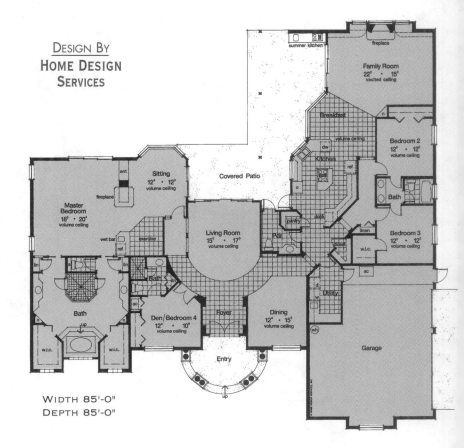

WIDTH 85'-0"
DEPTH 85'-0"

WIDTH 83'-10"
DEPTH 112'-0"

Bonus Room
24⁵ · 20⁵
Open To Below

DESIGN BY
HOME DESIGN
SERVICES

DESIGN 8692
Square Footage: 4,222
Bonus Room: 590 square feet

The striking facade of this magnificent estate is just the beginning of the excitement you will encounter inside. The entry foyer passes the formal dining room to the columned gallery, which leads to all regions of the house, with the formal living room at the head. The living room opens to the rear patio and the show-piece pool lying flush against the dramatic rear windows of the house. Expanding the entertaining options, a sunken wet bar serves the living room and the pool via a swim-up bar. The contemporary kitchen has a work island and all the amenities for gourmet preparations. The family room will be a favorite for casual entertaining with extras such as a built-in media center, fireplace and a breakfast nook with doors to the covered patio. The covered patio is fully equipped with a summer kitchen and dramatic steps to the pool and spa. A bonus loft overlooking the family room adds a new dimension to casual living. The family sleeping wing begins with an octagonal vestibule and features three bedrooms with private baths. The master wing opens with double doors to a minor foyer and private garden that segments the sleeping chamber from the opulent bath. A see-through fireplace and twin double doors join the bedroom to the rear patio and spa.

DESIGN 8034

First Floor: 2,639 square feet
Second Floor: 1,625 square feet
Total: 4,264 square feet

DESIGN BY
LARRY E. BELK
DESIGNS

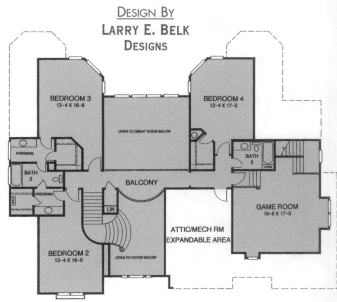

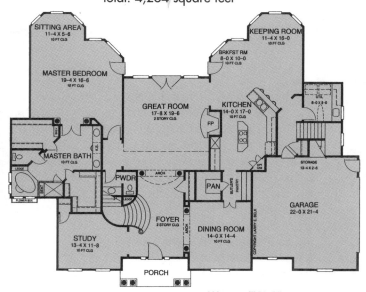

WIDTH 73'-8"
DEPTH 58'-6"

Rear

European traditional style is the hallmark of this best-selling plan. The stucco finish provides an elegant look to a home that is as beautiful from the rear as it appears from the front curb. Available in a 3,800-square-foot version as well, this home is a perfect blend of charm and practicality. The two-story foyer is graced by a lovely staircase and a Romeo balcony overlook from upstairs. Two columns flank the entry to the great room, notable for its beautiful window wall facing the rear grounds. Two-story double bays on the rear of the home form the keeping room and the breakfast room on one side and the master bedroom and its sitting area on the other. A huge walk-in pantry and an adjacent butler's pantry connect the dining room to the kitchen. Rear stairs from the kitchen join the family gathering area with the three bedrooms and game room upstairs. With a large study downstairs, this home provides all the amenities needed for today's busy family.

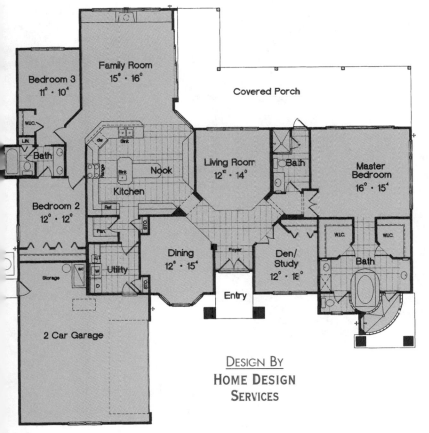

Bedroom 3
11⁰ · 10⁴

Family Room
15⁰ · 16⁰

Covered Porch

W.I.C.

LIN

Bath

Kitchen

Nook

Living Room
12¹⁰ · 14⁰

Bath

Master Bedroom
16⁰ · 15⁴

Bedroom 2
12⁰ · 12⁰

Ref

Pan

W.I.C.

W.I.C.

Bath

Utility

Storage

Dining
12⁸ · 15⁴

Foyer

Den/Study
12⁰ · 18⁰

Entry

2 Car Garage

DESIGN BY
HOME DESIGN
SERVICES

WIDTH 71'-10"
DEPTH 72'-8"

This design is perfect for the growing family. The formal living and dining rooms are separated by angular tile work and are ideal for quiet evenings of dinner and conversation. The huge island kitchen becomes the center of family gatherings. The secondary bedrooms share a pullman-style bath just off the large family room, which features a windowed media/fireplace wall. Note the large pantry just off the laundry room. The den/study can easily become a guest room, with use of the pool bath. The master wing comes complete with a windowed bed wall and an excellent master bath with an island tub, glass block shower, His and Hers vanities and walk-in closets. The courtyard-style garage layout makes for an easy fit on a small lot.

J.N. HANSEN S.D.G.

DESIGN 8145

First Floor: 2,959 square feet
Second Floor: 1,055 square feet
Basement: 1,270 square feet
Total: 5,284 square feet
Expandable Area: 230 square feet

Designed for a sloping lot, this fantastic Mediterranean features all the views to the rear, making it the perfect home for an ocean, lake or golf-course view. Inside, the two-story great room features a full window wall to the rear. The breakfast room, kitchen, dining room and master suite also have rear views. A tri-level series of porches is located on the back for outdoor relaxing. Two bedroom suites are found upstairs, each with a private bath and a porch. The basement of this home features another bedroom suite and a large game room. An expandable area can be used as an office or Bedroom 5. This home may also be built with a slab foundation. Please specify your preference when ordering.

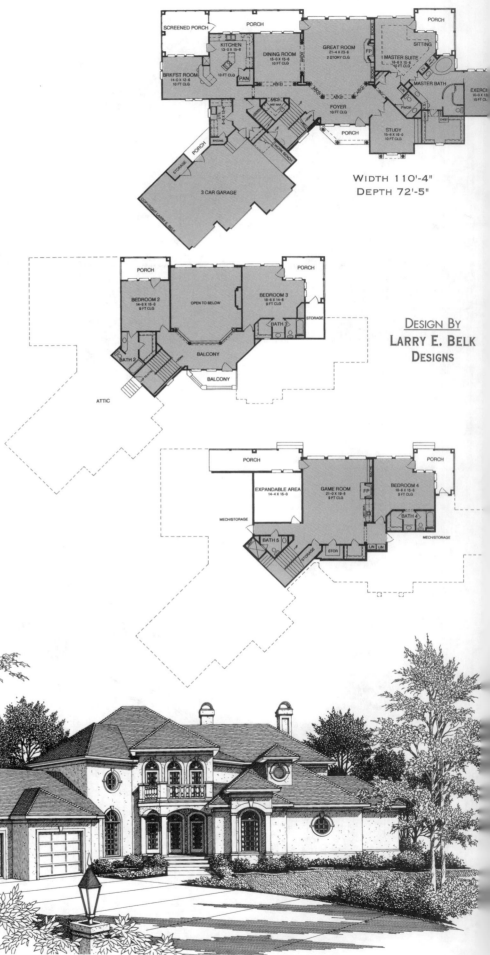

WIDTH 110'-4"
DEPTH 72'-5"

DESIGN BY
LARRY E. BELK
DESIGNS

COPYRIGHT LARRY E. BELK

Rear

DEIGN 6685

Main Level: 1,305 square feet
Second Level: 1,215 square feet
Total: 2,520 square feet
Unfinished Bonus Level: 935 square feet

WIDTH 30'-6"
DEPTH 72'-2"

DESIGN BY
**THE SATER
DESIGN COLLECTION**

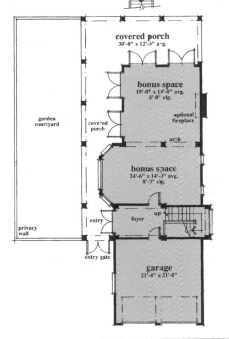

covered porch
30'-0" x 12'-3" avg.

bonus space
19'-0" x 13'-0" avg.
8'-0" clg.

optional fireplace

covered porch

arch

garden courtyard

bonus space
24'-6" x 14'-3" avg.
8'-3" clg.

entry

foyer

up

entry gate

privacy wall

garage
21'-4" x 21'-0"

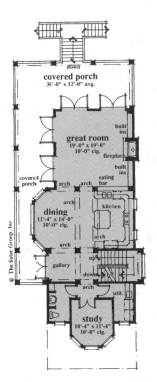

covered porch
30'-0" x 12'-0" avg.

great room
19'-0" x 19'-0"
10'-0" clg.

built ins

fireplac

built ins

eating bar

covered porch

arch

arch

dining
11'-4" x 14'-0"
10'-0" clg.

kitchen

arch

arch

gallery

up

down

arch

util.

study
10'-4" x 11'-4"
10'-0" clg.

© The Sater Group, Inc.

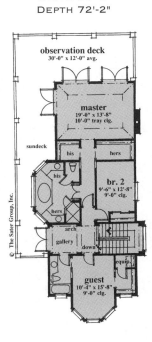

observation deck
30'-0" x 12'-0" avg.

master
19'-0" x 13'-8"
10'-0" tray clg.

sundeck

his

hers

his

br. 2
9'-6" x 12'-8"
9'-0" clg.

hers

arch

gallery

down

equip.

guest
10'-4" x 15'-8"
9'-0" clg.

© The Sater Group, Inc.

This elegant Old Charleston Row design blends high vogue with a restful character that says shoes are optional. A flexible interior enjoys modern space that welcomes sunlight. Wraparound porticos on two levels offer views to the living areas, while a "sit and watch the stars" observation deck opens from the master suite. Four sets of French doors bring the outside into the great room. The second-floor master suite features a spacious bath and three sets of doors that open to the observation deck. A guest bedroom on this level leads to a gallery hall with its own access to the deck. Bonus space awaits development on the lower level, which—true to its Old Charleston roots—opens gloriously to a garden courtyard.

DESIGN 6687

First Floor: 942 square feet
Second Floor: 571 square feet
Total: 1,513 square feet
Bonus Space: 167 square feet

The modest detailing of Greek Revival style gave rise to this grand home. A mid-level foyer eases the trip from ground level to the raised living area, while an arched vestibule announces the great room. The formal dining room offers French door access to the covered porch. Built-ins, a fireplace and two ways to access the porch make the great room truly great. A well-appointed kitchen serves a casual eating bar as well as the dining room. Upstairs, each of two private suites has a windowed tub, a vanity and wardrobe space. A pair of French doors opens each of the bedrooms to an observation sun deck through covered porches.

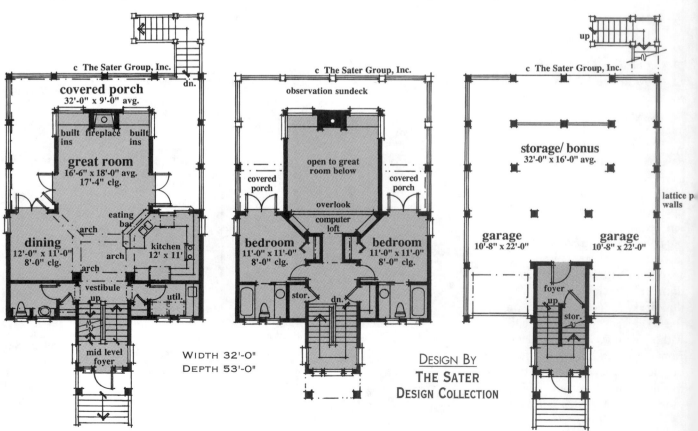

WIDTH 32'-0"
DEPTH 53'-0"

DESIGN BY
THE SATER
DESIGN COLLECTION

This eye-catching exterior features plenty of attractive windows, front and back porches, and a variety of rooflines. The two-story great room is the heart of this home, with its corner fireplace, built-in entertainment center and eating bar. Arches lead into this room from the foyer, the spacious island kitchen and the formal dining room. A covered porch is accessible from the two main rooms as well as the master suite, which includes a deluxe private bath. On the second floor, Bedroom 2 offers access to a private deck. A third bedroom and full bath complete this floor. Please specify crawlspace or basement foundation when ordering.

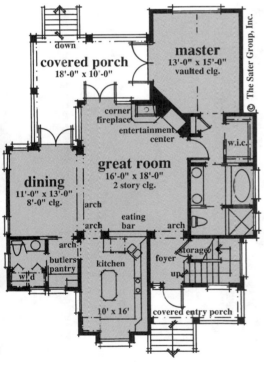

DESIGN BY
THE SATER
DESIGN COLLECTION

DESIGN 6683

First Floor: 1,290 square feet
Second Floor: 548 square feet
Total: 1,838 square feet

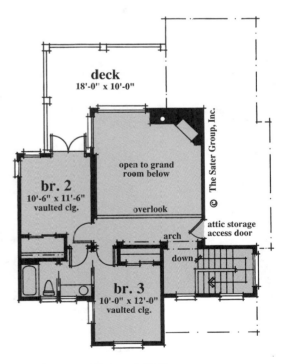

WIDTH 38'-0"
DEPTH 51'-0"

Rear

Louvered shutters, balustered railings and a slate-style roof complement a stucco-and-siding blend on this three-story narrow design. Entry stairs lead to the main-level living areas, defined by arches and columns. A wall of built-ins and a warming fireplace add coziness to the open, contemporary great room, while four sets of French doors expand the living area to the wraparound porch. Upper-level sleeping quarters include a guest suite with a bayed sitting area, an additional bedroom and a full bath. The master suite features His and Hers walk-in closets and vanities, and French doors to a private observation deck. The lower level offers bonus space for future use—a home office, perhaps—and another porch.

WIDTH 30'-6"
DEPTH 72'-2"

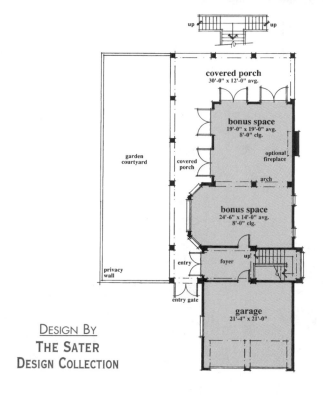

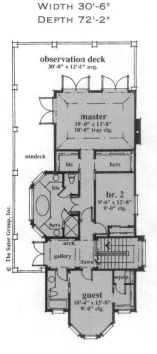

DESIGN BY
THE SATER
DESIGN COLLECTION

DESIGN 6700

First Floor: 1,305 square feet
Second Floor: 1,215 square feet
Total: 2,520 square feet
Bonus Space: 935 square feet

Rear

366

This retreat is pure heaven, decked out with a Charleston Row courtyard with a sun deck, spa and lap pool. Louvered shutters and circle-head windows speak softly of the past, while French doors extend the living areas. Gentle arches and decorative columns announce interior vistas as well as multi-directional views. Three sets of French doors extend an invitation to the covered porch, sun deck and courtyard. A bayed formal dining room is open to the gourmet kitchen, which shares its views. The second floor includes two secondary bedrooms—which share a bath—and a grand master suite with walls of glass that bring the outside in. A bonus room with a morning kitchen and a full bath could be built as a home theater or office.

DESIGN BY
THE SATER
DESIGN COLLECTION

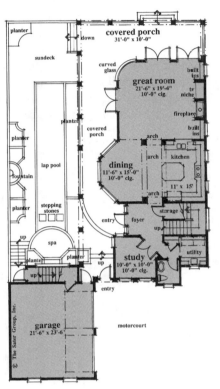

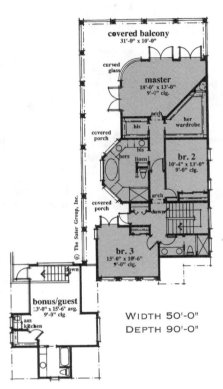

DESIGN 6688

First Floor: 1,293 square feet
Second Floor: 1,154 square feet
Total: 2,447 square feet
Bonus Room: 426 square feet

WIDTH 50'-0"
DEPTH 90'-0"

A unique tower with an observation deck will make this design a standout in any location. Inside, an impressive entry with a wrapping stair leads to three levels of livability. The main level includes a gallery leading to a formal dining room and a counter-filled kitchen on the left and a vaulted great room on the right. Five French doors on the main level access a covered porch spanning the width of the home. The upper level houses the master suite, with a sumptuous bath and a private deck, a guest bedroom and a large hall bath. On the lower level, the two-car garage is split and offers additional storage space.

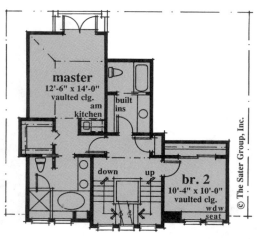

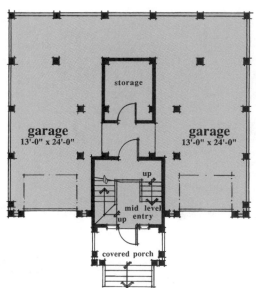

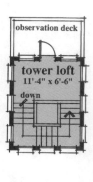

WIDTH 40'-0"
DEPTH 37'-0"

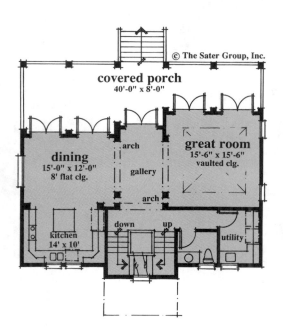

DESIGN BY
THE SATER
DESIGN COLLECTION

DESIGN 6681

First Floor: 906 square feet
Second Floor: 714 square feet
Tower Loft: 86 square feet
Total: 1,706 square feet

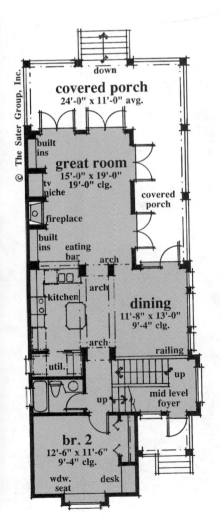

WIDTH 25'-0"
DEPTH 65'-6"

© The Sater Group, Inc.

down

covered porch
24'-0" x 11'-0" avg.

built ins

great room
15'-0" x 19'-0"
19'-0" clg.

tv niche

fireplace

built ins

eating bar

covered porch

arch

kitchen

arch

dining
11'-8" x 13'-0"
9'-4" clg.

arch

util.

up

railing

up

mid level foyer

br. 2
12'-6" x 11'-6"
9'-4" clg.

wdw. seat

desk

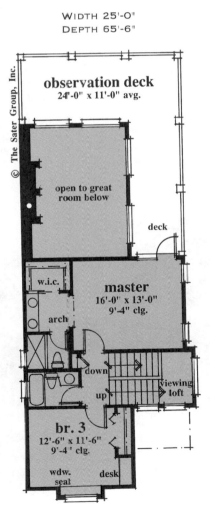

© The Sater Group, Inc.

observation deck
24'-0" x 11'-0" avg.

open to great room below

deck

w.i.c.

arch

master
16'-0" x 13'-0"
9'-4" clg.

down

up

viewing loft

br. 3
12'-6" x 11'-6"
9'-4" clg.

wdw. seat

desk

DESIGN 6686

First Floor: 1,046 square feet
Second Floor: 638 square feet
Total: 1,684 square feet

DESIGN BY
THE SATER
DESIGN COLLECTION

A Key West design that can be built any-where, this cozy three-bedroom home has plenty to offer. Built-ins and a media niche frame the fireplace in the great room, creating a cozy complement to the beauti-ful views from the wraparound covered porch. The formal dining room also opens to the porch and features direct access to the U-shaped island kitchen. A secondary bedroom on this floor has a nearby full bath. The second level is dedicated to the master suite, where the bed wall faces the private observation deck. A sensible bath offers a walk-in closet, an oversized shower and a compartmented toilet. A vestibule leads to a viewing-loft stair and to Bedroom 3, where a built-in window seat may be enjoyed.

DESIGN 6618

First Floor: 1,944 square feet
Second Floor: 1,196 square feet
Lower-Floor Entry: 195 square feet
Total: 3,335 square feet

In the deluxe grand room of this Floridian home, family and friends will enjoy the ambience created by arches and access to a veranda. Two guest rooms flank a full bath—one of the guest rooms also sports a private deck. The kitchen serves a circular breakfast nook. Upstairs, a balcony overlook furthers the drama of the grand room. The master suite, with a deck and a private bath opening through a pocket door, will be a pleasure to occupy. Another bedroom—or use this room for a study—sits at the other side of this floor. It extends a curved bay window, an expansive deck, built-ins and a full bath. The lower level contains enough room for two cars in its carport and offers plenty of storage and bonus room.

DESIGN BY
THE SATER
DESIGN COLLECTION

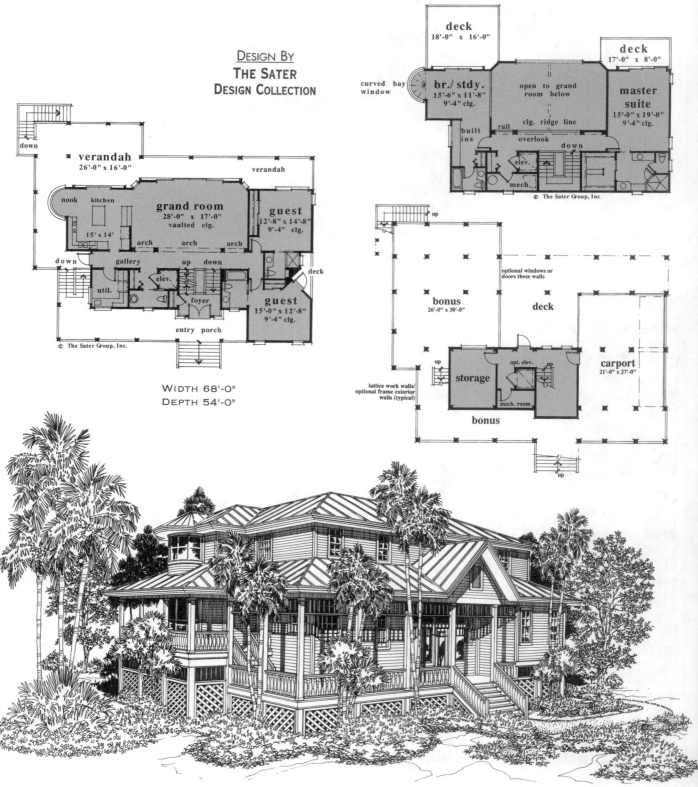

WIDTH 68'-0"
DEPTH 54'-0"

A faux widow's walk creates a stunning complement to the observation balcony and two sun decks. Inside, the open living and dining area is defined by two pairs of French doors that frame a two-story wall of glass and built-ins that flank the living room fireplace. The efficient kitchen features a walk-in pantry, a work island, and a door to the covered porch. Split sleeping quarters offer privacy to the first-floor master suite. Upstairs, two guest suites provide private baths. A gallery loft leads to a computer area with a built-in desk and a balcony overlook.

DESIGN 6693

First Floor: 1,642 square feet
Second Floor: 1,165 square feet
Lower-Floor Entry: 150 square feet
Total: 2,957 square feet

DESIGN BY
THE SATER
DESIGN COLLECTION

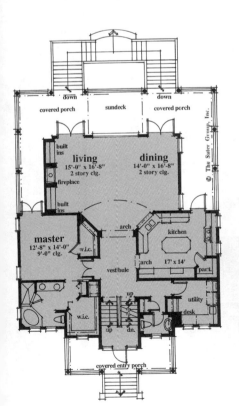

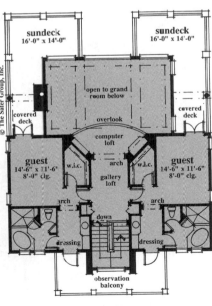

WIDTH 44'-6"
DEPTH 58'-0"

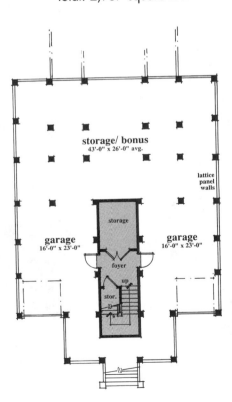

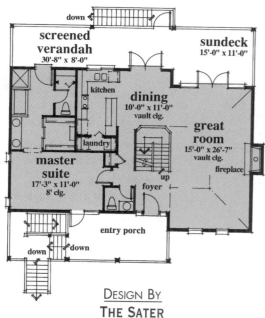

screened verandah
30'-8" x 8'-0"

sundeck
15'-0" x 11'-0"

kitchen

dining
10'-0" x 11'-0"
vault clg.

great room
15'-0" x 26'-7"
vault clg.

laundry

master suite
17'-3" x 11'-0"
8' clg.

up

foyer

fireplace

down

down

entry porch

DESIGN BY
THE SATER
DESIGN COLLECTION

DESIGN 6617

First Floor: 1,189 square feet
Second Floor: 575 square feet
Total: 1,764 square feet

An abundance of porches and a deck encourage year-round indoor-outdoor relationships in this classic two-story home. Both the spacious living room with its cozy fireplace and the adjacent dining room offer access to the screened porch/deck area. An efficient kitchen and nearby laundry room make chores easy. The private master suite offers access to the screened porch and leads into a relaxing master bath complete with a walk-in closet. Bedroom 2 shares the second floor with a full bath and a loft, which may be used as a third bedroom.

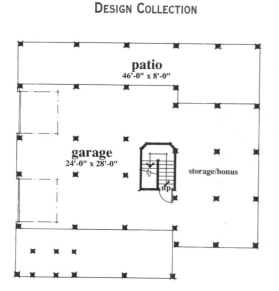

patio
46'-0" x 8'-0"

garage
24'-0" x 28'-0"

storage/bonus

up

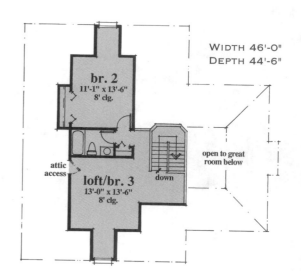

WIDTH 46'-0"
DEPTH 44'-6"

br. 2
11'-1" x 13'-6"
8' clg.

attic access

loft/br. 3
13'-0" x 13'-6"
8' clg.

down

open to great room below

© The Sater Group, Inc.

DESIGN 6615

First Floor: 1,736 square feet
Second Floor: 640 square feet
Total: 2,376 square feet
Bonus Space: 840 square feet

QUOTE ONE®

Cost to build? See page 434
to order complete cost estimate
to build this house in your area!

Lattice door panels, shutters, a balustrade and a metal roof add character to this delightful coastal home. Double doors flanking a fireplace open to the side sun deck from the spacious great room, which sports a vaulted ceiling. Access to the rear veranda is provided from this room also. An adjacent dining room provides views of the rear grounds and space for formal and informal entertaining. The glassed-in nook shares space with the L-shaped kitchen containing a center work island. Bedrooms 2 and 3, a full bath and a utility room complete this floor. Upstairs, a sumptuous master suite awaits. Double doors extend to a private deck from the master bedroom. His and Hers walk-in closets lead the way to a grand master bath featuring an arched whirlpool tub, a double-bowl vanity and a separate shower.

DESIGN BY
THE SATER DESIGN COLLECTION

WIDTH 54'-0"
DEPTH 44'-0"

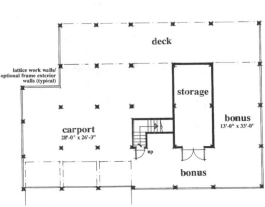

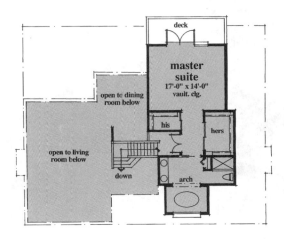

The captivating charm of this popular cottage calls up a sense of gentler times, with a quaint front balcony, horizontal siding and fishscale shingles. A contemporary, high-pitched roof harmonizes with sunbursts, double porticos, and a glass-paneled entry. In the great room, lovely French doors bring the outside in, and a fireplace framed by built-in cabinetry adds warmth. The formal dining room opens to a private area of the covered porch. The modified U-shaped kitchen sits between them and has a snack-bar counter to serve the great room. Double French doors with circle-head windows fill the master suite with sunlight and open to a private, sun-kissed deck. Two family bedrooms—or make one a study—share a full bath on the second floor.

DESIGN BY
THE SATER
DESIGN COLLECTION

WIDTH 27'-6"
DEPTH 64'-0"

DESIGN 6690

First Floor: 876 square feet
Second Floor: 948 square feet
Total: 1,824 square feet

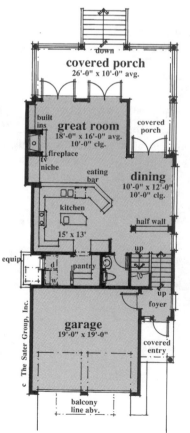

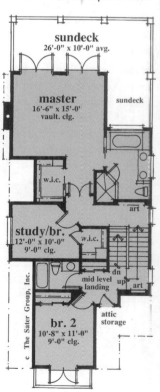

Rear

374

A captivating front balcony draws attention to this picturesque design. Inside, French doors open from the great room to views from the back covered porch. A fireplace and built-ins add to the grace of the great room. The kitchen features a large pantry and shares an eating bar with the dining room and great room. Upstairs, the master suite opens to a sun deck, while two secondary bedrooms access the front balcony. The master bath features a garden tub, separate shower and double sink. A walk-in closet is across the hall. The study could be used as a fourth bedroom and also has a walk-in closet.

Rear

DESIGN BY
**THE SATER
DESIGN COLLECTION**

DESIGN 6701

First Floor: 876 square feet
Second Floor: 1,245 square feet
Total: 2,121 square feet

WIDTH 27'-6"
DEPTH 64'-0"

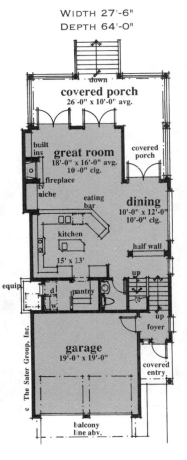

covered porch
26'-0" x 10'-0" avg.

down

built ins

great room
18'-0" x 16'-0" avg.
10'-0" clg.

covered porch

fireplace
tv niche

eating bar

dining
10'-0" x 12'-0"
10'-0" clg.

kitchen
15' x 13'

half wall

equip

d w

pantry

up

up

foyer

garage
19'-0" x 19'-0"

covered entry

c The Sater Group, Inc.

balcony line abv.

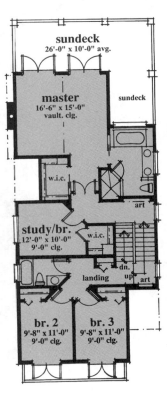

sundeck
26'-0" x 10'-0" avg.

master
16'-6" x 15'-0"
vault. clg.

sundeck

w.i.c.

art

study/br.
12'-0" x 10'-0"
9'-0" clg.

w.i.c.

dn.

landing

up

art

br. 2
9'-8" x 11'-0"
9'-0" clg.

br. 3
9'-8" x 11'-0"
9'-0" clg.

DESIGN 6680

First Floor: 1,007 square feet
Second Floor: 869 square feet
Total: 1,876 square feet

DESIGN BY
THE SATER
DESIGN COLLECTION

This dandy seaside home is just the right size with just the right amenities. The open plan begins with a side entry leading to a foyer and the great room beyond. A fireplace, entertainment center and double French doors to the rear covered porch adorn the great room. The dining area (another set of doors to the porch) and kitchen with eating bar and walk-in pantry are nearby. A bedroom with covered balcony and private bath finish the first floor. The master suite dominates the second floor. It has its own private balcony and a great bath. One additional bedroom with private bath joins the master suite on the second floor. A stair tower leads to a lovely lookout above the house.

covered porch
32'-0" x 8'-0"

entertainment center

corner fireplace

dining
12'-0" x 12'-6"
8'-0" clg.

great room
19'-0" x 16'-0"
2 story clg.

arch

hutch niche

eating bar

kitchen
12' x 12'

arch

arch

foyer

storage

covered entry porch

down

up

br. 2
11'-6" x 15'-0"
8'-0" clg.

covered balcony
12'-6" x 9'-0"

© The Sater Group, Inc.

© The Sater Group, Inc.

br. 3
11'-0" x 10'-6"
8'-0" clg.

open to grand room below

overlook

up

down

w.i.c.

master
11'-6" x 14'-6"
8'-0" clg.

covered balcony

stair tower

down

WIDTH 43'-8"
DEPTH 53'-6"

Rear

Variable rooflines, a tower and a covered front porch all combine to give this home a wonderful ambiance. Enter through the midlevel foyer and head either up to the main living level or down to the garage. On the main level, find a spacious, light-filled great room sharing a fireplace with the dining room. A study offers access to the rear covered veranda. The efficient island kitchen is open to the dining room, offering ease in entertaining. A guest suite with a private full bath completes this level. Upstairs, a second guest room with its own bath and a deluxe master suite with a covered balcony, sun deck, walk-in closet and lavish bath are sure to please.

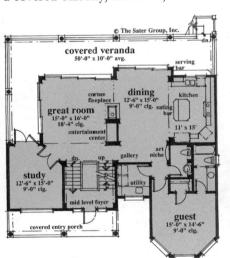

© The Sater Group, Inc.

dn.

covered veranda
50'-0" x 10'-0" avg.

serving bar

corner fireplace

dining
12'-6" x 15'-0"
9'-0" clg.

kitchen

eating bar

great room
15'-0" x 16'-0"
18'-4" clg.

entertainment center

11' x 15'

study
12'-6" x 15'-0"
9'-0" clg.

dn.

up

gallery

art niche

utility

mid level foyer

covered entry porch

guest
15'-0" x 14'-6"
9'-0" clg.

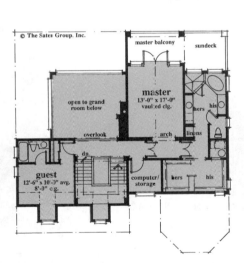

© The Sater Group, Inc.

master balcony

sundeck

open to grand room below

master
13'-0" x 17'-0"
vaulted clg.

hers

his

overlook

arch

linens

guest
12'-6" x 10'-3" avg.
8'-3" clg.

dn.

computer/ storage

hers

his

WIDTH 50'-0"
DEPTH 53'-0"

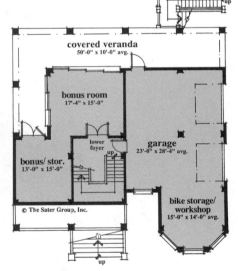

up

covered veranda
50'-0" x 10'-0" avg.

bonus room
17'-4" x 15'-0"

bonus/ stor.
13'-0" x 15'-0"

lower foyer

up

garage
23'-0" x 28'-4" avg.

bike storage/ workshop
15'-0" x 14'-0" avg.

© The Sater Group, Inc.

up

DESIGN 6682

First Floor: 1,617 square feet
Second Floor: 991 square feet
Total: 2,608 square feet
Bonus Space: 532 square feet

Rear

DESIGN 6654

First Floor: 1,342 square feet
Second Floor: 511 square feet
Total: 1,853 square feet

DESIGN BY
THE SATER
DESIGN COLLECTION

With influences from homes of the Caribbean, this island home is a perfect seaside residence or primary residence. The main living area is comprised of a grand room with a fireplace and access to a deck. The dining space also accesses this deck plus another that it shares with a secondary bedroom. An L-shaped kitchen with a prep island is open to the living areas. Two bedrooms on this level share a full bath. The master suite dominates the upper level. It has its own balcony and a rewarding bath with dual vanities and a whirlpool tub.

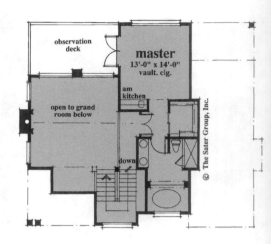

© The Sater Group, Inc.

observation deck

master
13'-0" x 14'-0"
vault. clg.

am kitchen

open to grand room below

down

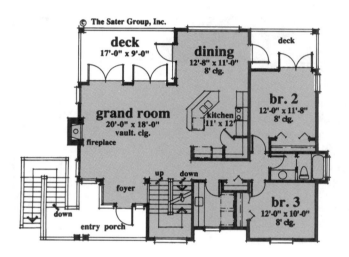

© The Sater Group, Inc.

deck
17'-0" x 9'-0"

dining
12'-8" x 11'-0"
8' clg.

deck

grand room
20'-0" x 18'-0"
vault. clg.

kitchen
11' x 12'

br. 2
12'-0" x 11'-8"
8' clg.

fireplace

foyer

up   down

entry porch

br. 3
12'-0" x 10'-0"
8' clg.

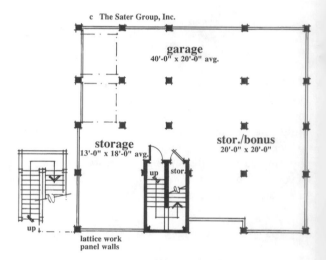

c The Sater Group, Inc.

garage
40'-0" x 20'-0" avg.

storage
13'-0" x 18'-0" avg.

stor./bonus
20'-0" x 20'-0"

up   stor.

up

lattice work
panel walls

WIDTH 44'-0"
DEPTH 40'-0"

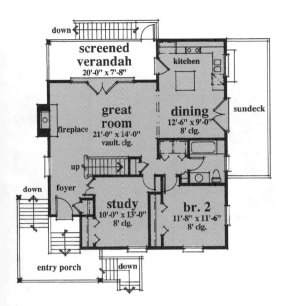

screened
verandah
20'-0" x 7'-8"

kitchen

great
room
21'-0" x 14'-0"
vault. clg.

fireplace

dining
12'-6" x 9'-0"
8' clg.

sundeck

up

foyer

down

study
10'-0" x 13'-0"
8' clg.

br. 2
11'-8" x 11'-6"
8' clg.

down

entry porch

down

open to
below

master
suite
12'-3" x 20'0"
8' clg.

down

loft

w.i.c.

WIDTH 41'-9"
DEPTH 45'-0"

DESIGN BY
THE SATER
DESIGN COLLECTION

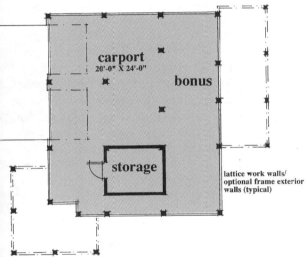

carport
20'-0" X 24'-0"

bonus

storage

lattice work walls/
optional frame exterior
walls (typical)

DESIGN 6616

First Floor: 1,136 square feet
Second Floor: 636 square feet
Total: 1,772 square feet

This two-story home's pleasing exterior is complemented by its warm character and decorative "widow's walk." The covered entry—with its dramatic transom window—leads to a spacious great room highlighted by a warming fireplace. To the right, the dining room and kitchen combine to provide a delightful place for mealtimes inside or out, with access to a side deck through double doors. Two bedrooms and a full bath complete the first floor. The luxurious master suite is located on the second floor for privacy and features an oversize walk-in closet and a separate dressing area. The pampering master bath enjoys a relaxing whirlpool tub, a double-bowl vanity and a compartmented toilet.

DESIGN 6689

Main Level: 1,642 square feet
Upper Level: 1,165 square feet
Lower-Level Entry: 150 square feet
Total: 2,957 square feet

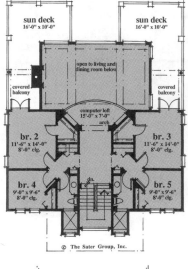

© The Sater Group, Inc.

Rear

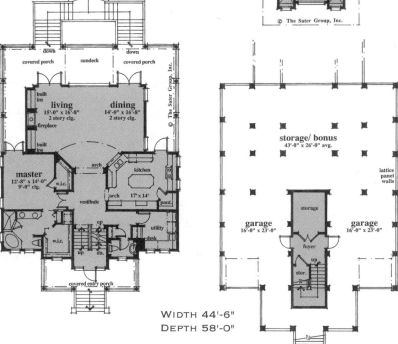

© The Sater Group, Inc.

WIDTH 44'-6"
DEPTH 58'-0"

Prevailing summer breezes find their way through many joyful rooms in this Neoclassical Revival design. Inspired by 19th-Century Key West houses, the exterior is heart-stoppingly beautiful with Doric columns, lattice and fretwork, and a glass-paneled, arched entry. The mid-level foyer eases the trip from ground level to living and dining areas, which offer flexible space for planned events or cozy gatherings. Two sets of French doors lead out to the gallery and sun deck, and a two-story picture window invites natural light and a spirit of *bon vivant* to pour into the heart of the home.

DESIGN BY
**THE SATER
DESIGN COLLECTION**

A classic pediment and low-pitched roof, topped by a cupola on this gorgeous coastal design, shows the influence of 19th-Century plantation houses. Living areas are on the upper level of this home, with unfinished space left in the lower level for a game room and additional storage space. Three bedrooms plus a study are found on the main level. They circulate around a central great room and kitchen with breakfast nook. The master suite, nook, great room and Bedroom 2 all feature sliding glass doors to the rear covered porch. The great room is graced by a wall of built-ins and an entertainment center.

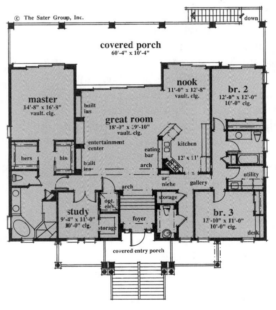

© The Sater Group, Inc.

covered porch
60'-4" x 10'-4"

down

master
14'-8" x 16'-8"
vault. clg.

nook
11'-0" x 12'-8"
vault. clg.

br. 2
12'-0" x 12'-0"
10'-0" clg.

built ins

great room
18'-0" x 29'-10"
vault. clg.

entertainment center

hers

his

built ins

kitchen

eating bar
12' x 11'

arch

utility

study
9'-4" x 11'-0"
10'-0" clg.

storage

arch

ar' niche

storage

gallery

foyer

br. 3
13'-10" x 11'-0"
10'-0" clg.

desk

opt. elev.

covered entry porch

DESIGN 6684

Main Level: 2,385 square feet
Lower-Level Entry: 80 square feet
Total: 2,465 square feet

DESIGN BY
THE SATER
DESIGN COLLECTION

WIDTH 60'-4"
DEPTH 59'-4"

Rear

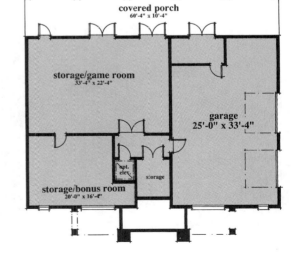

covered porch
60'-4" x 10'-4"

storage/game room
33'-4" x 22'-4"

garage
25'-0" x 33'-4"

opt. elev.

storage

storage/bonus room
20'-0" x 16'-4"

DESIGN 6694

Square Footage: 1,792

DESIGN BY
THE SATER
DESIGN COLLECTION

A blend of Southern comfort and Gulf Coast style sets this home apart. A covered porch runs the width of the home, creating a haven for family gatherings. Inside, decorative arches and columns mark the grand entrance to the living and dining areas, while the gourmet kitchen provides a pass-through to the dining room. On cold nights, a fireplace warms the great room, and on warm evenings, French doors to the covered porch let in cool breezes. At the rear of the plan, the master suite has private access to a sun deck, and French doors open to the covered porch. Two walk-in closets, a garden tub and a bayed sitting area add to the homeowners' comfort. This plan includes pier and crawlspace foundation options.

Rear

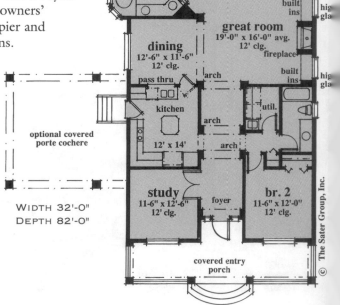

optional covered
porte cochere

WIDTH 32'-0"
DEPTH 82'-0"

master
12'-0" x 16'-6"
12' clg.

sundeck

his

hers

covered porch
19'-0" x 16'-0" avg.

built
ins

high
gla

great room
19'-0" x 16'-0" avg.
12' clg.

fireplace

dining
12'-6" x 11'-6"
12' clg.

pass thru

arch

kitchen
12' x 14'

arch

arch

built
ins

high
gla

util.

study
11'-6" x 12'-6"
12' clg.

foyer

br. 2
11'-6" x 12'-0"
12' clg.

covered entry
porch

© The Sater Group, Inc.

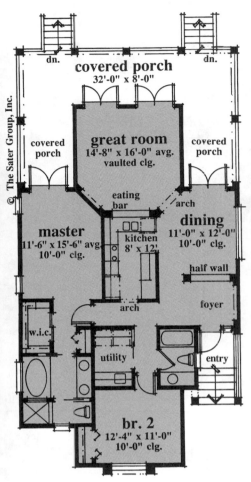

covered porch
32'-0" x 8'-0"

dn.   dn.

© The Sater Group, Inc.

covered porch

great room
14'-8" x 16'-0" avg.
vaulted clg.

covered porch

eating bar

arch

master
11'-6" x 15'-6" avg.
10'-0" clg.

kitchen
8' x 12'

dining
11'-0" x 12'-0"
10'-0" clg.

half wall

foyer

w.i.c.

arch

utility

entry

br. 2
12'-4" x 11'-0"
10'-0" clg.

WIDTH 32'-4"
DEPTH 60'-0"

This Tidewater design offers casual living in a modest square footage. Asymmetrical lines celebrate the Turn of the Century and blend with elements of Coast style. The heart of the home is the great room which features two sets of double French doors to the covered porch at the rear. Both the master suite and the dining room also have French doors to the porch. The kitchen is centrally located and has a snack-bar pass-through to the great room. A second bedroom at the front of the plan has its own bath.

DESIGN 6691
Square Footage: 1,288

DESIGN BY
**THE SATER
DESIGN COLLECTION**

Rear

383

DESIGN 6692

Square Footage: 2,068

DESIGN BY
THE SATER
DESIGN COLLECTION

The dramatic arched entry of this Southampton-style cottage borrows freely from its Southern coastal past. The foyer and central hall open to the grand room. The kitchen is flanked by the dining room and morning nook, which opens to the lanai. On the left side of the plan, the master suite also accesses the lanai. Two walk-in closets, a compartmented bath with separate tub and shower and a double-bowl vanity complete the homeowners' opulent retreat. The right side of the plan includes two secondary bedrooms and a full bath.

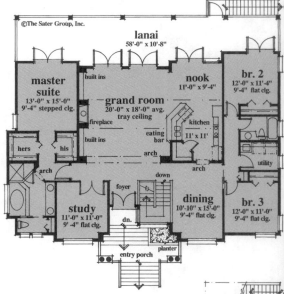

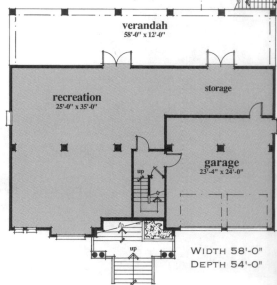

Rear

veranda
50'-0" x 10'-0" avg.

storage

stor./ bonus
14'-0" x 33'-0" avg.

garage
19'-0" x 32'-0" avg.

foyer

stor.

dumbwaiter

up

up

up

lattice
work walls

veranda
50'-0" x 10'-0"

down

dining
12'-0" x 14'-0"
vault. clg.

kitchen
10' x 13'

br. 2
13'-0" x 13'-8"
8' clg.

grand room
15'-0" x 27'-0"
vault. clg.

fireplace

down

up

foyer

util.

br. 3
13'-0" x 11'-0"
8' clg.

down

© The Sater Group, Inc.

master
14'-6" x 15'-6"
vault. clg.

am kitchen

down

© The Sater Group, Inc.

WIDTH 50'-0"
DEPTH 44'-0"

DESIGN 6655

First Floor: 1,586 square feet
Second Floor: 601 square feet
Total: 2,187 square feet

DESIGN BY
THE SATER
DESIGN COLLECTION

Lattice walls, pickets and horizontal siding complement a relaxed Key West island-style design that boasts a spacious sitting porch. Sunburst transoms lend a romantic spirit to this seaside destination, perfect for waterfront properties. Inside, an elegant interior doesn't miss a step, with an open foyer that leads to an expansive great room, made cozy by a warming hearth. Just right for entertaining, the living and dining rooms open to the veranda, which even invites a moonlit after-dinner dance—why not? A gallery hall leads to two family or guest bedrooms, one with French doors to the veranda. The upper level is dedicated to the master suite—a perfect, and private, home-owner's retreat. French doors reveal a vestibule open to both bedroom and bath. A sizable walk-in closet and a morning kitchen complement lavish amenities in the bath: a vanity with an arched soffit ceiling above, a dormered spa-style tub and an oversized shower with a seat.

DESIGN 6697

First Floor: 1,642 square feet
Second Floor: 927 square feet
Total: 2,569 square feet
Lower-Level Game Room/Storage:
849 square feet

DESIGN BY
THE SATER
DESIGN COLLECTION

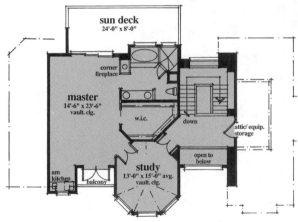

sun deck
24'-0" x 8'-0"

corner
fireplace

master
14'-6" x 23'-6"
vault. clg.

w.i.c.

down

attic/ equip.
storage

am kitchen

balcony

study
13'-0" x 15'-0" avg.
vault. clg.

open to
below

covered porch
24'-0" x 10'-0" avg.

sun deck
24'-0" x 7'-0"

down

open to
below

nook
11'-0" x 8'-6"
9'-4" clg.

built
ins

br. 2
13'-0" x 11'-8"
9'-4" clg.

great room
20'-0" x 15'-0"
9'-4" clg.

kitchen
14' x 11'

eating
bar

fireplace

built
ins

down

up

arch

utility

arch

arch

arch

balcony

dining
13'-0" x 13'-8"
9'-4" clg.

open to
below

br. 3
13'-0" x 11'-4"
9'-4" clg.

WIDTH 60'-0"
DEPTH 44'-6"

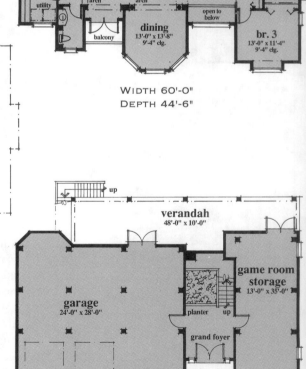

up

verandah
48'-0" x 10'-0"

garage
24'-0" x 28'-0"

**game room
storage**
13'-0" x 35'-0"

planter

up

grand foyer

workshop

entry

This stunning Gulf Coast cottage features wide windows to take in gorgeous views, while cool outdoor spaces invite festive gatherings, or just a little light reading. The staircase from the ground-level foyer to the raised living area enjoys elaborate views that make a powerful "welcome home" statement. Sliding glass doors open the great room to the main-level covered porch and sun deck, while a fireplace lends coziness and warmth. A columned archway announces the elegant formal dining room, while French doors open to a front balcony nearby. The gourmet kitchen is open to the bay-windowed morning nook and a single French door leads out to the veranda. The upper level is dedicated to a spacious master suite and a private, bayed study.

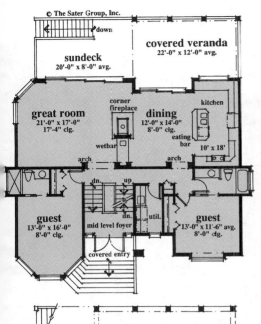

sundeck
20'-0" x 8'-0" avg.

covered veranda
22'-0" x 12'-0" avg.

down

great room
21'-0" x 17'-0"
17'-4" clg.

corner
fireplace

dining
12'-0" x 14'-0"
8'-0" clg.

kitchen

eating
bar
10' x 18'

wetbar

arch.

arch.

guest
13'-0" x 16'-0"
8'-0" clg.

dn.

up

util.

dn.

mid level foyer

guest
13'-0" x 11'-6" avg.
8'-0" clg.

covered entry

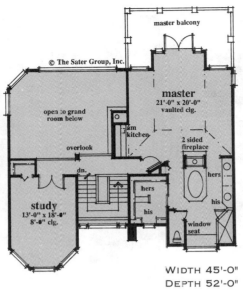

master balcony

master
21'-0" x 20'-0"
vaulted clg.

open to grand
room below

am
kitchen

overlook

2 sided
fireplace

dn.

hers

hers

his

his

study
13'-0" x 18'-0"
8'-0" clg.

window
seat

WIDTH 45'-0"
DEPTH 52'-0"

DESIGN 6698

First Floor: 1,684 square feet
Second Floor: 1,195 square feet
Total: 2,879 square feet
Unfinished Lower Level:
674 square feet

DESIGN BY
THE SATER
DESIGN COLLECTION

covered veranda
41'-0" x 12'-0" avg.

bonus room
24'-0 x 17'-6"

garage
19'-6" x 30'-0" avg.

lower foyer

up

bonus/ stor.
12'-8" x 20'-0"

bike storage/
workshop

up

This Key West design features asymmetrical rooflines that set off a grand turret and a two-story bay that allows glorious views within. Cottage charm gives way to practical comforts through the covered entry, with a mid-level foyer to ease the way. Glass doors open the great room to a sun-kissed deck, while arch-top clerestory windows enhance the casual atmosphere with natural light. A corner fireplace and a wet bar create warmth and coziness in the living and dining rooms. The gourmet kitchen boasts a center island with an eating bar for easy meals, plus a windowed wrapping counter. A winding staircase leads to a luxurious upper-level master suite that opens to a private master balcony, while a morning kitchen offers juice and coffee service. A two-sided fireplace warms both the bedroom and a bath designed for two. The gallery hall has a balcony overlook and leads to a secluded study, which enjoys wide views through a front bay window.

DESIGN 6619

First Floor: 2,725 square feet
Second Floor: 1,418 square feet
Total: 4,143 square feet

DESIGN BY
THE SATER
DESIGN COLLECTION

QUOTE ONE®

Cost to build? See page 434
to order complete cost estimate
to build this house in your area!

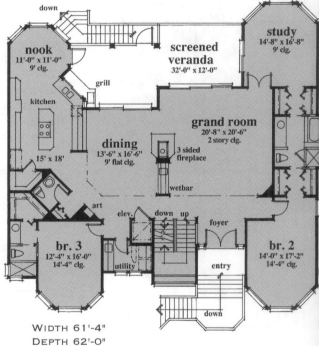

nook
11'-0" x 11'-0"
9' clg.

down

kitchen

15' x 18'

grill

screened
veranda
32'-0" x 12'-0"

study
14'-8" x 16'-8"
9' clg.

dining
13'-6" x 16'-6"
9' flat clg.

grand room
20'-8" x 20'-6"
2 story clg.

3 sided
fireplace

wetbar

art

elev.

down   up

foyer

br. 3
12'-4" x 16'-0"
14'-4" clg.

utility

entry

br. 2
14'-0" x 17'-2"
14'-4" clg.

down

WIDTH 61'-4"
DEPTH 62'-0"

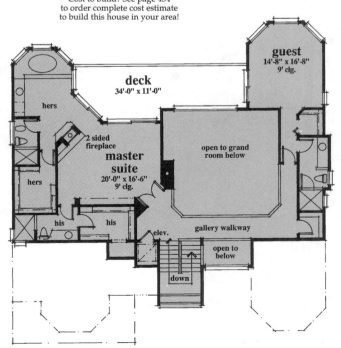

deck
34'-0" x 11'-0"

guest
14'-8" x 16'-8"
9' clg.

hers

2 sided
fireplace

master
suite
20'-0" x 16'-6"
9' clg.

open to grand
room below

hers

his   his

elev.

gallery walkway

open
to below

down

Florida living takes off in this grand design. A grand room gains attention as a superb entertaining area. A through-fireplace here connects this room to the dining room. Sets of sliding glass doors offer passage to an expansive rear deck. In the bayed study, quiet time is assured—or slip out onto the deck for a breather. A full bath connects the study and Bedroom 2. Bedroom 3 sits on the opposite side of the house and enjoys its own bath. The kitchen is fully functional with a large work island and a sunny connecting breakfast nook. Upstairs, the master bedroom suite is something to behold. His and Hers baths, a through-fireplace and access to an upper deck add character to this room. A guest bedroom suite with a bay window is located on the other side of the upper floor and will make visits a real pleasure.

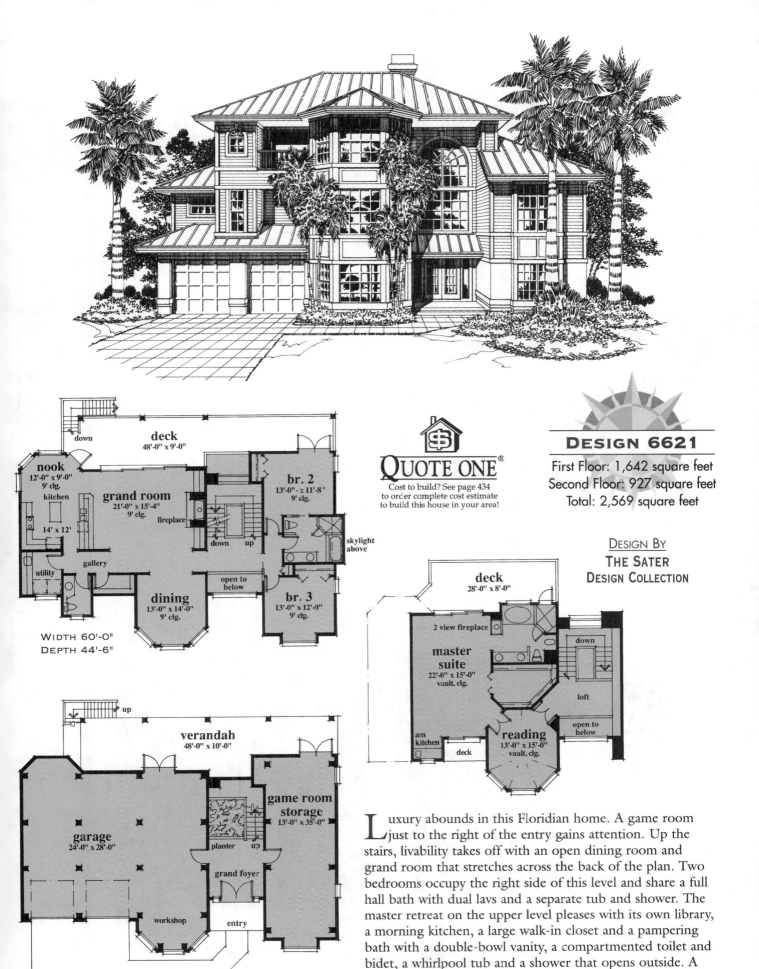

deck
48'-0" x 9'-0"

down

nook
12'-0" x 9'-0"
9' clg.

kitchen
14' x 12'

grand room
21'-0" x 15'-4"
9' clg.

fireplace

br. 2
13'-0" x 11'-8"
9' clg.

down   up

skylight above

gallery

utility

dining
13'-0" x 14'-0"
9' clg.

open to below

br. 3
13'-0" x 12'-0"
9' clg.

WIDTH 60'-0"
DEPTH 44'-6"

Quote One®
Cost to build? See page 434
to order complete cost estimate
to build this house in your area!

DESIGN 6621
First Floor: 1,642 square feet
Second Floor: 927 square feet
Total: 2,569 square feet

DESIGN BY
**THE SATER
DESIGN COLLECTION**

deck
28'-0" x 8'-0"

2 view fireplace

master suite
22'-0" x 15'-0"
vault. clg.

down

loft

am kitchen

deck

open to below

reading
13'-0" x 15'-0"
vault. clg.

up

verandah
48'-0" x 10'-0"

game room storage
13'-0" x 35'-0"

planter   up

garage
24'-0" x 28'-0"

grand foyer

workshop   entry

Luxury abounds in this Floridian home. A game room just to the right of the entry gains attention. Up the stairs, livability takes off with an open dining room and grand room that stretches across the back of the plan. Two bedrooms occupy the right side of this level and share a full hall bath with dual lavs and a separate tub and shower. The master retreat on the upper level pleases with its own library, a morning kitchen, a large walk-in closet and a pampering bath with a double-bowl vanity, a compartmented toilet and bidet, a whirlpool tub and a shower that opens outside. A private deck allows outdoor enjoyments.

DESIGN A307

First Floor: 2,297 square feet
Second Floor: 1,929 square feet
Total: 4,226 square feet

What a lovely Gulf Coast rendition with living levels elevated above double garages and a portico and balcony decorating the front. Up the double staircase lies a covered double entry which leads to a wide foyer with dining room on the right and guest suite on the left. The grand room dominates the back and connects to the rear deck and the private study with fireplace. A U-shaped kitchen with bayed breakfast room are on the right. The second floor includes three suites—all with private baths. The master suite is particularly spectacular, having double walk-in closets and a bath with separate shower and tub and dual sinks. Suite 3 also has a walk-in closet.

DESIGN BY
LIVING CONCEPTS
HOME PLANNING

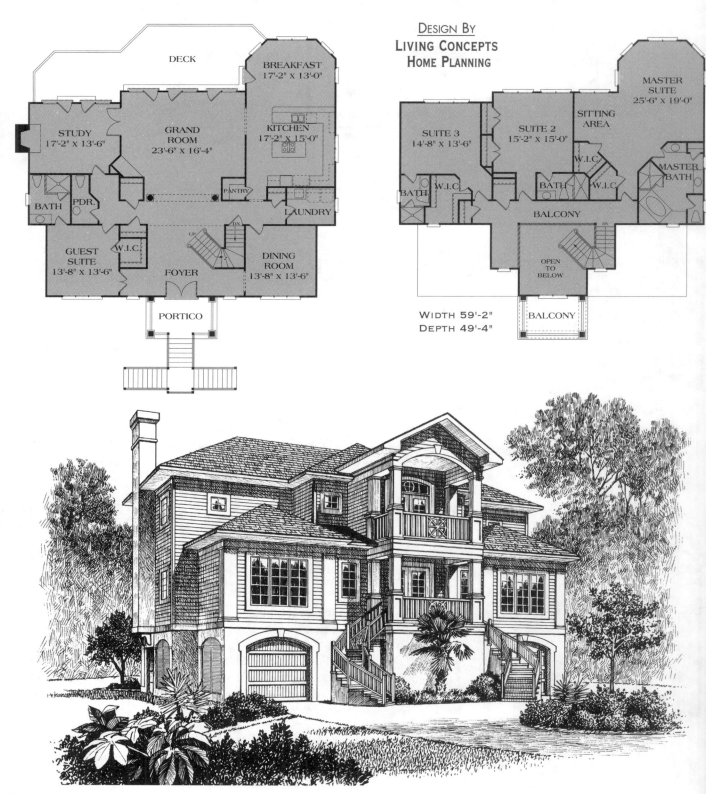

DECK

STUDY
17'-2" x 13'-6"

GRAND
ROOM
23'-6" x 16'-4"

BREAKFAST
17'-2" x 13'-0"

KITCHEN
17'-2" x 15'-0"

BATH

PDR.

PANTRY

LAUNDRY

GUEST
SUITE
13'-8" x 13'-6"

W.I.C.

UP

DN

FOYER

DINING
ROOM
13'-8" x 13'-6"

PORTICO

SUITE 3
14'-8" x 13'-6"

SUITE 2
15'-2" x 15'-0"

SITTING
AREA

MASTER
SUITE
25'-6" x 19'-0"

W.I.C.

BATH

W.I.C.

BATH

W.I.C.

MASTER
BATH

BALCONY

OPEN
TO
BELOW

DN

WIDTH 59'-2"
DEPTH 49'-4"

BALCONY

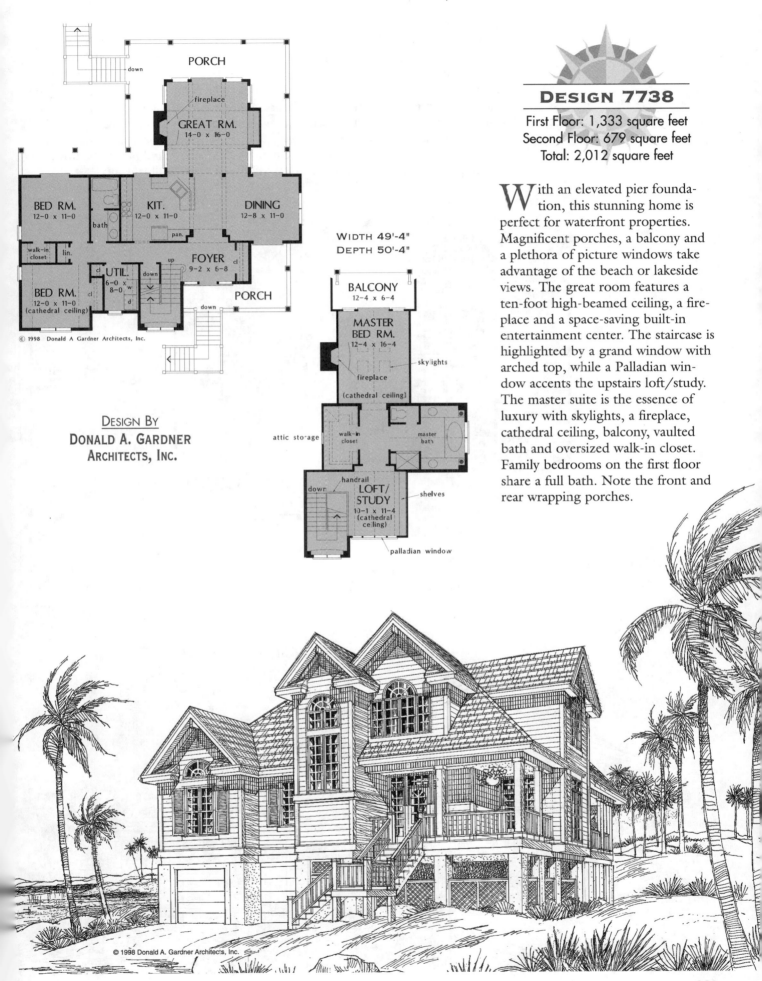

PORCH

fireplace

GREAT RM.
14-0 x 16-0

down

BED RM.
12-0 x 11-0

bath

KIT.
12-0 x 11-0

DINING
12-8 x 11-0

pan.

walk-in closet | lin.

BED RM.
12-0 x 11-0
(cathedral ceiling)

cl | **UTIL.**
6-0 x 8-0 | w
cl | | d

down | up

FOYER
9-2 x 6-8 | cl

PORCH

down

© 1998 Donald A Gardner Architects, Inc.

DESIGN BY
**DONALD A. GARDNER
ARCHITECTS, INC.**

WIDTH 49'-4"
DEPTH 50'-4"

BALCONY
12-4 x 6-4

**MASTER
BED RM.**
12-4 x 16-4

skylights

fireplace
(cathedral ceiling)

attic storage

walk-in closet

master bath

handrail

down

**LOFT/
STUDY**
10-1 x 11-4
(cathedral
ceiling)

shelves

palladian window

DESIGN 7738

First Floor: 1,333 square feet
Second Floor: 679 square feet
Total: 2,012 square feet

With an elevated pier founda-tion, this stunning home is perfect for waterfront properties. Magnificent porches, a balcony and a plethora of picture windows take advantage of the beach or lakeside views. The great room features a ten-foot high-beamed ceiling, a fire-place and a space-saving built-in entertainment center. The staircase is highlighted by a grand window with arched top, while a Palladian win-dow accents the upstairs loft/study. The master suite is the essence of luxury with skylights, a fireplace, cathedral ceiling, balcony, vaulted bath and oversized walk-in closet. Family bedrooms on the first floor share a full bath. Note the front and rear wrapping porches.

© 1998 Donald A. Gardner Architects, Inc.

DESIGN Q260

First Floor: 1,446 square feet
Second Floor: 1,047 square feet
Total: 2,493 square feet

This unique design is bedecked with a veranda that wraps around three sides of the home. The foyer is skylit and contains a curved staircase to the second floor. On the left are the living room with fireplace and bay window and dining room with sliding glass doors to the veranda. The living room has double doors to access the veranda. A family room is at the other end of the plan and holds a corner media center and a fireplace. Sliding glass doors open to the rear yard. In between is an island kitchen with breakfast bay. The bedrooms are upstairs and include a master suite with walk-in closet, vaulted alcove and private bath with whirlpool tub. Family bedrooms share a full bath with double vanity.

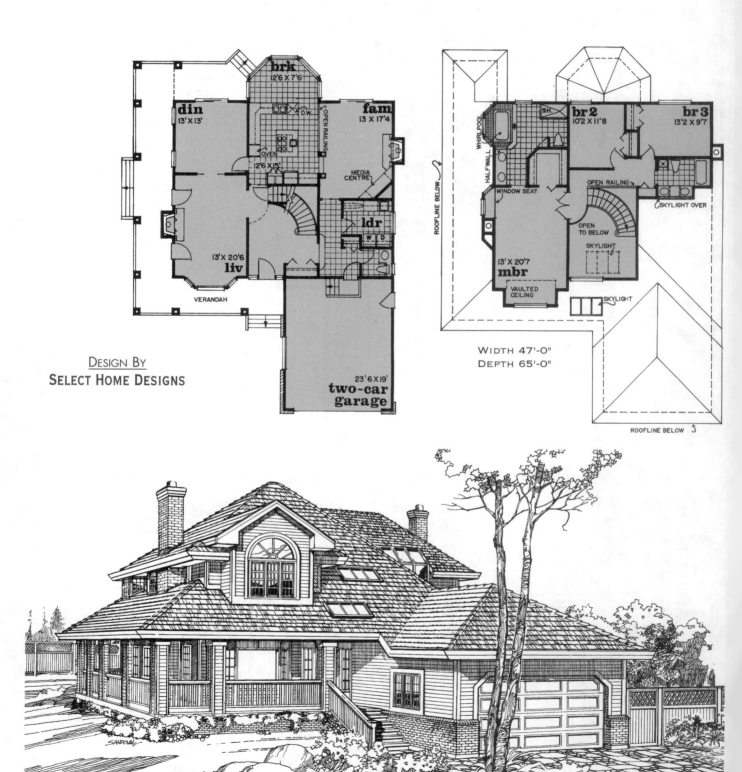

DESIGN BY
SELECT HOME DESIGNS

WIDTH 47'-0"
DEPTH 65'-0"

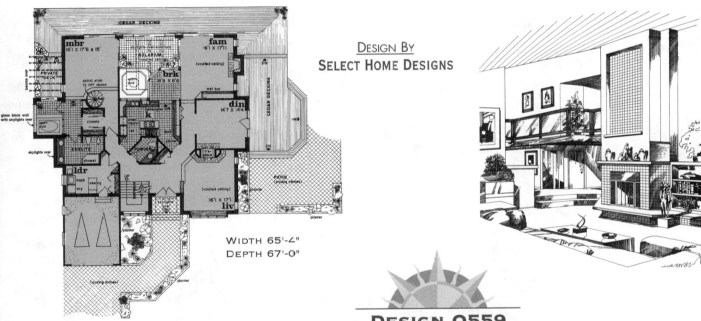

DESIGN BY
SELECT HOME DESIGNS

WIDTH 65'-4"
DEPTH 67'-0"

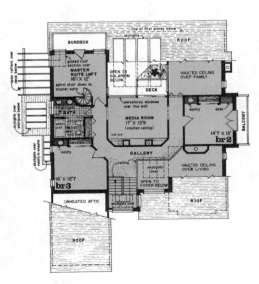

DESIGN Q559

First Floor: 2,690 square feet
Second Floor: 1,406 square feet
Total: 4,096 square feet

With contemporary styling, this seaside vacation home offers great livability and outdoor spaces. The foyer, solarium, living room, family room and media room all boast vaulted ceilings. The sunken living room shares a through-fireplace with the formal dining room; each has access to an outdoor area. Skylights illuminate the foyer, solarium, gallery and bathrooms. The sunken master bedroom has a private deck and a spiral staircase to the loft. The media room is graced by a wet bar, audio-visual center, clerestory windows and a deck overlooking the solarium. Each secondary bedroom has a private vanity; Bedroom 2 has a built-in desk.

DESIGN 6622

Square Footage: 2,190

DESIGN BY
THE SATER
DESIGN COLLECTION

QUOTE ONE®

Cost to build? See page 434
to order complete cost estimate
to build this house in your area!

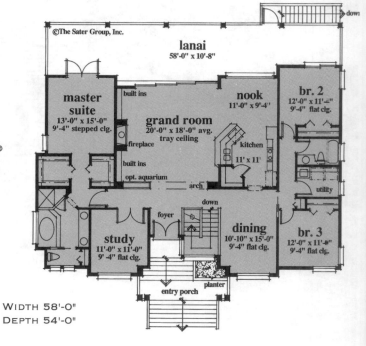

©The Sater Group, Inc.

lanai
58'-0" x 10'-8"

master suite
13'-0" x 15'-0"
9'-4" stepped clg.

built ins

grand room
20'-0" x 18'-0" avg.
tray ceiling

nook
11'-0" x 9'-4"

br. 2
12'-0" x 11'-"
9'-4" flat clg.

fireplace

kitchen
11' x 11'

built ins

opt. aquarium

arch

utility

study
11'-0" x 11'-0"
9'-4" flat clg.

foyer

down

dining
10'-10" x 15'-0"
9'-4" flat clg.

br. 3
12'-0" x 11'-"
9'-4" flat clg.

entry porch

planter

WIDTH 58'-0"
DEPTH 54'-0"

verandah
58'-0" x 12'-0"

recreation
25'-0" x 35'-0"

storage

up

garage
23'-4" x 24'-0"

up

A strikingly simple staircase leads to the dramatic entry of this contemporary design. The foyer opens to an expansive grand room with a fireplace and a built-in entertainment center. An expansive lanai opens from the living area and offers good inside/outside relationships. For more traditional occasions and planned events, a front-facing dining room offers a place for quiet, elegant entertaining. The master suite features a lavish bath with two sizable walk-in closets, a windowed whirlpool tub, twin lavatories and a compartmented toilet. Double doors open from the gallery hall to a secluded study that is convenient to the master bedroom. Two additional bedrooms share a private hall and a full bath on the opposite side of the plan.

Photo by Oscar Thompson

screened verandah
50'-0" x 12'-0" avg.

grill

kitchen

nook

study
12'-8" x 13'-4"
vaulted clg.

grand room
17'-6" x 18'-0"
2 story clg.

dining
11'-6" x 14'-0"
8'-6" clg.

18' x 14'

3 sided fireplace

wetbar

br. 3
10'-10" x 15'-0"
8'-6" clg.

elev.

up   down

br. 2
12'-8" x 14'-0"
8'-6" clg.

utility

foyer

entry

down

balcony

WIDTH 64'-0"
DEPTH 45'-0"

spa

deck

3 sided fireplace

master suite
20'-3" x 16'-0"
vaulted clg.

open to grand room below

w.l.c.

elev.   gallery walkway   storage

open to below

down

deck
50'-0" x 12'-0"

bonus

bonus
36'-0" x 17'-0"

garage
25'-0" x 27'-0"

opt. elev.   up

storage

bonus

DESIGN BY
THE SATER
DESIGN COLLECTION

DESIGN 6620

First Floor: 2,066 square feet
Second Floor: 810 square feet
Total: 2,876 square feet
Unfinished Lower Level: 1,260 square feet

This striking Floridian plan is designed for entertaining. A large, open floor plan offers soaring, sparkling space for planned gatherings. The foyer leads to the grand room, highlighted by a glass fireplace, a wet bar and wide views of the outdoors. Both the grand room and the formal dining room open to a screened veranda. The first floor includes two spacious family bedrooms and a secluded study which opens from the grand room. The second-floor master suite offers sumptuous amenities, including a private deck and spa, a three-sided fireplace, a sizable walk-in closet and a gallery hall with an overlook to the grand room.

DESIGN 8001

First Floor: 1,309 square feet
Second Floor: 1,343 square feet
Total: 2,652 square feet

DESIGN BY
LARRY E. BELK
DESIGNS

Clean, contemporary lines set this home apart and make it a stand out in any location. The metal roof and roof-top cupola rotated on a 45-degree angle add interest. Twin chimneys located on the right side of the house are constructed on a 45-degree angle to continue the theme. Stunning is the word when the front door opens on this home. Near the foyer, a 28-foot shaft opens from floor level to the top of the cupola. Remote control transoms in the cupola open automatically to increase ventilation. The great room, sun room, dining room and kitchen are all adjacent to provide areas for entertaining. Originally designed for a sloping site, the home incorporates multiple levels inside. Additionally, there is access to a series of multi-level outside decks from the dining room, sun room and great room. All these areas have at least one glass wall overlooking the rear. The master bedroom and bath upstairs are bridged by a pipe rail balcony that provides access to a rear outside deck. The master suite includes a huge master closet. Additional storage and closet space is located off the hallway to the office.

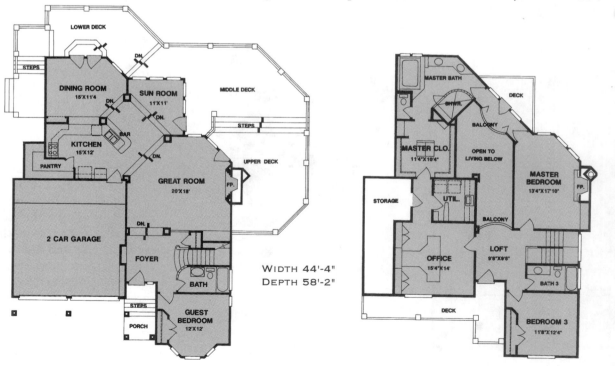

WIDTH 44'-4"
DEPTH 58'-2"

STEPS

PORCH

SITTING

MASTER BEDROOM
20' X 16'

REF.

RANGE

KITCHEN
12' X 13'

UTIL.

K/S

WP TUB

BUTLERS PANTRY

POWDER

SHOWER SEAT

D/W

P.

OPEN BAR

ARCH

UP

DINING ROOM
15' X 11'

WET BAR

ARCH

ARCH

LIVING ROOM
18' X 15'

FP

2 CAR GARAGE

PORCH

DESIGN BY
LARRY E. BELK
DESIGNS

DESIGN 8002

First Floor: 1,530 square feet
Second Floor: 968 square feet
Total: 2,498 square feet
Bonus Room: 326 square feet

WIDTH 40'-0"
DEPTH 66'-0"

DECK

BATH 2

BEDROOM 2
12' X 13'

BEDROOM 3
12' X 13'

BUILT-IN BOOK SHELVES

DOWN

LOFT

MECH. RM.

VOL. CEILING

BONUS AREA
17' X 20'

BALCONY

DECK

COPYRIGHT 1993 LARRY E. BELK

The timeless influence of the French Quarter is exemplified in this home designed for river-front living. The double French door entry opens into a large living room/dining room area separated by a double archway. The living room ceiling opens up through two stories to the cupola above. A railed balcony with a loft on the second floor overlooks the living room. A pass-through between the kitchen and dining room also provides seating at a bar for informal dining. The spacious master bedroom at the rear includes a sitting area and a roomy master bath with a large walk-in closet. Two additional bedrooms, a bath and a bonus area for an office or game room are located upstairs. With ten-foot ceilings downstairs and nine-foot ceilings upstairs, there is a feeling of spaciousness. The inclusion of fabulous decks on the front and back of the second story makes this home perfect for entertaining. Please specify basement or slab foundation when ordering.

DESIGN Q488

Lower-Level Entry: 175 square feet
Main Level: 1,115 square feet
Total: 1,290 square feet
Unfinished Lower Level: 626 square feet

DESIGN BY
SELECT HOME DESIGNS

With the main living areas on the second floor, this plan makes a grand vacation retreat. The covered entry opens to a foyer of 175 square feet. An open rail staircase leads to the living/dining room combination with fireplace and box window. Sliding glass doors in the dining room open to the wide sun deck that shades the patio below. The kitchen and breakfast nook are nearby. The kitchen has a U-shaped workcenter and a window over the sink. Three bedrooms are found across the back of the plan. The master has a full bath and large wall closet. Family bedrooms have walk-in closets and share a full bath. The central hallway has skylights to keep it bright. If you choose to finish the lower level, you'll add 626 square feet of space for a bedroom, a full bath and a family room. Note the large storage area in the garage.

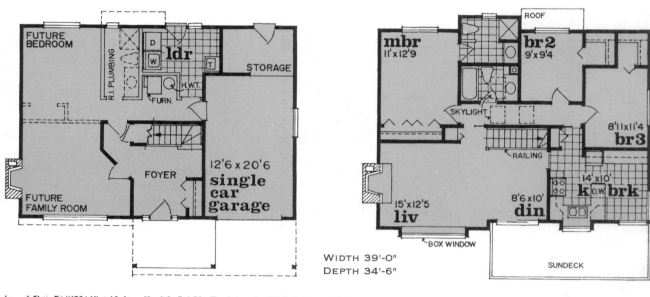

WIDTH 39'-0"
DEPTH 34'-6"

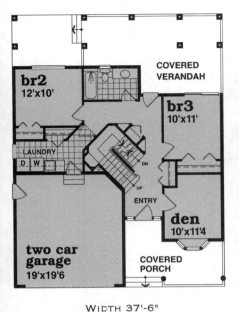

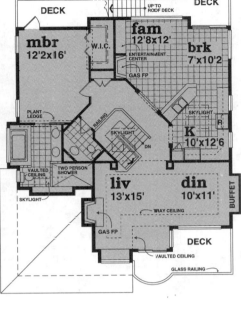

br2
12'x10'

COVERED
VERANDAH

br3
10'x11'

LAUNDRY
D W

DN

UP

ENTRY

den
10'x11'4

two car
garage
19'x19'6

COVERED
PORCH

WIDTH 37'-6"
DEPTH 48'-4"

DECK

DECK

UP TO
ROOF DECK

mbr
12'2x16'

W.I.C.

fam
12'8x12'

brk
7'x10'2

ENTERTAINMENT
CENTER

GAS FP

PLANT
LEDGE

RAILING

SKYLIGHT

SKYLIGHT

K
10'x12'6

R.

VAULTED
CEILING

TWO PERSON
SHOWER

DN

SKYLIGHT

liv
13'x15'

din
10'x11'

BUFFET

GAS FP

TRAY CEILING

DECK

VAULTED CEILING

GLASS RAILING

DESIGN Q482

First Floor: 832 square feet
Second Floor: 1,331 square feet
Total: 2,163 square feet

This two-level plan has a bonus—a roof deck with hot tub! A variety of additional outdoor spaces makes this one wonderful plan. The living spaces are on the second floor and include a living/dining room combination with deck and fireplace. The dining room has buffet space. The family room also has a fireplace, plus a built-in entertainment center, and is open to the breakfast room and skylit kitchen. Sliding glass doors in the breakfast room open to another deck. The master bedroom is on this level and features a private bath with whirlpool tub and two-person shower, walk-in closet and access to still another deck. Family bedrooms, a full bath and a cozy den are on the first level, along with a two-car garage.

DESIGN BY
SELECT HOME DESIGNS

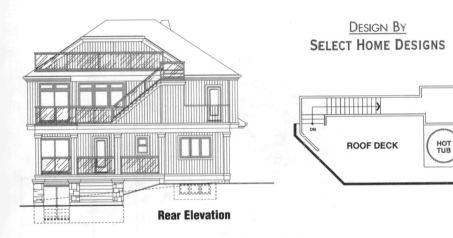

DN

ROOF DECK

HOT
TUB

Rear Elevation

DESIGN 7627

First Floor: 1,514 square feet
Second Floor: 642 square feet
Total: 2,156 square feet

Sleek contemporary lines, plenty of windows and a combination of textures give this home a lot of curb appeal. Great for entertaining, the formal dining room has a pass-through to the kitchen for ease in serving, and guests can drift into the spacious great room to gather around the cheerful fireplace for after-dinner cocktails and conversation. The large island kitchen will make meal preparations a breeze. Located on the first floor for privacy, the master bedroom suite features two walls of closets, a private bath and direct access to the sun room. Two bedrooms and a loft complete the second floor.

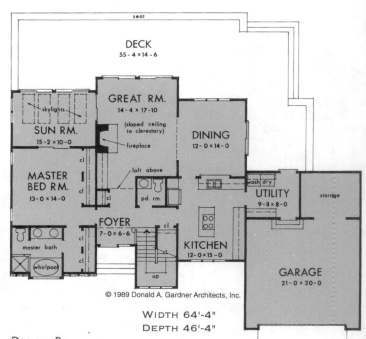

© 1989 Donald A. Gardner Architects, Inc.

WIDTH 64'-4"
DEPTH 46'-4"

DESIGN BY
DONALD A. GARDNER
ARCHITECTS, INC.

Rear

400

DESIGN G224

DESIGN BY
HOME PLANNERS

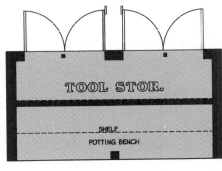

TOOL STOR.

SHELF

POTTING BENCH

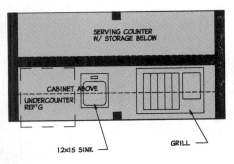

SERVING COUNTER W/ STORAGE BELOW

CABINET ABOVE

UNDERCOUNTER REF'G

12x15 SINK

GRILL

Here's a unique design that can be converted to serve a variety of functions: a tool shed, a barbecue stand, a pool-supply depot or a sports-equipment locker. Apply a little "what-if" imagination to come up with additional ways to use this versatile design to enhance your outdoor living space. As a tool shed, this design features a large potting bench with storage above and below. Second, as a summer kitchen, it includes a built-in grill, a sink and a refrigerator. Third, for use as a pool-supply depot or equipment storage, it comes with a locker to store chemicals or valuable sports equipment safely. This structure is designed to be movable, but, depending on its function, could be placed on a concrete slab.

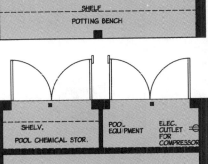

SHELV.
POOL CHEMICAL STOR.

POOL EQUIPMENT

ELEC. OUTLET FOR COMPRESSOR

SHELF

GAME STORAGE

WIDTH 8'-0"
DEPTH 4'-0"

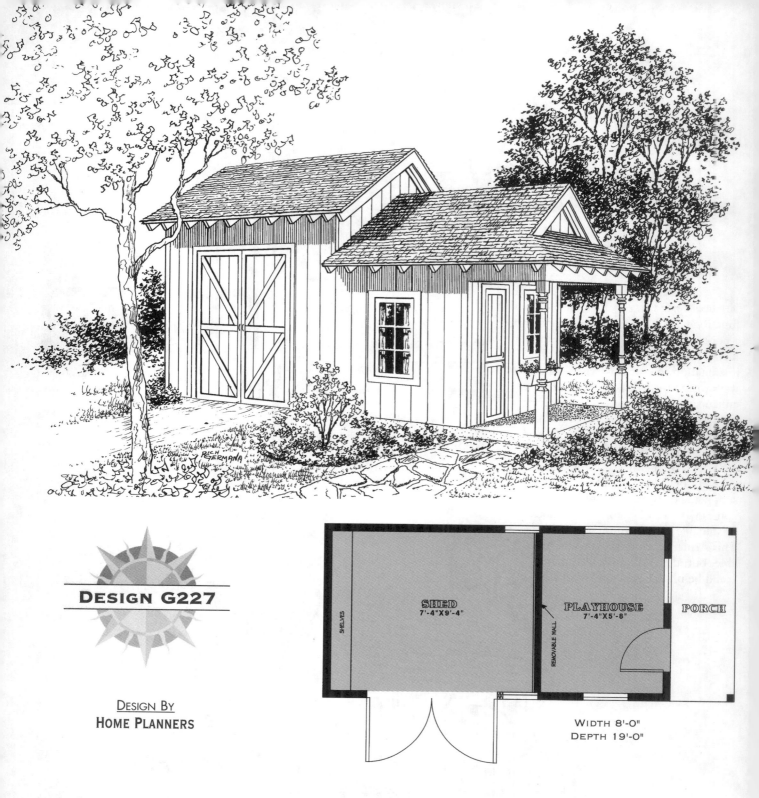

DESIGN G227

DESIGN BY
HOME PLANNERS

SHELVES

SHED
7'-4"X9'-4"

REMOVABLE WALL

PLAYHOUSE
7'-4"X5'-8"

PORCH

WIDTH 8'-0"
DEPTH 19'-0"

The kids will love this one! This functional, practical lawn shed doubles in design and capacity as a delightful playhouse complete with a covered porch, lathe-turned columns and a window box for young gardeners. The higher roofline on the shed gives the structure a two-story effect, while the playhouse design gives the simple lawn shed a much more appealing appearance. The shed is accessed through double doors. The playhouse features a single-door entrance from the porch and three bright windows. The interior wall between the shed and playhouse could be moved another 2-feet back to make it larger. Or, remove the interior wall completely to use the entire 128-square-foot exclusively for either the lawn shed or playhouse. The open eaves and porch columns give the structure a country appearance; however, by boxing in the eaves and modifying the columns, you can create just about any style you or the kids like best.

DESIGN G247

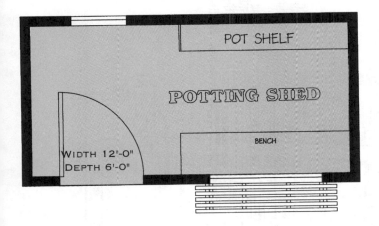

POT SHELF

POTTING SHED

BENCH

WIDTH 12'-0"
DEPTH 6'-0"

Designed to accent its surroundings, this cozy little building keeps all your garden tools and supplies at your fingertips. You can vary the materials to create the appearance best suited to your site. This structure is large enough to accommodate a potting bench, shelves and an area for garden tools. The window above the potting bench allows ample light, but electricity could be added easily. Designed to be built on a concrete slab, you could use pressure-treated lumber for the floor joists and sit it right on the ground. To convert this shed design to a playhouse, simply change the window shelf into a planter and add a step with a handrail at the door.

DESIGN G243

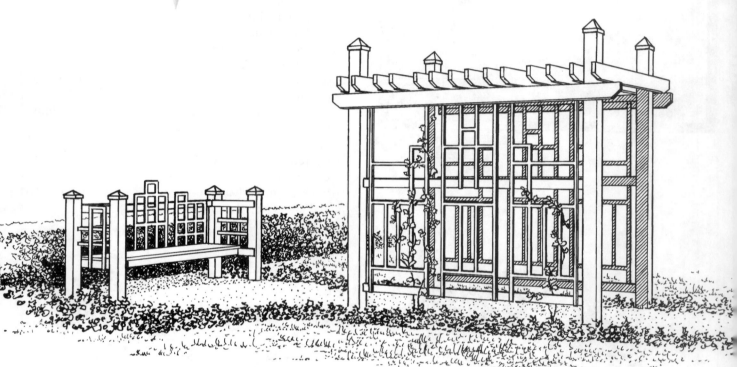

DESIGN BY
HOME PLANNERS

Build this impressive arbor to cover a garden path or walkway. Add the matching bench inside the arbor as a plant shelf or to provide shaded seating. Use the bench outside as an accent to both the arbor and the surrounding landscape. The 7'-11" patterned back and 5'-11" x 8'-10½" trellis roof are ideal for climbing vines or roses, giving this beautiful arbor even more of a garden effect. The 8'-11" bench is wide enough to seat four or five adults comfortably. The latticework design is repeated on the back and sides of the bench. The arbor is designed to sit on a slab or you can sink the support columns right into the ground using pressure-treated materials.

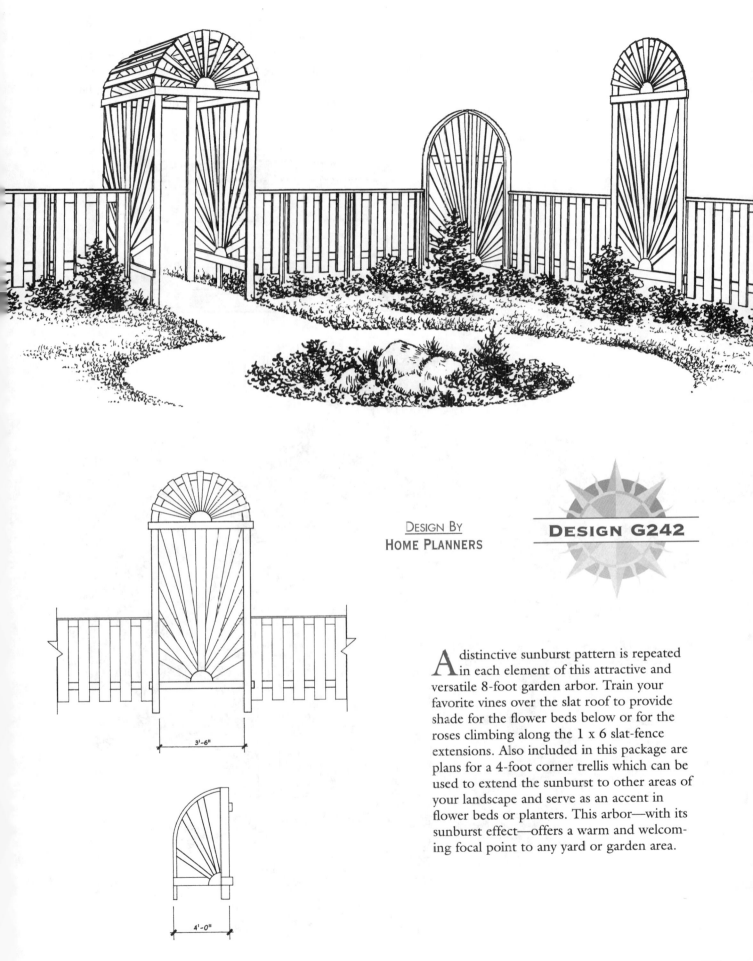

DESIGN G242

3'-6"

4'-0"

A distinctive sunburst pattern is repeated in each element of this attractive and versatile 8-foot garden arbor. Train your favorite vines over the slat roof to provide shade for the flower beds below or for the roses climbing along the 1 x 6 slat-fence extensions. Also included in this package are plans for a 4-foot corner trellis which can be used to extend the sunburst to other areas of your landscape and serve as an accent in flower beds or planters. This arbor—with its sunburst effect—offers a warm and welcoming focal point to any yard or garden area.

DESIGN G237

DESIGN BY
HOME PLANNERS

You can create a cozy shaded nook for reading or relaxing with this appealing strombella. It's simple to build as a glider or with a fixed seat. Either option provides ample room for two or three people to sit comfortably. Both designs use standard materials. For a fixed unit, attach it to a cement slab. To make it movable, use a wood base. Cover the roof with basic asphalt or fiberglass shingles, or use cedar shake shingles to enhance the appearance.

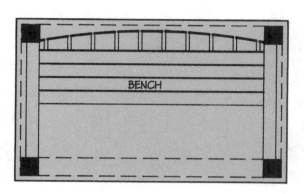

BENCH

WIDTH 6'-0"
DEPTH 3'-6"

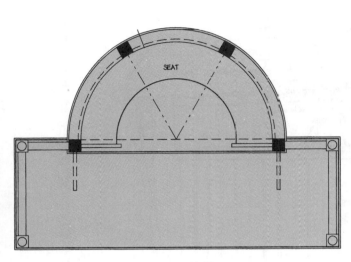

WIDTH 12'-0"
DEPTH 8'-0"

DESIGN BY
HOME PLANNERS

DESIGN G236

An accent to gracious living, this classic strombella will create an elegant focal point in any garden or landscape. Evoking memories of a more slowly paced era, the design is similar to those built in the late 1800s. The bench is large enough to seat up to six people. To increase its function, a half-round pole table could be added to provide a small picnic area or a nook for reading, cards or quiet conversation. The mill work can be purchased from your local supplier or from the manufacturer listed on the construction drawings. The generous entrance is 4-foot wide, which could provide space for additional seating if needed. You can build this structure with a wood base to allow for movable feasts, or secure it to a slab to make it permanent.

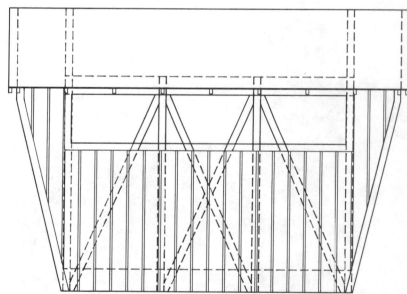

DESIGN G244

DESIGN BY
HOME PLANNERS

Nostalgia unlimited—this romantic covered bridge will re-create a unique link to history on your site. It is patterned after functional bridges built in the 1700s and 1800s, which were intended to provide a dry resting place for weary travelers. This current-day design offers expandable dimensions for a 12-foot, 14-foot or 16-foot span. To cross a wider area, the span can be increased by multiples of those dimensions, using large floor joists. Check with your local supplier for the span capability of the joists you employ in your project. The sides of this "glimpse into the past" have open window areas to allow air to flow freely. The generous 5'-3½" width allows for safe passage of any standard garden tractor or mower.

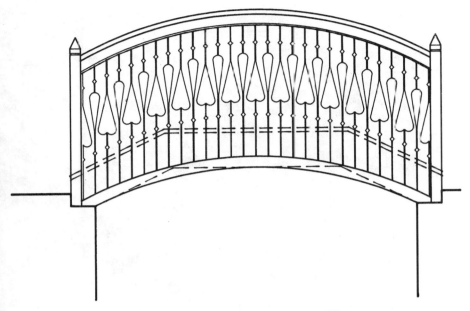

DESIGN BY
HOME PLANNERS

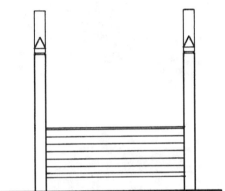

Combine form, function and beauty in this appealing bridge to enhance your landscape and provide easy passage over wet or rocky terrain. Entrance and exit ramps at either end of the bridge replicate the gentle arch of the handrail. The plans for this functional addition show how to build 6-foot, 8-foot or 10-foot spans to meet your needs. The decorative railing pattern will add a touch of elegance and charm to any site.

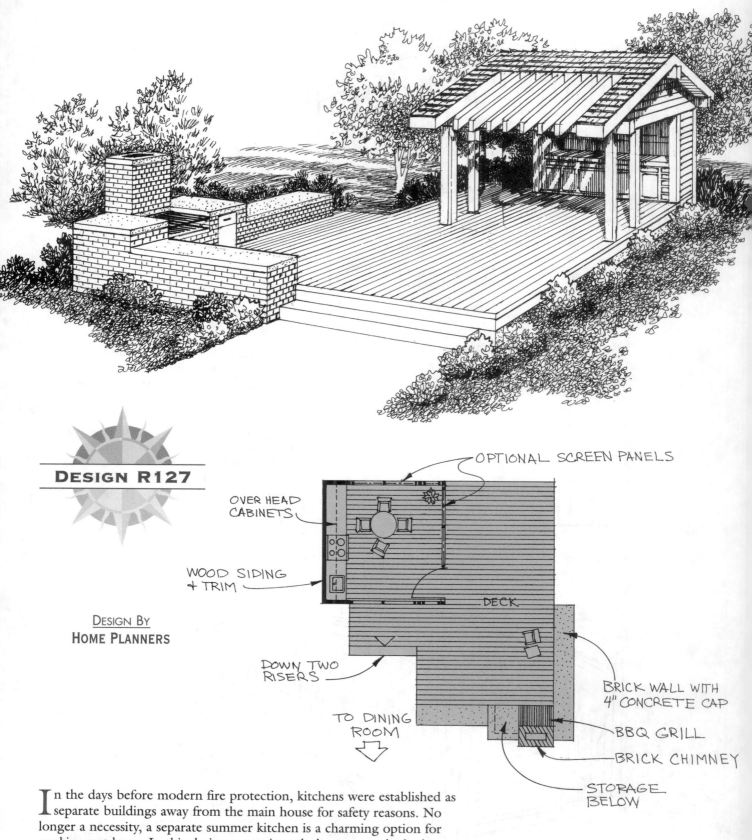

DESIGN R127

OPTIONAL SCREEN PANELS

OVER HEAD CABINETS

WOOD SIDING + TRIM

DESIGN BY
HOME PLANNERS

DECK

DOWN TWO RISERS

BRICK WALL WITH 4" CONCRETE CAP

TO DINING ROOM

BBQ GRILL

BRICK CHIMNEY

STORAGE BELOW

WIDTH 24'-8"
DEPTH 26'-0"

I n the days before modern fire protection, kitchens were established as separate buildings away from the main house for safety reasons. No longer a necessity, a separate summer kitchen is a charming option for cooking outdoors. In this design, a spacious deck connects the barbecue area with its generous counter space and storage, with the covered cooking area complete with sink, stove and refrigerator. Translucent panels in the roof provide lots of natural light. There is ample room under the roof for a table and chairs and you can enclose this area with screen panels to keep out flying insects. Built-in benches adjacent to the barbecue provide additional seating or serving space.

DESIGN G240

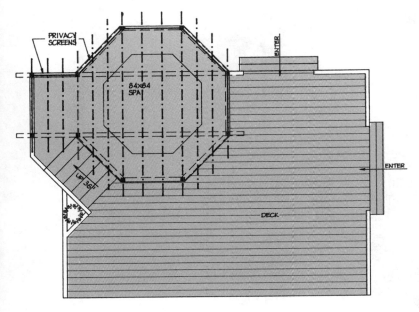

PRIVACY SCREENS

84X84 SPA

UP 36"

DECK

ENTER

ENTER

WIDTH 24'-4"

Secluded enough for privacy, yet open enough to view the night sky through a curtain of vines on the trellis roof, this private outdoor spa has its own deck with built-in benches and planters. Approximately 280 square feet in area, the deck of this outstanding unit offers plenty of space to entertain friends and family. In the design shown, three steps lead up from the ground to the deck, and six additional steps lead up to the 84" x 84" spa area. Patterned screens and a trellis roof provide privacy. You can place this spa adjacent to your house for convenient access, or install it as a free-standing unit in a secluded area of your property. Easy to build, this design will accommodate a spa of almost any style. The trellis roof can also be modified to a solid roof style or eliminated completely.

DESIGN BY
HOME PLANNERS

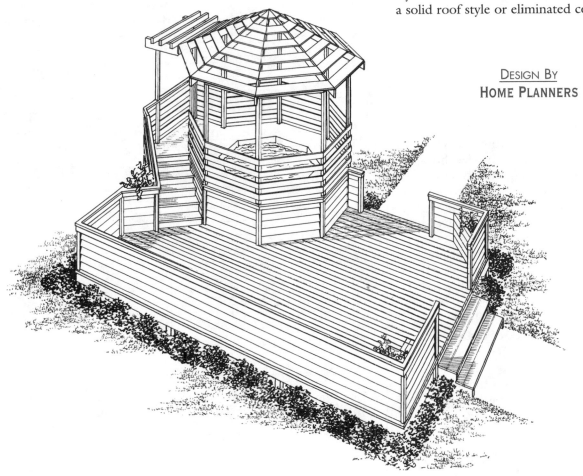

411

DESIGN BY
HOME PLANNERS

DESIGN G241

An outdoor kitchen and much, much more! For year-round, daylight-to-dark entertaining, consider this large outdoor entertaining unit. Nearly 700 square feet of floor space includes a deck for sunbathing by day or dancing under the stars after sundown. A 13' x 13'-2" screened room provides a pest-free environment for cards or conversation. And, the chef will rule with a flair over a full-service kitchen area that may include a grill, wet bar, sink, refrigerator and ample room for storage. You can locate this versatile structure adjacent to your pool, or place it as a free-standing unit wherever your landscape and site plan allow. Select material for the railings and privacy screens in patterns to match or complement your home.

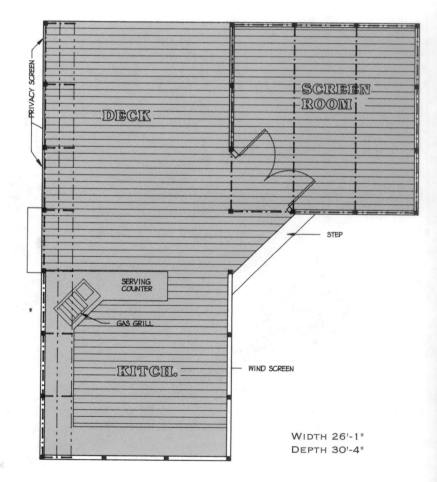

PRIVACY SCREEN

DECK

SCREEN ROOM

STEP

SERVING COUNTER

GAS GRILL

KITCH.

WIND SCREEN

WIDTH 26'-1"
DEPTH 30'-4"

DESIGN G234

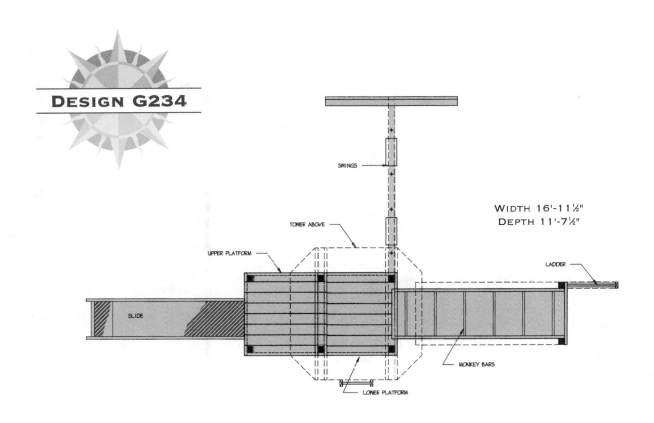

SWINGS

TOWER ABOVE

UPPER PLATFORM

WIDTH 16'-11½"
DEPTH 11'-7½"

LADDER

SLIDE

MONKEY BARS

LOWER PLATFORM

DESIGN BY
HOME PLANNERS

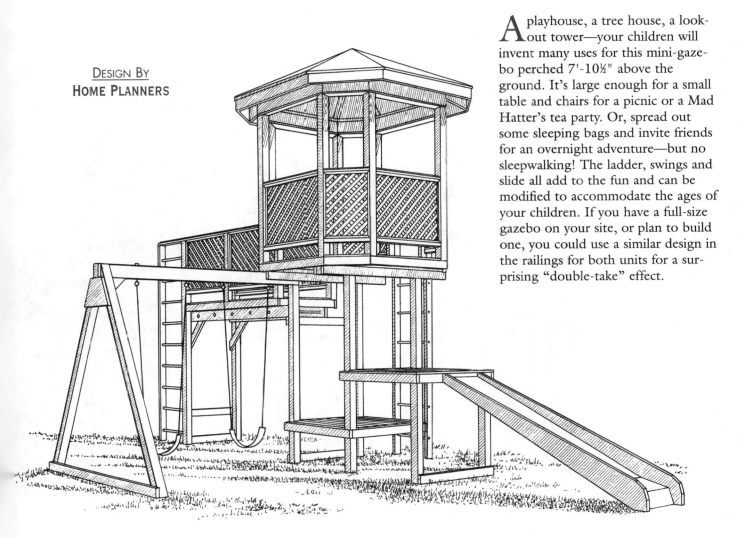

A playhouse, a tree house, a lookout tower—your children will invent many uses for this mini-gazebo perched 7'-10½" above the ground. It's large enough for a small table and chairs for a picnic or a Mad Hatter's tea party. Or, spread out some sleeping bags and invite friends for an overnight adventure—but no sleepwalking! The ladder, swings and slide all add to the fun and can be modified to accommodate the ages of your children. If you have a full-size gazebo on your site, or plan to build one, you could use a similar design in the railings for both units for a surprising "double-take" effect.

413

DESIGN G223

DESIGN BY
HOME PLANNERS

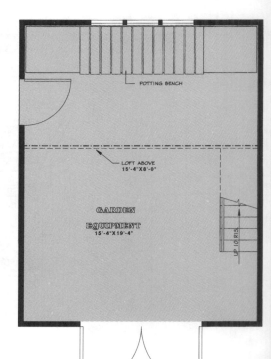

POTTING BENCH

LOFT ABOVE
15'-4"X8'-0"

GARDEN
EQUIPMENT
15'-4"X19'-4"

UP 10 RIS.

This large, multi-level garden shed can be easily modified to become a boat house if yours is a nautical family. It encompasses a generous 320 square feet, plus a convenient storage loft, and is totally contemporary in design. As a lawn or garden shed, there is ample room for all your garden equipment, with a separate area for potting plants. The built-in potting bench features removable planks to accommodate flats of flowers in various sizes. The roomy loft provides 133 square feet of safe storage area for chemicals, fertilizers or other lawn-care products. Natural light floods the interior through multiple windows in the rear wall and in the front, across from the storage loft. This practical structure can also be used as a studio or, placed at the water's edge, it can be easily converted to a boat house by adding 4' x 4' columns used as piers in lieu of the slab floor.

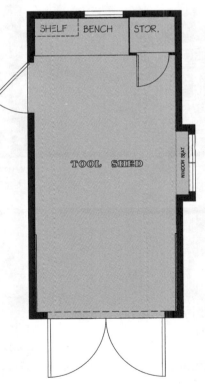

WIDTH 8'-0"
DEPTH 16'-0"

DESIGN BY
HOME PLANNERS

DESIGN G225

Lawn-shed extraordinare, this appealing design can be easily converted from the Tudor style shown here to match just about any exterior design you prefer. In addition to serving as a lawn shed, this versatile structure also can be used as a craft studio, a pool house, or a delightful playhouse for your children. The double doors and large floor area provide ample access and storage capacity for lawn tractors and other large pieces of equipment. A handy built-in work bench offers needed space for potting plants or working on craft projects. A separate storage room for craft supplies, lawn-care products or pool chemicals can be locked for safety. Strategically placed on your site, this charming building could be designed to be a reflection of your home in miniature.

DESIGN G226

DESIGN BY
HOME PLANNERS

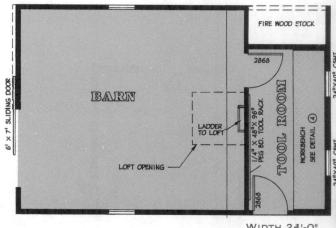

FIRE WOOD STOCK

BARN

TOOL ROOM

6' x 7' SLIDING DOOR

2868

24"X40" CSMT.

LADDER TO LOFT

LOFT OPENING

1/4" X 48"X 96" PEG BD. TOOL RACK

WORKBENCH SEE DETAIL ④

24"X40" CSMT.

2868

WIDTH 24'-0"
DEPTH 16'-0"

This large, sturdy lawn shed is not quite "as big as a barn," but almost! a combined area of 768 square feet includes a 24' x 16' loft area with access by ladder or stairway. The structure is built entirely of standard framing materials requiring no special beams or cutting. An ideal hideaway for the serious artist, this structure could serve a myriad of other uses including a second garage, a game house, or even as a barn for small livestock. Or, expand the design to include utilities and a bathroom to provide a secluded guest room. The large tool room at the back has a built-in work bench with plenty of natural light, plus entrances from inside or outside. Space is provided for a built-in wood stockpile area. The same space could be used to extend the length of the tool room. A 6' x 7' sliding-door entrance, with crossbars and a louvered cupola, accent the rural effect.

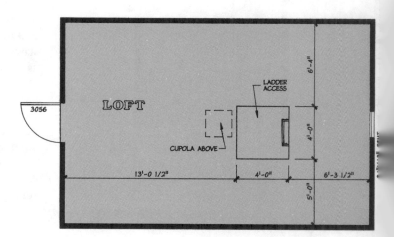

LOFT

3056

LADDER ACCESS

CUPOLA ABOVE

6'-4"

4'-0"

13'-0 1/2"   4'-0"   6'-3 1/2"

5'-0"

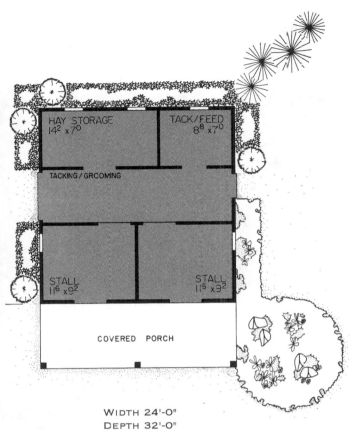

HAY STORAGE
14² x 7⁰

TACK/FEED
8⁸ x 7⁰

TACKING/GROOMING

STALL
11⁶ x 9²

STALL
11⁶ x 9²

COVERED PORCH

WIDTH 24'-0"
DEPTH 32'-0"

DESIGN G113

DESIGN BY
HOME PLANNERS

Right out of Kentucky horse country comes this all-in-one design for a two-horse stable, plus tack room and covered hay storage. Two generous 11'-6" x 9'-2" stalls provide shelter and security for your best stock, with easy access through Dutch doors. Against the far wall is a 14'-2" x 7' hay "loft" and next to it, an 8'-8" x 7' tack room. In the center is a large area reserved for grooming your mount or to saddle up for the big race.

DESIGN G109

DESIGN BY
HOME PLANNERS

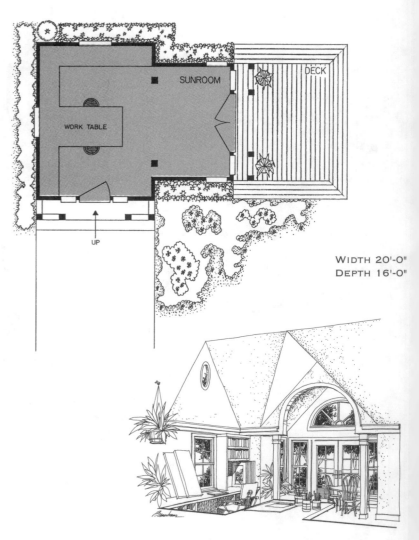

WIDTH 20'-0"
DEPTH 16'-0"

The ultimate luxury for any craft enthusiast—a separate, free-standing building dedicated to your craft of choice! Functional as well as a beautiful addition to your landscape, this 320-square-foot cottage provides ample counter space and shelving to spread out or store all your materials and tools. And at break time, relax from your endeavors in the attached sun room with vaulted ceiling, French doors and lots of elegant windows. Orient the structure on your property to face south for the sun room and the north-facing work area receives soft, even light. A built-in and well-thought-out work table is flanked by additional countertop work space. Outside, an open 10' x 12' deck off the sun room makes this little cottage just about perfect.

418

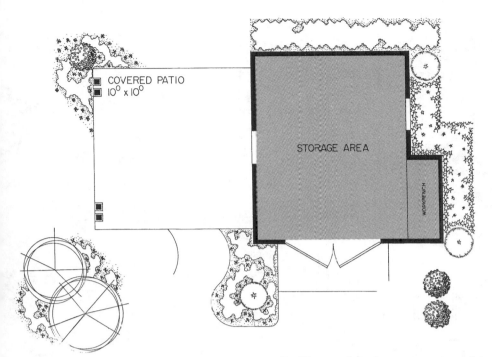

COVERED PATIO
10⁰ x 10⁰

STORAGE AREA

WORKBENCH

DESIGN BY
HOME PLANNERS

WIDTH 12'-0"
DEPTH 12'-0"

No words quite convey everything this generous storage shed/covered patio combination has to offer. The 120 square feet of storage area presents a delightful facade that belies its practical function. Grooved plywood siding and a shingled double roof are accented by double doors, shutters at the window, a bird house tucked in the eaves and a trellis for your favorite climbers. And if that's not enough—the extended roof line covers a 10' x 10' patio area complete with graceful support columns and topped by a jaunty cupola. Use the storage area as a potting shed, storage shed or workshop. You'll know immediately how to use the patio!

DESIGN G110

DESIGN BY
HOME PLANNERS

A mini-kitchen and an optional built-in table tucked in the breezeway of this double-room unit provide shelter for pool-side repasts no matter what the weather. You can enhance both the beauty and the function of your pool area with this charming structure. The exterior features include a gable roof with columns in the front, shuttered windows, horizontal wood and shingle siding and decorative flower boxes and cupola. The two rooms on either side of the breezeway area provide a 5'-8" x 7'-6" changing area with built-in seating and a larger area—7'-6" x 7'-6"—as convenient storage for pool supplies and equipment. This spacious cabana is sure to be a fine addition to an active family's pool area.

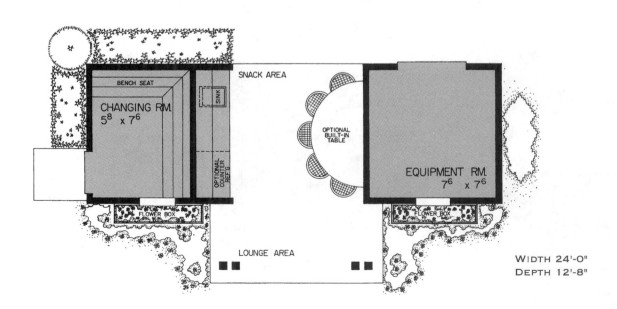

WIDTH 24'-0"
DEPTH 12'-8"

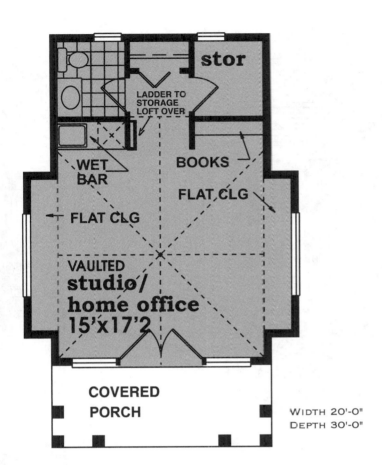

stor

LADDER TO
STORAGE
LOFT OVER

WET
BAR

BOOKS

FLAT CLG

FLAT CLG

VAULTED
**studio/
home office**
15'x17'2

**COVERED
PORCH**

WIDTH 20'-0"
DEPTH 30'-0"

DESIGN Q463

Square Footage: 432

DESIGN BY
HOME PLANNERS

Need a quiet place for a home office or a studio? You can't go wrong by choosing the plans for this cleverly designed structure. It is filled with amenities that make a small space seem huge. The ceiling of the main part of the building is vaulted and features clerestory windows to provide ample lighting. Bumped-out areas on both sides are perfect for desks and work areas. A built-in bookshelf along one wall is complemented by a large walk-in storage closet to the rear and an additional wall closet. A half-bath and wet bar round out the plan. The entry is graced by a columned porch and double French doors flanked by fixed windows.

Alternate Exterior

DESIGN Q461

Square Footage: 288

DESIGN BY
SELECT HOME DESIGNS

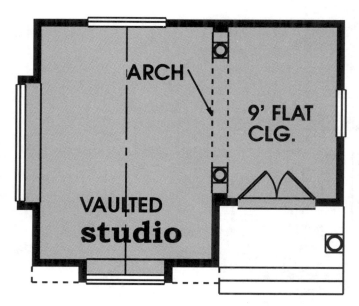

ARCH

9' FLAT
CLG.

VAULTED
studio

WIDTH 20'-0"
DEPTH 16'-0"

Though simple in design, this smaller studio/home office provides all the right stuff for your workspace. A covered entry shelters the double-French door access to a two-room area. The smaller space features a nine-foot flat ceiling and is separated from the main studio area by a columned arch. The main area seems larger than it is thanks to a vaulted ceiling and two bumped-out windows. Define your own work area with furniture, or modify this design to include handy built-ins.

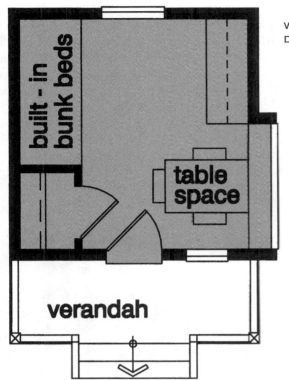

WIDTH 12'-0"
DEPTH 16'-0"

built - in bunk beds

table space

verandah

DESIGN Q459

Square Footage: 144

DESIGN BY
SELECT HOME DESIGNS

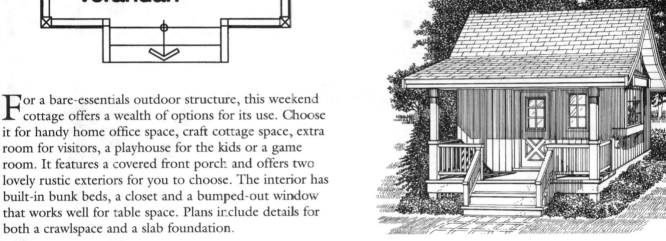

For a bare-essentials outdoor structure, this weekend cottage offers a wealth of options for its use. Choose it for handy home office space, craft cottage space, extra room for visitors, a playhouse for the kids or a game room. It features a covered front porch and offers two lovely rustic exteriors for you to choose. The interior has built-in bunk beds, a closet and a bumped-out window that works well for table space. Plans include details for both a crawlspace and a slab foundation.

DESIGN G238

DESIGN BY
HOME PLANNERS

The magic of this design is its flexibility. Use it exclusively as a changing cabana with separate His and Hers changing rooms, or, with a little sleight of hand, turn one of the rooms into a summer kitchen for outdoor entertaining. As changing rooms, each eight-sided area includes built-in benches and private bathroom facilities. The 15'-3½" x 15'-3½" kitchen option includes a stove, refrigerator, food preparation area and a storage pantry. A shuttered window poolside provides easy access to serve your guests across the counter. Linking these two areas is a covered walkway which serves as a shaded picnic area, or a convenient place to get out of the sun. Columns, arches and stained glass windows provide a touch of grandeur to this fun and functional poolside design.

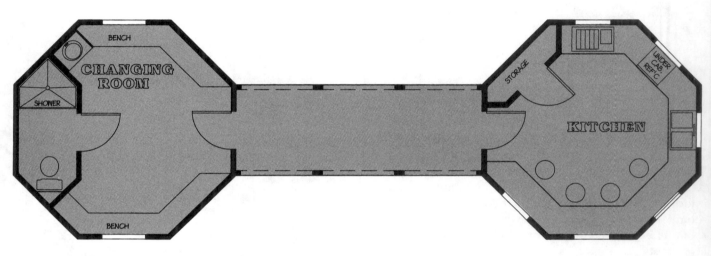

WIDTH 47'-7"
DEPTH 15'-4"

DESIGN G239

DESIGN BY
HOME PLANNERS

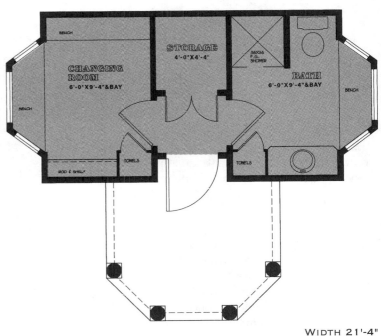

A changing room, a summer kitchen and an elegant porch for shade. Add the convenience of bathroom facilities and you're set for outdoor living all summer long. This pool pavilion is designed to provide maximum function in a small area and features built-in benches, shelves, hanging rods and a separate linen closet for towels. The opaque diamond-patterned windows decorate the exterior of the 10' x 6'-8" changing area and the mirror-image bath. The bath could also be made into a kitchen area, then simply add a sliding window to allow easy passage of refreshments to your family and guests poolside. When you've had enough sun or socializing, recline in the shade under the columned porch and enjoy a good book or a nap.

WIDTH 21'-4"
DEPTH 18'-0"

DESIGN G215

DESIGN BY
HOME PLANNERS

This all-American single-entrance gazebo is simple to construct and easy to adapt to a variety of styles. All materials are available in most areas with no special cutting for trim or rails. This gazebo is distinguished by its simple design and large floor area. The traditional eight-sided configuration and overall area of approximately 160 square feet allow for the placement of furniture with ample seating for 8 to 10 people. Build as shown, or modify the trim and railings to give a totally different appearance. If multiple entrance/exit access is desired, simply eliminate the rails as needed. Access to the ground is a single step which could be easily modified for a low ramp.

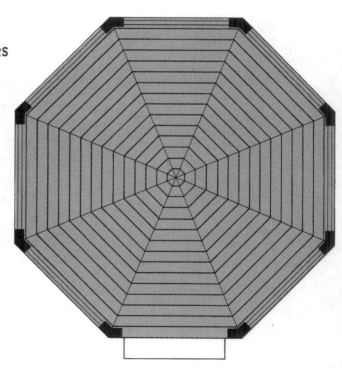

WIDTH 16'-0"
DEPTH 14'-9⅜"

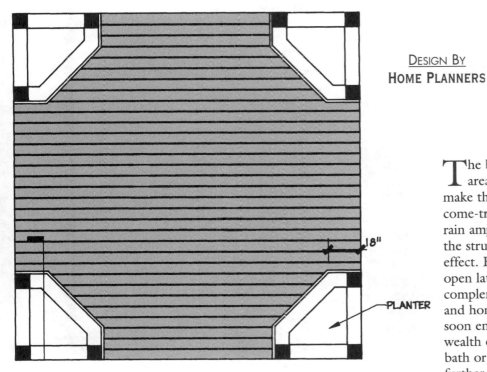

18"

PLANTER

WIDTH 16'-0"
DEPTH 16'-0"

The built-in planters and open roof areas of this multiple-entrance gazebo make this design a gardener's dream-come-true. The open roof allows sun and rain ample access to the planters and gives the structure a definite country-garden effect. Built with or without a cupola, the open lattice work in the walls and roof complements a wide variety of landscapes and home designs. A creative gardener will soon enhance this charming gazebo with a wealth of plants and vines. Tuck a bird bath or bubbling fountain into a corner to further the garden setting. The large design—256 square feet—ensures that both you and nature have plenty of room to share all that this gazebo has to offer. It easily accommodates a table and chairs when you invite your guests to this outdoor hideaway.

DESIGN G220

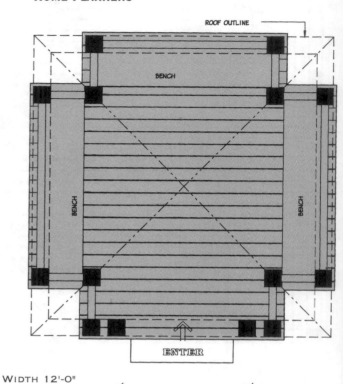

ROOF OUTLINE

BENCH

BENCH

BENCH

ENTER

WIDTH 12'-0"
DEPTH 12'-0"

Up, down and green all around! Light and airy, the unique trellis roof of this innovative single-entrance gazebo is just waiting for your favorite perennial vines. To extend the green-all-around look, modify the railings to a lattice pattern and train vines or grapes—or roses, for a splash of color—to experience nature all around you. The inset corners of the design provide plenty of space for planting. Simple lines make this delightful gazebo easy to construct, with no cumbersome cutting or gingerbread. The large area—100 square feet—provides built-in seating for nine people. This flexible design could be modified to a closed roof with any standard roof sheathing and shingles, and the single entrance design could be altered to accommodate multiple entrances.

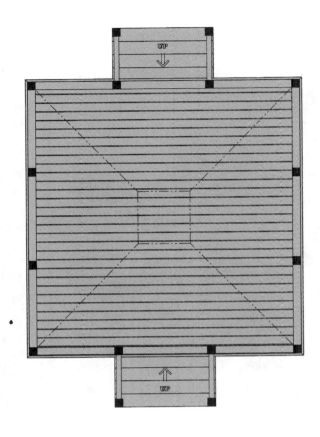

DESIGN G217

Dance the night away in this double-entrance, pass-through style gazebo. By day, the open-air construction provides a clear view in all directions. The large floor area of 256 square feet seats 12 to 16 people comfortably or nicely accommodates musicians or entertainers for a lawn party. The decorative cupola can be lowered, louvered or removed to create just the appearance you want. Or, add an antique weather vane just for fun. This gazebo has five steps up, which give it a large crawlspace for access to any added utilities. Its square shape allows for simple cutting and floor framing, plus easy assembly of the roof frame. The trim and hand rails are simple to construct or modify to achieve several different design effects.

WIDTH 16'-0"
DEPTH 22'-4"

WIDTH 12'-0"
DEPTH 12'-8"

DESIGN Q458

DESIGN BY
SELECT HOME DESIGNS

Victorian on a small scale, this gazebo will be the highlight of any yard. With a cupola topped by a weathervane, a railed perimeter and double steps up, it's the essence of historic design. Small enough to fit on just about any size lot, yet large enough to accommodate a small crowd, it is perfect for outdoor entertaining. Choose standard gingerbread details from your local supplier to make it your own.

DESIGN G246

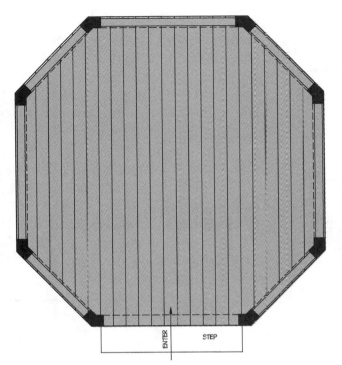

ENTER STEP

WIDTH 11'-8'
DEPTH 11'-7⅞"

Reflecting the image "gingerbread" is intended to convey, this delightful gazebo will be the focal point of your landscape. The floor area of nearly 144 square feet is large enough for a table and four to six chairs. Or, add built-in benches to increase the seating to up to 20 people. Painted white with pink asphalt shingles, this gazebo has a cool summery appearance. Or you can build it with unpainted, treated materials and cedar shakes for an entirely different effect. The jaunty cupola complete with spire adds a stately look to this single-entrance structure. The plans also include an optional arbor, which can be incorporated into the entrance of the gazebo.

When You're Ready To Order . . .

Let Us Show You Our Home Blueprint Package.

Building a home? Planning a home? Our Blueprint Package has nearly everything you need to get the job done right, whether you're working on your own or with help from an architect, designer, builder or subcontractors. Each Blueprint Package is the result of many hours of work by licensed architects or professional designers.

QUALITY

Hundreds of hours of painstaking effort have gone into the development of your blueprint set. Each home has been quality-checked by professionals to insure accuracy and buildability.

VALUE

Because we sell in volume, you can buy professional-quality blueprints at a fraction of their development cost. With our plans, your dream home design costs only a few hundred dollars, not the thousands of dollars that custom architects charge.

SERVICE

Once you've chosen your favorite home plan, you'll receive fast, efficient service whether you choose to mail or fax your order to us or call us toll free at 1-800-521-6797. For customer service, call toll free 1-888-690-1116.

SATISFACTION

Over 50 years of service to satisfied home plan buyers provide us unparalleled experience and knowledge in producing quality blueprints. What this means to you is satisfaction with our product and performance.

ORDER TOLL FREE 1-800-521-6797

After you've looked over our Blueprint Package and Important Extras on the following pages, simply mail the order form on page 445 or call toll free on our Blueprint Hotline: 1-800-521-6797. We're ready and eager to serve you. For customer service, call toll free 1-888-690-1116.

Each set of blueprints is an interrelated collection of detail sheets which includes components such as floor plans, interior and exterior elevations, dimensions, cross-sections, diagrams and notations. These sheets show exactly how your house is to be built.

Among the sheets included may be:

Frontal Sheet
This artist's sketch of the exterior of the house gives you an idea of how the house will look when built and landscaped. Large ink-line floor plans show all levels of the house and provide an overview of your new home's livability, as well as a handy reference for deciding on furniture placement.

Foundation Plan
This sheet shows the foundation layout includ-

SAMPLE PACKAGE

ing support walls, excavated and unexcavated areas, if any, and foundation notes. If slab construction rather than basement, the plan shows footings and details for a monolithic slab. This page, or another in the set, may include a sample plot plan for locating your house on a building site.

Detailed Floor Plans

These plans show the layout of each floor of the house. Rooms and interior spaces are carefully dimensioned and keys are given for cross-section details provided later in the plans. The positions of electrical outlets and switches are shown.

House Cross-Sections

Large-scale views show sections or cut-aways of the foundation, interior walls, exterior walls, floors, stairways and roof details. Additional cross-sections may show important changes in floor, ceiling or roof heights or the relationship of one level to another. Extremely valuable for construction, these sections show exactly how the various parts of the house fit together.

Interior Elevations

Many of our drawings show the design and placement of kitchen and bathroom cabinets, laundry areas, fireplaces, bookcases and other built-ins. Little "extras," such as mantelpiece and wainscoting drawings, plus moulding sections, provide details that give your home that custom touch.

Exterior Elevations

These drawings show the front, rear and sides of your house and give necessary notes on exterior materials and finishes. Particular attention is given to cornice detail, brick and stone accents or other finish items that make your home unique.

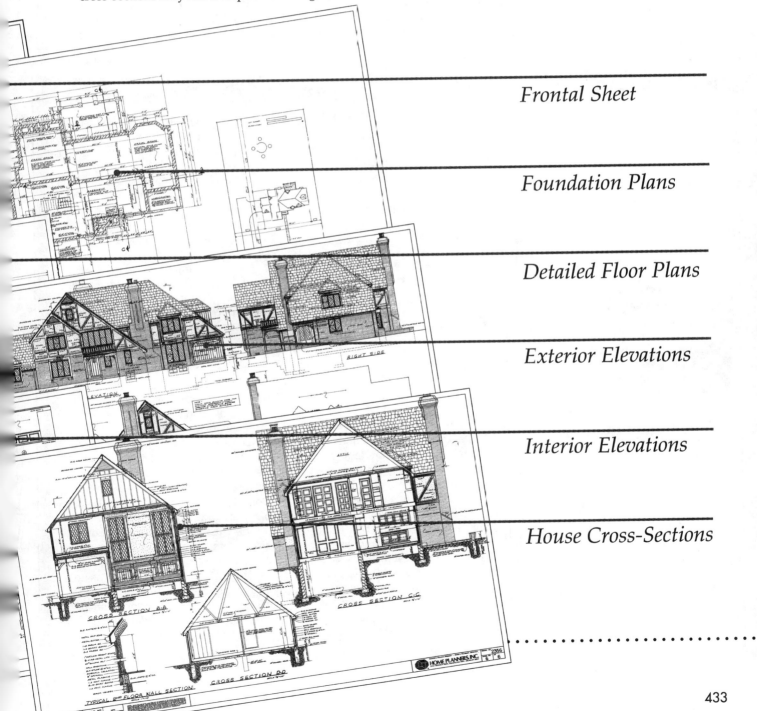

Frontal Sheet

Foundation Plans

Detailed Floor Plans

Exterior Elevations

Interior Elevations

House Cross-Sections

*I*mportant *Extras To Do The Job Right!*

Introducing eight important planning and construction aids developed by our professionals to help you succeed in your home-building project.

MATERIALS LIST

(Note: Because of the diversity of local building codes, our Materials List does not include mechanical materials.)

For many of the designs in our portfolio, we offer a customized materials take-off that is invaluable in planning and estimating the cost of your new home. This Materials List outlines the quantity, type and size of materials needed to build your house (with the exception of mechanical system items). Included are framing lumber, windows and doors, kitchen and bath cabinetry, rough and finish hardware, and much more. This handy list helps you or your builder cost out materials and serves as a reference sheet when you're compiling bids. A Materials List cannot be ordered before blueprints are ordered.

SPECIFICATION OUTLINE

This valuable 16-page document is critical to building your house correctly. Designed to be filled in by you or your builder, this book lists 166 stages or items crucial to the building process. It provides a comprehensive review of the construction process and helps in making choices of materials. When combined with the blueprints, a signed contract, and a schedule, it becomes a legal document and record for the building of your home.

QUOTE ONE®

Summary Cost Report / Materials Cost Report

A new service for estimating the cost of building select designs, the Quote One® system is available in two separate stages: The Summary Cost Report and the Materials Cost Report.

Make even more informed decisions about your home-building project with the second phase of our package, our Materials Cost Report. This tool is invaluable in planning and estimating the cost of your new home. The material and installation (labor and equipment) cost is shown for each of over 1,000 line items provided in the Materials List (Standard grade) which is included when you purchase this estimating tool. It allows you to determine building costs for your specific zip-code area and for your chosen home design. Space is allowed for additional estimates from contractors and subcontractors, such as for mechanical materials, which are not included in our packages. This invaluable tool is available for a price of $110 ($120 for a Schedule E plan) which includes a Materials List. A Materials Cost Report cannot be ordered before blueprints are ordered.

The Summary Cost Report is the first stage in the package and shows the total cost per square foot for your chosen home in your zip-code area and then breaks that cost down into various categories showing the costs for building materials, labor and installation. The total cost for the report (which includes three grades: Budget, Standard and Custom) is just $19.95 for one home, and additionals are only $14.95. These reports allow you to evaluate your building budget and compare the costs of building a variety of homes in your area.

The Quote One® program is continually updated with new plans. If you are interested in a plan that is not indicated as Quote One®, please call and ask our sales reps, they will be happy to verify the status for you. To order these invaluable reports, use the order form on page 445 or call 1-800-521-6797.

CONSTRUCTION INFORMATION

If you want to know more about techniques—and deal more confidently with subcontractors we offer these useful sheets. Each set is an excellent tool that will add to your understanding of these technical subjects.

Plan-A-Home®

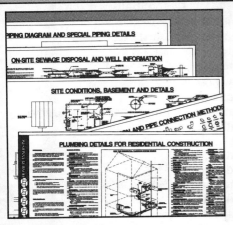

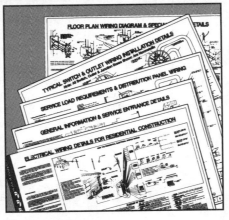

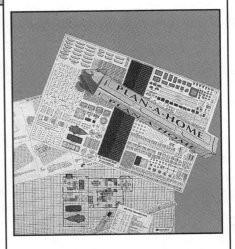

PLUMBING

The Blueprint Package includes locations for all the plumbing fixtures in your new house, including sinks, lavatories, tubs, showers, toilets, laundry trays and water heaters. However, if you want to know more about the complete plumbing system, these 24x36-inch detail sheets will prove very useful. Prepared to meet requirements of the National Plumbing Code, these six fact-filled sheets give general information on pipe schedules, fittings, sump-pump details, water-softener hookups, septic system details and much more. Color-coded sheets include a glossary of terms.

ELECTRICAL

The locations for every electrical switch, plug and outlet are shown in your Blueprint Package. However, these Electrical Details go further to take the mystery out of household electrical systems. Prepared to meet requirements of the National Electrical Code, these comprehensive 24x36-inch drawings come packed with helpful information, including wire sizing, switch-installation schematics, cable-routing details, appliance wattage, door-bell hookups, typical service panel circuitry and much more. Six sheets are bound together and color-coded for easy reference. A glossary of terms is also included.

Plan-A-Home® is an easy-to-use tool that helps you design a new home, arrange furniture in a new or existing home, or plan a remodeling project. Each package contains:

- **More than 700 reusable peel-off planning symbols** on a self-stick vinyl sheet, including walls, windows, doors, all types of furniture, kitchen components, bath fixtures and many more.

- **A reusable, transparent, 1/4-inch scale planning grid** that matches the scale of actual working drawings (1/4-inch equals 1 foot). This grid provides the basis for house layouts of up to 140x92 feet.

- **Tracing paper** and a protective sheet for copying or transferring your completed plan.

- **A felt-tip pen,** with water-soluble ink that wipes away quickly.

Plan-A-Home® lets you lay out areas as large as a 7,500 square foot, six-bedroom, seven-bath house.

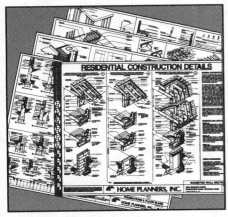

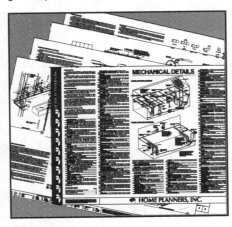

CONSTRUCTION

The Blueprint Package contains everything an experienced builder needs to construct a particular house. However, it doesn't show all the ways that houses can be built, nor does it explain alternate construction methods. To help you understand how your house will be built—and offer additional techniques—this set of drawings depicts the materials and methods used to build foundations, fireplaces, walls, floors and roofs. Where appropriate, the drawings show acceptable alternatives. These six sheets will answer questions for the advanced do-it-yourselfer or home planner.

MECHANICAL

This package contains fundamental principles and useful data that will help you make informed decisions and communicate with subcontractors about heating and cooling systems. The 24x36-inch drawings contain instructions and samples that allow you to make simple load calculations and preliminary sizing and costing analysis. Covered are today's most commonly used systems from heat pumps to solar fuel systems. The package is packed full of illustrations and diagrams to help you visualize components and how they relate to one another.

To Order, Call Toll Free 1-800-521-6797

To add these important extras to your Blueprint Package, simply indicate your choices on the order form on page 445 or call us Toll Free 1-800-521-6797 and we'll tell you more about these exciting products. For customer service, call toll free 1-888-690-1116.

⬛ *The Deck Blueprint Package*

Many of the homes in this book can be enhanced with a professionally designed Home Planners' Deck Plan. Those home plans highlighted with a ⬛ have a matching or corresponding deck plan available which includes a Deck Plan Frontal Sheet, Deck Framing and Floor Plans, Deck Elevations and a Deck Materials List. A Standard Deck Details Package, also available, provides all the how-to information necessary for building *any* deck. Our Complete Deck Building Package contains 1 set of Custom Deck Plans of your choice, plus 1 set of Standard Deck Building Details all for one low price. Our plans and details are carefully prepared in an easy-to-understand format that will guide you through every stage of your deck-building project. This page contains a sampling of 12 of the 25 different Deck layouts to match your favorite house. See page 438 for prices and ordering information.

SPLIT-LEVEL SUN DECK
Deck Plan D100

BI-LEVEL DECK WITH COVERED DINING
Deck Plan D101

WRAP-AROUND FAMILY DECK
Deck Plan D104

DECK FOR DINING AND VIEWS
Deck Plan D107

TREND SETTER DECK
Deck Plan D110

TURN-OF-THE-CENTURY DECK
Deck Plan D111

WEEKEND ENTERTAINER DECK
Deck Plan D112

CENTER-VIEW DECK
Deck Plan D114

KITCHEN-EXTENDER DECK
Deck Plan D115

SPLIT-LEVEL ACTIVITY DECK
Deck Plan D117

TRI-LEVEL DECK WITH GRILL
Deck Plan D119

CONTEMPORARY LEISURE DECK
Deck Plan D120

L The Landscape Blueprint Package

For the homes marked with an **L** in this book, Home Planners has created a front-yard landscape plan that matches or is complementary in design to the house plan. These comprehensive blueprint packages include a Frontal Sheet, Plan View, Regionalized Plant & Materials List, a sheet on Planting and Maintaining Your Landscape, Zone Maps and Plant Size and Description Guide. These plans will help you achieve professional results, adding value and enjoyment to your property for years to come. Each set of blueprints is a full 18" x 24" in size with clear, complete instructions and easy-to-read type. Six of the forty front yard Landscape Plans to match your favorite house are shown below.

Regional Order Map

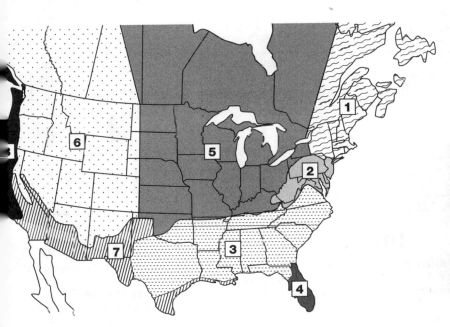

Most of the Landscape Plans shown on these pages are available with a Plant & Materials List adapted by horticultural experts to 8 different regions of the country. Please specify Geographic Region when ordering your plan. See page 438 for prices, ordering information and regional availability.

Region	1	Northeast
Region	2	Mid-Atlantic
Region	3	Deep South
Region	4	Florida & Gulf Coast
Region	5	Midwest
Region	6	Rocky Mountains
Region	7	Southern California & Desert Southwest
Region	8	Northern California & Pacific Northwest

CAPE COD COTTAGE
Landscape Plan L202

GAMBREL-ROOF COLONIAL
Landscape Plan L203

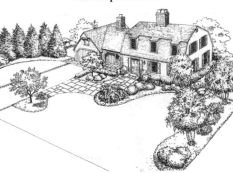

CENTER-HALL COLONIAL
Landscape Plan L204

CLASSIC NEW ENGLAND COLONIAL
Landscape Plan L205

COUNTRY-STYLE FARMHOUSE
Landscape Plan L207

TRADITIONAL SPLIT-LEVEL
Landscape Plan L228

Price Schedule & Plans Index

House Blueprint Price Schedule
(Prices guaranteed through December 31, 1999)

Tier	1-set Study Package	4-set Building Package	8-set Building Package	1-set Reproducible Sepias	Home Customizer® Package
A	$390	$435	$495	$595	$645
B	$430	$475	$535	$655	$705
C	$470	$515	$575	$715	$765
D	$510	$555	$615	$775	$825
E	$630	$675	$735	$835	$885
F	$730	$775	$835	$935	$985
G	$830	$875	$935	$1035	$1085

Prices for 4- or 8-set Building Packages honored only at time of original order.
Additional Identical Blueprints (standard or reverse) in same order ..$50 per set
Reverse Blueprints (mirror image) with 4- or 8-set order ....$50 fee per order
Specification Outlines ....$10 each
Materials Lists (available only for those designers listed below):
- ▲ Home Planners Designs...$50
- ● The Sater Design Collection $50
- ≠ Larry Belk Designs...$50
- † Design Basics Designs..$75
- ◆ Donald Gardner Designs..$50
- ■ Design Traditions Designs..$50
- ✹ Alan Mascord Designs..$50
- ✵ Living Concepts Home Planning $50
- ❖ Select Home Designs...$50

Materials Lists for "E-G" price plans are an additional $10.

Deck Plans Price Schedule

CUSTOM DECK PLANS

Price Group	Q	R	S
1 Set Custom Plans	$25	$30	$35
Additional identical sets	$10 each		
Reverse sets (mirror image)	$10 each		

STANDARD DECK DETAILS
1 Set Generic Construction Details ....$14.95 each

COMPLETE DECK BUILDING PACKAGE

Price Group	Q	R	S
1 Set Custom Plans, plus			
1 Set Standard Deck Details $35		$40	$45

Landscape Plans Price Schedule

Price Group	X	Y	Z
1 set	$35	$45	$55
3 sets	$50	$60	$70
6 sets	$65	$75	$85

Additional Identical Sets.................................$10 each
Reverse Sets (mirror image)............................$10 each

Index

To use the Index below, refer to the design number listed in numerical order (a helpful page reference is also given). Note the price index letter and refer to the House Blueprint Price Schedule above for the cost of one, four or eight sets of blueprints or the cost of a reproducible sepia. Additional prices are shown for identical and reverse blueprint sets, as well as a very useful Materials List for some of the plans. Also note in the Index below those plans that have matching or complementary Deck Plans or Landscape Plans. Refer to the schedules above for prices of these plans. All Home Planners' plans can be customized with Home Planners' Home Customizer® Package. These plans are indicated below with this symbol: 🏠. See page 445 for information. Some plans are also part of our Quote One® estimating service and are indicated by this symbol: 🏠 . See page 434 for more information.

To Order: Fill in and send the order form on page 445—or call toll free 1-800-521-6797 or 520-297-8200.

DESIGN	PRICE	PAGE	CUSTOMIZABLE	QUOTE ONE®	DECK	DECK PRICE	LANDSCAPE	LANDSCAPE PRICE	REGIONS
▲ 1404	A	276	🏠						
▲ 1406	A	250	🏠						
▲ 1425	A	288	🏠						
▲ 1427	A	290	🏠						
▲ 1432	B	244	🏠						
▲ 1433	A	283	🏠						
▲ 1435	A	291	🏠						
▲ 1444	A	169	🏠						
▲ 1448	A	251	🏠						
▲ 1451	A	249	🏠						
▲ 1468	A	297	🏠						
▲ 1470	A	247	🏠						
▲ 1471	A	157	🏠						
▲ 1472	A	156	🏠						
▲ 1475	B	268	🏠						
▲ 1482	A	272	🏠						
▲ 1486	A	220	🏠						
▲ 1491	A	248	🏠						
▲ 1499	B	245	🏠						
▲ 2420	A	168	🏠						
▲ 2423	A	221	🏠						
▲ 2425	A	218	🏠						
▲ 2427	A	267	🏠						
▲ 2428	A	278	🏠						
▲ 2431	A	243	🏠						
▲ 2439	A	222	🏠						

DESIGN	PRICE	PAGE	CUSTOMIZABLE	QUOTE ONE®	DECK	DECK PRICE	LANDSCAPE	LANDSCAPE PRICE	REGIONS
▲ 2456	B	274	✓						
▲ 2459	A	246	✓						
▲ 2461	A	277	✓						
▲ 2481	A	182	✓						
▲ 2485	B	241	✓						
▲ 2488	A	164	✓	✓	D102	Q			
▲ 2490	A	295	✓	✓					
▲ 2491	A	165	✓	✓					
▲ 2511	B	240	✓	✓	D108	R	L229	Y	1-8
▲ 2583	C	231	✓						
▲ 2679	C	238	✓						
▲ 2761	B	230	✓				L229	Y	1-8
▲ 2782	C	304	✓		D101	R			
▲ 2826	B	92	✓	✓	D116	R			
▲ 2878	B	7	✓	✓	D112	R	L200	X	1-3,5,6,8
▲ 2937	C	239	✓	✓			L229	Y	1-8
▲ 2947	B	20	✓	✓	D112	R	L200	X	1-3,5,6,8
▲ 3442	A	162	✓	✓	D115	Q	L200	X	1-3,5,6,8
▲ 3460	A	163	✓				L200	X	1-3,5,6,8
▲ 3481	B	167	✓	✓			L200	X	1-3,5,6,8
▲ 3496	B	219	✓	✓			L202	X	1-3,5,6,8
▲ 3658	B	270	✓	✓	D102	Q	L202	X	1-3,5,6,8
▲ 4015	A	279							
▲ 4027	A	237							
▲ 4061	A	137	✓	✓	D115	Q			
4115	B	242							
▲ 4153	A	293			D115	Q	L202	X	1-3,5,6,8
▲ 4210	A	282							
4293	B	287			D120	R			
• 6612	B	327		✓					
• 6615	D	373		✓					
6616	D	379							
6617	D	372							
6618	E	370							
• 6619	E	388		✓					
6620	E	395							
• 6621	D	389		✓					
• 6622	C	394		✓					
6644	C	305							
6654	D	378							
6655	C	385							
6680	D	376							
6681	D	368							
6682	D	377							
6683	D	365							
6684	D	381							
6685	D	363							
6686	C	369							
6687	C	364							
6688	D	367							
6689	D	380							
6690	C	374							
6691	C	383							
6692	C	384							
6693	D	371							
6694	C	382							
6697	D	386							
6698	D	387							
6700	D	366							
6701	C	375							
† 7246	E	91							
7431	C	192							
7445	E	215							
✸ 7464	B	187							
7469	B	205							
7471	B	73							
7494	C	185							
✸ 7495	B	196							
7508	C	193							
7509	B	233							
7510	B	232							
7512	A	87							
7515	B	204							
7516	B	235							
7534	C	195							
7535	B	194							
◆ 7621	D	77							
7627	D	400							
7631	D	186							
◆ 7632	C	154							
◆ 7654	C	140							
◆ 7665	D	229							
◆ 7671	D	114							
◆ 7678	D	49							
◆ 7680	C	188							
◆ 7682	C	11							
◆ 7688	E	56							
◆ 7689	D	35							
◆ 7693	E	189							
◆ 7694	D	147							
◆ 7695	C	32							
◆ 7699	C	33							
◆ 7701	C	141							
◆ 7727	D	79							

DESIGN	PRICE	PAGE	CUSTOMIZABLE	QUOTE ONE®	DECK	DECK PRICE	LANDSCAPE	LANDSCAPE PRICE	REGIONS
◆ 7733	B	166							
◆ 7734	D	130							
◆ 7736	E	133							
◆ 7737	D	76							
7738	D	391							
8001	C	396							
8002	C	397							
≠ 8013	D	44		⌂					
8034	E	360							
8051	B	75							
8064	B	36							
≠ 8071	C	46							
8088	D	88							
8114	D	125							
8143	D	122							
8145	E	362							
8161	D	57							
8164	C	85							
8170	B	29							
8178	A	41							
8179	C	83							
8180	B	40							
8181	B	31							
8183	B	45							
8229	B	26							
8246	A	15							
8251	E	201							
8252	E	53							
8253	D	50							
8257	C	47							
8263	E	198							
8265	B	4							
8600	C	312							
8601	B	315							
8603	C	306							
8610	A	336							
8611	A	330							
8612	B	320							
8620	C	318							
8624	C	325							
8629	B	184							
8630	B	332							
8631	B	334							
8632	B	331							
8633	B	333							
8635	B	354							
8636	B	316							
8637	B	321							
8639	B	319							
8640	C	353							
8644	B	310							
8645	C	317							
8646	C	313							
8648	C	103							
8653	D	307							
8659	B	355							
8662	B	314							
8663	C	51							
8669	C	311							
8672	C	344							
8682	C	309							
8690	D	358							
8692	E	359							
8693	A	335							
8709	C	361							
8732	C	308							
8792	D	52							
† 9200	C	18		⌂					
† 9201	C	39		⌂					
† 9202	C	34							
† 9204	D	38		⌂					
† 9206	C	67		⌂					
† 9235	C	113		⌂					
† 9238	C	62		⌂					
† 9251	D	110		⌂					
† 9252	C	111		⌂					
† 9256	B	19							
† 9274	D	123							
† 9298	D	115		⌂					
† 9310	C	108		⌂					
† 9362	C	43		⌂					
† 9366	E	82		⌂					
† 9371	C	17							
† 9375	E	42		⌂					
✳ 9431	A	6							
✳ 9509	B	234							
✳ 9525	B	72							
✳ 9532	A	63							
✳ 9534	B	197							
✳ 9536	D	199							
✳ 9537	D	356							
✳ 9551	E	203							
✳ 9557	C	117		⌂					
✳ 9587	C	200							

DESIGN	PRICE	PAGE	CUSTOMIZABLE	QUOTE ONE®	DECK	DECK PRICE	LANDSCAPE	LANDSCAPE PRICE	REGIONS
✳ 9588	C	112							
✳ 9590	C	202							
◆ 9608	C	135							
◆ 9609	B	155							
◆ 9613	C	303							
◆ 9614	C	302							
◆ 9620	B	104							
◆ 9621	C	128		🏠					
◆ 9622	C	93							
◆ 9632	D	127		🏠					
◆ 9645	C	131		🏠					
◆ 9661	C	54		🏠					
◆ 9663	B	136							
◆ 9664	B	21		🏠					
◆ 9666	C	139		🏠					
◆ 9679	C	22							
◆ 9690	C	129		🏠					
◆ 9697	B	138							
◆ 9702	D	106		🏠					
◆ 9713	C	105							
◆ 9723	D	132		🏠					
◆ 9726	B	23							
◆ 9734	C	37		🏠					
◆ 9749	C	107		🏠					
A138	D	210							
A141	D	126							
A154	B	124							
A169	E	89							
A185	D	66							
A186	D	80							
A203	C	190							
A205	D	357							
A239	A	65							
✳ A240	B	59							
A241	B	60							
A242	B	58							
✳ A243	B	64							
A244	B	61							
A250	C	175							
A253	C	109							
A262	C	81							
A263	D	206							
A264	D	207							
A266	D	90							
A267	D	217							
A268	D	211							
A269	E	212							
A271	F	214							
A274	F	213							
A296	C	172							
A297	C	216							
A298	D	86							
A300	F	208							
A301	C	116							
A307	E	390							
G107	$50	419							
G109	$50	418							
G110	$50	420							
G113	$60	417							
G215	$40	426							
G217	$40	429							
G220	$40	428							
G221	$40	427							
G223	$40	414							
G224	$20	401							
G225	$40	415							
G226	$50	416							
G227	$40	402							
G234	$40	413							
G236	$20	407							
G237	$20	406							
G238	$50	424							
G239	$50	425							
G240	$50	411							
G241	$75	412							
G242	$20	405							
G243	$20	404							
G244	$20	408							
G245	$20	409							
G246	$40	431							
G247	$20	403							
P444	C	145							
P445	D	27							
P446	E	48							
P447	D	143							
Q200	B	252							
Q201	A	292							
Q202	B	170							
❖ Q203	B	265							
❖ Q204	C	178							
❖ Q205	B	174							
❖ Q206	B	158							
❖ Q207	C	273							
❖ Q208	C	254							

DESIGN	PRICE	PAGE	CUSTOMIZABLE	QUOTE ONE®	DECK	DECK PRICE	LANDSCAPE	LANDSCAPE PRICE	REGIONS
❖ Q209	B	264							
❖ Q210	B	159							
❖ Q211	B	271							
Q212	C	269							
❖ Q214	A	301							
❖ Q217	A	183							
❖ Q219	B	142							
❖ Q221	A	152							
❖ Q222	C	98							
❖ Q223	C	226							
❖ Q224	A	236							
❖ Q226	C	149							
❖ Q238	A	294							
❖ Q240	B	275							
❖ Q241	B	296							
❖ Q243	C	352							
❖ Q246	A	74							
❖ Q247	A	225							
❖ Q248	A	84							
❖ Q252	C	96							
❖ Q255	B	148							
❖ Q260	C	392							
❖ Q267	A	142							
Q272	A	322							
❖ Q273	C	101							
❖ Q275	B	100							
❖ Q281	B	179							
❖ Q283	B	181							
❖ Q285	C	347							
❖ Q289	C	224							
❖ Q292	B	253							
❖ Q294	B	338							
❖ Q295	C	257							
❖ Q297	D	350							
Q313	A	99							
Q314	C	329							
Q316	A	328							
Q319	B	326							
Q325	B	171							
Q326	C	348							
Q327	C	349							
❖ Q329	C	346							
❖ Q330	C	337							
Q334	D	323							
❖ Q346	C	97							
❖ Q350	A	70							
❖ Q353	A	120							
❖ Q354	C	343							
❖ Q357	C	71							
❖ Q358	A	69							
❖ Q361	B	102							
❖ Q366	B	10							
❖ Q372	B	340							
❖ Q374	B	121							
❖ Q417	C	341							
❖ Q418	C	342							
❖ Q420	D	345							
❖ Q421	B	160							
❖ Q422	B	161							
❖ Q424	C	255							
❖ Q426	C	223							
❖ Q428	C	262							
❖ Q429	C	299							
❖ Q430	C	258							
❖ Q432	C	228							
❖ Q436	C	285							
❖ Q437	C	284							
❖ Q438	C	300							
❖ Q439	C	261							
❖ Q440	C	24							
❖ Q441	C	28							
❖ Q442	A	25							
❖ Q443	C	94							
❖ Q445	A	14							
❖ Q449	C	95							
❖ Q458	$35	430							
❖ Q459	$45	423							
❖ Q461	$65	422							
❖ Q463	$85	421							
❖ Q470	A	8							
❖ Q472	C	134							
❖ Q478	C	173							
❖ Q482	C	399							
❖ Q488	A	398							
❖ Q489	A	68							
❖ Q490	A	151							
❖ Q491	A	256							
Q492	A	260							
❖ Q493	B	263							
❖ Q494	A	286							
❖ Q499	C	259							
❖ Q500	A	12							
❖ Q501	C	118							
❖ Q504	A	13							

DESIGN	PRICE	PAGE	CUSTOMIZABLE	QUOTE ONE®	DECK	DECK PRICE	LANDSCAPE	LANDSCAPE PRICE	REGIONS
❖ Q505	A	9							
❖ Q508	B	298							
❖ Q512	B	16							
❖ Q513	B	5							
❖ Q515	B	150							
❖ Q516	B	280							
❖ Q518	C	146							
❖ Q519	B	281							
❖ Q527	B	227							
❖ Q530	B	177							
❖ Q537	C	180							
❖ Q545	B	176							
❖ Q546	B	266							
❖ Q559	D	393							
❖ Q598	C	351							
Q599	C	324							
❖ Q607	C	339							
❖ Q618	A	153							
❖ Q620	B	78							
❖ Q621	B	119							
▲ R127	$75	410							
■ T014	E	55		🏠					
■ T052	E	191		🏠					
T137	E	30							

Additional sets for Designs G107-G247 and Q458-Q463 are $10 each.

Before You Order . . .

Before filling out the coupon at right or calling us on our Toll-Free Blueprint Hotline, you may want to learn more about our services and products. Here's some information you will find helpful.

Quick Turnaround

We process and ship every blueprint order from our office within two business days. Because of this quick turnaround, we won't send a formal notice acknowledging receipt of your order. Note: Remodeling plans may require more turnaround time that two business days.

Our Exchange Policy

Since blueprints are printed in response to your order, we cannot honor requests for refunds. However, we will exchange your entire first order for an equal number of blueprints at a price of $50 for the first set and $10 for each additional set; $70 total exchange fee for 4 sets; $100 total exchange fee for 8 sets . . . *plus* the difference in cost if exchanging for a design in a higher price bracket or *less* the difference in cost if exchanging for a design in lower price bracket. One exchange is allowed within a year of purchase date. **(Sepias are not exchangeable.)** All sets from the first order must be returned before the exchange can take place. Please add $18 for postage and handling via Regular Service; $30 via Priority Service; $40 via Express Service. Returns and exchanges are subject to a 20% restocking fee; shipping and handling charges are not refundable.

About Reverse Blueprints

If you want to build in reverse of the plan as shown, we will reverse any number of blueprints (mirror image) from a 4- or 8-set package for an additional fee of $50. Although lettering and dimensions will appear backward, reverses will be a useful aid if you decide to flop the plan.

Revising, Modifying and Customizing Plans

The wide variety of designs available in this publication allows you to select ideas and concepts for a home to fit your building site and match your family's needs, wants and budget. Like many homeowners who buy these plans, you and your builder, architect or engineer may want to make changes to them. Some minor changes may be made by your builder, but we recommend that most changes be made by a licensed architect or engineer. If you need to make alterations to a design that is customizable, you need only order our Home Customizer® Package to get you started. As set forth below, we cannot assume any responsibility for blueprints which have been changed, whether by you, your builder or by professionals selected by you or referred to you by us, because such individuals are outside our supervision and control.

Architectural and Engineering Seals

Some cities and states are now requiring that a licensed architect or engineer review and "seal" a blueprint, or officially approve it, prior to construction due to concerns over energy costs, safety and other factors. Prior to application for a building permit or the start of actual construction, we strongly advise that you consult your local building official who can tell you if such a review is required.

About the Designers

The architects and designers whose work appears in this publication are among America's leading residential designers. Each plan was designed to meet the requirements of a nationally recognized model building code in effect at the time and place the plan was drawn. Because national building codes change from time to time, plans may not comply with any such code at the time they are sold to a customer. In addition, building officials may not accept these plans as final construction documents of record as the plans may need to be modified and additional drawings and details added to suit local conditions and requirements. We strongly advise that purchasers consult a licensed architect or engineer, and their local building official, before starting any construction related to these plans.

Local Building Codes and Zoning Requirements

At the time of creation, our plans are drawn to specifications published by the Building Officials and Code Administrators (BOCA) International, Inc.; the Southern Building Code Congress (SBCCI) International, Inc.; the International Conference of Building Officials; or the Council of American Building Officials (CABO). Our plans are designed to meet or exceed national building standards. Because of the great differences in geography and climate throughout the United States and Canada, each state, county and municipality has its own building codes, zone requirements, ordinances and building regulations. Your plan may need to be modified to comply with local requirements regarding snow loads, energy codes, soil and seismic conditions and a wide range of other matters. In addition, you may need to obtain permits or inspections from local governments before and in the course of construction. Prior to using blueprints ordered from us, we strongly advise that you consult a licensed architect or engineer—and speak with your local building official—before applying for any permit or beginning construction. We authorize the use of our blueprints on the express condition that you strictly comply with all local building codes, zoning requirements and other applicable laws, regulations, ordinances and requirements. **Notice:** Plans for homes to be built in Nevada must be re-drawn by a Nevada-registered professional. Consult your building official for more information on this subject.

Foundation and Exterior Wall Changes

Most of our plans are drawn with either a full or partial basement foundation. Depending on your specific climate or regional building practices, you may wish to change this basement to a slab or crawlspace. Most professional contractors and builders can easily adapt your plans to alternate foundation types. Likewise, most can easily change 2x4 wall construction to 2x6, or vice versa.

Disclaimer

We and the designers we work with have put substantial care and effort into the creation of our blueprints. However, because we cannot provide on-site consultation, supervision and control over actual construction, and because of the great variance in local building requirements, building practices and soil, seismic, weather and other conditions, WE CANNOT MAKE ANY WARRANTY, EXPRESS OR IMPLIED, WITH RESPECT TO THE CONTENT OR USE OF OUR BLUEPRINTS, INCLUDING BUT NOT LIMITED TO ANY WARRANTY OF MERCHANTABILITY OR OF FITNESS FOR A PARTICULAR PURPOSE.

Terms and Conditions

These designs are protected under the terms of United States Copyright Law and may not be copied or reproduced in any way, by any means, unless you have purchased Sepias or Reproducibles which clearly indicate your right to copy or reproduce. We authorize the use of your chosen design as an aid in the construction of one single family home only. You may not use this design to build a second or multiple dwellings without purchasing another blueprint or blueprints or paying additional design fees.

How Many Blueprints Do You Need?

A single set of blueprints is sufficient to study a home in greater detail. However, if you are planning to obtain cost estimates from a contractor or subcontractors—or if you are planning to build immediately—you will need more sets. Because additional sets are cheaper when ordered in quantity with the original order, make sure you order enough blueprints to satisfy all requirements. The following checklist will help you determine how many you need:

____ Owner

____ Builder (generally requires at least three sets; one as a legal document, one to use during inspections, and at least one to give to subcontractors)

____ Local Building Department (often requires two sets)

____ Mortgage Lender (usually one set for a conventional loan; three sets for FHA or VA loans)

____ TOTAL NUMBER OF SETS

The Home Customizer®

"This house is perfect...if only the family room were two feet wider." Sound familiar? In response to the numerous requests for this type of modification, Home Planners has developed **The Home Customizer® Package**. This exclusive package offers our top-of-the-line materials to make it easy for anyone, anywhere to customize any Home Planners design to fit their needs. Check the index on pages 438-443 for those plans which are customizable.

Some of the changes you can make to any of our plans include:

- exterior elevation changes
- kitchen and bath modifications
- roof, wall and foundation changes
- room additions and more!

The Home Customizer® Package includes everything you'll need to make the necessary changes to your favorite Home Planners design. The package includes:

- instruction book with examples
- architectural scale and clear work film
- erasable red marker and removable correction tape
- ¼"-scale furniture cutouts
- 1 set reproducible, erasable Sepias
- 1 set study blueprints for communicating changes to your design professional
- a copyright release letter so you can make copies as you need them
- referral letter with the name, address and telephone number of the professional in your region who is trained in modifying Home Planners designs efficiently and inexpensively.

The price of the **Home Customizer® Package** ranges from $645 to $1085, depending on the price schedule of the design you have chosen. **The Home Customizer® Package** will not only save you 25% to 75% of the cost of drawing the plans from scratch with a custom architect or engineer, it will also give you the flexibility to have your changes and modifications made by our referral network or by the professional of your choice. Now it's even easier and more affordable to have the custom home you've always wanted.

ORDER TOLL FREE!

For information about any of our services or to order call 1-800-521-6797 or 520-297-8200. Plus browse our website: www.homeplanners.com

For Customer Service, call toll free 1-888-690-1116.

ORDER FORM

 HOME PLANNERS, LLC
Wholly owned by Hanley-Wood, Inc.
3275 WEST INA ROAD, SUITE 110
TUCSON, ARIZONA 85741

THE BASIC BLUEPRINT PACKAGE
Rush me the following (please refer to the Plans Index and Price Schedule in this section):

_____ Set(s) of blueprints for plan number(s) _____. $_____
_____ Set(s) of sepias for plan number(s) _____. $_____
_____ Home Customizer® Package for plan(s)_____. $_____
_____ Additional identical blueprints (standard or reverse) in same order @ $50 per set. $_____
_____ Reverse blueprints @ $50 fee per order. $_____

IMPORTANT EXTRAS
Rush me the following:

_____ Materials List: $50 (Must be purchased with Blueprint set.) $75 Design Basics. Add $10 for a Schedule E-G plan Materials List.$_____
_____ **Quote One®** Summary Cost Report @ $19.95 for 1, $14.95 for each additional, for plans _____ $_____
Building location: City _____ Zip Code _____
_____ **Quote One®** Materials Cost Report @ $110 Schedule A-D; $120 Schedule E for plan_____ $_____
(Must be purchased with Blueprints set.)
Building location: City _____Zip Code_____
_____ Specification Outlines @ $10 each. $_____
_____ Detail Sets @ $14.95 each; any two for $22.95; any three for $29.95; all four for $39.95 (save $19.85). $_____
❏ Plumbing ❏ Electrical ❏ Construction ❏ Mechanical
(These helpful details provide general construction advice and are not specific to any single plan.)
_____ Plan-A-Home® @ $29.95 each. $_____

DECK BLUEPRINTS
_____ Set(s) of Deck Plan _____. $_____
_____ Additional identical blueprints in same order @ $10 per set. $_____
_____ Reverse blueprints @ $10 per set. $_____
_____ Set of Standard Deck Details @ $14.95 per set. $_____
_____ Set of Complete Building Package (Best Buy!) Includes Custom Deck Plan _____.
(See Index and Price Schedule)
Plus Standard Deck Details $_____

LANDSCAPE BLUEPRINTS
_____ Set(s) of Landscape Plan _____. $_____
_____ Additional identical blueprints in same order @ $10 per set. $_____
_____ Reverse blueprints @ $10 per set. $_____

Please indicate the appropriate region of the country for Plant & Material List. (See Map on page 437): Region _____

POSTAGE AND HANDLING	1-3 sets	4+ sets
Signature is required for all deliveries. **DELIVERY** No CODs (Requires street address -No P.O. Boxes)		
•Regular Service (Allow 7-10 business days delivery)	❏ $15.00	❏ $18.00
•Priority (Allow 4-5 business days delivery)	❏ $20.00	❏ $30.00
•Express (Allow 3 business days delivery)	❏ $30.00	❏ $40.00
CERTIFIED MAIL	❏ $20.00	❏ $30.00
If no street address available. (Allow 7-10 days delivery)		
OVERSEAS DELIVERY Note: All delivery times are from date Blueprint Package is shipped.	fax, phone or mail for quote	

POSTAGE (From box above) $_____
SUB-TOTAL $_____
SALES TAX (AZ, MI, & WA residents, please add appropriate state and local sales tax.) $_____
TOTAL (Sub-total and tax) $_____

YOUR ADDRESS (please print)

Name _____

Street _____

City _____State_____Zip _____

Daytime telephone number (_____) _____

FOR CREDIT CARD ORDERS ONLY
Please fill in the information below:
Credit card number _____
Exp. Date: Month/Year _____
Check one ❏ Visa ❏ MasterCard ❏ Discover Card ❏ American Express

Signature _____

Please check appropriate box: ❏ Licensed Builder-Contractor
❏ Homeowner

ORDER TOLL FREE!
1-800-521-6797 or 520-297-8200

Order Form Key
VSH

445

Helpful Books & Software

Home Planners wants your building experience to be as pleasant and trouble-free as possible. That's why we've expanded our library of Do-It-Yourself titles to help you along. In addition to our beautiful plans books, we've added books to guide you through specific projects as well as the construction process. In fact, these are titles that will be as useful after your dream home is built as they are right now.

ONE-STORY

1 448 designs for all lifestyles. 860 to 5,400 square feet. 384 pages $9.95

TWO-STORY

2 460 designs for one-and-a-half and two stories. 1,245 to 7,275 square feet. 384 pages $9.95

VACATION

3 345 designs for recreation, retirement and leisure. 312 pages $8.95

MULTI-LEVEL

4 214 designs for split-levels, bi-levels, multi-levels and walkouts. 224 pages $8.95

COUNTRY

5 200 country designs from classic to contemporary by 7 winning designers. 224 pages $8.95

MOVE-UP

6 200 stylish designs for today's growing families from 9 hot designers. 224 pages $8.95

NARROW-LOT

7 200 unique homes less than 60' wide from 7 designers. Up to 3,000 square feet. 224 pages $8.95

SMALL HOUSE

8 200 beautiful designs chosen for versatility and affordability. 224 pages $8.95

BUDGET-SMART

9 200 efficient plans from 7 top designers, that you can really afford to build! 224 pages $8.95

EXPANDABLES

10 200 flexible plans that expand with your needs from 7 top designers. 240 pages $8.95

ENCYCLOPEDIA

11 500 exceptional plans for all styles and budgets—the best book of its kind! 352 pages $9.95

AFFORDABLE

12 Completely revised and updated, featuring 300 designs for modest budgets. 256 pages $9.95

ENCYCLOPEDIA 2

13 500 Completely new plans. Spacious and stylish designs for every budget and taste. 352 pages $9.95

VICTORIAN

14 160 striking Victorian and Farmhouse designs from three leading designers. 192 pages $12.95

ESTATE

15 Dream big! Twenty-one designers showcase their biggest and best plans. 208 pages. $15.95

LUXURY

16 154 fine luxury plans-loaded with luscious amenities! 192 pages $14.95

COTTAGES

17 25 fresh new designs that are as warm as a tropical breeze. A blend of the best aspects of many coastal styles. 64 pages. $19.95

BEST SELLERS

18 Our 50th Anniversary book with 200 of our very best designs in full color! 224 pages $12.95

SPECIAL COLLECTION

19 70 Romantic house plans that capture the classic tradition of home design. 160 pages $17.95

COUNTRY HOUSES

20 208 Unique home plans that combine traditional style and modern livability. 224 pages $9.95

CLASSIC

21 Timeless, elegant designs that always feel like home. Gorgeous plans that are as flexible and up-to-date as their occupants. 240 pages. $9.95

CONTEMPORARY

22 The most complete and imaginative collection of contemporary designs available anywhere. 240 pages. $9.95

EASY-LIVING

23 200 Efficient and sophisticated plans that are small in size, but big on livability. 224 pages $8.95

SOUTHERN

24 207 homes rich in Southern styling and comfort. 240 pages $8.95

SUNBELT

25 215 Designs that capture the spirit of the Southwest. 208 pages $10.95

WESTERN

26 215 designs that capture the spirit and diversity of the Western lifestyle. 208 pages $9.95

ENERGY GUIDE

27 The most comprehensive energy efficiency and conservation guide available. 280 pages $35.00

Design Software

BOOK & CD ROM

28 Both the Home Planners Gold book and matching Windows™ CD ROM with 3D floorplans. $24.95

3D DESIGN SUITE

29 Home design made easy! View designs in 3D, take a virtual reality tour, add decorating details and more. $59.95

Outdoor Projects

OUTDOOR

30 42 unique outdoor projects. Gazebos, strombellas, bridges, sheds, playsets and more! 96 pages $7.95

GARAGES & MORE

31 101 Multi-use garages and outdoor structures to enhance any home. 96 pages $7.95

DECKS

32 25 outstanding single-, double- and multi-level decks you can build. 112 pages $7.95

446

Landscape Designs

EASY CARE	FRONT & BACK	BACKYARDS	BEDS & BORDERS	BATHROOMS	KITCHENS	HOUSE CONTRACTING	WINDOWS & DOORS

33 41 special landscapes designed for beauty and low maintenance. 160 pages $14.95

34 The first book of do-it-yourself landscapes. 40 front, 15 backyards. 208 pages $14.95

35 40 designs focused solely on creating your own specially themed backyard oasis. 160 pages $14.95

36 Practical advice and maintenance techniques for a wide variety of yard projects. 160 pages $14.95

37 An innovative guide to organizing, remodeling and decorating your bathroom. 96 pages $9.95

38 An imaginative guide to designing the perfect kitchen. Chock full of bright ideas to make your job easier. 176 pages $14.95

39 Everything you need to know to act as your own general contractor...and save up to 25% off building costs. 134 pages $14.95

40 Installation techniques and tips that make your project easier and more professional looking. 80 pages $7.95

ROOFING	FRAMING	VISUAL HANDBOOK	BASIC WIRING	PATIOS & WALKS	TILE	TRIM & MOLDING

41 Information on the latest tools, materials and techniques for roof installation or repair. 80 pages $7.95

42 For those who want to take a more-hands on approach to their dream. 319 pages $19.95

43 A plain-talk guide to the construction process; financing to final walkthrough, this book covers it all. 498 pages $19.95

44 A straight forward guide to one of the most misunderstood systems in the home. 160 pages $12.95

45 Clear step-by-step instructions take you from the basic design stages to the finished project. 80 pages $7.95

46 Every kind of tile for every kind of application. Includes tips on use installation and repair. 176 pages $12.95

47 Step-by-step instructions for installing baseboards, window and door casings and more. 80 pages $7.95

Additional Books Order Form

To order your books, just check the box of the book numbered below and complete the coupon. We will process your order and ship it from our office within 48 hours. Send coupon and check (in U.S. funds).

YES! Please send me the books I've indicated:

☐ 1:VO	$9.95	☐ 25:SW	$10.95
☐ 2:VT	$9.95	☐ 26:WH	$9.95
☐ 3:VH	$8.95	☐ 27:RES	$35.00
☐ 4:VS	$8.95	☐ 28:HPGC	$24.95
☐ 5:FH	$8.95	☐ 29:PLANSUITE	$59.95
☐ 6:MU	$8.95	☐ 30:YG	$7.95
☐ 7:NL	$8.95	☐ 31:GG	$7.95
☐ 8:SM	$8.95	☐ 32:DP	$7.95
☐ 9:BS	$8.95	☐ 33:ECL	$14.95
☐ 10:EX	$8.95	☐ 34:HL	$14.95
☐ 11:EN	$9.95	☐ 35:BYL	$14.95
☐ 12:AF	$9.95	☐ 36:BB	$14.95
☐ 13:E2	$9.95	☐ 37:CDB	$9.95
☐ 14:VDH	$12.95	☐ 38:CKI	$14.95
☐ 15:EDH	$15.95	☐ 39:SBC	$14.95
☐ 16:LD2	$14.95	☐ 40:CGD	$7.95
☐ 17:CTG	$19.95	☐ 41:CGR	$7.95
☐ 18:HPG	$12.95	☐ 42:SRF	$19.95
☐ 19:WEP	$17.95	☐ 43:RVH	$19.95
☐ 20:CN	$9.95	☐ 44:CBW	$12.95
☐ 21:CS	$9.95	☐ 45:CGW	$7.95
☐ 22:CM	$9.95	☐ 46:CWT	$12.95
☐ 23:EL	$8.95	☐ 47:CGT	$7.95
☐ 24:SH	$8.95		

Canadian Customers
Order Toll-Free 1-800-561-4169

Additional Books Sub-Total $_____
ADD Postage and Handling $ 4.00
Sales Tax: (AZ, MI & WA residents, please add appropriate state and local sales tax.) $_____
YOUR TOTAL (Sub-Total, Postage/Handling, Tax) $_____

YOUR ADDRESS (Please print)

Name _____
Street _____
City _____ State____ Zip _____
Phone (____) ____—_____

YOUR PAYMENT
Check one: ☐ Check ☐ Visa ☐ MasterCard ☐ Discover Card ☐ American Express
Required credit card information:
Credit Card Number_____
Expiration Date (Month/Year) _____/_____
Signature Required _____

 Home Planners, LLC
Wholly owned by Hanley-Wood, Inc.
3275 W. Ina Road, Suite 110, Dept. BK, Tucson, AZ 85741

VSH

Design 4061, page 137

OVER 3 MILLION BLUEPRINTS SOLD

"We instructed our builder to follow the plans including all of the many details which make this house so elegant...Our home is a fine example of the results one can achieve by purchasing and following the plans which you offer...Everyone who has seen it has assured us that it belongs in 'a picture book.' I truly mean it when I say that my home 'is a DREAM HOUSE.'"

S.P.
Anderson, SC

"We have had a steady stream of visitors, many of whom tell us this is the most beautiful home they've seen. Everyone is amazed at the layout and remarks on how unique it is. Our real estate attorney, who is a Chicago dweller and who deals with highly valued properties, told me this is the only suburban home he has seen that he would want to live in."

W. & P.S.
Flossmoor, IL

"Your blueprints saved us a great deal of money. I acted as the general contractor and we did a lot of the work ourselves. We probably built it for half the cost! We are thinking about more plans for another home. I purchased a competitor's book but my husband wants only your plans!"

K.M.
Grovetown, GA

"We are very happy with the product of our efforts. The neighbors and passersby appreciate what we have created. We have had many people stop by to discuss our house and kindly praise it as being the nicest house in our area of new construction. We have even had one person stop and make us an unsolicited offer to buy the house for much more than we have invested in it."

K. & L.S.
Bolingbrook, IL

"The traffic going past our house is unbelievable. On several occasions, we have heard that it is the 'prettiest house in Batvia.' Also, when meeting someone new and mentioning what street we live on, quite often we're told, 'Oh, you're the one in the yellow house with the wrap-around porch! I love it!'"

A.W.
Batavia, NY

"I have been involved in the building trades my entire life...Since building our home we have built two other homes for other families. Their plans from local professional architects were not nearly as good as yours. For that reason we are ordering additional plan books from you."

T.F.
Kingston, WA

"The blueprints we received from you were of excellent quality and provided us with exactly what we needed to get our successful home-building project underway. We appreciate your invaluable role in our home-building effort."

T.A.
Concord, TN